A NOBLE COMBAT

A NOBLE COMBAT

The Letters of Shiela Grant Duff
and Adam von Trott zu Solz 1932–1939

Edited by

Klemens von Klemperer

CLARENDON PRESS · OXFORD
1988

Oxford University Press, Walton Street, Oxford OX2 6DP
Oxford New York Toronto
Delhi Bombay Calcutta Madras Karachi
Petaling Jaya Singapore Hong Kong Tokyo
Nairobi Dar es Salaam Cape Town
Melbourne Auckland
and associated companies in
Beirut Berlin Ibadan Nicosia

Oxford is a trade mark of Oxford University Press

Published in the United States
by Oxford University Press, New York

British Library Cataloguing in Publication Data
Duff, Shiela Grant
A noble combat: the letters of Shiela
Grant Duff and Adam von Trott zu Solz
1932–1939.
1. Europe—Politics and government—
1918–1945
I. Title   II. Trott, Adam von   III. Von
Klemperer, Klemens
940.5'2'0922   D727
ISBN 0–19–822908–9

Library of Congress Cataloging in Publication Data
Grant Duff, Shiela, 1913–
A noble combat.
Includes index.
1. Grant Duff, Shiela, 1913–   —Correspondence.
2. Trotz zu Solz, Adam von, 1909–1944—Correspondence.
3. Great Britain—Intellectual life—20th century.
4. Germany—Intellectual life—20th century.
5. National socialism. 6. World War, 1939–1945—Under-
ground movements. 7. Foreign correspondents—Great
Britain—Correspondence. 8. Intellectuals—Germany—
Correspondence. I. Trott zu Solz, Adam von, 1909–1944.
II. Von Klemperer, Klemens, 1916– . III. Title.
PN5123.G714A4 1988   940.5'2'0922 [B] 87–20269
ISBN 0-19-822908-9

Set by Promenade Graphics Ltd., Cheltenham

Printed in Great Britain
at the University Printing House, Oxford
by David Stanford
Printer to the University

To the Memory of
Adam von Trott zu Solz
Who did Honour to his Country
and to his Friends

PREFACE

Correspondences between friends originally concern the writers alone, and in publishing them one runs the risk of invading privacy.

When I first visited Shiela Grant Duff (now Mrs Michael Sokolov Grant) in the Republic of Ireland some years ago in connection with my own work on the German Resistance against Hitler, she made it possible for me to read the more than three hundred letters that she and Adam von Trott zu Solz had written to each other during the nineteen thirties. These letters are the record of a friendship, and as such are of course private documents. At the same time, it is now clear that they express the aspirations and worries of a generation that came of age between the two wars, and of a class privileged—or condemned—to feel the political and ethical tensions of their time most keenly. Thus these letters have become something of a public document as well. Combining as it does the private and the public realms, the correspondence between Shiela Grant Duff and Adam von Trott is exceptionally interesting and illuminating for the historian who believes that both realms help determine the course of human experience. It is in fact a uniquely valuable document.

At the risk of invading privacy, then, I decided to edit this correspondence, with the generous permission of Shiela Grant Duff and the help of those who played a role in Adam von Trott's life and are still among the living. In editing this correspondence my intention has been to let the two writers—whom I shall from now on call simply 'Shiela' and 'Adam'—speak as much as possible for themselves, and to limit my own remarks to a brief introduction and necessary editorial notes. Originally, I planned to emphasize the more public passages at the expense of the private, but I was fortunately dissuaded from this course. The two realms were interwoven from the beginning, and should remain so in print.

The correspondence as it appears in this volume is not altogether complete. A few letters referred to in others have been lost: whenever possible I have identified these. Furthermore, I have omitted some letters and shortened others. In doing so, however, I have not censored anything or suppressed private matters to emphasize public ones. [1]

---

[1] I should, however, record here that I have seen fit to make one or two exceptions to the rule, omitting passages which if published would infringe upon the privacy of persons still alive.

Rather, I have cut out letters or parts of letters that seemed to me too inconsequential to merit printing, or so similar to other letters as to be repetitious. The letters altogether omitted are listed in the Appendix; omissions within letters are indicated by the conventional three dots; omissions in the original are marked by three unspaced dots. The letters I have selected for publication are those most likely to be of human and historical interest and most representative of the relationship between the two writers.

A good many of the original letters are undated: in such cases I have used internal evidence to assign to them the most probable dates, indicated in square brackets. The same holds true of letters where the place of writing is not given. I have arranged the letters in strictly chronological order, save in Chapters 4 and 5, which represent a time when the two writers were separated by vast oceans, and in which I thought that I could clarify the movement of the correspondence by coupling letters related to each other.

I have not tampered with the wording of the letters, in the belief that their style as well as their substance is significant. Shiela writes in the easy, literate manner that one would expect, given her upbringing and education. But the reader of Adam's letters may well exclaim, as she did on one occasion, 'You are so difficult to understand!' His English was in fact sometimes 'stilted' and 'clumsy', as he himself remarked: for him English was after all a second, acquired language. Futhermore, his writing no doubt suffered from the constraints imposed by Nazi censorship, under which he resorted to circumlocution and vagueness. The most important obscurities in his style, however, were due to his view of language which was in line with Karl Kraus's pursuit of the 'lebendige Sinn des Ganzen'.[2] He seems to have believed that words inhibit human understanding, that matters of value cannot be 'expressed' directly through them, but rather should be 'conveyed' through his language game.

These letters could not have been edited without the untiring assistance of Shiela Grant Duff. She has carefully checked the typed copies, commissioned in the sixties by the Hon. David Astor, against the originals. She has added some letters which had been missing from the collection. And she has patiently answered my innumerable requests for information about the letters' contents: having an extraordinary memory and supplementary documents, she has given me indispensable help for which I am most grateful.

---

[2] 'The live meaning of the whole'. Adam quoted this passage in a letter to Diana Hopkinson early in 1933; Diana Hopkinson, _Memoir of Trott's Life_, 1931–1940, typescript (1946), p. 14; Julie Braun-Vogelstein Collection, Leo Baeck Institute, New York.

Others, too, have provided me with valuable information. Adam von Trott's widow, Dr Clarita von Trott zu Solz, has been extremely kind and helpful to me, as have the Hon. David Astor, Mrs David Hopkinson (the former Diana Hubback), and Contessa Spinelli (the former Ingrid Warburg). They have each given me not only factual data and documents but also a vivid sense of the world—or perhaps I should say worlds—in which Shiela and Adam lived. I was helped over various historical hurdles by Henry O. Malone, jun., whose biography of Adam von Trott is a masterpiece of meticulous scholarship.[3] I owe thanks to my friend Ekkehard Klausa for his constant encouragement. To Tim Mason, I am especially indebted for steering this manuscript through some inevitable storms all the way to publication; without his generous engagement and wisdom this correspondence could never have seen the light of day.

My thanks also go to Miss Ruth Bryan and Mrs Renate Weber for expertly typing various versions of this volume, and to my daughter Catharine for taking a contagious interest in my work and for helping me to imagine what this collection of letters and the experience of the correspondents might mean to today's youth. In going over my text my wife Elizabeth has confirmed my wholesome awe of the English language. She also helped me to reduce the Introduction from fifty-five to fifteen typewritten pages.

Not the least of my thanks go to Ivon Asquith of the Oxford University Press for his patient supervision of the whole project.

[3] Henry O. Malone, *Adam von Trott zu Solz. Werdegang eines Verschwörers, 1909–1938* (Berlin, 1986).

LIST OF ILLUSTRATIONS

CONTENTS

'Ah, do not mourn,' he said,
'That we are tired, for other loves await us;
Hate on and love through unrepining hours.
Before us lies eternity; our souls
Are love, and a continual farewell.'

W. B. Yeats, *Ephemera*

Margaret then remarked, 'To me one of two things is very clear; either God does not know his own mind about England and Germany, or else these do not know the mind of God.'

E. M. Forster, *Howards End*

INTRODUCTION

When they first met in Oxford late in the autumn of 1931, Shiela Grant Duff and Adam von Trott zu Solz set out to form 'the best friendship in Europe'.[1] They shared a dream—that of finding a new social and political order for a civilization exhausted by the Great War—and also as time went on an immediate aim—that of resisting Hitler. But their friendship did not survive the strains caused by the gathering European crisis and by differences of circumstance and temperament. Their modes of resistance were bound to differ. Shiela, having worked her way into the guild of foreign correspondents, battled vigorously and openly against Britain's policy of appeasement. Adam's mode of resistance, especially in his conspiratorial activities, was necessarily covert: it became harder and harder for him to reveal himself fully as a 'good German', and increasingly difficult for his Anglo-Saxon friends to trust him.

This correspondence is, then, the story of two high-minded young people who set out to form what they liked to call a 'great European alliance',[2] and who fancied themselves, as Adam wrote in elation, 'children of a yet unborn civilisation'.[3] At the same time, it is the story about a European upper class in one of its last phases: it was in part out of *noblesse oblige* that Shiela was a radical and that Adam had distinct socialist leanings. More than this, Shiela's and Adam's letters are the record of a generation, troubled and at the same time excited, to whom the Great War had bequeathed a 'stifling world', as Shiela put it,[4] of social unrest and imperial self-doubt in Britain and of national humiliation and a struggling experiment with democracy in 'Weimar' Germany. Certainly the Victorian-Edwardian-Wilhelminian certainties had been shattered by the war and were impatiently questioned and indeed dismissed by Shiela and Adam and their friends, who were united both in rebellion and in hope for a 'new common Europe'.[5] That Europe would centre on the relationship between Britain and Germany.

[1] See letter Adam–Shiela, Peking, 20 July 1938; cf. also letter Shiela–Adam, Karlsbad, 27 Aug. 1936.
[2] See letter Adam–Shiela, Berlin, 5 Feb. 1937.
[3] See letter Adam–Shiela, Bellers, Hessen, 7 Sept. 1936.
[4] See letter Shiela–Adam *about* 7 Nov. 1935.
[5] See letter Adam–Shiela, Peking, 8 Sept. 1938.

Shiela[6] was born in 1913, the youngest child of Lieutenant Colonel Adrian Grant Duff, CB, third son of Sir Mountstuart Elphinstone Grant Duff, a leading Liberal MP who had served in both Gladstone Governments of 1868 and 1880 and was later Governor of Madras. Her father had worked as a Staff Officer in the Department of Military Operations in the War Office and had been concerned with the organization of the British Expeditionary Force destined for France in the event of German aggression. Later, as Military Assistant to the Committee of Imperial Defence, he had drawn up the War Book, a detailed plan, never before envisaged, by which all Government Departments knew the exact procedure they were to follow on the outbreak of war.[7] He resigned on receiving command of his regiment, the First Battalion of the Black Watch. He was killed less than six weeks after the beginning of the 1914–18 war.

Shiela's mother, Ursula, the eldest daughter of Alice Fox-Pitt and Sir John Lubbock, the first Lord Avebury, also a distinguished Liberal MP and a Victorian polymath, was left widowed after barely eight years of marriage with four little children to bring up. She also lost two brothers in the First World War and her only son, Neill, in the Second World War. Idealistic and compassionate, she brought up her children not to hate Germany but to hate war. She fully accepted Shiela's friendship with Adam, the first German Shiela had ever met. On every Armistice Day she would take her children to the ceremony at the Cenotaph in Whitehall; in 1936 she took Adam along and was 'very moved' to have him at her side.[8]

Adam was born four years earlier than Shiela, in Potsdam. In 1920, however, his family moved to Imshausen, the Trotts' ancestral seat south-east of Kassel, capital of Hesse-Nassau. Throughout his life he remained strongly attached to the remote eighteenth-century manorhouse and village, the fields and secret forests of that landscape. But the Trotts were more than country squires. Like Shiela's, Adam's forebears on both his father's and his mother's sides had played important parts on the national, even the international, scene. His father, August von Trott zu Solz, joined the Prussian administration when Hesse became a Prussian province after the war of 1866 between Prussia and Austria. In 1909 he became Prussian Minister of Culture and Education, and after leaving the ministry upon Chancel-

---

[6] For more information about Shiela see also her autobiographies, *Fünf Jahre bis zum Krieg, 1934–1939: Eine Engländerin im Widerstand gegen Hitler* (Munich, 1978) and *The Parting of Ways: A Personal Account of the Thirties* (London, 1982).

[7] Shiela Sokolov Grant, 'The Origins of the War Book', *Journal of the Royal United Service Institution*, 117 (1972), pp. 65–9.

[8] See letter Shiela–Adam, Prague, *about* 12 Nov. 1936.

lor Bethmann Hollweg's resignation in 1917, he took over as *Oberpräsident* of Hesse-Kassel and also represented the province of Hesse in the *Reichsrat* until his retirement in 1920. Adam's mother's family, the Schweinitzes, were Prussian Junkers of Silesian stock. The family had an interesting and not unimportant American connection: as ambassador to Vienna, Adam's grandfather, Lothar von Schweinitz, had married the twenty-three-year-old daughter of the American ambassador John Jay, grandson of John Jay, the first Chief Justice of the United States. While Adam's mother, Eleonore (von Schweinitz) von Trott, saw herself as a German, and faithfully fulfilled her function as the wife of a high-ranking Prussian official, she remained mindful of her American inheritance, including the Jays' abolitionist tradition.[9] Deeply religious, she took an active interest— rather unusual among her German peers—in the Ecumenical Movement in Geneva, and spoke out vigorously whenever she thought that basic human rights were threatened.

Adam began his early education at the Französisches Gymnasium in Berlin, studied at Kassel and at home, and spent four years at a boarding-school of the Cloister Loccum in Hannoversch-Münden, passing his *Abitur* in 1927. As a university student he spent some time at Munich and Berlin as well as at Göttingen, where he worked towards a degree in law. In 1929, thanks to some ecumenical connections of his mother's, he was invited to spend the Hilary term at Mansfield College, Oxford.[10] During this first close exposure to life in England Adam not only took courses in theology (since this was what Mansfield College had to offer), but also made a number of friends, including A. L. Rowse,[11] the historian and Shakespeare scholar and since 1925 Fellow of All Souls. The sojourn proved to be a decisive experience for Adam, confronting him for the first time with the intricacies of the Anglo-German relationship which would from then on be one of his chief concerns.

Back in Göttingen Adam finished his doctoral dissertation and examination, *summa cum laude*, on the connection between Hegel's

[9] The Jays were originally Huguenots who left France after the Revocation of the Edict of Nantes by Louis XIV and made their way first to England and then America. John Jay himself, as Governor of New York, signed the act abolishing slavery in that state; his son William and grandson John were active in the abolitionist movement.

[10] Mid-Jan.—mid-Mar.; Mansfield College, a Congregationalist foundation at that time not yet formally associated with the University, offered places to students working towards a BA degree in theology.

[11] (1903–); Elizabethan scholar and poet; Emeritus Fellow of All Souls; see A. L. Rowse, *Poems of Deliverance* (London, 1946); *All Souls and Appeasement: A Contribution to Contemporary History* (London, 1961); *A Cornishman Abroad* (London, 1976); *A Man of the Thirties* (London, 1979).

philosophy of state and international law.[12] Immediately upon his return from Oxford, however, he wrote an essay entitled 'Impressions of a German Student in England', an attempt to get at the roots of what he perceived to be the differences between the German and the English post-war student generations. While his German fellow-students, he said, were 'lost in the bewildering mazes of the world of thought' and plagued by the uncertainties of a broken past, their more fortunate English counterparts could formulate objectives and translate their energies into action.[13]

Shiela and Adam went up to Oxford in the autumn of 1931, Shiela as History Exhibitioner at Lady Margaret Hall and Adam a Rhodes Scholar at Balliol.[14] Balliol's Master, A. D. Lindsay,[15] a philosopher, took particular interest in him, and the friendship between the two withstood the strains of the war, during which Adam was able to keep in touch with friends in Oxford through connections in neutral Europe. Adam's regular tutor, Benedict Humphrey Sumner,[16] a distinguished historian of Eastern Europe and later Warden of All Souls, also became a friend. Meanwhile Adam formed close ties with some of his class-mates at Balliol, notably David Astor, the second son of Lord and Lady (Nancy Langhorne) Astor. The Astors' London house in St James's Square welcomed Adam whenever he was in England, but their connections in the latter half of the thirties with the Chamberlain Government and its appeasement policies made Adam's association with them harmful for his reputation in England. David Astor, who served during the war in the Royal Marines, remained a loyal defender of Adam's political integrity.

Shiela's and Adam's Oxford friends and acquaintances constituted a cross-section of the University in the thirties, an era of transition between the frivolity fashionable during the twenties to a sober, even sombre, mood. His circle did include a number of the so-called 'Oxford wits',[17] who dazzlingly defied the humourless and unlovely,

---

[12] Adam von Trott zu Solz, *Hegels Staatsphilosophie und das internationale Recht* (Göttingen, 1932; repr. 1967).

[13] The essay, containing some 4,800 words, is in the Trott Archive. An abbreviated version was published in *World's Youth*, vol. V, no. 9 (Nov. 1929), pp. 135 and 138.

[14] This was the second year since Rhodes Scholarships for Germans, discontinued during the First World War, had been reinstated.

[15] (1879–1952), from 1945 Lord Lindsay of Birker; Master of Balliol 1924–49; Vice-Chancellor of Oxford University 1935–8.

[16] See letter Shiela–Adam, Chelsea, 15 Oct. 1934, n. 1.

[17] Cf. Noel Annan, ' "Our Age": Reflections on Three Generations in England', in *Generations*, ed. Stephen R. Graubard (New York and London, 1979), pp. 81–109.

if not levelling, demands of public life. At their centre was Maurice Bowra,[18] literary critic and classicist, friend of the *jeunesse dorée*, at that time Fellow and later Warden of Wadham. They also included Isaiah Berlin,[19] the son of Russian immigrants, whose chief concerns were philosophy, literature, and music: he was an undergraduate at Corpus Christi in Adam's first year, elected Fellow of All Souls and appointed philosophy tutor at New College in 1932, and later Professor and then President of Wolfson College.

Both Adam and Shiela moved in and out of Bowra's and Berlin's orbit, amused and puzzled, if not mildly disapproving. Meanwhile they both gravitated towards the political set at Oxford: Adam quite deliberately sought his friends in that quarter as he began to see his mission as that of cementing the relations between his country and Britain. Moreover, both Adam and Shiela were attracted by socialism, which was becoming a cult at Oxford and which made the past war appear as the work more of capitalists and imperialists than of wicked Germans. Adam and Shiela and nearly all their immediate friends joined the Labour Club, in those days largely a social centre dominated by future Labour Cabinet Ministers like Michael Foot[20] and Anthony Greenwood.[21] Adam attended the Oxford Union, the training ground for British statesmanship, and twice addressed its meetings. And while he frequented people of all political hues, including such conservatives as Lord Lothian of All Souls,[22] the Secretary of the Rhodes Trust, and Lionel Curtis,[23] the crusader for Commonwealth and father of the Royal Institute of International Affairs, he became regarded at Oxford as a 'red'.[24] Quite naturally, he and Shiela shared the view, prevalent among English intellectuals at the time, that the past war and its sacrifices had been a tragic waste and the Versailles settlement unjust.

Although Oxford was traditionally a setting for friendships among men, this correspondence is evidence that women were beginning,

---

[18] See letter Adam–Shiela, *beginning of* Mar. 1937, n. 3.

[19] See letter Shiela–Adam, *about* 8 Nov. 1933, n. 6.

[20] The Rt. Hon. Michael Foot (1913–); Pres. of the Oxford Union 1933; Honorary Fellow of Wadham; leading Labour politician and statesman.

[21] The Rt. Hon. Anthony Greenwood (1911–); from 1970 Baron Greenwood of Rossendale; Labour MP 1946–70; Minister of Housing and Local Government 1966–70.

[22] See letter Adam–Shiela, Glasgow, 22 July 1933, n. 2.

[23] See letter Adam–Shiela, Glasgow, 22 July 1933, n. 4.

[24] This fact came to the ears of Adam's father through a report by a family friend and high German official in the field of higher education (His Excellency Dr Friedrich Schmitt-Ott, who had been Chairman of the Rhodes Scholarship Selection Committee before the First World War and successor in 1917 of August von Trott as

figuratively, to scale its venerable walls. In fact the connection between Adam and Shiela was part of a large web of relationships between the two sexes. This may have seemed quite natural to Adam, as he had not been prepared for an exclusively men's world by an English public school. At any rate, his letters show that he did not separate his sense of service and mission from his relationships with women, which were important to him. Shiela was not the only or even the first woman in his life. At the University of Göttingen he had fallen in love with Miriam Dyer-Bennet, an American *divorcée* with five children, and almost twenty years older than he, who was studying for a doctorate in philosophy. She continued as an anxious presence in his life throughout the thirties. At Oxford Adam also met Diana Hubback who came to mean a great deal to him. Diana (now Mrs David Hopkinson), the daughter of a classicist descended from Jane Austen's family, and of Eva (Spielman) Hubback, an outspoken feminist from England's *haute juiverie*, was Shiela's former schoolmate and closest friend.[25] Meanwhile Shiela met Goronwy Rees, a poet, scholar, and journalist from Wales who had come to New College on a scholarship in 1928, was elected fellow of All Souls in 1931, and in 1933 after sojourns in Berlin and Vienna became leader-writer for the *Manchester Guardian*; throughout her Oxford days he meant more than anyone else to her. These relationships which came first for each of them provided the basis for a tender friendship, strong and loving, between Adam and Shiela, which survived several hard tests before it broke down.

Notwithstanding the heady atmosphere of Oxford and their various friendships, Adam and Shiela were increasingly aware of ominous developments in the larger world. Adam could not but feel the ambiguity of his situation as a German student abroad. Much as he enjoyed his time in England, one of his closest friends from Balliol,

---

Prussian Minister of Culture and Education, and who in 1920 founded the 'Notgemeinschaft der deutschen Wissenschaft', an organization designed to further research at all German academies and universities) who had been on a visit of inspection to Oxford to gather information on the conditions of the German Rhodes scholars; it took a long letter by Adam to his father to explain that his 'in many respects socialist views' were quite honourable; see the letter from Adam to his father, most likely written June 1932, quoted in Clarita von Trott zu Solz, *Adam von Trott zu Solz. Eine erste Materialsammlung*, typescript (Reinbek, 1958), pp. 31 f. Adam's sense of service was to the state and the world as they 'should be'.

[25] See Diana Hopkinson, *The Incense-Tree* (London, 1968). She also conducted a lively correspondence (1932–42) with Adam which has been preserved and deposited in the Library of Balliol. Mrs Hopkinson also has written a Memoir in which she quotes elaborately from Adam's letters; Diana Hopkinson, *Memoir of Trott's Life*.

Charles Collins, recalled, 'he was never unmindful of the real business of his life which was the future of Germany' and 'he knew that even in the most favourable circumstances that future would be difficult; he feared that it would be tragic'.[26] And while he spoke his mind freely at Oxford about his distaste of National Socialism,[27] he stood up for what he considered the legitimate rights of his own country, and insisted that the wrongs of Versailles should be righted. He felt it vital to maintain the distinction between Germany as a continuing nation and National Socialism as the illness which had seized a large part of it. But he found it increasingly hard to maintain this without giving the impression of ambiguity.

It was in the Balliol Junior Common Room that Adam first read, in the evening paper, of the fatal events of 30 January 1933. 'He knew at once', his friend Charles Collins remarked, 'that a terrible disaster had befallen his country' and 'that the prospects of his own future had undergone a fundamental change'.[28] But although Adam thought momentarily of prolonging his stay abroad, he very soon realized that he could get his bearings in an altered Germany only by going home. Emigration he never considered seriously. A couple of years later he was to say to a friend who meant to emigrate, 'Go if you must. I shall stay behind, since someone must stay . . . I shall stay and lead a double life. I shall get a position from which I can fight secretly against National Socialism. But I shall do it from here, not from abroad.'[29] In the mean time he pondered the questions that faced him: should he, to be at all effective, join the Party and try to change the new regime from within? Could he find a career that would not compel him to surrender his basic convictions—in the university, in industry, or in public service? Of course his decision to return to Germany was liable to misinterpretation by his English acquaintances.

Adam went down from Oxford in 1933 and Shiela in 1934, and in the summer of 1934 she visited him and his parents at Kassel and Imshausen.[30] 'In the coming struggle for power', he announced to

[26] C. E. Collins, 'Notes on Adam von Trott' (19 Nov. 1946); from the papers of the Hon. David Astor.

[27] Thus during the first month of his stay he took issue with the Nazis in the German Club, only to be reminded by his mother, herself by no means in sympathy with the movement, that this was not the thing to do outside one's own country.

[28] Collins, 'Notes'.

[29] Margaret Boveri, 'Variationen über die Treue', *Merkur*, 23 (1969), p. 663; cf. also Christopher Sykes, *Troubled Loyalty: A Biography of Adam von Trott zu Solz* (London, 1968), p. 178.

[30] See Shiela Grant Duff, *The Parting of Ways: A Personal Account of the Thirties* (London, 1982), pp. 57 ff.

her as the two parted at the railroad station near Imshausen, 'we must be in the right places'.[31] Hitler's evil presence made itself felt not only in Germany, where it lay as a dreadful barrier across Adam's loyal wish to serve his country, but equally in England. The warm and tragic glow of forgiveness and brotherhood, with which films like *All Quiet on the Western Front* and the poems and auto-biographies of the First World War poets had coloured the teens of this generation, gave way to a renewed spectre of war encased in the pages of *Mein Kampf* and given substance by preparations towards such an eventuality which Hitler pursued, year by year: leaving the League of Nations in 1933, declaring conscription and general re-armament in Germany in 1935, sending troops into the Rhineland in 1936, giving military aid to General Franco in the Spanish Civil War, and finally doing the same on an even greater scale in Austria in 1938 and Czechoslovakia in the following year.

While Adam spent the three years between the autumn of 1933 and the summer of 1936 completing his legal apprenticeship, Shiela sought a career which would involve her with people reporting on international affairs and determined, just as she was, to prevent the outbreak of another European war. Through Adam's and Goronwy's friend, J. Peter Mayer, she was introduced to Edgar Ansel Mowrer, the Paris correspondent of the *Chicago Daily News*, whose book *Germany Puts the Clock Back*, published a month before Hitler's seizure of power,[32] warned against the resurgence of German nationalism and militarism. He took her into his office and set about correcting the erroneous views about German intentions which he felt she had imbibed from her studies at Oxford and which were now held by the British Government.

Shiela saw quite a different image of Germany from the one Adam so dearly loved and venerated. She witnessed the overwhelming defeat of the German anti-Nazi parties in the Saar Plebiscite of 1935, judged German rearmament and the reoccupation of the Rhineland in altogether different terms from Adam's strong stand against the Versailles Treaty, and went to Czechoslovakia in 1936 as correspon-dent for the *Observer* with the avowed intention of thwarting Nazi manœuvres against that country. She also put a mission to Franco's Spain on behalf of the Spanish Government before a promised fare-well meeting with Adam before he left Europe in 1937. Later in the same year she resigned her position with the *Observer* because of its

[31] Diary of Shiela Grant Duff for the summer of 1934; cf. also letter Shiela–Adam, Paris, 11 June 1935.

[32] Edgar Ansel Mowrer, *Germany Puts the Clock Back* (New York, 1933).

editor's[33] pro-German and anti-Czech policy. She continued to write prolifically on these issues, both as free-lance journalist, and as the author of a pamphlet and a book.[34] She also developed her contacts with British politicians, especially Winston Churchill,[35] in a further effort to attract attention to the dangerous policies being pursued by the British Government and the Foreign Office in Central Europe.

Meanwhile Adam, feeling that he must escape the pressures of Nazi society, set off in March 1937 on a long trip around the world that took him first to the United States and then, in July, to the Far East. He went out to study the broader dimensions of a world headed for the war which he dreaded, and moreover to explore, in China, the Confucian sources of political wisdom. Inevitably Shiela's and Adam's separate experiences clouded their political exchanges. Isolated, as he was, first behind Nazi censorship until 1937 and thereafter by his sojourn in the United States and the Far East until the end of 1938, he desperately feared that all this would tear them apart. A long letter of protest which he wrote on 20 July 1938[36] seeking agreement and acquiescence, in fact brought even greater disagreement and doubt into the open but did not yet bring open hostility. Their meeting in Paris, as Adam passed through on his journey home, although it led to no quarrel, was in no way a meeting of minds.

Adam returned to Germany in November 1938 resolved to take an active part in the opposition to Hitler. He took upon himself the task of preparing abroad a climate that might be propitious for a change of regime at home. The missions to England which he undertook in February and June 1939, however, took place in an atmosphere of growing tensions between his country and Britain, and the very fact that through the Astor connection he was able to reach the Foreign Secretary and even the Prime Minister only served to feed suspicion of further appeasement on the part of his Oxford friends and acquaintances. Particularly was this so with Shiela in consequence of her active involvement in the Sudeten German crisis of 1938 and her opposition to the Munich Agreement.

[33] J. L. Garvin.

[34] She wrote regular unsigned articles for the *Spectator* and *Time and Tide* and longer articles for the *Contemporary Review*. The pamphlet *German and Czech: A Threat to European Peace* (London, 1937) was commissioned by the New Fabian Research Bureau; the Penguin Special *Europe and the Czechs* (Harmondsworth, 1938), which sold 198,000 copies in three weeks, only appeared the day the Munich Agreement was signed—too late to alert public opinion.

[35] See Martin Gilbert, *Winston S. Churchill*, vol. v. *1922–1939* (London, 1976), pp. 863, 897, 957–8, 976, 985–6, 1017.

[36] Letter Adam–Shiela, Peking, 20 July 1938; see also letters Adam–Shiela, Peking, 9 Sept. 1938 and Shiela–Adam, 24 Oct. 1938.

These circumstances inevitably cast Shiela and Adam in contrasting roles. Whereas Shiela, however reluctantly, had come to the conclusion that war was inexorably approaching and had withdrawn from active political involvement, Adam now strongly took up the cause of preventing a European war which he envisaged as a calamitous fratricide reminiscent of that of the Greek city states.[37] The maintenance of peace, he came to believe, was a prerequisite for a coup against the Nazi regime.[38]

After their meeting in Paris Shiela and Adam saw each other twice more, both times at Clock House at the Lubbock family estate 'High Elms' in Kent. Adam stayed there in February 1939 and again on 18 and 19 June the same year, when Shiela made an unsuccessful attempt to bring him together with Winston Churchill. But the friendship between Shiela and Adam was overwhelmed by the realities of politics and pride. The last letter of the correspondence between the two was written by Adam on 25 August 1939, just six days before the outbreak of the war which finally forced them to go their separate ways.

In June 1940 Adam joined the Foreign Office (*Auswärtiges Amt*), and it was under cover of this position that he worked for the Resistance and eventually, in 1944, took part in the 20 July plot to assassinate Hitler. As is well known, the plot failed; Adam, with his fellow-conspirators, was executed.

The letters of Shiela Grant-Duff and Adam von Trott offer a careful, almost systematic analysis of the problems and ills of the post-Versailles order and of the challenges that came from Bolshevik Russia and Nazi Germany. What is particularly impressive about our two correspondents is that in the turmoil of the nineteen thirties, when ever so many of their contemporaries surrendered to the lure of extremism and ideology of one kind or another, neither of them would surrender to despair or intoxication. At the same time, the inevitable parting of their ways, the widening gulf between them, gives their relationship not only the features of a 'noble combat' but also a personal and tragic character.

[37] Letter Adam–Lord Lothian, Peking, 4 Dec. 1937; Rhodes Trust, Oxford.
[38] See below: Editor's note, pp. 354–6.

I

A PROMISING FRIENDSHIP
OXFORD AND AFTER
May 1932–10 September 1935

EDITOR'S NOTE

Shiela and Adam met in their first term in Oxford when Shiela was 18 and Adam 22. Their friendship was immediate though not very close, for the main attention of each of them was directed elsewhere and as undergraduates their freedom of access to each other was hindered by college rules.

Their friendship really became close only after both had left the University, and Shiela stayed in Kassel and Imshausen for the first time in the summer of 1934.

Balliol[1] Wednesday night
[11 May 1932]

My dear Shiela,
I wanted you to have flowers rather than a letter[2]—but the shop was closed. Be happy in your new year—and let the beauty of life grow richer and stronger for you every day—as I believe it will and should for you.

I trust it will be one of these best Oxford summer days for you to-morrow—It would please me to take you on the water or see you in the evening but I presume you will be very busy (and also there is the concert!) I have just been out: willows and water were lovely.

Bless you—

A.

[1] Adam's College at Oxford while he was a Rhodes Scholar (1931–3). Balliol was Adam's choice partly because Eberhard von Schweinitz, an uncle of his, had studied there.
[2] This was Shiela's 19th birthday.

Lady Margaret Hall.
Oxford.
16th May 1932.

I cannot begin properly to you because I have no name for you but I am looking for one.[1]

Here is Kafka's Amerika.

I would love to go for a walk on Wednesday with you. I will have to be back by 5 pm as I am riding at 5.30. Where shall we go? If we went to the wood we walked through last term I would meet you by the Martyrs' Memorial at 2.30. Would that be early enough. It is a long way.

The blue-bell picnic of next week-end is on Saturday and not on Sunday. Will that be allright? I do hope so.

It was a lovely walk on Saturday.

Shiela G.D.

[1] Among Shiela's friends Adam was generally spoken of as 'von Trott'. Obviously this could not continue in a direct friendship; but the change to 'Adam' was not natural either at this stage.

Balliol College,
Oxford.
13th June, 1932.

Dear Shiela,

Can you meet me tomorrow at about 9.30 somewhere near those trees under which we once sat after the 'New Babylon'?[1]

I could not write to you as I had intended during these days as long as I don't know whether I can still presuppose in you the friend's and not the critic's attitude.[2] Although I believe there is much to give and take where confidence prevails between us—I have got nothing to say in an atmosphere of suspicion. Is the first going to subside into the latter after all?—

That is what I want to see you not write about—

I associate in our relation what is true and sane in and around us in this place—and should regret it deeply if I was mistaken.

Yours
A.

[1] Most likely some musical or dramatic performance in Magdalen College.
[2] Shiela had reproached Adam for his part in an incident which Diana records in her autobiography *The Incense-Tree*, pp. 89–90. Confidence was quickly restored

(letters omitted). Shiela and other friends joined Adam and Diana in her mother's Cornish cottage that summer, after which Shiela when on to Germany and the Soviet Union with Goronwy and Neill, her brother. *The Parting of Ways*, Ch. 4.

22 Rue Victor Greyson
Brussels.[1]
[December 1932]

My Dear Shiela,
    I wonder how you are getting on with the Kant. Often I think of our morning together in London—talking of my philosophies in your amiable though reserved and dignified English streets and of Greece in the Museum.[2] You must remain interested in philosophy for it gives such integration to your thoughts once you have dug your own way through what first seems sheer wilderness. One learns not to waste one's wits on moods—a waste which is not always as considerable as it would be in your case. People with a strong native attitude in life—if they resist the temptations of cleverness—must gain enormously through a trained and consciously controlled contact of their own senses with the common meaning of things outside us. And real character and personality, I believe, start only when one begins to educate one's native powers into a willed and enjoyed unison with the world or rather one's world as one thus understands it. To me it seems the very basis for freedom, courage, and fullness in experience, though I assure you that I am—at any rate now—more thickly in the *process* of getting there rather than in any sense of its end. . . .
    The 'Kritique'[3] [*sic*] was a great mental experience to me though, I believe, partly only because of my previous wrestlings with Hegel.[4] But its essential lesson, I am sure, applies to any stage of intellectual experience, i.e. to teach one the unity of one's internal processes of thought and their problematic relations to what one usually takes for granted as known. All we can know are those internal processes, Kant argues, and they all spring from a magic source which establishes our spontaneous capacity of having them: Imagination. . . .
    Diana writes me that you are happily together with Goronwy— and I know he commands the better way of conveying the order of imagination, i.e. its aesthetic form. I wish I was an artist and not a political doctrinaire—no, that is like wishing to be a boy when you are a girl (or rather the other way around?) and we agreed that is no good. . . .
    Brussels is in many, many respects different from what I had

expected it to be—not exactly in the way of people; they seem rather sinister, much like your Thuringians.[5] Most of my time I spend over books, partly in a perfectly horrid library—but one must not be complaining. Will we ride next term again and walk along that lovely long and almost Roman looking road? Will you see Diana over Christmas? I hope you will both have a happy Christmas! Give my love to Rees.

Yours
Adam

[1] Adam spent the Christmas vacation in Brussels to prepare for his final examinations at Oxford and also to work on his French.

[2] Reference to a previous visit by Shiela and Adam to the Greek statues in the British Museum.

[3] Immanuel Kant, *Kritik der reinen Vernunft* (1781).

[4] Adam had been an avid student of the German philosopher Georg Wilhelm Friedrich Hegel (1770–1831) on whom he wrote his doctoral dissertation at the University of Göttingen (published in expanded form as *Hegels Staatsphilosophie und das Internationale Recht* (Göttingen, 1932)). In this thesis he made a case for the coexistence in Hegel's philosophy of the state of the concepts of sovereignty and of international law. Adam's preoccupation with Hegel caused much dismay among his English friends who, little concerned with the fine points of Adam's thesis, identified Hegel with German muddleheadedness. Later in his life Adam himself conceded to his brother Heinrich that he had been 'bewitched' by Hegel.

[5] Shiela had told Adam after the summer of the previous year spent with Goronwy in Wickersdorf, a progressive school in the hills of Thuringia, that she found the landscape there 'sinister'.

Holsteinisches Ufer 17
bei Kunz
Berlin W
[March 1933]

My Dear Shiela,

My chief reason for writing to you so soon is wanting to get an answer. You are now in Cornwall I expect, enjoying sun, winds, and spring colours, while I am moving in gloomy grey streets, libraries, and at best the somewhat barren surroundings of Berlin.—However I have not really regretted (even for the less personal reasons) to have come here to experience at close sight a first rate political crisis[1]—or rather a transformation of human and social fates on the biggest scale. One will have to rub one's eyes before one will really see what has come about—and not only its being yet too early is a good reason for not writing too much about that.

Oxford seems very far and unreal—but that is probably the same in your case—don't be too unhappy however going back because summer makes it beautiful enough almost for any claims—I am writing this stupid letter in a Restaurant—'Berliner Kindl' while the Radio has been howling a report of the German–French football match which fortunately just ended with the result 3:3. It was pleasant to hear the enthusiastic cheers of the crowds when France scored. We are a simple and sometimes (it seems to me) almost imbecile race—all our talents are unsocial and there are all our sins too, the worst of which being, that unable to run our public affairs properly, we leave them to most extraordinary forces and figures. This I agree is bad enough, but the mix-up that is the consequence of this fouling is no more due to the German 'national character' but to a mixture of normality with those abnormal delegates.[2] It is like wanting to play marionettes and real theatre on the same stage. . . .

In my personal affairs, dear Shiela, I am not very fortunate. M.[3] is extremely unwell and really almost ill most of the time; everything else you know. Disquietness about so many things but above all the most obvious here in this country is in no way helping me on with my work. . . .

I am glad to think of you as peaceful and happy—never mind my clumsy words, it is more the foreigner than their own meaning that it comes from. . . .

A.

[1] On 27 Feb. the Reichstag went up in flames. The Nazis denounced this as a Communist plot and President von Hindenburg subsequently issued emergency decrees suspending the constitutional guarantees of free speech and free press, as well as other liberties.

[2] The representatives of Nazi Germany.

[3] Miriam Dyer-Bennet, an American *divorcée*, mother of five children, whom Adam knew from his last year at Göttingen University (1930–1). They formed a close, though tempestuous, friendship which outlasted their student years. See Introduction above.

Cornwall.

29th March, 1933.

Dear Adam,

Thank you for your letter which I answered immediately but in such a subtle and conspiratorial way that it was too laughable to send.

How are you? I would like to hear more often from you for I have a tragic imagination and read the Manchester Guardian, but I do not really deserve to have letters if I do not write.

I am in Cornwall, at first I was alone here with Peggy,[1] but now Diana's sister has come and a girl-friend of hers, and Douglas Jay.[2] We have occasional clashes over home-rule but they are underground streams and only bubble out when Peggy blunders in and asks why I am hostile. They are nice but difficult to live with. I am growing rest-less but I do not want to leave the sea. It has been sunny and warm here, cloudless sky and a china blue sea, but now it is breaking up, the sky is chequered with clouds and the sea is a cold fierce green—I like it better like that—it is more suited to its character. Sometimes I feel very defiant of the sea. I stand a long time on the head-lands and watch the waves rolling in in steady ranks across Treyarnon and Constantine Bays[3]—I no longer feel so awed with it, but rather scornful of its servility to wind and tide and defiant of its power which, after all, is helpless to do anything but drown one. But of course, it is fine, and something steady and unchanging through all that's happening. I do not know if it is cowardice to turn to the sea and cliffs now; qua human being one must get on with one's life I suppose, and make that as good as possible—but I spend it in impo-tent rage. I only hope what you said is true, and it is the 'abnormal delegates' who are to blame. . . .

Are you still in Berlin? I am awfully sorry about your personal affairs.—Is there anything I can do to help? I would do anything. How is M. I do hope she is better. Does she know what makes her ill? There must be good doctors in Berlin. Do you make her sad? Give her my love. I wish I could help you. . . .

My little cat is here with me—very gentle and affectionate, but my poor dog, whom we used to have on our walks, has had to be killed. He got hysteria and bit everyone. He was a very fine dog with a lion-heart and I am very unhappy for him. Sometimes I want to take everyone and everything I care for onto an island where nothing can hurt them, but it's no good, and the whole earth's a battle-field. I feel very strong and the sea is green and cruel, and there's no pretence left of a china existence.

I still want to go round the world. I am of pure thought. I read Leibniz religiously.[4] It seems not only madness but wickedness to be so concerned with substance and perception, but perhaps it is like the sea, and the world one escapes to and yet holds in defiance. I am rather excited by living and resent the camp behind the lines as it were, that girls are sent to.[5] There we disagree; perhaps one day I shall perform my offices dutifully in the camp, but there is no need yet—surely you agree to that. . . .

Shiela.

[1] Peggy Garnett, friend of Shiela's, from St Paul's Girls' School in London and Oxford; married Douglas Jay (see n. 2 below).

[2] Douglas Jay, Fellow of All Souls; Labour politician; friend of Shiela's.

[3] Due west of Padstow in north-eastern Cornwall, Treyarnon and Constantine Bays are adjacent to each other. In Treyarnon Bay Diana's mother had built Trethias Cottage.

[4] Gottfried Wilhelm von Leibniz (1646–1716); German universal scholar and philosopher.

[5] Marriage.

2/4/33

Dear Shiela,

 . . . No, it is not only abnormal delegacy, but a dangerous crowd that has got hold of things. Individual happenings are *not* the character of the whole thing—but the whole thing has put business on a move. The western capitalist states will make a lot more of the disorders here than is legitimate in view of the veiled brutality of any capitalist state. I am sure that fear of the setting in of a revolutionary transformation of even the economic side—is one of the sources of indignation and hostility. It is here that the friends of European and world development must be careful with their criticism. . . .

 Will I encounter much anti-German feeling now?—It makes me think very especially of my few real friends as I know I shall be safe with them. Please let's stick to the plan of meeting more regularly in those few weeks that are left.[1]

Yours

A.

[1] At Oxford; this was to be the last period in which Shiela and Adam ever lived in the same place engaged in their own work. This accounts for the enormous correspondence interrupted only by very short and contrived meetings outside the regular operation of their lives.

The Central Hotel,
Glasgow.
22 July, 1933

My Dear Shiela,

 I have been walking through the crowded streets of this place in search of somewhere quiet to write to you as I long intended to do. People's expression is so different here from London—and much pleasanter on the whole. They look much more shabby, more worn, and harder—but at the same time human, friendly, and very much alive.

I have come back just an hour ago from Jura[1] which is a lovely island where I stayed four days—two at the East and two on the Atlantic coast. I like your Scotland though at first its woodlessness and uninhabitedness made me feel a little lost. I walked hours and hours seeing nothing but bare hills, stags, and seagulls of most varied types. Part of the time I stalked with a Scottish keeper whom I could hardly understand, he made terrific strides wearing long rubber boots with which he simply walked through bogs and streams—leaving me to jump them. I shot a wild billy-goat with fascinating horns about $1\frac{1}{2}$ feet long—it was most exciting in storming rain and clouds on the top of a rocky hill.—The sea had become too stormy to return by motor-boat, so we had to sail back with two most delightful fishermen who live in the caves of Jura island. The younger one of them said that 'from his point of view' lobsters did not return to the deep sea in winter but to the coast—though the dominating opinion holds the opposite. . . .

I was so sorry, Shiela, to see so little of you in London—though the one time I saw you was as good a success as might have been expected from a charity dance. Will I perhaps see you in Germany?— Don't waste your opportunity of going there on a casual week-end! I think a great deal about the implications of my returning home this time—the balance of possibilities lies with its being a final return. Lord Lothian,[2] who is or was a Fellow of All Souls,[3] and especially concerned with Rhodes Scholars, has told somebody I know that my chances of getting in are nil and Lionel Curtis[4] (do you know the man?) has said something to the same effect. I don't take this as ulti- mate, but I think I must acknowledge it as the prevailing bias. I don't want the argument *pity* to be used in my favour. I would take the f'ship mainly because of then not having to be humiliated by the Hit- lerites—but I would not exchange this exemption for another humi- liation. It is humiliating to be an emigrant—and this I think I least want to be. I think you know and understand.

I passed the statue of the Duke of Wellington just now—you know he had a very strong and impressive head, but he was hard to brut- ality; it is that one must be, I felt, to be a politician.

In contrast to that I have a sensation of not belonging to that world of happenings which rules and upsets my chances—and almost cynical realisation of homelessness which is most unnerving and which I must get out of. To read on the brick walls of a Glasgow slum 'Fight or Starve!'—or reading of the split amongst the French

Socialists[5]—or a pamphlet on Fascist activities in Germany, seem nothing but confirmation of something.—And together with all that fragments of personal relations and endeavours conveying a clear feeling of my unimportance—like a glass container which hinders no insight into the crude and mixed facts. Some people think a great deal of reducing themselves to this state—I think Keats must have meant something very similar when talking of 'negative capability'[6]—and maybe when no selfish ambition hinders your assimilation of experience one must really put forward truth.

I hope a great deal from a period of rest and it looks as if I will have it in August.

Are you happy, Shiela, working at your history and your own world to which I feel a great deal of solidarity and affection—do you accept that? What I really wanted to write to you about is that gift you have which made me write the last sentence. I think it is a great liability as well, because it mainly rests in your effect on other people—providing you if you want to take it with a big scope for influence and help. Your world being very definitely and genuinely your own, your presence challenges people to be themselves, and clear as to what that means to them. I think this true even if you are not aware of it—and it certainly has been a great value to me to know you. It is time to stop—will I perhaps see you the week after this one—my Viva[7] is 25th—I'll be in Oxford on and off till Sunday—then come to London—I'd like to see you very much—

Bless you—

A.

---

[1] After a trip through the industrial Midlands with David Astor and another friend, Adam and David travelled for a few days on the island of Jura due West of Glasgow.

[2] Lord Lothian (1882–1940), the former Philip H. Kerr; Secretary of the Rhodes Trust 1925–39; British Ambassador to the United States, 1939–40.

[3] The most prestigious of Oxford Colleges; founded in 1437, it has a large endowment for sixty Fellows; traditionally it has had close links with the British political and ecclesiastical establishments. Adam's academic performance at Oxford was not sufficiently outstanding (he did not get the much-coveted first) to help him obtain a Fellowship at All Souls.

[4] Lionel Curtis (1872–1955); Fellow of All Souls; an untiring advocate of the Commonwealth idea; founder of the Royal Institute of International Affairs (Chatham House); author of a mammoth work with the ambitious title *Civitas Dei* (London, 1934—).

[5] This is evidently an allusion to the lack of unity between the Radicals and the Socialists.

[6] ' . . . *Negative Capability*, that is when man is capable of being in uncertainties, mysteries, doubts, without any irritable reaching after fact and reason . . . ' John Keats to George and Thomas Keats, Sunday [21 Dec. 1817], Hampstead; John

Keats, *Selected Poetry and Letters*, ed. Richard Harter Fogle (New York, 1964), pp. 303 ff.
  [7] Viva voce: an oral examination; at Oxford, part of the final examinations or 'Schools', taken after the written papers, to determine the final degree class.

Imshausen.
28th. Aug. 1933.

Dear Shiela,
  . . . I have not found my feet yet, quite. While the general look of things was more depressing in the big towns, (Hamburg, Berlin) there are the most encouraging features in the countryside. I think you would even find your sinister Thuringians woken up to a better form of life and awareness. My future field of activity, Rotenburg,[1] is completely occupied by the 'men of the trees'[2]—and the rest of the province seems to be in the most promising chaos.
  In order to learn things from within and to anticipate being forced to, I am to take part in one of the 'camps'[3] for these first weeks of September. It will be near Marburg. . . .
  Diana has been here now for a few days and it is lovely with the most beautiful weather. She likes my home and the hills. . . . The peasants asked me to tell her how very quiet everything was. It is very quiet here—but I can only enjoy it in passing. The next stage will be very unquiet—and Oxford seems far, far away. . . .

Yours ever,
Adam.

  [1] A Hessian town on the Fulda river near Imshausen, where Adam was to serve from Oct. 1933 to the end of Jan. 1934 as *Referendar* (clerk of court) at the County Court.
  [2] The Nazis.
  [3] *Wehrsportlager*; a paramilitary training camp in which Adam served in Sept. 1933.

Rotenburg
[*beginning of*] November 1933

Dear Shiela,
  I wrote you a letter some time ago—describing all the circumstances and surroundings of this new life—but then it seemed so trivial and tiring that I left it unfinished.
  You see the great change appears in a somewhat gratifying if theatrical cloak in this old residence of some petty prince of Hesse. That

same petty continuity works at the bottom of the bourgeois mind unconscious to himself in his new pride, but in his eternal commitment to something superior, be it just a courtier's cloak, they treat one with extraordinary, non-interfering loyalty. It is quite clear to them now—so far as I come into contact with them at all—that I do not belong to them or their silly factions, but so far I haven't had a single rebuke. In the court, I am the only non-party man, I believe, except one judge. It is a silly stupid game to know that they think I am not because I belong to the petty prince rather than the petty bourgeois—it's like making the bear dance though it might well eat one. The pathetic self-deception shines through very rarely, but I have caught glimpses of its realisation in most unexpected, encouraging and solidaric, momentary meetings with people.

There is a large core of the most loyal, decent, and idealistic following, and they are by far the majority in the rural districts. Naturally, 20th century conditions of social life cannot be loyally handled with the peasants' world of concept without hypocrisy, and hypocrisy will eat a sinister and satanic rift into the moral unity of the whole. The situation then arising will be life and death of this country. The alternatives are too tremendous to sustain a cynical judgement on the present changes—they will initiate quite clearly the last great European decision. The western countries may find that in taking a positive or negative attitude they will involve their own existence.[1]

Did you really get a taste of what this country is really like when you were here those few times? Of this quite extraordinary potential power if only it finds its way to ordered creativeness? This extraordinary simplicity behind a screen of big words and the hard wide beauty of its most typical landscape? Nature is hard and somewhat ungenerous here, and it has made men poor and fierce at places, but extremely open to friendliness and persuasion. I hate their wasteful clumsiness, and their petty pride and many other qualities which I sense very definitely in myself too—but they are the only people in Europe I know which cannot yet be simply identified with their social and political pattern—however much doing so feeds the pens of unkind observers—and this may be the real reason for all justified fear and hatred: that their true form of social and political self-expression has not yet been reached. Naturally that is a danger to any established system—the unrest is much deeper than any war-scare that capital and press can produce. They may try to snatch the opportunity before the issue has fully ripened but they will do it to their own disaster. Time, however, will work against them and the necessity to find new forms of life rather than mutual decay will force the peoples together against their own stupid will. There is in the mean time no reason for either hectic impatience or emotionalism—but for definite steady work which I am very unhappy to perform so inadequately at my present station. Most of my day is occupied with more or less mechanical legal work—interrupted only by fascinating contacts with the peasants and poor themselves who come from various parts to seek their right. (My English is getting bad already, isn't it?) . . .[2]

Winter will completely surround and isolate me very soon now as it has probably never quite succeeded to do like this—I hope it will be a spur to better and happier work than so far.

I shall send my love to nobody else in this letter—as I want it to be for you alone—. I hope you are happy and prosperous.

Yours,
Adam.

[1] In this paragraph, Adam proposes to maintain, in spite of his basic rejection of Nazism, an open view towards its agricultural reform programme aimed at rescuing the peasantry.

[2] This unusually convoluted passage reflects Adam's struggle to come to terms with the events in Germany. His love of home and loyalty to country are coupled with forebodings concerning the new regime, and his basic optimism makes him hope that his country will be able to resolve its problems and find its 'true form of social and political self-expression', if only 'capital and press' do not interfere by forcing a war.

[about 8] November, 1933

Dear Adam,

I am working in Rhodes House Library.[1] What a lovely place it is. I wish I had come here before when you used to come. Today is full of memories of you. I have been in Balliol to a room near your room. I miss you very much here. It is funny how when one misses a person very much one keeps forgetting they have gone away, or perhaps it is that one keeps remembering. Often and often I find myself looking out for you, and thinking you may come out of doors I have seen you come out from. It is very sad that you cannot—but I don't expect you mind very much. Do you think about Oxford at all? You said in your letter that you were not home-sick, so perhaps you never do. If one thinks at all, one is apt to romanticise all the moments when one was most miserable. When I am not in Oxford, I think with great regret of wet evenings which I have particularly disliked, and they seem absolute pinnacles of intense living! . . .

I am very excited by the thought of perfect worlds. I am reading the history of Chartism[2] and all the working-class movements of the 19th century. They do seem incredibly real and vigorous compared with the motives and intentions of the politicians over the same period. Did you come across Feargus O'Connor, 'The Lion of Freedom?'[3] The Chartist leaders are wonderful men. Perhaps working class leaders are always like that. I want to know what the working classes are really like. Any life which is not in touch with them must be, of necessity, superficial and limited. Perhaps that is why Oxford life seems unreal and yet perhaps I have a romantic conception of the lower classes, and too great a faith in them. Are the people you have to deal with mostly town workers or peasants? You talked of peasants. I hope what you said was true, but have they really these almost 'feudal' loyalties? I think it must be very difficult for an English person to understand Germany. We have no peasants. Every countryman is near a large town and in close relationship to the artisans and townworkers. That must have a great effect on the character of political movements. I think we have not the same elements for a fascist government as Germany and Italy had, but I'm not sure of that, since I'm not sure either what elements those are, or what people here are really like.

There is a strong public feeling against Germany. The Sunday papers have headlines about the armaments you're having, and a great deal of anger was caused by your leaving the League.[4] I don't understand the diplomatic details of that, but I cannot help sympathizing, and wishing England was not so self-righteous and complacent in foreign affairs. It is monstrous to have probationary periods, 15 years after Versailles, and a certain amount of strength and boldness might have led to disarmament immediately in every country—but there is always so great an atmosphere of fear and suspicion in international councils, I wonder they continue at all. I don't know what will happen now.

I am learning all about constitutions and theory of government. It is very interesting. My work is the most intense form of pleasure now—except when Goronwy[5] comes, and then we listen to music. Shaiah[6] has the Spring Sonata,[7] which is really so beautiful and moving that everything changes. And the Fledermaus songs still excite me terribly, I can understand Shaiah's life, which makes one so angry sometimes for its placid continuity, is to him, full of intense and vivid feeling. I want a life of 'incredible splendour and beauty'. . . .

I send you my love, very much of it.

S.

¹ The Library of Rhodes House at Oxford specializing in international and Commonwealth affairs.
² English working-class movement founded in 1836; its 'People's Charter', published in May 1838 included the demand for six basic political freedoms.
³ Feargus Edward O'Connor (1796–1855), one of the foremost leaders of the Chartist movement and its most powerful speaker.
⁴ In Oct. 1933 Hitler withdrew from the Disarmament Conference and from the League of Nations.
⁵ Goronwy Rees (1909–79), author, fellow of All Souls 1931–7; leader-writer for the *Manchester Guardian* 1933; assistant editor of the *Spectator* 1936; Shiela's friend and also a good friend of Adam's. See *A Bundle of Sensations* (London, 1960); *A Chapter of Accidents* (London, 1972).
⁶ Isaiah Berlin (1909–); from 1957 Sir Isaiah, fellow of All Souls; friend of Shiela's and Adam's. He became a well-known philosopher and historian of ideas; Chichele Professor of Social and Political Ideas at Oxford and President of Wolfson College, Oxford, 1966–75.
⁷ Beethoven violin sonata (F major, opus 24).

Rotenburg
[*about* 10] Nov. 1933.

My Dear Shiela,
Thank you for a lovely letter. I too miss you—a great deal, and life will always seem the poorer for never being able to see or talk to you. But you made me feel at home with your new life at Oxford and so as if I had not really gone away.—I too am in danger of starting 'grand' scraps to you, which afterwards never go to the post. Why should that be? I think you are right to say that there is simply too much to write about. The 'general situation' is too distorted by the antagonistic backgrounds from which we draw our daily impressions, but also I don't think we would find agreement very hard there. . . .

Do you think I should ever see Diana again? I want to very much—yet you know the obstacles and objections (you raised them very strongly during our last hours together). You must give me a sisterly and very discrete advice, because, you see, I am rather ashamed of not being able to solve this question all by myself. Is it a terribly serious fault in one's caring for someone if it does not include the thought of marriage? I am very conscious that it shifts the burden of unhappiness seriously onto the one side. Can that be avoided? . . .

I have been reading Tolstoi which is exactly what I want—I am still indulgingly content in a purely provincial life, in which it is not too hard to be a 'resigned politician'.—What you say about the popular suppositions about Fascism is extremely true. Our population here is almost exclusively rural. Legal contact with peasants can be fascinating—almost always instructive. I feel you are more right about the working classes than about Chartism—There is a stiff job between the former and a perfect world.

I am afraid of arguing a kind of bureaucratic cruelty in view of the repetitive impression of destitution and misery one has. Who could enter into it all? I suppose Christ did.—On the other side I often have a burning idea that the world is perfect whatever its inhabitants are doing to it and themselves. Tolstoi knew how to express that—do you remember Andrej Bolkonski's[1] vision over the wide grey sky over the battlefield of Austerlitz? To be free in the midst of toil and pain would make one able to live a perfect life.

Mine is all but perfect yet—though there are times when I catch a glimpse of where my real toil is to lie. And I know you will still be my friend when I find it. . . .

Devotedly Yours,
Adam.

[Postscript omitted]

[1] Prince Andrej Bolkónski, member of Kutúzov's staff; one of the principal characters in Tolstoy's novel *War and Peace*; wounded in the battle of Austerlitz on 2 Dec. 1805 (Pt. III.).

Lady Margaret Hall,
Oxford.
11th Nov. 1933.

Dear Adam,

. . . Oxford is very exciting politically these days. The October Club[1] has been banned and meets secretly in public houses. It arose out of a fuss about the OTC[2] and the Anti-War Association—the proctors[3] objected to it being called the Oxford University A-WA and banned its meetings—then they had a meeting for free speech and that was banned. Jane[4] and I went to that—it was in Ruskin, very orderly and quiet. Everyone went in at the back door because the proctors banned the front door. There were some young men from London University who spoke about freedom of speech in their university—and then everyone passed a resolution against the proctors, and broke out in a mass into the street—In spite of a great many bulldogs,[5] most people escaped. Those who didn't have been gated for two terms. The papers write lurid accounts of it, but I do not think it is of any great importance. In a way it is exciting because it is reminiscent of Russian books in which the students have a great deal of political activity. . . .

. . . Peggy is very much married and tells us all to marry—but I do not think I like marriage too much. It seems to me to have all the problems of government attached to it, and being only one person, I do not see why one should sacrifice liberty to order inside oneself. Still I am very fond of Goronwy, and that unfortunately makes one not so singly one person.

Do you know Rembrandt's picture of Christ? I think it is in Berlin. It is very beautiful and moving. I have a copy of it above this table where I work.

Write to me one day.

Love,

S.

[1] The Communist-inspired student club at Oxford which had splintered off from the Labour Club.

[2] Officers' Training Corps.

[3] University officials.

[4] Jane Rendel was one of Shiela's closest friends from school and subsequently went with her up to Oxford to study at Lady Margaret Hall.

[5] University policemen.

Rotenburg

Nov. 14th 1933.

Dear Shiela,

. . . Thank you for writing to me so generously for a second time; your notes give me a very vivid feeling about Oxford that is pleasing and yet sad. In spite of what I said before, it is rather true that at times I dare not recollect all its beauty and loveliness because I cannot be there any longer. I am very fond of Oxford and of England and of you.

I went home with my small car at lunchtime (it's about ten miles) to see if there were any letters and was so pleased to find your writing. It now really is winter here—the trees are all bare and all the dead leaves cover the cold wet ground. There is a most monotonous grey haze over everything, and it is night almost at four o'clock. But I am happy with my work and reading. Yesterday I found that I would not mind if I had to spend my whole life as a small provincial official. With the long hours of the evening to myself and the wonderful world of imagery that the best hands of all ages have built up in their work. . . .

Perhaps this sounds all rather petty—it is so utterly different from academic excitements. The law-court is an extremely 'adult' institution; yet if one just penetrates the surface of its formalism it is pathetically real. I quite agree with your view that I am 'well out' of All Souls, though the possibility had fascinated me. It is no longer a possibility and sometimes I have the feeling as if there is an exceedingly kind power or providence in charge of my fate—'how blind I was not to see that I had to go back to the country for some time now,' it then strikes me. Yesterday night I went up the hill behind my house on a dark road which in daytime overlooks the whole valley—I just saw the lights of the town beneath. Two banks of white mist seemed to come down from higher up in the air. One could just see the trees in a few feet's distance. There was a coldish breath down the hill and a smell of wet soil and leaves. No stars and only the rounded stony road under my feet. It was all so strong and simple. Perhaps you can understand from this bad description.

In a way I am glad that this is your last year in Oxford—it is too stifling and excited a place. Its politics too seem rather strange to me now, I mean quite apart from their obviously childish elements—but maybe my misjudgment is rather obsolete on that point at present. . . .

In my house there is a secondary school teacher who was four times wounded in the war. He told me about it last night—his left eye and brow were shot away, otherwise he would look exactly like Lenin—whose views he does not share. He seems an honest and strong man, very much like a warrior. Very much anti-militarist and a great lover of birds. He catches them in huge nets only to put a ring on one of their feet with a number. Very often he finds birds that he numbered one or two years ago. He says that is science, and that there is a huge organization of people who do the same. He says the last war defeated the Prussians, and this was the first chance for real Germany, which meant a great chance to us Hessians. He is very proud of this specific quality of ours.—You can see how remotely I am living because he lives next door to me; yesterday was the first time we had a conversation. . . .

Is Oxford still happy—and does it make the prospect of going abroad at Christmas seem altogether absurd?

Love,
Adam.

Hanau[1]
20.2.34.

Dear Shiela,

This is just to tell you a dream I had tonight before I should forget it again—

I was lying on my sofa in the room at Balliol reading (in a voluminous French book bound in red-brown linen) the speeches of delegates on some international congress of professors. Under a thick black line the Russian was summing up his remarks on nationalism— saying that when the work was accomplished it would show in all its branches and forms a strong national character which belonged and could only belong to his country. But in the meantime they considered the issue to be the accomplishment of that work—the creating of possibilities to earn and to live and that talk about the other was superfluous and wrong. Another professor interjected: But of course there is the problem of the generations still! Of course, replied the Soviet. All this was made more vivid by an extremely old-fashioned caricature of the proceedings: Several professors in morning coats with a stiff collar and a somewhat shabby elegance, their hair parted in the middle, spectacles, an untidy moustache and beard were sitting extremely leisurely in a small class-room lighted by an oil-lamp under which the young Russian stood on an elevated platform, rather idealised in his looks and rhetoric gesture—like Stalin.

I had been looking at all this when I remember there was a long pause during which I dozed—suddenly I heard you rushing up the stone steps—I could tell from your movements and the noise of your rather hard rain-coat flapping—you stopped at the door to listen whether I was in. I wanted to call you in and—couldn't. I tried to move and found I was completely paralysed. A few anguished seconds went by and when I at last managed to draw up my knees to rise from my sleep I seemed to hear your steps on the gravel below, departing to some lecture or so. After that I woke up.—I am afraid all this seems rather absurd to tell, one cannot convey the strange intensity of such dreams.

Will we keep a relation of real persons to each other when we neither see nor hear anything of each other any more?

A.

---

[1] Between Jan. and July 1934 Adam served as *Referendar* at the District Court in Hanau, East of Frankfurt-on-Main.

[*beginning of* March 1934]

Dear Adam,

It was a very strange dream you had. I hope it is not true and that you are not dragged into this curse of nationalism. I'm afraid you are, because even when you were here, you thought in that way—the more I read of history, and the more people I meet from other countries, the more obstructive and wrong national divisions seem. I am reading modern history—1913–34, and all the evils of post-war Europe, and indeed of the whole world, seem in large part attributable to the Versailles Treaty, and its construction on the basis of independent sovereign states—perhaps the world was not ready then for any greater unity, but at least something might have been done to make it so, instead of perpetuating divisions, creating new conflicts, and hedging in your country and Austria in such a way as to make independent economic existence impossible.

I am very moved and appalled by events in the world. This business in Austria is absolutely terrible,[1] and the whole thing is made more poignant and vivid at the moment by the action of the hunger marchers here. There is a huge meeting in London on Sunday of the unemployed in protest against the new Unemployment Bill. They came through Oxford and stopped and fed in the Corn Exchange. I went down there—there was no need of help, but I talked to some of the people, and it is awful how worn and haggard they are. They live like animals; all their pleasures are those of material comforts and then these are denied them—and through no fault. I had meant not to go there again, for the first time I was too easily moved and helpless to do anything, and it was what Shaiah calls 'Tolstoyan sentimentality' that the organisers of the people most hate—but then I saw them again marching out of Oxford, with banners flying, and they were singing and crying 'Hunger, hunger!' and I recognised faces among the crowd of men whom I had talked to and whom I had watched eating the miserable food given to them, and who afterwards lay down on the floor from sheer weariness. The whole thing was so dreadful, one must make up one's mind not to have these tender Tolstoyan sympathies and at the same time co-operate in a system which by its evils evokes them. The whole question is so difficult and bewildering, and I become worse at thinking every day. Economics, which is the basis of the whole question, I find quite impossible, and philosophy, which should be the ground-work of one's faith, is empty and incomprehensible to me. And meanwhile there is the most beautiful spring, the birds singing again, and the snowdrops and crocuses lifting their heads, and all day a warm and soft sunlight over everything. I wander through the fields instead of doing my work, and the trunks of the trees are warm to touch, and the grass alive again. I read Milton—first because of the slaughter in Vienna— 'Avenge O Lord, Thy slaughtered saints'[2] and the passages in 'Paradise Lost' about immortal hate and the unconquerable will—and now, for the Spring, Lycidas and L'Allegro.[3] He is a most beautiful poet. Everyone is reading Yeats now because he has published a collected edition. There are poems there on revolution—of a terrible beauty which is born, and all changed, changed utterly,[4] and love poems, full of moonlight, and half-closed lids, a sort of darkness not in my life, but very moving—I do find the world so wild and exciting—this incomprehensible mixture of terror and misery and pain, with the softness and tenderness of the Spring and flowers. All these mean more somehow than people actually in one's life, yet through it one's own life is more and more intense—I feel I ought to write to you about people and actual events, and changes of daily life, about people you knew, and the places and kinds of thing that happen, and yet, to write so seldom would give no real account of these—and now, if we are to go on knowing each other and being friends, it will not be on that basis any more—You have left, and soon I will too— and our being friends depends so little on that. I want to go on being friends. I wish I could see you and talk to you—sometimes I miss you very much—people here are very few whom I know, and then great chasms one falls into between one and them—the walks we went were shy, but I was very happy, and wish we could go again. Write to me—tell me if it is possible what you are doing, what you will do. I read a letter from you to the M-G. Voigt questioned your observatory powers. I only hope you are right.[5]

   Write to me again. I like having letters from you. I started to write a long time ago, but interrupted, I could not go on. I put it in with this, but it is not true now because my work is distracted by other things, by the terrors of the working classes and by the spring and sunlight.

Love,
S.

[Postscript omitted]

[1] On 12 Feb. 1934 Austrian Chancellor Engelbert Dollfuss moved against the Socialist party and trade union headquarters in Vienna and used artillery against the Viennese workers who had barricaded themselves in their tenements, notably the Karl Marx-Hof.
   [2] Milton, 'On the Late Massacre in Piedmont'.
   [3] Milton, 'Lycidas' (an elegy); 'L'Allegro' (an ode to gaiety).
   [4] ' . . . All changed, changed utterly: A terrible beauty is born. . . . from 'Easter

1916', in W. B. Yeats, *Selected Poems and Two Plays*, ed. M. L. Rosenthal (New York, 1966), pp. 85 ff.

[5] In Feb. 1934 Adam got involved in a controversy in the letters column of the *Manchester Guardian*. Late in Jan. the paper had carried on article in two instalments (22 and 23 Jan.) on the persecution of the Jews in Germany since the Nazi seizure of power, citing especially the situation in Hesse with its large Jewish population. Adam, who was despite his hostility to the Nazis, always sensitive to attacks upon his country and especially his native Hesse (concerning which, he thought, the article was in error), decided to write a letter to the *Manchester Guardian* in refutation of the charges. Immediately after writing it, it occurred to him that it might be subject to misunderstanding, and he wrote to his mother that he hoped his 'somewhat foolish letter' would not be published. But it appeared on 21 Feb., causing considerable agitation in subsequent issues of the paper, and, moreover, causing much distrust in Britain of Adam as a bona fide opponent of National Socialism. Frederick A. Voigt, a leading British journalist, was correspondent for the *Manchester Guardian* in Berlin. For the *Manchester Guardian* episode, cf. Christopher Sykes, *Troubled Loyalty: A Biography of Adam von Trott zu Solz* (London, 1968), pp. 104 ff: Henry Ozelle Malone, *Adam von Trott zu Solz: Werdegang eines Verschwörers 1909–1938* (Berlin, 1986), pp. 116 ff.

Hanau
7th May, 1934.

My Dear Shiela,

I have been very bad about writing lately, and you have written me such a beautiful letter which I have carried in my pocket and have just reread. Now this will be just in time for your 21st birthday, and my letter will probably be swamped by the flood of friendly letters you will receive from everywhere, so you too must do me the favour to reread mine some other calm time!—But then, it is right that you should enjoy this festival occasion and have it as grandly as possible. I know you like that, really belonging like myself to that squirearchy for which the coming of age has always been of special importance, to renew the devotion of all sorts of dependents. You should survive this, even if your new style[1] may have made you spend this day away in the country or at one of those democratic parties at All Souls. If you were a sovereign lady coming of age I should like to be your gardener or forester preparing the flowers or game for your great banquet, and a specially beautiful specimen to present to you at the morning of the great day. I am sure I would be a very good gardener for you, your garden would have to become a wonder of landscape gardening—perhaps in the style of the bridge at Blenheim—and there would be fresh flowers of all colours before your house and windows at every time of the year, (I will not go into the forester's services for I have just been reading Lady Chatterley![2] forgive me)—yes, I think you would be the most wonderful person to form the centre of a great festival, and I do hope your birthday this time will be a little bit like that!

And what you say about being friends, depending less in future on people, actual events, and changes of daily life, is I think very true, and seems even more emphasised by the fact of your having become a legal adult as well. If only this hasn't the consequence of letting our relationship become all impersonal too, which I think would be a crude falsification. I too would like to walk and talk with you, and that there should still be ways that you remember having gone with me gives me great pleasure. There are some that I hardly dare to remember yet. One of the most vivid memories of you though was a warm summer evening in London when you walked down to the river with me—you were bare-footed, and we talked and the night seemed very beautiful.

I was interrupted by an old jeweller who is being sued by a London firm and who, after having all his claims put to paper went on to tell me a lot of his experiences in London. What a contrast to all I had just been writing about! As a young goldsmith, (he said) (I don't believe him), he beat up a policeman who had asked him to shut up, and when told by some people in a pub that the Kaiser was a fool, he had answered Queen Mary was a mistress of Kitchener.[3] In the mornings he had for some time cleaned windows in the City, while in the afternoons he was walking with a silk hat in the West End, and drew jewellery for diamond merchants, till one of them recognised him as the window-cleaner of the morning and gave him a commission for £1500. I think he is a wild liar, but quite amusing—he said he still knew 'every pub' in London, and was well-known there—

I am sorry you should have thought I was being drawn helplessly into the curse of nationalism—but it reminds me of your saying that (at any rate in the beginning) you like to listen to me without understanding one word of my Hegelian English. No, Shiela, I am not drawn into that curse; and if one has to accept the order of independent nation states, because as it stands, they are the only means to maintain any order at all, one assents neither to the invidiousness of the Versailles Treaty nor to rampant nationalism, which are the two extremes brought on one by the other. I should like to talk to you about many things—about what you write about philosophy and economics and poetry and faith in things and people!—I am quite sure schools[4] will be allright for you. There is a great clarity in the sentences of your letter, and the very tentativeness of your judgements is extremely persuasive. My papers in schools were lacking both, so I am sure you will do better than I did. And I heartily hope that you will. I am sorry that I cannot walk with you and stimulate your all too modest self-consciousness which is so much preyed upon by many sides of Oxford.—And last, not least, schools and universities are not really the place for a person like you, and therefore you are dealing with them best when you take them as a passing show. But you hate people being patronising—and I won't be, though somehow I always like being patronised by you!

Love
A.

[1] Shiela at this stage of her life followed the desires and customs of her friends more than those of her family which, with the exception of her mother, did not mean much to her; as for what Adam termed the 'squirearchy', she greatly scorned it.
[2] D. H. Lawrence, *Lady Chatterley's Lover* (1928).
[3] Horatio Herbert Kitchener, 1st Earl (1850–1916); British general and war minister.
[4] Final examinations at Oxford.

Bath
[early July] 1934

Dear Adam,

Thank you for your letter, which was a little short and severe, but nice to have.[1] Please write again and tell me how you are and what you are doing. I wish you were here. It is a most wonderful place, with a rose garden below the house like a swimming bath. I want to dive from the buttresses of the house into rose petals. I am in a very excited and bewildered state—but I would not exchange it for happiness—Do you know how it feels?—as if all one's nerves were uncovered and open like the strings of a piano when it is in bits—one feels very responsive, rather delicate and apprehensive and a little melancholy, but also very excited—(I shall get like Shaiah with this Anatomy of Melancholy[2]—all his moods have anatomies). It is leaving Oxford and all my friends, and meaning to leave England and all my family—I have never felt such a revolution in my life[3]—Everything is new and strange, and one minute I think it is and will be very fine and beautiful, and the next I think it is and will be the decay of the past, and the substitution of second rate for first rate things. Do you remember at Oxford I used to say 'I do not know what I want to be' and you used to say I was lucky to feel I had the choice. I feel I still have it, but perhaps it is self-deception.

I have been reading a wonderful book about Japan—called La Bataille, by Claude Farrère[4]—Because of this imperialism of theirs in China, I had hated the Japanese, but now I admire them very much.

I'm afraid it is impossible for me to understand them—I wish I were not English with such closed sympathies. Do you know the story of the Japanese prince who had the most beautiful garden—say of roses, and the Emperor, hearing of it, asked to see it. When he came he could see no garden—the beautiful lawns of flowers he had been led to expect were not there—. Then the prince led him to the most beautiful and perfect flower, standing all alone in absolute perfection. 'This', he said, 'is my garden'.—and he had destroyed all the rest to accentuate this one perfection. It is a philosophy of life—very splendid and noble. But I do not know if I could live it. I am back to thinking of philosophy as I thought of it before I went up to Oxford—as an explanation of the universe, and as a modus vivendi. Is that how the Greeks thought of it? I went to Oxford a Stoic, I believe, and left it an Epicurean—but that is probably untrue—and as my friends said when people talk like this—'It is only a fact about myself.'

I wish we could talk about you—I am a little afraid to write. I think I understand how you feel, and admire you for it, but I wish you did not feel it. Patriotism is a primitive instinct and is a narrowing of sympathies—but if you feel it, as you do—so strongly, you must obey it. With you it does not take the form of hating other countries and people—and perhaps I shall one day think you are right, and one must promote the welfare of one's own country first—. I am glad I am not a man, so that I cannot be called upon to promote it at the expense of other things which I value. For the freedom one loses, there are other freedoms one gains—I wish there were any absolute freedom, but I have read Bradley[5] with too much conviction to believe there is. It is so silly writing to you this way—but I do not know how else to write—everything must seem meaningless and terrible to you and it is heartless and cruel to write about rose gardens and freedom.[6] I wish I could see you. Would it be any good from the point of view of seeing you if I came to Germany in the next few weeks? I am free now except for a viva[7] on the 26th July. I am only bounded in by money now—and I can scrape that together. I am a capitalist you know, and can sell my capital and live like a rich woman for a few years in the expectation of dying at the end. It will probably be the fate of most of ours—and the lives of those who don't die will hardly be worth living in any case. I can't think how people can bear to grow old—they're duped by this family business, I suppose. I mean what I say about seeing you. I would come to Germany if I can do anything for you. One must be loyal to one's friends.

My love,

S.

[1] Adam's letter lost.

[2] Allusion to Robert Burton, *The Anatomy of Melancholy* (1621).

[3] Shiela had just taken her Finals in Philosophy, Politics, and Economics, and felt the need of having a year of her own away from Oxford in order to find out where she stood and what she wanted to do; Grant Duff, *The Parting of Ways*. p. 56.

[4] Claude Farrère, *La Bataille* (Paris, 1921).

[5] F. H. Bradley, *Ethical Studies*, 2nd edn., (Oxford, 1927).

[6] This passage is an allusion to the news on the 'Night of the Long Knives' in Germany, the so-called Röhm Purge of 30 June 1934 in which Hitler rid himself of the chief of his Stormtroopers (SA) Ernst Röhm and numerous other actual and potential political foes within and without the Nazi Party.

[7] See letter Adam–Shiela, Glasgow 22 July 1933, n. 7.

Imshausen.
18th July, 1934.

My Dear Shiela,

I have been home now for three days and often I thought of you, wanting to communicate to you the delight of summer in these fields and woods, the beauty of which I hate to describe with words—I thought how lovely it would be to show to you these waves of ripening cornfields, the fresh green of grass and moss under pine trees and the violet yellow of rye in the sunset. A few hours breathing in this sphere at home restores to me a sense of living that I have always missed in the towns—however necessary and sensible it may be to stay there.

Your letter this morning arrived together with one that indicated to me the rejection of my transference to Berlin which I had very much hoped would come about. There has been one thing after another like that, and if Oxford has ever made me an Epicurean, things have tended to teach me the opposite since. But to go back to Hanau, which they wanted me to, I obstructed, so I rang up the offices where these things are decided, and by persuasive politeness to some powerful subaltern I managed to be transferred to Kassel instead.[1] That is not too far from here—

Your letter delighted me, Shiela—it is not so much the words—though I like the story of the prince's garden—but your readiness to remain for me the good friend you are. Mine was not meant to be 'short and severe'—but you see, I am horrified by the idea that as a friend I should in any way be a burden to you. So I wanted you to feel that though things were edged and difficult at present, for an outside view perhaps even confused and distressing, that I am not desponding. (The harder you have to fight for it, the more precious freedom becomes). And also I wanted you to see that however complex temporary estrangement might seem, I was aware of a keen loyalty between us. Well, and that your letter confirms—that's why it made me very glad indeed.

Unless you mean by 'if I can do anything for you' that on your own account you would rather not come, I would ask you very earnestly to come now. Whatever else is true, it is beautiful here now—many of the fields may be stubbles by then, but I still think there is this sound beauty that Hesse can offer to you. For myself it would be a very great joy to see you—it's a very strong wish in fact that suffers from no doubts whatsoever except perhaps that you may find I have little to offer.

But do come. It seems a right stage to meet again. You can live and travel very cheaply in Germany. You would come to Kassel—a rather beautiful town in its way, though inhabited by wicked dwarfs I always think (all the less reason for us to be disturbed by them), there's a river, parks, woods (plenty), a Rembrandt Gallery, a charming library—I won't have too much work, and we would drive here for the week-ends. Tell me soon, and I shall find you a nice room—it would not be as violent a start on life as Paris, but free enough from all familiar associations and a calm basis for planning your own for the coming year.

I see that it is very important for you not to be hindered in this by your loyalty to your friends, Shiela, and I shall not be hurt if you turn down the plan after all. I want you to be of help to me—which quite undoubtedly your presence would be—only if I am sure that I am at the same time of help to you.

There's no loyalty—not even patriotism—which is right without promoting the best of our real self, that's why it is right and noble to be selfish in this sense—One of the reasons why I have always liked you is that I have thought you to be selfish in this sense.

I don't know whether I told you why I wanted to go to Berlin—the reasons remain though I shall have to wait and see now. There are so many things to explain and tell, but also to learn from you, that letters are no good for. . . .

I hope the larks will still be singing when you come

Love

A.

---

[1] Adam was transferred to the Public Prosecutor's office in Kassel, the capital of the Prussian province of Hesse-Nassau.

Imshausen.
Aug. 19th 1934.

My Dear Shiela,
You were away long before you had gone,[1] and the stupour of separation had seized me while I tried to be still gay with you. Now it
has left—but this morning I had a letter from M.[2] which apparently
puts an end to everything. She is definitely in love with that Scandinavian boy, and does not want to see me again. It destroys a very great
deal which—by analogy to the one embracing love you have had—
you will understand. You said I must not 'take comforts'—and yet it
is exactly what seems impossible not to at times. Without that I
might have realised before that the new direction might threaten to
turn a pure and honest devotion into the idea of your distrust which
is truly unbearable. It is unjustified.
One must not burden anything new with the pains of the past, they
must be born out to the full first. In a sense I feel that after this one
greatest failure—and it was my failure—I shall never legitimately
attach myself to one person, nor shall I have any right to expect trust.
Your life seems so clear and unbroken and hopeful to me. I want
to be unselfish in my love for it, though I cannot for given reasons
expect you to be entirely in your relation to mine. Let's be calm
undisturbed friends trusting to time what we cannot to present
efforts between us.
Yesterday I spent a beautiful though sad evening in the woods, and
this morning I went to the ballot[3] after reading Kleist.[4] Now you are
listening to Mozart and perhaps after a few hours are already carried
by the tidal waves of old and other friends. Dear Shiela—I have finished Flaubert—it is the most disillusioned book, most foreign to
your view of life, but beautiful. You must give a great amnesty for
distrust and set free thereby a lot of prisoners and judges for happy
weeks like ours.

Love,
A.

[1] In mid-Aug. Shiela visited Adam in Kassel; then the two proceeded to Imshausen where Shiela met Adam's parents. Towards the end of her stay Shiela got
involved in a discussion with Adam's mother on Germany's place in the world which
ended rather acrimoniously—with Adam's mother standing up for Germany's pride
and Shiela attacking; cf. Grant Duff, *The Parting of Ways*, pp. 57 ff.
[2] Miriam.
[3] Reference to the plebiscite of 19 Aug. after the death of President von Hindenburg on the question of Hitler's assumption of the Presidency.
[4] See letter Adam–Shiela, Kassel, 31 Oct. 1934 n. 1.

Salzburg.
20.8.34.

Dear Adam,

... It is so beautiful and so much a place to be happy in, and alone it is a little bit sad. It was very nice with you. Thank you very much for taking me to your home and for showing me so many beautiful places. The woods I liked specially. It would be wonderful to be a roebuck in them except for the danger of being shot by philistines like you and Bobbi.[1] You are very lucky to have a home—not just a house with a family in it, but a whole place where you belong and which you can make into what you want. I do so hope you will be able to divide it up as you want to and that it will not be a Tolstoyan plan like Levin's, but what you mean it to be. It would be very satisfying to take Candide literally,[2] and make a community on such a basis. Perhaps the Dark Ages will be repeated in detail and as well as the broad political chaos we seem to be getting into, there will be a return to small community life. You are a great Paternalist, except in your friendships—there, not at all, I don't think. Your friends have to look after themselves and the relation is one of sovereign states. It is a very good thing, but I am not sure how many people can stand it. Most people look for comfort rather than anything else in their friends—that's why they make such bad friends—perhaps that's not true. ...

I wish I went home by Kassel so I could see you again and visit all the palaces with squirrels and woods with deer, once again.

Much love,

S.

I hope you voted.[3]

[1] Adam's cousin, whose real name was Friedrich von Trott zu Solz.
[2] Konstantin Levin in Leo Tolstoy's novel *Anna Karenina* had vision of transforming his country estate into a co-operative farm as opposed to Voltaire's prescription at the end of *Candide* 'we must cultivate our garden' which sets individaul and concrete well-being above the visionary abstraction.
[3] See letter Adam–Shiela, Imshausen, 19 Aug. 1934, n. 3.

Kassel.
[About 22. Aug.] 1934.

[Dear Shiela,]

I was just about to get absurdly unhappy about your absence, silence, and general unattainableness, when I found the letter in green ink coming home. ...

Yes, there must be sovereignty in friendship, but the very fact that there's another sovereign state—they are rare—is a great comfort I find and alliance with it a great aid in dealing with internal up-heavals. . . .

My Love to you,

A.

I did vote.[1]

I wish you were here and then I wish there were no frontiers. You must not be sorry for a single more second to have 'quarrelled' with my mother, she told me that your talk afterwards had brought you nearer than if you hadn't previously misunderstood each other—that she liked you a great deal and was extremely sorry for her impatience, very apologetic indeed for she felt she had spoilt something with it for us—It was entirely due to her extremely bad nervous condition at the present, and there's truly no cause for the slightest depression—you are *very* affectionately remembered at I.

---

[1] This is a cryptic answer obviously for reasons of censorship. But Shiela after Hindenburg's death entered into her diary as follows: 'Adam, if he votes, will vote against. He voted against Hitler last time, tho' he voted for leaving the League. As his mother said, no responsible person did not vote for leaving it. . . .

Salzburg.
22.8.34.

Dear Adam,

I am most terribly sorry to hear about Miriam[1] and I wish I could be with you now if I could comfort you in any way, because I would comfort you willingly. I cannot bear you to be unhappy nor have a great deal destroyed nor feel you can never legitimately attach your-self to any one person, nor expect trust. She must also have felt that when you met Diana—and indeed before, that first summer in Oxford when you were doubting. I cannot explain why you should neither of you feel it—or perhaps you should feel it. Do you know the Shakespeare sonnet

> Love is not love
> Which alters when it alteration finds
> Or bends with the remover to remove

I have never known what it means—whether it means one's own love should not alter, if a person changes, or if the love of that person changes. I think it is probably the latter and means, for you, that you must not cease to love her, or forget that you have loved her—and for her, that she also must remember that she has loved you and be true to that memory, even in loving someone else. It is perhaps, because she feels that, that she does not want to see you again. I don't know. I'm afraid to come in where I am not wanted, and can only be a lesser comfort to a greater sorrow. Only please, Adam, do not feel bitter . . . and trust people still, and expect trust from them. Trust me, and expect trust from me. We will be calm, undisturbed friends, and hope that what time adds of good to our lives will be added to our friendship. I wish you could be here with me now. In the garden you could read and work at your Kleist with the mountains round you, and beautiful sunshine, and seclusion from the people we know in Salzburg—except in the evenings when we would listen to music. . . . I would comfort you, tho' not for comfort's sake, as I feared you were seeking it. I forget why you do not expect me to be unselfish towards your life, tho' you are to mine—Let's both be unselfish.

Love,
Shiela,

¹ See letter Adam–Shiela, Imshausen, 19 Aug. 1934.

Kassel
24.8.34

My very dear Shiela,

I think I have finished the Kleist essay.¹ I shall rewrite it again though, and when I have time I shall translate it and send it to you, to whom in a way it belongs. For you helped me a great deal. Your last letter did—it made my trust go out to you and embrace you in gratitude. The fact that you are not mixed up with all sorts of friends, but are staying in your lovely place all by yourself makes me particularly thankful. Because one is always honest when one is alone—and that you should then say you wish I were there, to work in the garden and to be comforted by you though not for comfort's sake—dear Shiela, it makes me almost forget that I was unhappy. You see, you come in in such a strange and important way—as far more than a 'lesser comfort!' I have from the beginning sensed in you sympathy and respect for something like my love for Miriam. The older I grow, the more conscious its meaning becomes for me, parts recede into, and parts merge from mystery. Doubt, pain, and finally bitterness—the effects of distance in age and place I feel have been undermining this possession for a very long time. I never know how much one crisis means, but the process I fear has been a gradual and certain one. In a way it has meant a constant dying for me, death of all the great many realisations that at long last I seemed to have found in this love. Beforehand you see there was constant desire for some person to understand and share—something never fulfilled full of promise but frustrated. When I met M. I told you this frustration had just been of a most devastating nature. I knew that I was embarking on a new great undertaking with risks, dangers and very uncertain reward, but I did it consciously and with a somewhat resigned determination. Then in that summer at Göttingen it flowered into something so complete and beautiful that my conception of emotional value must always I think derive from then. It was a very nearly complete sharing of heart and mind, yet undreamlike joined to all the parts of ordinary practical and even political life. I should be a scoundrel if ever I forgot this—no I honour it as a still living thing in my life, though all it entailed I cannot still quite see in its strange growing away from my own life. It is not that I have shirked the pains of great happiness, leaving it when they come. They have been abundant, violent and dreary, but I have tried hard to accept and mould them to that experience of bigger, more joyful life. The demands of the lesser life—examination work especially, the insistent time pressure, the fear of Miriam's necessary departure in summer 31, health and all came in to challenge our triumphs. She left in the middle of July from Kassel where we walked the night before in the known park—you see, and then the year came part of which you know, and the fearful gradual preponderance of pain and doubt between us. Even then we did not give up, it was a terrific struggle—of which outside happenings, including even my relation to D. were symptoms never sources to what really mattered. Clearly I behaved unimaginatively and in consequence cruelly, but it was not that I didn't still know and desire what was right between us. My capacity to act up to it was numbed I think by failure and my life refused to stand still and concentrate. It was then I think that the ground began to shift under our feet—starting a most desperate violent upheaval in her and a profound cold discouragement in me. Yet in the whole following year and after Miriam's second return to America I have not given up trying and hoping, to give up did not only seem to me like letting down treacherously another human being but a giving up of my entire ideal of immediate personal loyalty and all it may bring between people. The pressure on Miriam was unbearably stronger, she must have all along felt that I had failed her finally already—a realisation which weighed heavily on my discouragement—and now, you see, she has given up trying.

Thank you for making me see from your note that you realise the extreme vital importance of all this—you see it is really that I shall never feel trust in that side of life and oneself again—Miriam used to say that this was not as important to me as it was to some people. Yet, what can be important, if this isn't? I write to Miriam now with a feeling that all my words—and they flow very scarcely now too—are nothing but a vain escape from something irretrievable. That makes them pitiful and empty, so the honester thing seems to be silence, and even now I know that Miriam suffers badly when I don't write.

Please don't feel burdened by all this, dear Shiela, there seems such a lot that I would rather write about yourself—(your intentions are of great personal interest to me!)—you have mocked yourself being a moralist but any person reading this letter (there will be no one beside you please!) would think me a most pressing moralist for urging onto you the role of father confessor in matters so distinctly my own. You see I do now want absolution from you, but perhaps trust in my continued efforts to be loyal to all that Miriam means. And you see, somehow life seems to have singled you out for giving me this. Please in return let me show to you that I can be a loyal unselfish friend. I know you can understand the importance of this wish—let me be there for you whenever and however you might need me. I know life does not repeat itself, but just because of this I feel that you of all people including even Miriam could alone realise what importance initial great failure of heart means to someone who does not ultimately accept being severed into the parting streams of intellect and sense. However argued this letter may sound, Shiela, it is to neither of them that I appeal in you.—You need not answer in length, short of an unexpected turn that makes me unreal to you again, I do not now believe that you and I will lose sight so easily.

Love and many thanks to you,
Adam.

D. has announced her coming for Sept. 1! It will be lovely to see her.

¹ See letter Adam–Shiela, Kassel, 31. Oct. 1934, n. 1.

Salzburg.
25.8.34.

Dear Adam,

Thank you for your letter, which has been to the Toscanini concert with me and for a ride on the back of a motor bicycle, and back a long walk alone in the moonlight. I was late for the concert and did not have time to read it so I took it with me, and ran down the road and a man on a motor bicycle offered to me a lift—and there being a general amnesty, I took it and he was most charming and I enjoyed it very much and thought how exciting is must be to have a young man with a motor bicycle. Then I shook hands with him and he went away. The concert was incredibly grand socially—all the elite of money and intellect—but far far grander musically. It was absolutely wonderful—the Haffner Symphony is beautiful[1]—but most moving of all was the Beethoven 7th Symphony. Do you remember it? I'm afraid it made me think of my own life. The first movement is absolutely terrible—full of past gaiety and joy which is so sad to remember, and the 2nd movement is a Funeral March in which unhappiness is fine and pure. Then it breaks into new life in the 3rd movement, and the 4th is superb and splendid victory. I am hung, as it were, over the first three movements—or perhaps the second is yet to come, but I pray not.

. . . Stephen[2] is here . . . writing a long poem about the Viennese troubles. He is full of despair about central European politics and says they are absolutely corrupt, I talked to a young Austrian here who is a National Socialist and says all Austrian men are—Stephen doesn't believe it's true. I wish you could meet Stephen—he is extremely nice. He is extremely nice. He said he liked you. I said you had asked me to send him the Cossacks[3] a long time ago and I would do so. . . .

A terrific storm has suddenly come. I heard it coming, like a train, and now it's tearing at my window. There are heavy black clouds stretching from the mountains and the wind is full of leaves and sticks which knock at the window. It was you who brought me home safely when there were no clouds and bright moonlight because I wanted to write to you—now I would be rather afraid to come in the dark, even with your letter. Growing up is becoming afraid of fewer and fewer things and becoming a sovereign state. Let's have an alliance. I wish it could also be an alliance of a new Germany and a new England—if only our countries regarded each other as we do, there would be greater hope in Europe—but they're all such fools. International morality should be identical with personal morality— selfishness, suspicion, fear, bitterness, revenge, should be as discreditable feelings for a country as for a person.

The storm is stupendous—there is lightning, a great wind, but no thunder. It is as if the wind were made by the lightning breaking the air. Somewhere there must be thunder—in the mountains perhaps— There is a gash in the sky behind the Untersberg. I want to know the history of Europe in the last 20 years—or at least since the War— why such peaks of idealism, hope and bravery are followed by such pits of despair, anarchy, and oppression. I want to write a book about it, not the events of history, but the sufferings and hopes of the people, showing the frightful price paid for every international move—for every economic change, the long run effects of the war on freeing people and making them more hopelessly servile to fear and leadership than ever before. I want to do two things—one is to write the history—the unwritten part of history, of the last twenty years in the form of a novel—perhaps many, it will have to be—and it would take years and years to do,—and the other, if possible, to contribute something to prevent war and bring about better peace conditions in Europe—especially in Austria and Germany—that is the vague outline of my ambitions—the latter, very vague indeed, and I fear very much the former, but to attempt either and fail is infinitely better than not to attempt—even though neither seem to have much place in the Universe—tho' I can't find any places there, nor any point or purpose. . . .

Bless you Adam—do not feel great wealth has gone—you cannot lose what you have had, tho' it is the 1st movement of the 7th Symphony and great pain to remember, but there are the 3rd and 4th movements to come for you.

Love to you
S.

The last sentence of your letter was quite incomprehensible—'the truest diplomacy which is as near to the issues of history as to the struggle of internal resources to be mutually brought up to it'?

Isn't it nice to think England's frontiers are the Rhine! But it would be so much less silly if I and not Baldwin[4] had said it.

---

[1] Mozart, Symphony no. 35 in D (K. 385).
[2] Stephen Spender *Vienna* (New York, 1935); see also letter Shiela–Adam, beginning of Mar. 1934, n. 1.
[3] Leo Tolstoy, *The Cossacks* (Oxford, 1853).
[4] Stanley Baldwin (1867–1947), from 1937 first Earl of Baldwin; Prime Minister of Great Britain, May 1923–Jan. 1924, Nov. 1924–June 1929, and June 1935–May 1937: 'When you think of the defence of England you no longer think of the chalk cliffs of Dover; you think of the Rhine. That is where our frontier lies'; 30 July 1934, *House of Commons Parliamentary Debates*, vol. 292, col. 2339.

Munich
27.8.34.

Dear Adam,

. . . Thank you for your letter. Thank you above all for believing I can understand—perhaps I can, only because I pretend to no experience. I understand what you have lost because it is what I have never thought possible—I cannot help believing in the utter separateness and eventual solitariness of everything living, and human sympathy is somehow the cruellest of all creations because it is helpless—it is terrible to believe, but I hope one day it will be different with G[1]—only one must face the other first. I wish now Adam, I could persuade you to trust that side of life and yourself again—since you have both believed in it and realised it, your failure this time should not take away your faith. You know it is possible and you have fought against the dangers of it—then surely it is possible and you can fight again—You must be brave enough not only to admit failure, but to face further attempt. You cannot now, and have no wish to—leave it, do your work, write to Miriam—It cannot be more honest to leave unsaid to her even those things which you said to me. Try and write—she will be glad of it and not ashamed or unhappy if she realises she has given you more than she can ever take away and left you stronger and brave and not broken. I'm sorry to write so morally to you—you don't need it—I respect very much what you feel now, but I hate you to say you will not feel trust in yourself or that side of life any more, because it must be the greatest thing in the world. When I do take marriage seriously that is what I mean by it—it is the way of life under which love and perfect understanding are alone possible. This Shelleyan-Epipsychidion[2] kind of love is more worldly than the other, but in Shelley's hands it assumes a more ideal character because he sees what a falsehood marriage is for most people, how it blocks out even gentle human kindness for other people—and also perhaps because he over-estimated the capacity of most human beings to understand each—Have you read Epipsychidion? Read it and tell me what you think. . . .

Love
S.

---

[1] Goronwy Rees.
[2] See letter Shiela–Adam, Chelsea, 14 Sept. 1934.

Kassel
[30 Aug. 1934]

[Dear Shiela,]

The grievance I confided to you seems to be truer even than I thought for I dare not accept your sweet and generous offer for fear that rather than restoring it would further this dissolution of loyalties.

Dear Shiela, I took your letter up into the woods where we were together—do you remember that bench way over the lights of the city and the plain, framed in widely by tall, slender beeches? And I find you must not go out of your way now to help me, for what help can I really accept when the core of it all is well realised past and present failure within my own life? I want to become truly calm and undisturbed before I see you again, and I want a complete absence of qualms and worry for you too. . . .

I know I have not reached anything like a satisfactory attitude about M. and I must not (as I have been) simply drown it in books and other things and people, and I know I must not let down D. whose role is guiltless though unrealising as far as M. is concerned. Dear Shiela, how entangled I must seem to you, and yet I know if you sat here with me under these beeches you would see without much comment. Let's save our comeradeship for gay hard co-operation. . . .

Give me the Shelley you recommend when you get back, will you? . . .

Sometimes I wish you were a man and would live with me, go to the law and work with me all the time, without its meaning any complications—but then it wouldn't be you really, would it? No, I think it might. . . .

Ever love,

A.

Basel.

2nd Sept. 1934

Dear Adam,

I can't quite make out what is happening to you—whether your troubles are personal or public—at least whether they are both. I was not sure of the reason why you put off Diana, and your letter being so cryptic, I concluded it was public trouble, so wrote to her according to that—which may have been wrong, but doesn't matter. I don't know what you can do for her, except show her how big the world is, and how full of interest even without you in it. (dear Adam, I'm glad you are in it). You are right probably to sort out your own life now, and us meet again when you are calm and undisturbed, and in possession of yourself. I too wish I were a man, tho' my not being shall make no difference to us being friends—tho' to our lives, but remember Balzac, 'la dissemblance des destinées est presque toujours un puissant lieu d'amitié.'[1]—but perhaps if I were a man I could help you more now, which I would like to do, though I think you are right and it is only your own battle—but please Adam, if it is very hard, ignore my own words as to the helplessness of sympathy and prove them untrue—and above all if I could help you 'publicly'. . . .

Love,

S.

[Postscript omitted]

¹ 'The dissimilarity of destinies is almost always a powerful bond of friendship.'

Imshausen.

Sept 2nd, 1934

[Dear Shiela,]

I have just come back from that hill over the woods where there is the wildest view; we were there together one evening you remember? From the distance I heard the village lads and girls sing their rustic melancholic songs on the road between Solz and our valley. The woods were beautiful, with a tinge of autumn over the crowns and a blue haze joining them on to the pale night sky. The horizon in the west and the volcano-like mountain you will remember were bathed in flaming red to a kind of sulphur colour making it look all wide and like the edges of the world.

Dear Shiela, I always try and entrust the things that happen to these solemn hills and trees and old familiar forms so that when I next come to them they relate the things of one's life that are important and permanent . . . You truly belong to my home now as an inalienable part of it. Please don't find this a queer form of nature-worship—it is very simple. Yesterday night I spent a rather wild night drinking and dancing with all the cousins in Solz.¹ I came home at half past three in beautiful pale moonlight—the meadows and bushes were all silver, and the arches beneath the beeches like secret castles of nymphs. And it was so reassuring to walk quietly on the gravel of the white road with all its apple trees on either side. I once drove down it with you on the back of an over-loaded car and once up it in mine but you wouldn't remember that!? Listening to the songs of the villagers tonight I felt strongly why had I been made not to stay with them ever since 15 years ago when I started to become a highbrow. You would have liked me better then, Shiela, I am sure; at any rate I would have deserved being liked ever so much more. I hope you are finding all you wanted at Montreux, I hope indeed that you are happy and strong—I worked today, but it was none too good. When could you take your degree in October, when will you leave for Paris?

Love and many thoughts from
A.

---

[1] Branch of the von Trott family living in nearby Solz; Adam frequently visited the Solz cousins.

Chelsea.
14th Sept. [1934]

Dear Adam,

Thank you for two letters.[1] You sounded depressed and bewildered and I am very sorry. I do not think of you as on a sick bed so you should not think my enquiries as for a sick person.

I know very well how it is—I think perhaps in every grown person's life there comes a break, a time of great change and bewilderment and often unhappiness before one can become whole. Stephen said that illness often marked this in people's lives—We grow up without being ill. . . .

Do you remember wondering what loyalty was? I think it is keeping each of the relations one has, unhurt and unaffected by the others. It is never denying what one is to one person when one is not with them—never allowing one love to drive out another. It is not the negative virtue conventional morality makes of it. It is something constructive, embracing one's whole life, all love. But this satisfies conventional morality also because the main relation of one's life—such as marriage would be, is the highest of all loyalties. It is the love which demands the greatest of one, that one should be strong, wise, gentle, and of widest sympathies—so that loyalty to it is loyalty to oneself and to all the qualities of the world one admires—so any lesser love which threatens to hurt that, must be sacrificed.

Here is the Epipsychidion poem for you. I will not send you the whole because I hate most of the rest.

> Thy wisdom speaks in me, and bids me dare
> Beacon the rocks on which high hearts are wreckt.
> I never was attached to that great sect
> Whose doctrine is, that each one should select
> Out of the crowd a mistress or a friend,
> And all the rest, though fair and wise, commend
> To cold oblivion, though it is in the code
> Of modern morals, and the beaten road
> Which those poor slaves with weary footsteps tread,

Who travel to their home among the dead
By the broad highway of the world, and so
With one chained friend, perhaps a jealous foe,
The dreariest and the longest journey go.

True Love in this differs from gold and clay,
That to divide is not to take away.
Love is like understanding, that grows bright
Gazing on many truths; . . .

> . . . Narrow
The heart that loves, the brain that contemplates,
The life that wears, the spirit that creates
One object, and one form, and builds thereby
A sepulchre for its eternity

Mind from its object differs most in this:
Evil from good; misery from happiness;
The baser from the nobler; the impure
And frail, from what is clear and must endure.
If you divide suffering and dross, you may
Diminish till it is consumed away;
If you divide pleasure and love and thought
Each part exceeds the whole; and we know not
How much, while any yet remains unshared,
Of pleasure may be gained, of sorrow spared:

At the end of the poem, he says—

We shall become the same, we shall be one
Spirit within two frames, oh! wherefore two?[2]

What I understand by loyalty covers, I think,—both loving one person and loving many. It is, if only one can love, the same—It is only if one cannot love properly, or one is not a whole person that there is conflict between them, and one must choose 'one chained friend' or a multitude of superficial affections.

Does it bore or worry you to read all this now? . . . But your natural inclination to live in the 'wide crystal clear cold atmosphere outside' must not make you despair of love as you were doing. Please do not—but I will not write to you any more about it—I also go to Paris to work. My intentions are clear and firm. I shall live by myself in a sort of hotel there in Montparnasse, and find if I can a Professor at the Sorbonne who will help me study what I want. If there is none there, I shall have to learn from politicians. I have an enormous and intense desire to know everything and understand. I am reading a book by a countryman of yours—Burckhardt[3]—about the Italian Renaissance. It is wildly exciting. To know what the 'I' really is you must read about the Renaissance, when men suddenly grasped the making of Individuality. It was the flowering of art, culture, and learning.—Now we are turning against all that. I hate it—I am an individualist tho' the sufferings it causes to millions if society is built that way, makes me want to die but not to deny individualism. Are you a Hegelian? Do you remember Stephen's poem about the 'I'?[4] It is in his book I think.

> Only he who has learned everything
> said Ghiberti 'is nowhere a stranger;
> Robbed of his fortune and without friends,
> He is yet a citizen of every country and
> Can fearlessly despise the changes of fortune.[5]

Write to me if you can, Adam. . . .

Love
Shiela.

This letter too long and love boring on paper usually.

[1] One of Adam's letters missing.
[2] Shelley, *Epipsychidion* (London, 1821).
[3] Jacob Burckhardt (1818–97), a native of Basle, Switzerland, was the major nineteenth-century historian of the Italian Renaissance; *The Civilization of the Renaissance in Italy* (London, 1878).
[4] Stephen Spender 'An 'I' can never be a great man', *Poems* (London, 1933), p. 18.
[5] Burckhardt, *The Civilization of the Renaissance in Italy* (Vienna and New York, 1937), p. 72.

Kassel.
19th Sept, 1934.

Yes, Shiela, love must be something immediate, something to touch me and see, otherwise it becomes untrue. Only sometimes a sudden realisation brings back to me in the morning, when sunrays come through the open window, how you had been here in this very room, and how warm and delightful your presence. Or I remember you at my side in the car with your Scandinavian scarf looking so joyous and——[1] or I remember that afternoon at the pond near Wilhelmstal[2] where I gave you two big white feathers to put in your hair—But usually these warm moments and you seem very far away.

Thank you for your letter with Shelley's lines that I must reread. Your Theory of Love is beautiful but it never works . . . I do not think it is lack of wholeness—nothing surmounts it more truly—but distance that breaks love.

There is now complete silence everywhere and I can hear the wind sing. I saw a magnificent grey evening sky driving through the country from the West tonight—it seemed like a drama of 'cosmic profundity' (this expression struck my mind when I banged the garage door).

I came across at the courts this story of a young man who fell in love with the youngish wife of his farm-employer. They were apparently wildly so—lovers, and she demanded of him to give up his bride. He was 20, and this hurt him terribly. The conflict seemed to consume him entirely. Life became intolerable to him and he decided to commit suicide.—A friend of mine had to question him about all this.—So he went out one evening into the fields by himself, where quite unexpectedly he met the old farmer. That man had known and even had talked about the young man's relation to his wife. But sudden and quite inexplicable fury beset him when he saw the farmer walk towards him. He seized a plank of wood and killed him with innumerable blows over the head.—The young man is a good, gentle, sympathetic, almost soft creature. He is now in the convict for 15 years. Can you understand at all?

Shiela, don't cease to write 'because love is boring on paper' (thank you for this sentence!)—it is presence in some curious way—and more and better in your writing than in mine. . . .

My love to you

A.

---

¹ Blank in the original letter.
² A rococo castle and park near Kassel.

[*Postcard of Goya's 'The Duel'*]

London
[*end of* September 1934]

[Dear Adam,]

Here are some duellers I bought for you a long time ago. I hope you will like them. Your letters are a little incomprehensible. I can't write you a long one now because I am going to Berlin to-morrow.¹ I only decided to to-day. It is rather unexpected—but I have almost ceased to expect things. . .

[Shiela]

---

¹ To visit Goronwy Rees who had written an anguished letter to Shiela from Berlin; see Grant Duff, *The Parting of Ways*, p. 64.

[*Postcard*]

2.10.34

[Dear Adam,]
    Do you want some money? If so I could give you some from Jane! But will you send me a cheque for 3/-, or your monetary affairs cannot be wound up.
    It is very warm and nice here—still summer— tho' in England it was far away. We are going to Grunewald[1]—this afternoon. I hear your brother lives there, tho' I am afraid he will not be there now. I would like to see him. This morning I admired your countrymen's pictures. They reveal all sorts of national characteristics. If you want to tell me about the English character I will tell you about the German. We are going to Fidelio tonight.

Love,
S.

Are you going to England in Oct? Is there any point? You have to pay a lot of money for a degree, and it would be much kinder to D. not to reawaken all that—and she is worried you do not write—when you did not say you were not going to.

    [1] A large pine forest to the south-west of the German capital, a favourite resort of Berliners.

Kassel.
3 Oct, 1934.

Dear S.—
    Yes, I need some money badly—could you let me have 150 M? It is not safe to send that cheque.
    It was a little painful to have my letters summed up as 'incomprehensible'. I am sorry I wrote them. Anyhow it is probably better and happier to leave me to myself. It would be a little funny too for me now to explain that diffidence in caring for people may temporarily change into unreflected protest against the whole physical, emotional, intellectual isolation. It, the protest, is however, temporary and over now.
    . . . It is indeed the most beautiful autumn. The days are wide, light blue, red and gold, and the nights silvery white. The stags are beautiful at night. Their roaring is so far away from equivocal mediation between the sexes—wild and unmistakeable.
    The whole of yesterday I spent with the others in woods (those

.

stretching north-east from the other side of Kassel valley) and the evening in a village pub till late.

There's a grand fair on in Kassel at the moment to which we went after coming back. It was great fun to take the little street girls over the toboggan railway. From the top you see all the lights moving beneath you, and then diving up and down is wonderfully exciting. I have always thought that much nicer than the 'flying swing.'—what do you think?—After that we went to a very doubtful house in the Altstadt[1] where one of us had a long discussion with the mother-keeper. It was fascinating but horrible to listen. In the end she chucked us out because she took our lack of serious intentions as indication of our being informers. So we went to a Tirolienne Bar whose existence I had forgotten, where we found a lovely peasant girl singing her songs. I had a long discussion with a Roman Catholic who said that he was first that and afterwards a German and everything else. He was very excitable and nervous and I remember him claiming at least three times that I had offended him. . . .

What are your plans? You have excluded me a little suddenly. Will you go straight to Paris from Berlin? . . .

Give my love to Goronwy and to yourself!

A.

[1] The old part of the city.

Chelsea
11. Oct. 1934

Dear Adam,

. . . I talked to Arnold Toynbee[1] about studying International Relations—he was very sympathetic about my revulsion against academic study and suggested I should be a foreign journalist. Douglas Jay objects that it needs 'real talent' and hard work: I want to meet journalists and see how they live and work. Mayer[2] is going to introduce me to Mowrer[3]—because of Goronwy not because of me. Do you know any journalists in Paris? But I want to live a real private life too—Read the Russians and the French and go to concerts and see pictures. All these political wrangles and chaos are worse even than the assassination. I cannot help being excited even by the Times account of the murder of King Alexander,[4] and when the British Cabinet condole with Yugoslavia over the 'cowardly assassination.' I have great admiration for Keleman.[5] It is, after all, an extremely heroic personal action, and he paid the penalty pretty fully, and knew he would.

Will you wish Monika[6] the very best wishes and happiness from me. I would write but she would be burdened rather than otherwise with it. I was very shocked by the story of your brother. They are beasts. Goronwy has 105 marks for you—which is £6 that Jane has given me. Write to me if you have time. I would just get it Monday if I send this air-mail. How is Kleist?

Love,

S.

[1] Arnold Toynbee (1889–1976); English historian; 1925–38 research director of the Royal Institute of International Affairs; author of *A Study of History*, 6 vols. (London, 1934–9).

[2] J. P. Mayer; socialist and scholar of socialism; editor of the early writings of Karl Marx and of a standard work on Alexis de Tocqueville (London, 1939). He was connected with the circle around the *Neue Blätter für den Sozialismus*, a journal founded in 1930 and dedicated to the renewal of German socialism. Adam, who had attended meetings of this group since 1931, re-established contact with it in Berlin in 1933. Adam and Mayer were political associates for a number of years after 1933, but they later parted company. In 1936 Mayer emigrated to England where he taught at the London School of Economics and later at the University of Reading.

[3] Edgar Ansel Mowrer (1892–1976), one of the very distinguished American foreign correspondents in the nineteen thirties, reporting for the *Chicago Daily News* from Paris; author of *Germany Puts the Clock Back* (New York, 1933). He launched Shiela's journalistic career in the autumn of 1934 and became her political mentor; cf. Grant Duff, *The Parting of Ways,* pp. 68 ff.

[4] On 9 Oct. 1934 King Alexander of Yugoslavia together with the French Foreign Minister Louis Barthou were assassinated by a Croat revolutionary in Marseilles.

[5] The name of the assassin was Petrus Kalemen.

[6] Monika Eleonore (Onken), Adam's younger sister.

Chelsea.

15th Oct. 1934.

Dear Adam,

. . . My plans have changed again—tho' I'm not sure how much since I wrote on Thursday. G. suggested I should work in the Times office—they take people unpaid apparently in their foreign offices—I would learn that way to earn my living one day, and learn also all the things I want to know—or some of them. I would have a status too, which I find myself slightly in need of—and I need money too and anything which would help me earn some is welcome. Do you approve of journalism at all? You know better than anyone what makes me want to do it—it is the same train of thought as was begun

with you when I read the 'Brothers Karamazov', and was continued
in Munich and here in London. It made me write to Sumner[1] and see
Webster,[2] and finally Toynbee who suggested journalism. Douglas,
as I told you, is sceptical about my capacities which just makes me
more determined—anyhow, I'll tell you of the upshot of all this.
What do you think about it? I am longing to go to Paris, for a room
to myself—even Oxford had that advantage, and time and peace to
read in, and look at pictures and sort things in my own mind. . . .

Love,
Shiela.

[1] Benedict Humphrey Sumner (1893–1951); Oxford historian; Adam's turor at
Balliol. Shiela's examiner in Schools.
[2] Charles K. Webster (later Sir Charles; 1886–1961); English historian.

31.10.34.
Kassel.

My Dear Shiela,
    . . . Continually I have thought of D. and of the doubtful rightness
to break all the beauty of contact with her. She is a beautiful person,
quite apart from appearance, you know. . . . She gave me a great deal
that no one else has ever given me, and certainly no one will dream of
giving me now. . . .
    . . . There seems no commonly shared centre in the lives of my
friends—I know you too have periods of unkind judgments. I think it
is something extremely disillusioning to have unless it's a mere
caprice. And one should see enough of one's friends to tell them
clearly about one's doubts and disapprovals. They too should have a
continuous vision of one's own stand of battle, and accept or reject
the values one adopts. Communication should not be based on
general sympathy, agreement in ideas, etc, but a clear and open view
of the trend where one believes one's best efforts are concentrated.—
This in people, and heavy professional work is what I shall try this
time to find in Berlin. My present work, Shiela, is awful. Long
drawn-out criminal cases, dark and impenetrable in their substance,
vague partly unjustifiable conclusions to revise and possibly alter at
best. With nobody's particular fault most mismanaged coincidences
of fate. While I am actually working at them—only a mechanical,
legal part of me is active—all goes reasonably well. But soon after it
comes back to me how all fundamental issues of good life are given
up and compromised in the dealings of criminal law. It is not a sentimental hurt, but an ugly deterioration of standards with which such

work poisons one's life. Only the missionary type would remain pure
in continuous contact with these spheres.—One must choose the
work of one's life with extreme care, otherwise—with it and the
human contacts and extremes it involves—the little moral confidence
one has must go.—I am sorry, all this may sound rather weak and
over-serious, but soon I shall have finished with the criminal section
and will work at international cases. Did I tell you that the publisher
refused to print my 'Kleist'[1] in the original form, and that I am trying
to find another one, because I don't want to alter it? . . .

Love, as ever

A.

[1] Adam was working on an edition of the political and journalistic writings of the
German poet and dramatist Heinrich von Kleist (1777–1811). The ostensible purpose of the publication, in particular Adam's introduction, was to expose Kleist's
valiant stand against the Napoleonic domination. But Kleist's condemnation of
Napoleon's despotism in fact was to serve as a cover for the book's real purpose
which was to attack Nazi oppression. The Protte Verlag originally rejected the
manuscript but eventually published it under the title *Heinrich von Kleist, Politische
und Journalistische Schriften*, Ausgewählt und eingeleitet von Adam von Trott (Potsdam, 1935).

Paris[1]

13th November, 34

Dear Adam,

At last after all this time—I have the heart, the will, and the opportunity to write to you—all together. It is shocking how short an
absence develops bad habits—but it didn't make any difference
before, and shall not now—and even if our idiotic governments made
absence longer, fiercer, and more certain, it still shall make no difference; and Adam, how I loathe and detest this militariness, cowardli-
ness, and lack of generosity into which every country, government
and newspaper seems to have fallen. Perhaps you don't notice it very
much in Kassel, and are working hard and go often into the country
and your home—but here, reading French, English, and parts of German, Italian, Czech, Belgian, Polish, Russian newspapers all day, one
reads hardly anything else, but new expenditure on armaments, new
recriminations, and new fears.—But still—my life is exciting, I like
my work and my office; I like the street of public bars in which I live,
and I like the grand restaurants where the walls are made of glass and
have a sky and sea and trees painted on them with love-birds and
canaries flying through lighted fountains—oh, it's a gay and beautiful
place.

... Are you happy about Diana? I am glad of what you say about her. Certainly I have never seen such love and constancy and courage. ... There was a poem Diana and I read at school, but I don't know if she remembers it—which goes

> A prophet that, Cassandra-like, tells truth without belief
> For headstrong youth will run its race, altho' it goal be grief.

Diana has no fear of unhappiness. I admire that so much since I have such a horror of it. God knows if you were right to break it—but I always felt it was not a power you had—to keep it or break it—only the power to kill it or let it wither slowly. It is inevitable you should miss all that she gave you, and realise how beautiful it was. But you must not be sad now—the past is past and must be. I never realised before what 'Leave the dead to bury the dead' meant—now with so great a cleft between past and present it is clear what it means. Loyalty to people and things means only one must not falsify what one has done or felt or thought—either directly or by doing other things which make a nonsense of it. Am I very sententious? I'm afraid, rather—only God knows how not to be—that is a special English quality not being sententious—they get out of it through reserve. I am looking forward to being told what the English are really like, and seem like to foreigners. I would tell you what the Germans were like except that the only ones I know are you and Hasso[2] and Mayer and Borsig[3]—and your national characteristics are—according to opinions abroad—absolutely different—oh I would like so much to see you again—to be able to smoothen those national characteristics.

... Dear Adam—I like you so much but you are so difficult to understand. 'Communication should not be based on general sympathy, agreement in ideas etc., but a clear and open view of the trends where one believes one's best efforts are concentrated.' What is your trend—what is my trend? Our best efforts at present seem to be concentrated on hating each other—nationally speaking—yet surely, sympathy, agreement in ideas, common liking, private life—all those are what our communication is built on. Oh—that the world could stand still for one moment and there could be only one long summer where everyone lived a private, natural, and unafraid life.

Write to me often and at length—write soon when you get mine—then it's easier—and I will too. I have told you so much what I am doing—it is, what I write to you in the summer about—except that I am not writing at all—but I am trying to understand people and above all, events of the last ten years—write to me, remember me, as I do you—very clearly, so that I want to laugh as you come in at the door—so tall, and with your round green straw hat on top of your head!

Love,
Shiela.

¹ Shiela was determined to try her luck as a journalist in Paris. After having failed to persuade *The Times* to give her an assignment there, she took off on her own, with the assurance of £3 a week, to Paris with the 'highflown resolve to prevent war and save the world'. She accepted an unpaid position with Mowrer. This connection turned out to be decisive for Shiela; see Grant Duff *The Parting of Ways*, pp. 64 f, 66 ff.

² Adam's friend Hasso von Seebach; he was a socialist and worked in Berlin for the United Press; he later emigrated to the United States with his older friend Julie Braun-Vogelstein (see letter Adam–Shiela, beginning of Mar. 1937 n. 4); after the war he returned to Germany.

³ Arnold von Borsig, a member of the well-known Berlin industralists' family; he had socialist leanings and was friendly with J. P. Mayer. His apartment was often used by socialists for clandestine purposes. In Dec. 1934, when Adam moved to Berlin, he stayed in Borsig's apartment during the latter's absence in Italy.

Kassel
19.11.34.

Darling Shiela,

Thank you for your letter—No, our bad habits do not affect mutual sympathy; except in my present position one tends to be a little over-sensitive. You sound very vigorous and firm, and I wonder how you manage to read newspapers all day and yet maintain the joy of life. It is remarkable—but then we want to be strong enough to surmount all these modern discrepancies. My country, and provincial life of course makes me see things 'from too harmless an angle' but I wonder whether journalists do not often commit the opposite mistake. You will never become like them, if I know you—and for your final purposes you certainly seem to be in a centre now from which to understand things and people and the development of the last ten years. But do not remain 'eccentric' in your views of Germany, you know more of it than me, . . . and yours will not be an outlook of the 'safe world of democracy' which seems to me as unsafe spiritually as any other human world I know with the possible exception of certain parts of Russia.

Was my letter and the quotation you extracted from it really as complicated and obscure? Read the first few chapters of Turgenev's 'Virgin Soil', and you will know what I mean by the 'vital trend of one's best efforts.' My belief in the intrinsic impotence of those edifices of cultural concepts with which 'Times' leader-writers furnish their phrases, is growing, the more I realise the extreme rareness of personal consistency—I mean that kind of inner concentration which makes people and their mental outlook worth bothering about. But you are right, only God knows how not to be sententious, and there are very few men whose very alliance with God is *not* sententious— as i.e. Pascal or Swift, or in their atheistic way Lenin and— Flaubert. . . .

Winter is rather beautiful now, the clouds are torn and there's a beautiful pale light over the soaking fields and the dusky horizons. There has been little or no frost yet and that gives the contrast of still vividly green patches to the violet-coloured earth. There is an extreme restfulness in this sleep of Nature—somehow (perhaps that is an association of pre-Christmas-time from early childhood) it is a strange atmosphere of piousness over it all. It is moving and in no way an anachronistic vision to see Christian Germany re-emerge powerfully beneath the already crumbling artifices of newer experiments. . . . [1]

My going to Berlin on Dec. 11th is now a decided matter. I am starting work with one of the most important German lawyers,[2] an extremely interesting firm which will be very profitable for my legal progress. I shall see this other 'centre' from a very close, though luckily detached angle. I shall work hard. In the way of American journalists in Berlin I could perhaps supply you with connections—as I shall know two quite important ones, and a cousin of mine who is Councillor in their Embassy.[3] Have you any links with yours?—May I enclose this snap-shot of Bobbi and myself and may I too ask you for one? I like you very much and I am very glad of you—sorry to be pompous—

A.

---

[1] This is undoubtedly a reference to the role of the Confessing Church (*Bekennende Kirche*), which, in opposition to the efforts of the 'German Christians' to nazify German Protestantism, served as a rallying point for Protestants to reaffirm their faith. Adam's mother, a deeply religious person, had close ties with it. Also, Adam was much heartened by the sermons of Cardinal Michael von Faulhaber in Munich which were sent to him by his friend Ingrid Warburg; Diana Hopkinson, 'Memoir of Trott's Life 1931–40', typescript (Leo Baeck Institute, New York, 1946), p. 56.

[2] With the help of various friends Adam obtained a five months' release from his duties in Kassel to work with Dr Paul Leverkühn. A former Rhodes scholar, Leverkühn headed a distinguished law firm specializing in international law; its offices were at the Pariserplatz adjacent to the Brandenburg Gate.

[3] Friedrich ('Bobbi') von Trott zu Solz.

Paris,
26.11.34.

Dear Adam,

Thank you so much for such a nice letter, post-card and photo-graph—I send you one of 48 for 2 marks. It is among the few in which I am not looking half-witted, maudlin, or religious. If you don't like it you can send it back and you can have a religious one instead.

Dear Adam—I am very glad of you too, and like you very much. In moments of fever, insanity, or depression I think of you, and you give proportion back to my life. Do you know that feeling of being very fond of somebody, but of them making you unreal and destroying, or rather sending away from you, all your life? With you it is the opposite—when I think of you my life is whole and there is sense and order in it. I don't know why that is—it is strange when you think that the first 20 years of our lives, and still all the background and setting, are absolutely different—Yet you do not seem a stranger at all—and I wish very much you could come in my country home where I spent all my holidays as a child. I hope I shall go there for Christmas—living alone gives me a passionate desire to establish continuity with myself—and as with you in the summer, I feel far nearer and more deeply about the pre-Oxford time than about Oxford. But I do think often about Oxford and how incredibly beau-tiful it was, and how nearly perfect life could have been there. It is very sad that when one is there one does not know what one wants, but tries a lot of things and makes a muddle and confusion of it. But it was lovely all the same, and I think with much home-sickness of days there, of walks in the country, of friends, of my dogs and my rooms and books. Do you think of it too?—perhaps not, because you live in a very beautiful place already. Paris is beautiful too, in a way, but I miss the country very much, and the silhouettes of Oxford buildings. I went to Versailles yesterday for the first time. It is incredi-bly grand and splendid—the late 17th and 18th centuries were won-derful. Their houses and pictures and books are incredibly humane and civilised in comparison with ours. I regard the 19th century, with its early romantic poets and its later realist novelists as the beginning of the return to barbarism which we have now begun—but con-sciousness of centuries should free one of any historical process, and one should be able to choose, and not have imposed on one, the life one will lead. Anyhow, even if that's not true—which I suspect—it is comforting to think that in decadent civilisations, art flourishes and science declines.

Do you attack the 'safe world of democracy'? Who calls it 'safe' anyway? It is a curious description of it, but all the same it is still the most admirable form of government possible. Natural aristocracies are perhaps better—or at least have been realised more often, but the ruling aristocracies of today, if you can call any government that, are pretty disagreeable. You seem to attack culture too—I hope you only mean the ideas of 3rd Leader writers of the 'Times'—because other things—books, poetry, beautiful houses, seem to have more value every day, as more and more people ignore their existence. Modern concern with politics is a pretty bad sign of their going wrong— anarchism is the most tolerable state to live in, but I'm afraid it demands too much of human intelligence and virtue.

What you say in your letter of 'Christian Germany' re-emerging is very hopeful and encouraging, and I'm terribly glad if it's true—but I wonder what you mean by Christian Germany. I'm told Rosenberg[1] describes God as being the nation. He is certainly a genius of great originality.[2] From the things I read in your papers, I believe your hair must be falling out because of the rivers of peroxide—How is your hair now? I hope it is growing more firmly attached. . . .

Write to me soon and often. I wish I could come to Wilhelmshöhe[3] and see you and walk in the forests again—but it must be very cold in your car. . . .

Much love,
S.

[1] Alfred Rosenberg (1893–1946), one of Nazi Germany's chief racist theoreticians and ideologists. His main work was *Der Mythos des 20. Jahrhunderts* (Munich, 1930).
[2] This is, of course, ironic.
[3] Eighteenth-century castle and park near Kassel; while working in Kassel Adam rented a room in the residential area of the suburb.

Imshausen.
7.12.34.

Dear Shiela,

I wrote a long letter to you in a little Wilhelmshöhe cafe a week ago. But I found its English intolerable bad—it sounds so childish and irresponsible that I must suppress it. Yours was a lovely letter, and it must have seemed an unfair exchange to you for a long time already. But I think my Anglo-Saxon friends soon acquire a kind of indirect manner in reading what I want to convey rather than what I express.

That last week in Kassel I was very busy . . . On the whole it was a kind world I said good-bye to there, but a damnably inadequate one. I am full of anticipations and good intentions now. Yes, how wonderful it would be to have a real friend like you with me at that start in Berlin. It seems an awful waste not to meet till next summer! For I must leave B. in May or June: before you get there! This is very sad and I resent it. But I suppose nothing will keep you now from returning to your country for Christmas! (Thank you for asking me to come there one day—I certainly shall if you still want me to come when I am in England again—) Is there no chance whatsoever that you would save me from an entirely lonely Christmas in Berlin (for I am not returning home)? I should have asked you earlier and perhaps that change would have appeared to you more within your own 'Continuity' than a short glimpse of your home. Now, I am afraid my arguments will sound rather selfish to you, which of course they are in a way. But couldn't perhaps your noble boss send out to have an 'interview' with one of the leaders at Berlin and you go to one or two of the famous artists' dances with me.—You see, allied states must really talk over their mutual policies from time to time— . . . .

My whole mind and soul is bent on the future, and yet this seems unfair on others. So I turn my back again and again, but my very readiness to meet these demands seems poisoned, and against my will increases the hurt. Who can of himself solve the cruelties of life?—Friendship and love when turned into a kind of religion is I think the most irreligious hybrid attempt.—People should be humble and strong in their intercourse and resigned in their mutual expectations.

As to the political arguments, I think, Shiela, we agree about essence and appearance of democracy much more than you seem prepared to take for granted. I wrote a long thesis about this to you in that letter from the Cafe—but I shall leave it at that. I was aiming at the insanity of making 'the world safe for democracy' by a fratricidal war, and afterwards making the world or rather the beaten equally safe for dictatorship by a fratricidal peace. There will either be a solution on the fraternal European basis, for which you and I work—or there will, after the collapse of Germany and Europe in the old sense, follow an united Russo-German front against the western imperialist powers.

Smuts[1] seemed to me the only humane voice to me in all this mess. But since you wrote the tension seems to have relaxed a little. . . .

Can't I see you at Christmas, Shiela—it would be so good to talk over some things seriously. . . .

Love
Adam.

[1] Jan Christiaan Smuts (1820–1950), South African general and statesman; a leader of the Boers, he became a proponent of the British Commonwealth of Nations.

Berlin.
29.12.34.

My Dear Shiela,

... Why should your life, both 'spiritual and material' be so upset? You are obviously too much of a Teuton for slim Paris and your wish to change it for Berlin is so much the call of your better nature. Do come Shiela—but I should if I were you under no circumstances leave out the Saar.[1] What an opportunity of a most promising experience. Not that there will be much going on—but a most curious incident of the Teuton combatting the Latin spirit. And then make the evident victory of the first the signal for your return here....

In the mean time I had one of the most interesting experiences of my life—my first time in East Elbian squirearchy.[2] I have met with human greatness in struggle that made my heart jump with joy and pride. And I have met with life 'solid and ordered' as one does rarely nowadays. Think of infinite planes of acres with hard (no longer sinister) lines of pine-trees along which horses are galloping with the light carriage, my friend explaining to me the cultivation and history of their administering it. Though I was a little ill, I was extremely happy there.

Yesterday I came all the way (very near our Eastern frontier) with a little open car I borrowed, with a thick fox-fur coat, taking 8½ hours driving in all, because most roads were iced and snowed.

And how good to have had your letter this morning, with your old tone and character in it—seconded by a lovely one from Diana. How wonderful to have two friends like you! Tell me you are both coming in the middle of Jan. and Hasso and I will find you the loveliest flat in B.

As always, Love,
Adam.

[1] In Dec. 1934, A. M. Rendel asked Shiela to take his place in covering the Saar Plebiscite for the *Observer*. By the terms of the Treaty of Versailles the Saar area had been turned over to an international administration, and France given the right to exploit the coal resources for a period of fifteen years, after which a plebiscite was to be held. It was scheduled to take place under League of Nations' auspices on 13 Jan. 1935. Ninety per cent of the population voted for reunion of the region with Germany; see Grant Duff, *The Parting of Ways*, pp. 76 ff.

[2] Over Christmas Adam visited a friend, P. C. von Kleist, at his estate in Pomerania. There he met Ewald von Kleist-Schmenzin, 'a model of a true country squire' (letter Adam to his father, Berlin, 28 Dec. 1934, Trott Archive, Letters to the Parents). Kleist-Schmenzin was one of the principle conservative opponents of Nazism. Before Hitler's seizure of power, he published a pamphlet on the threat of

National Socialism (*Der Nationalsozialismus—eine Gefahr* (Berlin, 1932)) and was twice arrested in 1933. In Aug. 1938 he was sent by Admiral Wilhelm Canaris, chief of the Armed Forces Intelligence Service, on a secret mission to London to warn the British Government of Hitler's aggressive plans and urge it to stand firm; he had talks with Lord Lloyd, Sir Robert Vansittart, and Winston Churchill. After consultation with Lord Halifax, Churchill handed him a letter to take home assuring him of Britain's determination to stand firm against Nazi aggression. After the unsuccessful attempt against Hitler on 20 July 1944, Kleist-Schmenzin was arrested and the letter was found by the Gestapo. He was guillotined on 16 Apr. 1945. In the months following their first meeting in Dec. 1934, Adam and Kleist-Schmenzin met regularly in Berlin; see Bodo Scheurig, *Ewald von Kleist-Schmenzin. Ein Konservativer gegen Hitler* (Oldenburg, Hamburg, 1968).

                                                        Chelsea.
                                              [*about* 1 January 1935]

Dear Adam,
    . . . You long as much as any of your 60 million country-men for the victory of the Teutonic over the Latin race—but it would be a terrible thing—There is no struggle between them, not even in the Saar—and if there was, it would be worse than the end of the Roman Empire—O, Adam—don't be taken in. I wish very much I could come to Berlin[1]—you're all going dotty. . . .
                                                   My love to you,
                                                        Shiela.

[*Postscript omitted*]

    [1] Adam begged Shiela and Diana to come and visit him in Berlin; Diana went; see Hopkinson, *The Incense-Tree*, pp. 131 ff.

                                                        Berlin
                                                        3.1.35.

Dear Shiela,
    . . . I was surprised at you taking my reference to the Latin and Teuton race as more than a gamble of words which it was—and your thinking we are 'dotty and taken in'. Or were you being vicious?
    There's a sky, stars at night, lakes, trees, even occasional human beauty (though as everywhere very much of its opposite) and I don't see why you deny goodness and reality to one's life. You must not become a Western hypocrite!—They seem to me laying one crust over the other on top of this world's real issues and to be scorning

and mocking all those who (in good and bad faith) are really at grips at them. . . .

My true love to you dear Shiela

Adam

[*Postscript omitted*]

Saarbrücken
13.1.35.

Dear Adam,

. . . I am here in the Saar—for two weeks I have been the correspondent of an English newspaper and I have had the honour to be banned in Germany.[1] The foolishness of certain types of government is to increase people's importance. Fascism, by banning their bad-wishers, and making all their friends into officials, destroys every national value and gives everyone an inflated self-importance which is regrettable.

Well—what do you think of the world? I find it shocking and sometimes want to leave it for a country life, peace and quietness—but it is exciting too and my life here is immeasurably fine—half of it is conducted in this hotel, which is just like an American film—and half in the Saarbrücken streets, which today are clogged and cluttered with snow. In the main streets it is filthy, but down by the river, or in the quieter slopes, where no wheeled traffic goes, children toboggan and slide, snow covers all the ledges and roofs of the houses. It is strange to be in a country where snow is the normal bad weather in winter.—Everyone takes it for granted—no snow-men are made, few children play snow-balls.—In England it has only to snow to produce a feeling of intense excitement and strangeness, and people look at the new world which snow makes of familiar places, with enormous astonishment and happiness.

The opposition people here are rather splendid but fight a losing battle; you—well-propaganded, I suppose—look upon them as 'idiots and traitors.' I had the honour to eat opposite Herr Bürckel,[2] and learn of the educational efforts he will make after the plebiscite. The trouble with them here is their shocking physique and frailty. I find it very moving and feel like a thermometer with its red liquid mounting up a tube—however—tant pis. I'm glad you didn't mean your Teutonic-Latin speech seriously. The French are, of course, untermensch. I, on the other hand, am an enormous social success with the Übermensch[3]—or whatever they're called. There is a rather nice Nazi journalist here, whom I dance with, and others whom I meet.—We perhaps get on better for my not being able to speak German—conversation, I've decided, is at all times quite unnecessary, and the only reason why people speak is because it's the laziest way of communicating, and they feel embarrassed not to communicate at all. It is exceedingly nice to have an excuse of silence.

What do you think about and what books do you read? I sent you a beautiful Botticelli picture for Christmas—but it was returned to my office in Paris—I believed in an address in Pariserplatz 6—What was that? . . .

Anyway—I have taken European politics too much to heart to leave them for the moment. I feel very strongly about the Saar question, and perhaps will go to Geneva. I don't at all want to go back to Paris—only my respect for Mowrer will take me back. He is an exceedingly fine and splendid man, and I was very moved to see him again on Saarbrücken station, in ski-ing trousers and boots and a rucksack over his shoulder. His correspondent in Berlin[4] is also exceedingly nice—high-minded civilised Americans are rather charming after all—I had never liked Americans before.

There are a curious crowd of people here—hot—chicken-food rats with whiskers and all very thin and hungry—large, brutal, red-faced agency men, and a sprinkling of intellectuals.—It is a curious society to have made one's home in. I like its free coming and going and friendliness, and its democratic and international spirit. The French journalists are nice and it suddenly gives me a great pleasure to listen to and speak French. Your language was described as 'la langue élégante de Goethe' at a press meeting the other day. I am terribly much a press girl (the only one).—I have a sly picture of myself stuck on a card with which I walk boldly thro' police cordons and barred doors.—It is not a life for always but I learn fast about the world.— Oh—I do all I wanted—and I learn it is shocking and brutal and corrupt and lying—and that it is noble, brave, gentle and gay—I [am] full of infinite hope and possibility of achievement one minute, and depressed and weary the next. . . .

Anyway—bless you—let me know what happens to you—

Love
S.

. . . I'm sorry this is not a very nice letter. I started to write to you in the middle of this Bürckel speech in Kaiserslautern,[5] but that too was difficult—I don't know quite what it is, perhaps nationalism, that is the matter now—I must come and see you. There are so many things I want to talk about and discuss with you, and I feel jumpy that we disagree on things I feel very strongly—I think it was going to Kaiserslautern—I felt sick—it's bloody and hateful.

¹ *Observer*; it was banned for its reports from Saarbrücken in Jan.
² Josef Bürckel (1895–1944), Nazi *Gauleiter* of the Rhineland-Palatinate; as Plenipotentiary for the Saar area (since 1934) he successfully organized the return of the Saar area to Germany.
³ A facetious play on the Nazi term *Untermensch* meaning members of an inferior race; *Übermensch* would be members of a superior race, i.e. the Germans.
⁴ Wallace Deuel, *Chicago Daily News* correspondent in Berlin.
⁵ In Kaiserslautern Shiela witnessed a Nazi rally for the first time.

[*Postcard with picture by Franz Hals, 'Group d'enfants'*]

15.1.35

Shiela dear,
 Thank you for your long letter and *come to Germany* if you are not banned in person. In itself I think it more important that we should meet and talk again than that your stay should necessarily coincide with Diana's. It is very uncertain when she will come as there is every kind of suspense about jobs. But she will come and it is right.—Damn you for remaining frivolous about my being 'propaganded' in spite of my reproaches. Yes: there is no more lying cynical profession than the press, you must not remain one of them. I wrote such nice things about you to Miriam yesterday. They are quite incompatible with the 'press girl' side of yourself. But I know its only a tiny fraction of your person and all the rest of your wickedness is essentially charming. I hate to disagree on serious points with you too and I don't believe we really do.

Love
A.

Saarbrücken
23.1.35

Dear Adam,
 . . . I wish too that I could come to Berlin. I think I will quite soon—This is what I mean to do now—probably—tho' I am going to London for the week-end, and that may change my intentions a bit—I mean to stay here with a family till the middle of March—then I will have learnt a good deal of German, a good deal of politics, and a good deal of journalism—Then I would like to live in Wedding¹ in a working-class family—because, as the Führer says—those are the

most valuable people in the country—doesn't he say so? and do you not think it a good idea? Of course I will see a lot of you and Hasso, and other people I know—but I think it would be very good for me and teach me a lot, to live among workers. I loathe the class system, and aristocracy is an illusion these days—Something new has got to be rebuilt, some alternative to the present drift of politics—that one can only learn from the people whom politics most nearly concern, and those are the lower classes. Of course one ought to learn such things in one's own country—but in yours I think one can learn more at the beginning 1). because foreigners have no class, and I will not give myself away by my accent as I would in Whitechapel, and 2). because politics are more pronounced and important, and national socialism is something which should be understood. What do you think of that? I would like to know—Hasso says politics are dirty—but that's no argument against the need to do something—From my own point of view, I think women are best out of them—and men too if they want to live quiet and good lives—but then, can one lead such a life? (I see it so clearly—the country, animals, books, a house, friends—when there is so much need to keep the world civilised? I, myself, shall never 'go into' politics—but I want to understand people, and have a wide experience, and wide understanding.

The alternative to all this is to go back to Paris, as I was—to read and learn, and live among diplomats and journalists in such a beautiful place—very pleasant but not very admirable. I admire Mowrer, and am sorry to give up job, office, and all that I had there—but you think it right to do this, don't you? I shall more nearly have a job here than in Paris, because I continue attached vaguely to 2 big English newspapers, and that alone is a good thing in the Saar—all sorts of things go better when the lights are on. . . .

Love
S.

¹ A working-class district of Berlin.

96 rue de Grenelle.
Paris VIIe
11.4.35.

Dear Adam,

Thank your for another very nice picture: it is very nice to have letters on pictures. I wish I could write you a real letter but now till I see you I'm afraid it will always be difficult. I doubt very much I will be able to come to Berlin while you're there. Goronwy has come here now and is likely to stay a long time so I can't very well leave Paris for Berlin. When you go to England, can you not go through Paris? . . .

My goodness international politics! . . . The only people who understand each other's language are Mussolini, Stalin and Hitler. . . . I think I shall give up journalism and study history, it is more interesting and less harrassing. Contemporary life is very waring. I start fresh and happy every morning and end every day jumpy and on edge. What do you think will come of Stresa?[1] There was a wonderful letter in the Times (serious) saying 'After Stresa, I hope we'll have plenty of other meetings . . . ' The summer is coming and is too beautiful to spoil, but I suppose they'll spoil it. I am very pessimistic about politics. Hasso says they're dirty, as if one should have nothing to do with them—but after all, they're about Peace and War, and whether people have enough to eat, and decent houses and warm clothes—one can't prevent either war or poverty without thinking about politics—but the Chinese poem is much lovelier

> that so many of the poor should suffer from cold what can we
>   do to prevent?
> To bring warmth to a single body is not much use.
> I wish I had a big rug 10,000 feet long
> Which at one time could cover up every inch of the city.

The Chinese are—were—wonderful people—very worldly in the sense of having no really great philosophy, nor even very spiritual religion—and yet in the world, they didn't want all the things that European poetry frets about . . . power and battles and love and distinction and romanticism, but rather friendship, leisure, and calm— 'refusing with a bow, retire to a cottage in the country.' They are lovely and make me very happy.

What do you think of and what do you read? I so seldom read books, only books about things. It is a great pity. Is your life jointed and does it go as you wish it? Mine is always unjointed and disjointed—ship on the sea, very excited and sails very fast—but no rudder. At least always changing rudders. I hate to be so nearly related to the world, so much affected by people I never see or speak to like Sir John Simon.[2] Let's all live on an island or a ship. How difficult it would be! a suicide every day.

I'm writing this in bed while I eat my breakfast. I must start the day again—dear Adam, I long to see you and laugh again—I'd like to begin again and be at Oxford.

Much love always . . .
Shiela.

¹ The Stresa Conference, 11–14 Apr. 1935, between Great Britain, France, and Italy, considered action against German rearmament.

² Sir John Simon (1873–1954); from 1940 Viscount of Stackpole Elidor; elected to Parliament in 1906; Solicitor General 1910–13; Attorney General 1913–15; Secretary of State for Home Affairs 1915–16, 1935–7; Secretary of State for Foreign Affairs 1931–5; Chancellor of the Exchequer 1937–40; and Lord Chancellor 1940–5. This is most likely a reference to Sir John Simon's unsuccessful talks of 25–26 Mar. in Berlin (with Anthony Eden, Lord Privy Seal) with Adolf Hitler. They dealt primarily with the question of German rearmament. Hitler remained adamant.

Paris.

June 11th, 35.

Dear Adam,

. . . Dear Adam—I find everything you say incomprehensible and yet I feel I understand you and your life so clearly. I s'pose that's what all liking is—a clear perception and immediate sympathy with all the processes of thought left out.¹

I think it is true that, as you say, we are both experiencing the gulf, rather than the bond between us—but, not for a minute, since last summer, will I disbelieve in the bond or ever relinquish it without fighting for it. . . .

It is depressing what you say about decadence and decay—it is what Mowrer here says too—and I think he represents all that is best, most spiritual and most vital in the Americans. I have been staying with him in the country, and was infinitely moved by his stories of Red Indians, of the rivers and falls and forests of North America, and all the human qualities that go with uncomplicated and still natural life. He thinks too that Europe is doomed, because it cannot adapt, because in trying, it contradicts its own qualities—It seems to me there is only one way of growing—it is the essence of all intelligent conservatism, it is organic growing through tradition to a new life—I can't say what I mean exactly—Burke said it in the inverse when he said 'The state without the means of change is without the means of its own conservation.'² Today, what needs to be realised is 'The state, without its own conservation, is without the means of vital change.' So states are changing now only to die—Even your country confuses the meaning of vitality—If you find England effete and decadent besides Germany, it is only because one is dying by strangling, the other by apoplexy. I think all that's true—but I think also, we're able to alter truth—one man's saved a country before now, and there's hope till the end—So we can keep, as you say, a 'laughing vitality, aware but invulnerable.' Do you remember your half-laughing remark on the station at Bebra[3] 'In the coming struggle for power . . .'[4]

Well—all this being so—one's got to plan one's life accordingly—I want to learn—learn about the world—we forget and think Europe's the world—it's the dying part we've got to dope up a bit—so I'm going round the world.—I feel I've hung about aimlessly long enough now—it was my fault if it was aimless—M. abuses us as a generation, says we are without conviction, intellectual vitality or will—He's right in a sense—but our world's bigger than theirs was—they only had one bag of hay, we've got two, and one poor donkey starving between them—What about all that? Let's make a pact and fix it all up? Dear Adam—I want to see you again—not in the rain after a long journey—let's meet in China—Puff! for your moral tyranny. Goronwy and I decided last week you were governed entirely by intelligent self-interest—So am I—and I like you because you laugh at yourself with me—... I like your attitude to presents and girls and everything else. You ought to have been a Red Indian rather than a German. Let's chuck our nationalities—it's all bunkum anyway. Man's a man for all that—

Much love always
S.

---

[1] Adam's letter lost.
[2] 'A state without the means of some change is without the means of its conservation', Edmund Burke, *Reflections on the Revolution in France* (New York, 1961), p. 33.
[3] The railway station nearest Imshausen.
[4] The sentence continued: ' . . . we must be in the right places'. In her diary (Kassel, summer 1934) Shiela commented: 'I think he is in the right place.'

Paris.
[*middle of* June 1935]

Dear Adam,

What a cross letter.[1] I wrote you an equally cross one, not really because I was cross, but because I didn't see why you should have the pleasure alone. What made you so angry?—my new conservatism . . . finished now . . . my not understanding you, or my crediting you with a low moral plane . . . not really low? All three, I agree, might have done it, but not one was meant to.

The conservatism is now over, and I am at the opposite extreme, where I am always tending to go, but never seem able to arrive. Not understanding you is your fault and not mine, though perhaps I ought to regard your letters with more mental effort, but you know, philosophy at Oxford gave me considerable distaste for mental effort of that sort. As for your morals, I think they're a very fine set, and that was more praise than criticism. I don't think anyone can act except from intelligent self-interest, the moral value of the act depends on the extent of the intelligence, and in what directions a man finds his self-interest satisfied. Criminals find it in crime, you find it in a certain way of life, in the desire to accomplish social ends, it is saying nothing about a person's morals to say they act from intelligent self-interest. Anyhow I don't think you were really cross. . . .

I have at last met somebody who knew your brother. He wants to know how your brother is, what he's doing, because he has lost touch with him. Like everyone whom I have spoken to about Werner, he had a very great admiration for him and was also very much influenced by him. . . . [2]

Dear Adam, it is really the biggest barrier that my letters are not written for you alone[3]—there are so many things I want to tell you, ask you, and cannot. I loathe it. Paris is very beautiful and I am really very sad to leave it and feel life anywhere else will be poorer, because every other place is less beautiful. They floodlight many of the buildings, and every night I walk by the Seine and watch the black river and the lights all the way along. It is an incredibly wonderful place. My conservatism is ended, because I think a more radical attitude is the only way in which so much beauty and the life which is lived in it, can be preserved.

Do you remember last summer I said I thought loyalty was the capacity to reconcile, inside oneself only perhaps, all the important things of one's life, and if one loved someone, one could be loyal to them, only if that love made such reconciliation possible. You never said what you thought of that. I still want to believe it, and yet there are such conflicts one doubts they can ever be reconciled and one can only ever have one thing by sacrificing another. It is typical of convention and society that they have made fidelity a purely physical concept, as if the greatest infidelity were not spiritual, and the real difficulties were not conflicts of a purely spiritual nature. Now you can get your own back by not understanding what I say. I am very much occupied by 'spiritual' thoughts these days; I know very well, when one is not occupied by them oneself, other people's spiritual thoughts are apt to make nonsense to one.

I have been meeting a lot of your countrymen lately. They like me too easily. It's a very bad thing... bad for my vanity, bad for my estimation of them... still, for all that they are pleasant to be with, and I find social relations are freer, more natural, and generally pleasanter with your countrymen than with my own . . .

Write to me again, not so crossly. Please be not cross about my not coming to Germany before the end of the summer. I very much feel it's time I was serious about some work.

Love always.

S.

---

[1] Adam's letter lost.

[2] Adam's elder brother Werner (1902–65) was an unusually stern, brooding, and strong-willed man who in anguish over the conditions in his country withdrew into himself. While in 1931 he joined the Communist Party and in 1942 became a Roman Catholic, he always remained a loner in search of some mystical communion with the land and his fellow men. He virtually tyrannized his younger brothers and especially Adam whom he loved dearly. He disapproved of Adam's explorative and outgoing ways. The man whom Shiela met in Paris was the German Expressionist writer Johannes R. Becher, after the Second World War one of the leading cultural influences in the German Democratic Republic.

[3] Almost all of Adam's and Shiela's letters were opened by the censor and resealed with the official label: *Zur Devisenüberwachung zollamtlich geöffnet* (Opened by the Customs Office for foreign exchange inspection).

Kassel.[1]

26.6.35.

Dear Sheila—

In my best and happiest moments I think of you, with love, and wish you were there to prolong them. I know, I am probably a rather harassing and uncertain friend for you, but please be glad of this important place you have, and be frank and unimpeded in the things you want to have me understand, and don't think you hurt me when you prefer to stay or go somewhere else rather than come here!

I found these Chinese stanzas for you:

> Men say that on the road to Southern Province
> Hill monkeys hang from every tree.
> In each house their cry like a cough can be heard:
> Send one for me as small as my fist,
> Smile a little at its Barbarian face,
> And its playfulness when it sees the horse-whip.
> I would buy one that is intelligent and lively;
> My tiny boys when they carry it should go mad for joy.

And this is the Kleist for you. You may like to look at the mask even if you cannot like my veiled and indirect introduction. I am happy to be able to put it in your hands now—you are the first English person who gets it. You would have loved and admired Kleist, his chivalrous, hard and noble life. Sweet Shiela, I remember telling you about him in the Reinhardswald² when we were sitting under the beeches waiting a rain to pass.

Yesterday around midnight I bathed in the Fulda river, and lights of the town in some distance and a magnificent varied night-sky spreading over me. It was beautiful and serene, the water flowing quietly, and a gentle warm breeze relieving the heat of the day. The world comes near to one, challenging one's meagre ways of inhabiting its generous beauty and calling for a childish gratitude. You know these moods, don't you?

I met the lawyers afterwards that I had left to battle by myself, and I took them to drink in the place where we once danced—you remember: the semi-underworld place. It's now called the 'Neue Welt' and we had great fun encouraging people to dance faster and drink more. These fellows I am with sometimes (working law to make up for my abominable gaps of legal knowledge) are extraordinarily crude, but good-natured. You would probably dislike them. . . .

I am now even perfectly prepared to be taken from my work a good deal by you and do everything to make your time here as full of pleasure and play as you like. Not only do I think it would be conducive to my work, but good all round. On the other side, I firmly believe that our friendship—lovely, simple, clear, and strong—will not suffer if we delay meeting, till we can do so at a more convenient time for you. I repeat that I should love having you. . . .

Love always,
A.

¹ At the end of May Adam returned to serve his second term as *Referendar* in the Kassel County Court.
² Near Kassel.

Chelsea.
30.6.35.

Dear Adam,

Thank you very much for a lovely letter and a beautiful book—I am very proud to be the first English person who gets it. Your books are like works of religion to me—my Latin Bibles, which I cannot read, and so begin to treasure their physical rather than their spiritual significance! It is very, very nice in its physical properties, and the mask is moving, and I shall learn German if only to read it. Thank you very much.

Thank you for your letter too—it is one of the nicest you have ever written to me and makes me very happy. The Chinese poem is charming too—Everything is very nice, and I am feeling very happy—and being in a best and happiest moment think of you with love too—really Adam—all that's best and least confused and most aspiring in my life is connected with you. Whenever I have ideas or clear intentions, I want to tell you about them—and I am very ashamed when, as at Oxford, I seem to have none to tell you about! But now I am full of them, and I want to come to Germany to tell you about them—but I think I cannot, because my coming there would be turning away from my intentions. I want terribly to work, learn Russian, write a chapter for a book on International Affairs—and read a great deal. I think I shall probably spend the summer in a cottage in England with Goronwy and we would both work very hard and be very happy. One so wants to lead a good life with people one loves. Thank you for seeing I couldn't come to Germany without telling him—I couldn't in ordinary circumstances—telling lies is very complicated, sometimes one tells them in order that the real truth should be understood, but with people one loves, they must understand the truth through the truth. . . .

As for my coming, I think now it will not be till September or October even—unless I can find no job in Russia.[1] I would have liked very much to go to Germany as a journalist, but it might have been disastrous, and anyway would have been done too much out of a spirit of adventure and emotion rather than serious intention.

I'm afraid if I were a man, I would be nothing but an adventurer, it is a constant effort now to adapt love of excitement to 'creative' intentions, but the first without the second grows stale, and puts one's teeth on edge. I've been feeling a little bit like that the last week for an internal adventure—that is partly why I particularly want to work hard now—and be quiet and in the country for three months, and then have a life in Russia where they are connected again. I am writing this in bed on a Sunday morning. I would like to write you a long confessio fidei—no, that's what our king is[2]—I don't know what I mean—but I'd like to tell you all the things you used to tell me in Oxford which I only half understood because I had not thought that way myself—about how one must take a political part.

Bless you always Adam—I'm glad you were born and are still alive—thank you for Kleist very much.

Much love,
Shiela.

---

[1] About that time Shiela toyed with the idea of going to Russia as a journalist.
[2] An allusion to the King as Fidei Defensor?

Berlin.[1]
21.8.35.

Dear Adam,

... There is a shocking spiritual poverty in the world today—your friend Schumacher[2] thinks it's because of the masses. 'No doubt,' he said, 'Being a friend of A v. T. you know about Hegel. Well he said the 19th century was the beginning of the advance of the masses. Today, they've arrived.' It's more the retreat of the others and their selfishness, greed and lack of sympathy or generosity—F. S. included, but he's rather nice, and has nice lines in his face. ...

Write often—don't be cross, hurt, or anything but affectionate.

Love

S.

[1] During the summer months of 1935 Shiela took a secretarial job in the Berlin office of the *Daily Telegraph* at which she did not prove a great success. But she used the time to inform herself as best she might of conditions in Nazi Germany, visiting a Nazi labour camp and staying a weekend with a socialist worker's family in their tent in Wannsee; see Grant Duff, *The Parting of Ways*, pp. 95 f.

[2] Ernst Friedrich Schumacher, a friend of Adam's from Oxford; later became well-known as an economist and author of *Small is Beautiful: Economics as if People Mattered* (New York, 1975).

Berlin.
[*About* 10 September 1935]

Dear Adam,

... Your reference to your 'unusually flattering views on women'[1] is funny, and also that you think I am annoyed by it. I know you like them perhaps too much, but like all people who find themselves in that apparently unfortunate position, I suspect you correct the balance by pretending to yourself that you despise them. In fact I don't know any man except Brian[2] who has an attitude to women which is entirely free from barbarism. I am reading the 'Revolt of the Masses' so, like Ortega y Gasset,[3] I see barbarism in everything. It is a very remarkable and important book, and when people have finished with this stage of barbarism, it will be read as were read the works of the last Romans. ...

[Shiela.]

[1] Adam's letter lost.

[2] As President of the Oxford Union, Brian Davidson advocated admission of women.

[3] José Ortega y Gasset, *The Revolt of the Masses* (New York, 1932).

2

THE ESTRANGING SEA
BETWEEN HAMBURG AND LONDON
End of September 1935–7 July 1936

EDITOR'S NOTE

Shiela and Adam had not seen each other for one whole year. During that period she had been working as a journalist in Paris, the Saar, Paris again, and then Berlin while Adam had been engaged in legal work in Kassel, Berlin, and again in Kassel. Adam had invited Diana to Berlin for a long visit in the early winter months of 1935,[1] and she visited him again during the summer, as did various other Oxford friends. Now, having completed the exploratory year she had promised herself to sort out her plans and her feelings about Goronwy,[2] Shiela returned to England with the intention of marrying Goronwy. She routed her journey via Hamburg where Adam, as a required step in his legal training, had taken up a post with the Hamburg Levant Line, engaged in passenger and freight traffic with the Near East. She was now 22 and Adam 26. On their first weekend he took her to stay with Count Albrecht von Bernstorff at his Stintenburg estate in Mecklenburg,[3] and on the second to the Baltic port of Travemünde. There she informed him of her intention, and he suddenly proposed marriage to her. This probably altogether unpremeditated move on Adam's part took her wholly by surprise. Obviously she refused him, and they agreed to keep the whole episode strictly between themselves.[4] Adam, however, was unable to disguise it completely and, since Adam and Shiela did not meet again until the following July, the ensuing complications dominate this phase of the correspondence.

[1] See Hopkinson, *The Incense-Tree*, chap. IX.
[2] See Grant Duff, *The Parting of Ways*, pp. 56, 64, 96.
[3] Count Albrecht von Bernstorff (1890–1945), a former Rhodes Scholar and a friend of Adam's. He was strongly and openly anti-Nazi and resigned from his post as Senior Counsellor of the German Embassy in London in 1933. In 1940 he was imprisoned by the Nazis in Dachau Concentration Camp and murdered by them in Apr. 1945.
[4] See Grant Duff, op. cit., pp. 96 ff; Hopkinson, *The Incense-Tree*, p. 158; Sykes, *Loyalty*, p. 164; Clarita von Trott zu Solz, *Adam von Trott zu Solz. Eine erste Materialsammlung*, typescript, pp. 76 ff.

Hamburg.
[*end of*] September 1935.

Shiela Darling,
    I hope you slept well and are not sad. . . .
    Let's try and eliminate that tyrannical category of marriage from our love—it frightens both of us and makes us see our mutual difficulties from the wrong angle. And for God sake don't try and suppress the non-casual signs of your also liking me. Let's be free and above all these oppressions and let us truly make it into something that works positively. If you promise to spare me the *unnecessary* pain of being suspected as insincere by you (however much your natural inclination nourishes that), I shall promise you to cope with my pride and my disappointment. You will have to cope with your indecision. I see it as a real threat to your life and to your friends. Perhaps a month of definite work here would clarify and settle your opinion of this country and its more personal aspects for you. All the secondary aspects are indeed very, very difficult.
    But I feel quite strong and determined this morning, and in my work I shall also work for our relation to be what by its nature it ought to be. We'll find that out together and I am happy that you're still here.

                                                                    A.[1]

---

[1] Adam left this note for Shiela in Hamburg the morning after the weekend before he went off to his office. Shiela left for Paris soon afterwards.

Paris.
2 Oct. 1935.

Darling Adam,
    It is difficult to write to you because it is difficult not to believe I will be seeing you again when you come back from your office. It is time for that now, and as if I had been waiting for it all day, only now, when I should be with you, it is possible to write.
    Partir, c'est mourir un peu[1]—never before has it been so true. Not only are we parted and a little bit dead, but the world in which we were is split and divided. That is the difference between love and friendship.
    Friendship is something which two independent lives can share

and create from two different worlds. Love is making one life of two lives, one world of two worlds. Darling Adam—perhaps in talking with you, I have minimised the differences between love and friendship, fearing the gravity of my answer. If I have seemed insensitive to that gravity, ungrateful for the honour you gave me, unaware of the consequences of my answer, it is only from the impossibility of expressing all I have thought, and, if you can understand, from the respect in which I held your feelings.

I know that in offering you friendship for love, I am offering you something which you have not asked for, and refusing something which it would be an honour to give—but darling Adam, let me give what I have to give, which is a deep affection for you, a real desire to share in your work and always to be a warm and steadfast element in your life.

Darling Adam—I have meant all I have said. Friendship goes very very far—all the way while loyalty to oneself and to the life one has chosen, remains.

But if this now seems impossible or accepting something secondary, I will not be hurt if you refuse—only please do not because I value what it could be very much. Bless you always, and always thanking you.

Shiela.

---

[1] To part is always to die a little.

[Hamburg]
[About 2 October] Autumn 1935.

[Dear Shiela,]

I have a feeling you did not go to Paris after all, but stopped in Bremen to take the boat on Thursday. And I won't know it before you write from England.

The new period of my life—marked by your final absence—enveloped me in a large grey mist in which one does things numbly and without joy. The autumn in the street where I had brought you so many times was empty and cold. Siebert[1] alone had an expression of warmth; I am glad he is here. But tonight I will stay alone. Soon, though not now, I may have to tell you a number of things.

This is just to tell you that you must not be sad or uncertain about me. You have been constant and beautiful and considerate in your attitude to me. I could not help admiring you for it even though it was but a reflection of the new life you have set your heart on.[2] It was very moving to see how brave and simple you are and yet capable of the further and sincere desire for a friendship as you want it with me. That, if nothing else, would call for my truest efforts.

Time will make them easier, and as I said I can't do anything before this mist hasn't gone.

Bless you always fair darling Shiela—

A.

[*Postscript omitted*]

[1] Hans Siebert, a Communist friend of Adam's; they met when Adam was *Referendar* in Kassel and Siebert was in jail. Subsequently Siebert spent a short time in a concentration camp; after his release he found work in Hamburg and with the help of Adam and Diana early in 1936, managed to leave Germany for England where Shiela's mother took him in.

[2] A reference to Shiela's plan to marry Goronwy.

Paris.

3.10.35.

[Dear Adam,]

Thank you for your letter, and for saying what you do, but please do not be sad, and in a large grey mist, numb and joyless. I know how it feels, and have felt it myself in these last two days, and tho' I did not have to stay on in a cold and empty world, as you did—the new one I came to was strange and lonely.

I did not stay on in Bremen, of which you suspected me, tho' my heart nearly failed, then and at Köln, on that journey. It was very long and empty. I read the Trial of Socrates,[1] which gives one courage. From Köln I slept most of the way, in spite of my seven companions and the numerous frontiers we crossed. Paris is charming at 7 o'clock in the morning, the bars already open and the streets still and empty. I climbed to Sacré Coeur and looked at Paris and watched the rather ironic and self-mocking air which the scavengers of Paris have. All day I spent here on the hill. It was like being in a village, there is no boundary between road and pavement, and the streets are cobbled. I like Paris more this time and jokes come more readily and I feel strange and more detached. That is a little because of you—do you know how strong and idealistic you make me feel. You would be proud if you knew.

Today I descended into the town—descent in every meaning. I hate that low, occupied, urban life there. I saw Mowrer—the office transformed with maps and papers—no longer the brandy-drinking, joke-making office of my time. M. is excited and pleased with the English and angry with the French, which is unwonted. Paris is full of news headings, 'Italians break the frontier at 5 places,'[2] 'General mobilisation'—but the real crisis is the League vote a few weeks hence[3]—then we'll know, darling Adam, whether to make something of this world or die in its ruins. . . .

I am very excited by a United States of Europe—everybody wants it—only nobody will believe it. O, there's such a lot to be done—we are not ready to die.

I think tomorrow I must go home. I am sorry to leave my village. I could stay here very sadly happy for three weeks. My room looks over a cobbled steep corner, bounded by a house with blue shutters and a garden wall. There's a square with trees under my window, where the old people sit and the children play. It is beautiful here. I wish I could share it with you, perhaps one day.

What are the things you may have to tell me soon? Please tell me everything which you want to, and do not be afraid. You said we think so differently and it is difficult to be friends with an Anglo-Saxon. I do not think that is true, or if it were true, it would be so much modified by natural sympathy. You seem to admire that one can have one single-hearted love, and yet be capable of a sincere desire for friendship.—But love is something generous and brave, which transforms the world and makes all things possible—Darling Adam—I am grateful to you above all for one thing—that I have learnt thro' you there is no conflict in love. In every case, love is something pure and unique and if it seems to conflict with one's love for other people, it is because of one's own poverty and weakness. I think I believe really the philosophical definition of love—that it is the feeling one has before goodness. Marriage is a relation one chooses to have with one person, a relation of complete harmony, which makes possible, rather than excludes, all other relations.

Darling Adam, I cannot bear you to feel confused and hurt and weakened, when you have given me strength and clearness and joy. Time will give you what you have given me, and us both all the good of which we are capable.

Meanwhile, be brave and strong and if it is any comfort to you, remember how much I care for you, and how sad I am to have gone away.

always my love,
Shiela.

Here is the poem. It is more than a year old, but the second verse has more meaning now. It is what I mean when I say I want to be friends.

> One word is too often profaned
>   For me to profane it;
> One feeling too falsely disdained
>   For thee to disdain it.
> One hope is too like despair
>   For prudence to smother,
> And pity from thee is more dear
>   Than that from another.
>
> I can give not what men call love:
>   But wilt thou accept not
> The worship the heart lifts above,
>   And the Heavens reject not:
> The desire of the moth for the star,
>   The night for the morrow,
> The devotion to something afar
>   From the sphere of our sorrow?[4]

[1] Presumably Plato's *Apology*.
[2] The Italians invaded Ethiopia on 3 Oct. 1935.
[3] On 7 Oct. the League of Nations Council declared Italy the aggressor; on 11 Oct. the League Assembly voted to impose sanctions on Italy; on 18 Nov. sanctions were put into effect, but they did not affect coal and oil shipments and were ineffective. On 9 May 1936 Ethiopia was officially annexed by Italy.
[4] Shelley, 'To——'; *The Poetical Works of Percy Bysshe Shelley*, ed. Thomas Hutchinson (London, 1905), p. 639.

Hamburg.
4.10.35.

My dear Shiela,

Thank you for your lines whose firm tenderness was helpful in spite of the resignation underlying it. It makes, if you can sustain it, that no question of wounded pride can arise and that we shall each face clearly the peculiar and different difficulties that our bond to the other involves. This difference I suppose is the first stage of a new friendship—but remember that the first stages of any new growth are inarticulate and be patient and trusting. Life will go on streaming through cliffs and through broad plains with still more dangerous shallows and since it is not one life—as you denied and I tended towards assuming—we must be clear of never quite fathoming the stage of the other.

And yet I want to submit to no depression that we have witnessed the eclipse of what—let me please believe—was a strong tendency to meet and unite in both streams. For it makes it superbly clear that it was never a casual and sentimental affinity that brought us near again and again—but something which it would now be reckless to doubt.

It is surely the gravest test in maturing to see at turning points of one's existence almost imminently before one lovely wide plains of harmony and enrichment and then willingly see their impossibility and break your way through hills in another direction. And not all rivers end in the ocean to meet again, but some get swallowed up in the lakes and swamps and lose their freshness and solidarity. But there seems sufficient dry land ahead yet and also, though divisions between streams in the mountains are not far but steep—land further on between them often is the most fertile and communicative. At present the change seems a bit like freezing, but that may help to push aside certain rocks. And I cherish your pureness and your beauty and though I have not been much good at times, I shall not betray you in the end, sweet Shiela.

A.

Hamburg
9.10.35.

Darling Shiela,
  I trust you don't let yourself be disquictened [*sic*] through me and that you are happily returned to your old realms of joy.
  Life seems changed since you have gone and I still am not quite sure what to make of this change. And I wonder how and whether it affects you. To love and still more I believe, to be loved makes one feel a whole person and to have that taken away—the opposite.[1]
  However to-night I am better off and can tell you that I fed the ducks in the Alster on my way home from the office—lovely green heads in the sunshine the male ones had. And day before yesterday I quarrelled with the young flute playing doctor and his nasty little wife said she didn't care two pins when he suggested that I should be a little fatter. But he was sorry for having quarrelled and came to see me this afternoon. He wants to have his two little girls christened on Saturday—but I shall be in the country. . . .
  There's a beautiful verse on Autumn in the booklet of Chinese poems you gave me. The leaves hold surprisingly tight to their

branches in Hamburg. Somehow I would have thought it kinder if a brisk winter atmosphere had set in immediately.

[Adam.]

---

¹ Several lines scratched out.

10.10.35.

[Dear Shiela,]
    Try and type me a letter.
    Yesterday I found the part of Hamburg we missed: a whole street spanned by arches of electric light making it appear like a tunnel of sparkling rays, lined on both sides by pleasure resorts with shabby livery-bearing porters and pompous doorways pouring forth jazz. I went with a serious young man I know to the Indra-Wonder-Palace—a half lighted biggish hall with a light blue stage for the band in the background. Tables all round the polished square in the middle and boxes one story higher. Although everything was modelled on elegance of sorts nobody seemed to care very much, sailors spending their money in the short hours of leave and whores—some of them really nice I thought—busy making life seem pleasant for the boys. A great number seemed to be halfbreeds, some girls and men actually Chinese. When they danced the only illumination was a kind of searchlight from the balcony changing colour every few minutes—its blue green and red gave a fantastic artificiality to the whole scene— very much like marionettes. In the intervals there was a boxing match and later on a lady with a veil and not much else performed a queer kind of dance. Though extremely commercial every detail of it all to be had for money the whole seemed romantic and generous for its honesty including the tough porter clearly intended for refractory kilis [*sic*] and the blackcoated overseer who vainly asked for a premium for the winner in the intervals of the boxing match. Quite unsentimentally I wished you were there to share this sensation. . . .

[Adam.]

Friday 11.10.35.

My darling Shiela,
    I came up my stairs with sad reflections as to my powerlessness about your silence—for if I requested news from you it would have

come from the sense that you 'ought' to write now—useless to me!—
and if I didn't request you probably just wouldn't. Yesterday morning I even caught myself laughing out bitterly when there was no
mail. Why cannot I believe you? For when I entered my room there
was your airmail note and many sweet and kind sentences in it, making me grateful and glad.

Your advice to find an elderly and unworrying mistress for myself,
you see, doesn't work at all—for where should I find her? Instead I
am finding the paragraphs of my law and the notices of the shipping
press and the autumnal beautiful visions of Alster and town quite an
inadequate remedy.—I find your saying that it is difficult to write
'when suddenly all that one understands and expresses by is taken
and there are only words . . .'[1] very treacherous indeed.

You want to know how 'freezing' feels—it is when you have found
yourself rather softly unfolded to the world and what moves you in it
and then find some of those folds contracting or even decaying and
reduced to a hard cold something with which you can break rather
than gather the world. It is when you see a very high pale moon in a
cold whitish sky and you feel this chilling clarity exactly what you
should aim at too—and when you know that your moods and sorrows are and should be important only for yourself and only in so far
as they contain some trace of the way out of them—to some plain
that one can share.

I have written to Diana that since true love is denied to me I want
and need to be solitary.

When you refused me I had to deal with things squarely. It has also
thrown me back upon myself and I cannot trust approximate relationships. England too moved further away—though in a strange
impersonal way it has come nearer home. I feel more like the time
when I first visited it being 18. . . . I still want you in this violent kind
of way but I cannot fight for it because of the inadequacy of what I
have to offer. To alter that I must be free and, I suppose, without
you. Come and live with me, darling Shiela, if you know it otherwise.
How can I be warm and happy as it is? But I know how to be alone. I
have known it for a long time and it will not defeat me. Be good and
understand my position and respect it. I embrace and kiss you.

A.

---

[1] The letter in which Shiela expressed these thoughts is lost.

[*n.d.*]¹

Darling Adam,
   Thank you terribly much for your long letters to-day, not hearing
from you is difficult to meet and your trusting I am not disquietened²
through you of no avail when you do not write. I feel as if I am standing in the dark by a precipice perhaps between two deep holes like
the walk over the cliffs to Trevose lighthouse,³ but I have lost my
way and no longer know which side is the precipice. It is dreadful to
feel. Do you know the end of Prometheus Unbound?

> Neither to change nor falter nor repent;
> This, like their glory, Titan! is to be
> Good, great and joyous, beautiful and free;
> This is alone Life, Joy, Empire and Victory.⁴

The lines before are beautiful—I will send them to you one day—but
the first line is what I want and fall so short of. What you say is true
and brave, ones moods and sorrows are and should be important
only for oneself and only in so far as they contain some trace of the
way out of them. I wish, like you, I could find the moon to freeze by
and could have a physical solitude to match the solitariness I feel
inside.

[Shiela.]

   ¹ This note, unfinished and unsent, was written on the back of a postcard from
Ingrid Warburg's house, Blankenese, Kösterberg.
   ² See letter Adam–Shiela, Hamburg 9 Oct. 1935.
   ³ Lighthouse at Trevose Head. At the north-western edge of Padstow Bay, near
the summer residence of Diana's family in Cornwall.
   ⁴ Shelley, 'Prometheus Unbound' (1820).

Hamburg
13.10.35.

Shiela dear,
   Your note¹ proved of great value—it was too bad to think you had
been submerged in the waves of new life and not a bit disturbed by
crude separation. Every day I meet new things in this place that it
seems absurd not to have seen with you and with thoughts that so
much want to be shared with you and hours in the evening when it is
difficult to know you so far away. But your little note made me rather
more tranquil than happy—for though it is a comfort to feel you too
are sad I am not pleased by your being sad for it is such a waste. The
times fly past and we don't even gather the harvest offered to us.
   I know the want of adventure is only one side of life—not the most

but a very important side—and there is the province of calm systematic endeavour which must be guarded from intrusions. Specially
when they are not full blooded, for the 'aberrations' of true nature
carry their own remedies. Only half-fulfilment is dangerous and morbid.

You oughtn't yet accept that 'daily round' in which seeming indifference to happiness or unhappiness is expected of you. Are you sure
you don't really detest all the remnants of bourgeois 19th Century
culture and values? One wastes oneself over them if one does not
make up one's mind clearly as to which one accepts and rejects.
There is a lack of freedom in you somewhere—though I prefer it to
the unbounded chaos that I find in people over here so often. The
'New Statesman' and what it pictures as typical for what you and I
might become rather shocks me, but the 'Spectator' would probably
do so even more. . . .

I believe you think I am cheating when I think that in order not to
fall from bourgeois greed and stingyness [*sic*] into pseudoproletarian
amorphicness [*sic*] one must stand for certain valuations of the feudal
Middle Ages. They were full of vitality, adventure and yet discipline
and self sacrifice. I think it is their virtues that we need more than
anything else.

Shiela darling, since by your departure we have removed what you
consider a danger for yourself and our friendship—let us keep it clear
and free of cautious reserves and suspicions. I think it better to sail
straight into spheres of pain and danger than to cruise in sheltered
waters. You are brave in so many ways and yet you want to do the
latter as well.

This I say not to attack you but because I love you and want to
know you free to be yourself. If you aren't I am in danger of building
up a myth of a Shiela that isn't really there at all and put us both in a
very uncomfortable position. I think the danger is hardly there at all
the other way round—for I think you have no or, if so, very restricted
illusions about my person and prospects. You don't even think I am
suited to finding any job when I am finished with this law business.
Sometimes that pinches my vanity a little bit, but on the whole it is
better than the opposite.

The Renoir² of which I enclose a very inadequate reproduction is
wonderful in its mastered sensuality—the plastic mould of light
greyish green horses impresses one with vital power that seems to
burst out of the framed plane towards you and the lady seems to
breeze [*sic*] with such certainty of joyful nights passed and to come,
that the unambiguity of triumphant living fills one with uncritical
wonder.

The picture of Degas[3] I referred to was more repressed and a little bit melancholic, its grace, constituted by a sweet potentiality of fulfilment.

Thank you for being there at all—for it is joy to love you and feel that at any rate I do not just belong to the 'many' who do.

A.

[1] Shiela's note lost.
[2] Shiela does not remember which picture is referred to.
[3] Shiela does not remember which picture is referred to.

Tuesday. [most likely 15 October 1935]

Darling Adam,

It was a great relief to get your letter[1] and the Renoir picture, and even renewed attacks on me. Your silence made me feel suffocated and lost—'I always knew what I desired before, nor ever found delight to wish in vain'[2]—but as you say one's moods and sorrows should be important only for oneself and only insofar as they contain some trace of the way out of them. I do not accept the daily round in which seeming indifference to happiness or unhappiness is expected of one. Heaven knows if I can ever accept any 'daily round' and yet that is the condition of a whole life. I must learn—I no longer feel the grown-up I felt when I first came to Hamburg. It is awful having to grow up so many times.

What do you mean by all the remnants of bourgeois 19th century culture and values?[3] I think there is so such thing as 19th century culture, there is just one continued European culture, by which I mean all the arts which Europeans have created, their music, painting, houses, books, and that I value. I think you may mean something different, because 'Kultur' means a sort of way of living, doesn't it—then certainly I don't accept 19th century standards though I have none others; how I live is determined almost entirely by circumstances and my character, and neither of these can rightly be called a standard. If one lives by no standard one must live chaotically or accept a lack of freedom, self-dictated, and tentative. But have you, darling Adam, made up your mind which of European cultures and values you accept or reject?

I wonder whereabouts your feudalism fits in? I don't think you are cheating exactly when you try and escape bourgeois and proletarian values by substituting feudal ones—I only suspect you do not really know what you mean. You have a vague idea of society based ultimately on the land, and a vague idea of relations between people of 'mutual' service, rather like your relation with Siebert. But how you relate these ideas to a world of industrial towns, of a large illiterate working class, and an even larger middle class of incredible pride and stupidity, I can't understand—but perhaps I don't understand your ideas and they are clearer and more appropriate. Perhaps you must mean the qualities of vitality, adventure, discipline, and self-sacrifice, but they, I think, have less to do with the Feudal ages than with the preceding and succeeding ones. Vitality and adventurousness are qualities of the mind primarily, and the Feudal Ages are well-known to be the ages in which intellect was most restricted. Discipline and self-sacrifice, perhaps were more common than in the Renaissance, but in the Church, not in the Feudal System.

When I was staying with you at Bernstorff's,[4] I thought a lot about tradition and all these ideas of the rich, and tried to think what they meant, and what was good in them that we could have today. I think there is a real thing tradition, which is not just the out-worn vanity of a ruined class. 'Tradition' to Bernstorff and, I think, to you, is a sense of service to the state, and a pride in your family which always has served the state and which has respected certain values and given expression to its steadfastness by associating itself to a certain part of the country. I think that was admirable to a certain extent, but that now is dead. There is no continuation of it possible. We're living in a new world in which it has no place. But that doesn't mean rejecting the whole past, or saying tradition is dead. Tradition in that sense is a sort of primitive stage of nationalism, and is as valuable if it represents pride in contributing to an enduring whole—the state in the case of family tradition, Europe in the case of nationalism—but I think that both are evilly understood today and represent bad things—the state, a sort of totalitarian and meaningless machine, and nationalism an exclusive and unwarranted and deluded arrogance.

Darling Adam, I give you a long lecture (which you will not bother to read except that it would be rude not to comment a little on it in your answer) and you will reaccuse me of cruising in sheltered waters when you hide behind metaphors when you accuse me. How have I sheltered in relation to you? My silence as to my feelings since I have been home is not from fear of hurting myself, but because I felt utterly confused and lost, and respect myself and you too much to burden you with that. Slowly it grows better though I wish like you I would find the moon to freeze by, and could have a physical solitariness to match the solitariness I claim inside.

. . . I see Diana quite often but we do not talk about you. I believe, though she is not happy with me because she does not care for me deeply, that she is stronger with me than she may be with you or

Jane. For that reason too I think it would be bad to tell her. I do not feel dishonest with her and when we talk about you I respect absolutely her love for you and your caring for her and as something unaffected and untouched by my existence . . . My relation to you binds me closer to her for both your sake and for hers.

This is a long long letter and it is nearly three o'clock in the morning. It makes day of the night to make such a noise of writing, and this night, of all nights, is most beautiful, and the moon as freezing as either of us could wish to be, and the stars as sharp and clear. Bless you, Adam darling. I will try to be free to be myself and not let you build up a myth of me which will have no existence. You can help me so much if only you will, because you love me and attack me. Darling Adam, you are a bold and generous person to be loved by, thank you very much.

Always my love,

S.

I can't leave uncommented your remark that I do not hope for you to get a job after you have finished your training and that I have no danger of creating illusions about you. If you do not get a job it would not be for any reason for which I would be disillusioned but would rather make me respect you all the more. Success is mostly to be despised, and in your country a little more than in most. For you, at any rate, it is true that what you are, rather than what you do, is what matters. I will send you 'Prometheus Unbound'. It is very moving and especially the last part when Conquest is drawn captive through the deep:

> These are the spells by which to reassume
> An empire o'er the disentangled doom.

Oh, I'll send it to you, and risk your feeling I have delivered a sermon. Next time I'll write to you all about the autumn and the red buses and whom I meet and what they say. Bear with it this time and tell me if you could bear with it perhaps once in six weeks. I fall deep into the discovery of platitudes every few months... that is also an operation which does not remove the seat of evil, only makes the patient a bit stronger to go on.

Bless you again. Love,

S.

---

1 See letter Adam–Shiela, Hamburg 13 Oct. 1935.
2 From Shelley, 'Prometheus Unbound'.
3 See letter Adam–Shiela, Hamburg 13 Oct. 1935.
4 See above: Editor's note, n. 3, p. 77.

Chelsea,
17 October 1935

[Dear Adam,]
Diana came to me last night very unhappy because you had told her you were in love with someone. She thought I would know who it was since I had been with you last. I told her—I could not have done otherwise. She could not believe it and could not understand it. I could not explain it to her. I only could tell her what you said and what had happened, what I said and how we had parted. She asked me if I would see you again and if I loved you. . . .

We have perhaps deceived ourselves that this—or anything which we feel or do—belongs to us alone. Though I felt it taken away from me by Diana and these weeks I have struggled very hard to keep it between us, that you had to tell Diana and I had to make a wall between me and Goronwy behind which to hide it, means really that one's relations are not independent of each other.

I told Goronwy. He will tell nobody and he respects it. I told him that I loved you, as I have told you, and I told Diana. She asked if I were in love with you and I said I did not know. I think I do know and I am not in love with you. I am in love with nobody in the world. I love Goronwy and could never never leave him, though whether I will marry him or not, I do not know and it is no immediate question.

To us, telling or not telling can make no difference. I would not have told anyone had this not happened but I do not regret that it has. I think it will make a break easier for Diana and I think I can help her, though how she will feel to-day and in these next few months may not be how she felt last night. I will do everything I can for her. I am very touched by her and very fond of her. I think perhaps now you should make a real break with her, neither writing nor seeing her.

Darling Adam, I do not know how you will feel about all this. I think one must not let oneself be hurt or the quality of what one has endangered by other people coming into it. I think you will see that I had to tell Diana once she came to me. That she would come to me you could not have realised or perhaps you would not have written. Once she knew you loved someone, it was a lesser pain to know it was me than to fear an unknown person with whom you were happy in Hamburg. I denied to her and to Goronwy knowing that you wanted to marry me. That was more, perhaps, from wanting to keep something of all this to myself.[1]

It is perhaps wrong to want strongly complete privacy for one's feelings. It would at any rate be wrong for[2] me to put mine before

Diana's. Everything in me, after all, should be untouched by her feeling a part in this—everything in her is touched by the part she is. I will do everything I can for her. I think you can do nothing but let her live without you.

Bless you, darling Adam. I wish I were with you to say these things to you and be able to talk to you. The Alster is so beautiful and calm to walk beside. I hope it may be a companion to you now in these months.

my love,
Shiela

[Postscript omitted]

¹ Two lines scratched out.
² Two words scratched out.

Hamburg.
Oct 22, 1935.

Dear Shiela,

Nothing indeed has been taken away from you.

There will be no continuation of the dispute and of the extra difficulties I seem to have raised for you. I did not then realise that Diana would come to you so that you would then have to tell her. But since my telling her had to happen—my hope to keep it impersonal and attain D's respecting this wish was unfounded—the other was inevitable,—I see that now. But nothing essential is changed.

I am very grateful for your not sharing out everything to others, and keeping the core of my personal feeling to yourself. And I do not believe that it still just bewilders and astonishes you. I do not want to complicate your clear warm life. If I had known G. was still in London and that you might have to read them to Diana I would have written different letters—but their spring would have been the same.

Your writing that the Alster must now be my companion was strange, because I read and opened your letter coming home over the water last night. I could see the blue sky and water melt into the dusky silhouette of spires and scarcely lighted buildings. It was cold, but very calm and beautiful.

The warmth and courage I felt in spite of what you said may have been due to my seeing in the morning—when I came back from Berlin in the train—for a very short moment that meadow and wooden bridge near Friedrichsruh in the Sachsenwald. Do you remember it? Nobody can hurt what truly belongs to oneself.

Berlin, again, brought back to me the full hard world of things that belong to me and I am glad they will be hard and absorbing. Something quite new is beginning and you belong to it too.

There is another thing I want you to keep to yourself entirely: I may be in London for just one day in the near future and we can stop all nonsense between each other.

About Diana I cannot write to you nor to her about you—Goronwy's respect I return wholeheartedly and to you I feel nothing that should burden or bewilder you. Tell me what happens or whether you want to stop writing to me.

Love.

A.

Chelsea.
25th Oct. 1935.

Dear Adam,
. . . We are all working very hard for the Election.[1] Diana has a real job and has to work very hard, writing a newspaper and typing letters. I have menial jobs and address envelopes and take them to the people I've addressed them to. I get very excited in local politics and the slum population of Chelsea is splendid. Though it is incredible that anyone can raise themselves out of the squalor and enforced intimacy and dreadful poverty and ugliness of the slums. I have fierce quarrels with Peggy[2] because the Labour Party has no interest in the heads and hearts of the working class. Peggy says how can they have any heads and hearts when their bodies are so miserable. How can they indeed but they do, and they're cheated and starved at every turn by all the tricksters. Do you remember what Burke said—'The age of chivalry has gone, and that of sophists, calculators, and economists remains.'[3] That's what politics are like in England now.

I hope your visit to Berlin was a success. When and why will you come to London? What is this nonsense we will stop between us? By all means let's stop it. Why should I want not to write to you? I do not feel burdened or bewildered by you, only an incredible desire for us to get on with our lives and deal with the world as it really is, and not as it is when our shadows loom over it and obscure everything which is not ourselves. . . .

I feel excited and welcoming of everything that will happen. I want to belong to what is beginning for you. Something new is beginning for the whole world, I want to belong to that too. It may be absolute hell these next years, but I still believe in Socrates that no harm can come to a good man, and if we are not good we will not recognise the harm.

Come to London. Tell me what it is that is beginning. Trust me and remember what I said the night we came back from Bernstorff's if ever you are in trouble you can ask anything of me.

Meanwhile don't lets think so much about ourselves . . .

Love
S.

[1] The General Election scheduled for 14 Nov. 1935.
[2] Peggy Jay (Garnett).
[3] 'But the age of chivalry is gone. That of sophisters, economists, and calculators, has succeeded; and the glory of Europe is extinguished forever'; Edmund Burke, *Reflections on the Revolution in France* (New York, 1961), p. 89.

Hamburg.
29.10.35.

Shiela darling,

Letters and distance are clearly not the medium in which our friendship thrives. What we need is definitely an outer world to share, street, land, houses, water, people, politics, and little rabbits, and puppies—and without it all the 'inner world' and its ideas and notions and heavy letters becomes a little shabby and unreal. You are wrong when you think I spend all my days talking to myself about myself and then want to hand an accumulated amount of all that over to my friends.

But the things I am concerned with I cannot pour freely into letters[1] that are anything approximatingly as nice as your better letters. It is because probably Germany is really so very different in so many respects and because what I indicated to you as something quite new is nothing but a still more fascinating and a queer sense isolating exploration of my own country. This is not nationalism or reaction, but a search for solidarity in the particular phase we are in—the only way to make it creative and join up with that in other countries when we see our own future form more clearly. You must not forget that in a way you left Germany behind as a kind of hopeless proposition and my very life is bound up with not accepting that as right. All I hint at in connection with mediaeval virtues etc. belongs to entirely different requirements and backgrounds than those you are connected with. When you say you don't think I know what I mean—it is true enough for you canvassing in Chelsea slums or writing for the Economist . . . but may not necessarily be all nonsense regarding what is needed over here. And that being more difficult in some ways does not call for the short dismissal it so often finds—personally I probably deserve it more often than not, and you were kind and argued point for point—but in general there is no denying that the worlds that fill our thoughts and hopes—especially the selfless thought—are in an immediate and very important sense different worlds. So we must not waste our time in arguing things which we must by the nature of things see differently—all the more since I suspect that this makes you a little cross and bored. That in turn tends to make me feel extremely uncomfortable—especially when you go on to say that you wonder whether we are all real persons. Anyhow I am and I have felt more like one these very last weeks than for a long time before.

However much I agree with you that one must not let questions of self get on top of one, I resent tucking them away, pretending they're all right when they're not. From my point of view our relationship is far from all right, but if you prefer my not mentioning this any more, I will comply. . . .

But now I don't think the trip to England will come off and you will not want to come back to Germany.

Siebert is in my room, wondering why I type so very slowly on the type-writer we bought today. We went to a circus yesterday and it was great fun to see him laugh very hard—he looks very Chinese then. Often I see lots of people in the evenings and even go dancing with women—sometimes they are like a nightmare.

Suddenly I understand that you were very angry with me when you wrote that last letter before going to the country and probably you still do so now—this scrappy letter will hardly placate you and while saying I can always ask your help when I'm in trouble you will move further and further away in your distant and different life until very much later we will meet again and you will tell me why it suddenly became impossible to really tell each other things. If you cannot be my lover as I want you to be, we had hoped to be something like brother and sister and I have involved you in nothing that should have made that impossible. Or have I—tell me openly when I fail.

Always my love,

A.

---

[1] A reference to German censorship.

Thursday, [31 October 1935]

Darling Adam,

Really I wasn't cross, type-writing always looks cross, except yours, which is wonderfully typed, and too handsome and bold to be cross. But I'll write to you in writing— . . . Letters and distance certainly do not make us better friends, and now you have decided not to come here, which is very sad. Is that quite certain? You know I can't come to Germany. How can brothers and sisters meet each other so little? There is surely a Nordic law which commands them to see each other. Tell me why from your point of view our relationship is far from all right—or is it because you want to be lovers and think sister and brother an impossible and anyway a second best relation? Please not—in the circumstances of our two lives, our wanting to be whole and honest people, in my loving Goronwy, and us of necessity parted most of the time, I think friendship is the first and best relation we could have—I know we are both finding it hard to be friends, but if I move further and further away, it will be a little your fault, and it has not really become impossible to tell each other things—only is becoming, and the reason is because we neither can bear, or dare to speak of what we hold so important—Goronwy for me—Diana for you—and also G. for you, Diana for me—If I was a little resentful when I wrote to you, it was perhaps it was because I felt you had involved me in what I had always condemned—your relation to Diana—and if I go more further from you now, it is because I will not be involved. She wants me to tell her about you these months when you cannot write to her—and later you two resume your relationship. I do not know what she means by your being cowardly to tell me. I regret only that you did not wait and try and make it possible for us to share the same world for a short time in Hamburg. If you had always loved me, I think you deliberately chose what was not love, but was easier, when you made love to Diana. I cannot understand in any case why you did not know I loved Goronwy. Diana said you had always taken it for granted between you.—Still all this is nothing to do with now unless the writing of these things made you suddenly realise you did not love me as you thought in Hamburg— but as a brother. Do you think perhaps you made a mistake then? Admit it if you did—I would not think anything different of you. . . .

You asked me to tell you where you fail, and why and how you make it not possible to be something like brother and sister—I think you fail because you are not quite honest with me—I don't know whether from design, or unclearness in your feelings—I think half-conscious design—Please, darling Adam, try and say it—whatever it is—I feel sufficiently much your sister not to falter at anything you say. In our relationship you must regard me as the unchanging part, and yourself as the changing—though my letters may grow distant— I will be the same whenever we meet.

Love then,
Shiela.

. . . Your letters to me are always opened.

16 Mulberry Walk,
London SW3
3 Nov 1935

Dear Adam,

Forgive and do not be worried by the return to typescript which has no sinister or unfriendly significance. There was lots in your letter which I did not answer, nor did I thank you for the very nice portrait of Lamb[1] which makes me like him much more than I have ever done before.

Why do you say that we must not waste time in arguing about things which we must of necessity see differently? I should have thought those were the only sort of things people did argue about. Also I think in your attitude to Germany,[2] which you share with practically all your countrymen, that it is a sort of mystical entity which can only be understood and should only be judged by Germans themselves, is very dangerous both for Germany and for the Europe of which it is a part. I have been reading the introduction of Sieburg's Es werde Deutschland[3] and though one cannot help feeling some sympathy for his point of view, I think one must also condemn it if one wants Germany to play a part as a grown up nation and the equal of other European powers. He says about Germany to-day 'there are to be no more human beings in Germany but only Germans.' I think that is what shocks people outside Germany. Have you read Was Europe a Success yet?[4] His objection to communism was chiefly that it deliberately denied, and by its policy made impossible, the continuation of European culture. I think that is now true of Germany also. And when you affirm your German character, you deny your European character and when you deny that, you deny not only what is best and most highly civilised in you now but also all the great people who have made you of any account in Europe. German rearmament will not really make Germany any more respected in Europe, and when it goes with a fanatical assertion of Germany rather than Europe and you cease to share in the intellectual and religious and artistic movements of the rest of Europe, you become more and more like the Turks.

I am sorry if I am insulting you by supposing you need to hear these things but it sounds awfully as if you did when you talk about 'isolating exploration' of your own country or 'entirely different requirements and backgrounds from those' I am concerned with. Either you are part of Europe and we are all concerned with what you do in Germany and share very similar conditions, ideals, and traditions, or else you deliberately cut yourself off from Europe and since at the same time you are arming yourself to the teeth the only alternative for the rest of Europe is to surround your frontiers with defensive alliances and give you the isolation you yourselves demand till you are once more a grown up nation. Still you better read Sieburg because you are very alike in your attitudes and your search for solidarity is met by his 'Since I wholly accept Germany, I must for good or ill accept too those elements of her life which excite of criticism, even the aversion, of the outside world.' But it's such a queer way of looking at things. Since I accept England, I wish to change those things in England which excite the aversion of other nations.

It is not true that I left Germany as a hopeless proposition. On the contrary I left it with an almost exalted desire and hope that there would one day be a United State of Europe of which Germany would be a real and important part. In a Memorandum on German Foreign Policy, Sir Eyre Crowe wrote 'It cannot for a moment be questioned that the mere existence and healthy activity of a powerful Germany is an undoubted blessing to the world. Germany represents in a pre-eminent degree those highest qualities and virtues of good citizenship in the large sense of the word, which constitute the triumph and glory of modern civilization.'[5] We went to war with you when you tried to impose your will on other countries even when we believed in your representing 'the triumph and glory of modern civilisation.' Now that we are questioning that and you have resumed your civilising mission the same thing will happen with worse consequences than before. I think anybody with any serious patriotism must do their utmost to prevent that and by isolating yourself you are making it more likely. I suppose it is inevitable that I should care most about German foreign policy and you about domestic affairs, and that you should feel I misjudge and summarily dismiss what you say, but you should go on saying it all the same. Or is it really you who is bored and not wanting to go on talking about these things. We can't write very often or very long if we write only about the things about which we are not thinking about particularly at the moment, like your gay evenings and my new friends. . . .

I am enjoying myself very much working for the election. The Chelsea people are practically all working class people and more extreme than the Labour Party. There is even one anarchist who is mocked a great deal by his more serious fellows for belonging to a different party at every meeting he goes to. I like everybody very much and we have a lot of jokes. I have cut my hair off and am afraid look more like a boy again and less like a woman. I went to a fair last night with my cousin and won a toy monkey and a coconut which we gave to some nice children in the street. Now I am going to an Open-Air-Meeting in Trafalgar Square with my brother, Sunday afternoon occupation. . . .

Darling Adam, I'm afraid this letter will confirm your ideas that typed letters are of evil omen, please not. I wish you had been coming to England after all though perhaps a secret visit would have shaken more nerves. Have you read the story of San Michele?[6]

Love

S.

---

[1] Charles Lamb (1775–1834); English essayist and critic.

[2] See letter Adam–Shiela, Hamburg, 29 Oct. 1935, para. 2.

[3] Friedrich Sieburg, *Es werde Deutschland* (Frankfurt-on-Main, 1933); Engl. trans.: *Germany: My Country* (London, 1933).

[4] Joseph Wood Krutch, *Was Europe a Success?* (New York, 1934).

[5] Sir Eyre Crowe (1864–1925); British foreign servant; 1920–25, Permanent Under-Secretary for Foreign Affairs; 'Memorandum on the Present State of British Relations with France and Germany', 1 Jan. 1907, in G. P. Gooch and Harold Temperley (eds.), *British Documents on the Origin of the War 1898–1914*, vol. iii; 'The Testing of the Entente 1904–1906', App. A, p. 406.

[6] Axel Martin Fredrik Munthe (1857–1949), Swedish physician and author; wrote several books of reminiscences, most notable of which was the *Story of San Michele* (New York, 1929), widely read in England at the time.

Hamburg.
Nov. 4th 1935.

[Dear Shiela,]

I missed you very much yesterday when I drove through the country to see my farmer friend who once was shepherd in Siberia. It was a cold and grey, but beautiful day, with burning yellow leaves among grey veils of mist. And his farm is lovely—a river all around it, two mills, and lots of little fishing ponds connected by a little stream. It must be quite perfect in summer and his wife too I liked to a certain extent. Then I went to see another family not very far from there, of a former Rhodes Scholar who is now lawyer in Hamburg. He has a very nice little farm, beautiful cows and calves, a big wolf-dog, and good fields and pasture near a little river. He is an enormous big man and in his way quite admirable, he has had a very difficult time recently. Driving home through the dark, I reflected what I should answer to your nice sleepy letter with its neatly embedded accusations and doubts. Mainly I thought you must be told to stop doubting and accusing for it makes life more difficult than is necessary. You did *not* doubt my sincerity when you were here and your doing so now must reasonably be attributed to other factors than my own untrustworthiness. So, please stop that, because I cannot defend myself effectively against these charges—which can only spring from an unsympathetic perspective of my relationship to you. And for God sake go on refusing to get 'involved' in D's relation to me. It really has nothing to do with us and I was most anxious for her to respect my wish not to let her know who it was that made it impossible for me to carry on with her as I used to be able to. That I had to give her the reason for that you will see; and it was lack of imagination for me not to know that she would try to find out from you, and that this would eventually lead to a conference of powers in which my position would be disputed and attacked like that of Italy in Geneva[1]— me facing the constant threat that my chief ally will suddenly be my chief condemner. He seems already to try and extract from me admissions that I sinned against our alliance before the 'incident'[2] occurred and yet, I really believe, he can only be agitated by the bother arising from the incident and not the alliance. It would be dishonest of me to say that I had been dishonest here or at the Ostsee[3] and I remind you again that you believed me and that you promised to believe me. Why destroy that?—

I admitted freely that I had lots and serious doubts about the ultimate happiness of the solution I suggested—but I insist that the suggestion was completely sincere and backed by all that I considered best in me. I feel no need to go back on that.

Also I admitted that I considered the true friendship between us as only beginning after the change I desired and seemed to need. I told you more than once that I am acutely aware of frequent lacks of understanding and solidarity which I was sure to conquer on the path I suggested. Now, you have refused it, those difficulties exist as much as before and there are new ones on top of it. And that is why there is unclearness and uncertainty in me about the chances of our friendship and sadness about this distance on all fields.

When you went and something of your warmth was still with me, I thought happily that the 'brother and sister' adjustment would be easy and creative. But gradually a kind of starved feeling—which has a lot to do with my general conditions of life—took the place of that hope. And then your attacks and your distrust in my sincerity became a bit wounding. But I know that you would be the same fair Shiela if we met and I don't blame you for considering my representations a little unconvincing and bloodless compared to the living love that surrounds you and that you return.

Still I am ready to make the required adjustment and don't think it ultimately need to fail. It is neither the better or the lesser, but the only way before us now, I suppose. And I think we can best find it by being a little resigned and not expecting too much. We will be very good friends during the short times we will be able to meet in the future and for the rest we will always labour under the lack of immediacy in our communication. Letters are almost nothing (though I must for a while see myself deriving a disproportionately joy from any kind thing you say in your letter—i.e. your remembering that Smoke[4] had been to tea with me when at the moment you found him the only bearable company in the house) but we must keep the contact which will prevent us from meeting as strangers when we meet. . . .

It is an oppressive and absorbing hope ever to find someone who could respond and share with one the simple side of one's complex and heterogeneous encounters with the world. Yet I begin to look on that rather as an added richness than as an absolute requirement. Why should one face those complexities any less determinedly if one has made up one's mind that every friendship one has touches only one part of one's existence. Perhaps toning down one's wishes in that respect makes for harder and more realistic work. And yet one can hardly remain or become joyful as a whole being that way.

It is silly and childish to talk with one's friends about the things one can *not* share—and sometimes it is very unfair and cruel to make conjectures about them.

But if you look backward and forward, Shiela, there are a great number of things we might share still and have already shared. It is a clear and indubitable continuity, I think, that nothing we did has as yet broken.

Nor should you 'condemn' my tie with D.[5] (God knows what will become of it now). This is, in a sense, the time for me to realise how much she has given me, in a complete and reckless generosity, and what comfort I derived from her interest in the details and troubles of my life. Of course I miss her, and am hurt of hurting her.—I am sure you gave G. no feeling whatsoever that he must destroy your confidence in me. It shouldn't be worth his while. There is no dishonesty

or unclearness, at heart we all know where we stand now and I love
you and shall try to be a brotherly friend.

                                                                    A.

¹ See letter Shiela–Adam, Paris Oct. 1935, n. 3.
² See Editor's note preceding letter Adam–Shiela, Hamburg, end of Sept. 1935.
³ The Baltic Sea where Travemünde is situated.
⁴ Shiela's cat.
⁵ Diana; see letter Shiela–Adam, Thursday 31 Oct. 1935.

                                                          6.11.35.

Dear Shiela,

  You are right when you warn me not to fall back into that mystical
isolationism that makes so much that is happening over here dangerous and ridiculous. Surely you know that I am all in favour to put as
many 'mere human beings' into positions of power in our various
nations as possible. (God knows there are few enough in any of the
parties concerned!) But why I was saying these things had two main
reasons: a) when one has trouble with one's friends personally one
tends to withdraw into retreats of which one can safely say: Anyhow
you know nothing or little about this! and more seriously b) I do not
think that the easy identity of the task before us all that is expressive
in what is usually held against the new German mysticism, the jargon
of the new statesmen and of those many minds that are guided by the
journalists of the 'grown-up' nations—is at all adequate to mould
what I should consider a new Europe worth all our best endeavours.
Have you read the 'first prize' poem of the N. St. & N. competition
of last week? (I will use it as typing practice for it isn't really worth
reprinting)

> It is a fact for which quite a lot can be said
> That, after a number of unfortunate people are gassed,
>   bombed, and otherwise unpleasantly dead,
> Europe will not have changed much.
> It may be a little worse or a little better.
> Which is no unduly important matter.
> For many of us there will continue to be women, sun, cafés,
>   music, old cities.
> The fact that the dead won't see them is admittedly
> A thousand pities . . . ¹

The motto was 'A cheerful view of the future of Europe'! I think this
is not entirely untypical of your cultured politicians of the Left.

  There's undoubtedly a lot of truth in the things Krutch points out in his book. One has often felt the same things—but when you put it away and ask yourself what it all amounts to, you have a taste of defeat and resignation in your mouth. It is very nice to know which things you like, and which you don't. But if you want to change the world you must have deeper preferences. That your democratic system of elections gives a semblance to the important things coming about according to personal preferences... —this semblance I think is a very dangerous illusion, in many respects as resigned, unclear, and uncertain as this tendency of mysticism you attack in me. I think, however, we can safely join hands in agreeing that we want each to defeat the great fraud in our respective social system and begin doing that by trying to be as free and human as possible in our stifling surroundings and create an open and honest outlook around us of the things that really matter. This sounds vague enough and till I have some power to do and see things a little more concretely you cannot expect me to have a set programme in these generally altered complexities. To see through them for my self and not according to the patter of any of those 'progressive parties' of the old democracies is really all I mean when I say I cannot very well do it and translate what I see into the terms of another world at the same time. Personally as friends *when we are together* we quite naturally share the beautiful common worlds of human beings doing their best; but while we are apart we must trust each other going on trying, even though a hundred difficulties prevent us reporting our results.

It was very nice of you indeed to write me that little note when you had been working all evening and I hope you didn't think me pathetic or complaining. I am all right though I don't think much of myself at the moment nor of things and people around me, I know it's my own and nobody else's fault.

Write to me when are you inclined and I will write when I have a little more to say.

LOVE

A.

[1] This strikingly prophetic poem was printed in the *New Statesman and Nation*, 245, 2 Nov. 1935, p. 654 over the signature 'Zilch'.

[*about* 7 November 1935]

Darling Adam,

Thank you for your letter and the drunken one.[1] It is . . . nice to be a golden girl in your defiant and drunken thoughts. You seem to be very gay with your sailors, I wish there were some sailors in London.

It is very staid as always, and the only café in London is the Café Royal, and you know what that's like. Looking at its brightest side it has only the interest of Holbein with some of the gruesomeness, in a new form, of Hogarth. You would find lots of food for your comtempt and despair of the 'grown-up' nations there. It's full of so-called statesmen of the Left... but I think you misjudge these and you'd better stop reading the *New Statesmen* before you condemn all England under its cover. The poem is far from typical of our 'cultured politicians of the left.' To begin with the whole trouble with them is that they are not cultured, and then nowhere so much as on the left is war hated and feared as the absolute wrecker of anything we have and want to have now which is of any value. The people who think that way are in a minority of about twenty to 20 or 40 million of the population. Still, I agree with you, and there is something profoundly wrong with the whole of Europe, as Ortega y Gasset says, even the Russian attempt is nothing new, just the old ideas of western Europe tried on an eastern country, and there is nothing new in Germany now, just a greater and further reaction to things which most people had rejected a few hundred years ago. The question, though, is what to do about it. As we've lived here all our lives and been brought up in this stifling world are we able to say anything about it or see it as it really is? And if it is really finished and decadent, is there any hope of prolonging its life or any point in easing its death? Why don't we leave it? Goronwy and I are seriously thinking of going to the Far East, preferably China, in about a year. He is very excited by reading a speech of Smuts 'I feel that great continent moving again.' I'm very willing to go, because though I had hoped to do something here, the whole spirit of it all is so awful and a world in which every thought and every action is one blind groping to ward off evil and chaos is fundamentally without interest. The issues are only peace and war, poverty and the perpetuation of the present social system, or changing it for another under the threat of starvation and violence. Of course it is a matter of life and death, but matters of life and death aren't of much interest. Every question in Europe seems to be on the plane of material interest. Even your mysticism is nothing more except that and psychological ill-health . . . I heard a rather unpleasant countryman of yours on Germany and the present situation at Chatham House, it is pleasant to hear how profoundly peace-loving you are and you are behaving very well about sanctions.[2] If only the League would turn into a United States, there might be some hope in a new world and we could think about different things than politics and frontier issues and empires.

Darling Adam, why do you not think very much of yourself? You should work very hard and be independent through your exam and then examine everything again. My sisters have babies. It seems such a pity we can't all die off and let them begin a new world all of their own, or that we can't teach them and make a new world for them. I would like to have some beautiful sons and bring them up in the Chinese mountains beside a waterfall till they were twenty-one then send them into the world to make it again. Love and write to me.

S.

[1] Letter Adam–Shiela, Thursday 31 Oct. 1935 (not reproduced here): 'it is long after midnight and I have spent hours at drinking with sailors and people ... darling golden girl, good night.'
[2] See letter Shiela–Adam, Paris 3 Oct. 1935, n. 3.

Hamburg.
11.11.35.

Shiela Darling,
Thank you for the lovely sentence about 'some beautiful sons and bringing them up in the Chinese mountains beside a waterfall' and the context in which it was not so very clear who they all belong to. I had not expected from you all that acclamation to my pessimistic remarks about Europe, nor is it right to follow out moods like those of Ortega y Gasset. His book was translated by a beautiful and clever woman I used to know at Göttingen with whom I went for a long and interesting walk,[1] ... and really I thought what thin stuff all this 'aristocratic' musing she and her author went in for was compared to Hegel whom I was admiring tremendously during that time. Hegel for all his reputation as an esoteric writer is full of warm power and participation in the contexts we are created to be part of. Nor is he (or I) an example for the mysticism you call psychological ill-health. Yet he is nearer to that than to the scanty rationalism which makes piecemeal of everything. That rationalism when it is not even backed by warmth of heart is truly awful. I admit that our 'mysticism' is too.

I am rather disturbed about the increasing indifference I feel about my juridical stuff. Other factors too hinder me from just sitting down and working hard at nothing but the exam and leaving other things till later. . . .

From next week onwards there is to be a tremendous fair in this town to which I invite you and G. It has been held for 1000 years and this is the 1001st time which I think will be especially beautiful and enjoyable. But I'm sure that many important things like your election and learning to cook etc. will hinder you from coming.

This is a silly letter and I wanted to write and complain and be comforted by you about a great number of things, but when it came to saying them, I don't think at present you are the person for it. . . .

Sometimes I think you are a very restless person and should go to China or somewhere to get out of all your unsettling associations and then it seems positively criminal to let you have anything to do with my life, the mental and circumstantial unrest of which at present even unsettled an old very nice lady of 76 to whom I talked the other day. So far she is the best girl-friend I have in this place. . . .

. . . When you are abstract, darling Shiela, you are nice and funny and one knows exactly what kind of thing will bring you back to reality (you find that more frequently necessary with me, don't you?)—but when I have to write to you that is technically impossible and so it remains all very abstract and one does not know which terms to use for it and knows exactly that any strong tide of real life on either side would sweep away those terms anyway.—But please do write when you feel a little more than kindly.

Love,

A.

¹ Hélène Weyl.

Chelsea.

15th Nov, 1935.

Darling Adam,

Thank you for one of the nicest letters you've ever written me,¹ so funny and like you and inconsequent. Don't find letters stupid and subaltern when you write such nice ones and I like having them so much—tho' I agree, they are an unsatisfactory form of communication, and more than ever so when one is restless, changing, and uncertain of everything. It is not criminal for me to have anything to do with your life because of its mental and circumstantial unrest—mine is too full of unrest already to be affected evilly by yours, tho' I wish I could be more steadfast and unchanging so that I could be of help to you, and you could complain to me and I could comfort you. I'm sorry you will not let me.

The results of the General Election² are truly appalling, and the comments all around upon them are even worse. The British public is complimented on its steadiness, tradition, and God knows what, when the whole election is the result of blind panic. All the depressed areas voted conservative, all the best young Labour men were defeated. Bill Astor, the brother of your one,³ has turned out Wilmot entirely by snobbishness. I feel like despising the whole electorate for its stupidity, cowardice and snobbishness—and the awful thing now is that the next General Election (if there is one—Douglas says this is probably the last and there will be war within two years) will take place at the beginning of an even worse slump than the one which wrecked the 1929 Labour Govt. That makes one despair even of working for the Labour Party except for working inside it to make it a really strong and efficient party able to take over in a crisis. I want very much to be secretary to Hugh Dalton.[4]

I feel about everything as Mowrer feels about the International Situation—it's a cross-word puzzle where all the letters keep wandering about. One must have something to hold onto in a changing world—I suppose that's what made people such blind believers in the Unknown—at least God cannot be proved *not* to exist—the same holds for all spiritual values—but I feel very much lost and feel I have taken a wrong turning somewhere in my life—a long way back—or perhaps it is just what made Wordsworth write his Ode on Immortality. I feel terribly

> It is not now as it hath been of yore;
>   Turn wheresoe'er I may,
>   By night or day,
> The things which I have seen I now can see no more.[5]

I feel almost as if the only things which can make me truly happy are those of the physical world, the trees and fields and rocks and sea, and the air when it is cold and fresh under the winter sun—it was most beautiful by the Baltic.

You must not take any notice of this despair and melancholy—it will grow better if I am strong. Perhaps I should not express it—but one must get rid of it and one can only do so by facing it. I am going to Oxford tomorrow, I long for it very much, it was so stupid to be so discontent when one lived in such a beautiful place and did not know how lying and stupid politics were, and still believed that by thought one could solve everything.

Darling Adam—and I meant to write such a bright happy letter in answer to yours—I wish we could come to the Fair for the 1001st time. I wish you would be at Oxford tomorrow.

Love,
S.

---

[1] See letter Adam–Shiela, Hamburg, 11 Nov. 1935.
[2] In the mid-November General Election the National Government of Baldwin was returned to power with 431 seats. The Conservatives won 381 seats and Labour,

divided between those who supported the government and those who opposed it, 154 seats.

³ William Waldorf Astor (1907–66), elected Conservative MP in 1935; from 1952 3rd Viscount Astor; brother of Adam's friend the Hon. David Astor.

⁴ Hugh Dalton (1887–1962); from 1960 Lord Dalton; Labour expert on foreign affairs; Shiela worked for him as honorary secretary 1935–6.

⁵ Wordsworth, 'Ode on Intimations of Immortality from Recollections of Early Childhood' (1802–4).

[*Postcard*:
Baz Bahadur and Rupmati reading by moonlight; Indian 18th century.]

British Museum
[*n.d.*]

[Dear Adam,]
    Do you think these are the people of whom Smuts said 'Sleeping Asia is awaking, is stirring from one end to the other. Two thirds of the human race are on the move . . . no one knows whither'. I am very excited and think the world of an incredible beauty and splendour in the East, and of all the colours which our slums and poverty shut out of Europe.

    I am writing this chapter about the present situation and it is very difficult indeed. I work in the British Museum which I like, because I used to work here a long time ago, and because it is full of madmen. There is one with long red clothes and sandals and long hair down his back and rather a nice gentle face. I went to a Tchekhov¹ play last night, called the Three Sisters. It is very depressing. They wanted to go to Moscow and were always frustrated. For two acts it is just very depressing, then tragedies happen which is a great relief. . . .

    Do you think these poor Abyssinians are dying to save us, like the Vivisection animals, and now there is at last hope of peace and a real League? Your country is behaving very well. . . .

S.

¹ *The Three Sisters* (1901).

Hamburg.
Nov. 17th 1935.

Shiela Darling,
    Did the last sentence of my last letter stop you writing? The whole of it wasn't very satisfactory I suppose. . . .

I was out the last two nights till almost daylight and gained more bitter tastes about life and people and me with them. I think I am entirely spoilt for it in one sense—though I find men freer and more comradely than before. But, you are right, there's no peace in Europe—and peace there must be if you want to create. As it is, being harnessed and equal to the tidal motion around one is the nearest approach to truth and stability. . . .

I have been more or less offered a job in the big German chemical concern (I.G.)[1]

Siebert just came and told me of the China–Russia agreement[2] which may mean a tremendous change. If only you had returned a strong Labour Govt, it might have been the time to stem effectively the tide of Italian and Japanese Imperialism. As it is you will probably be lenient to the first and friends with the latter. And China will cease to be the ideal resort for us from Europe—if your Empire helped the Abyssinians speedily and effectively it would be a very good thing—but will you?

The bourgeois mind dominating in all the 'advanced' countries (this time including Germany) will go on adjusting and readjusting itself on the revolutionary tides that move the world until the rest of rational mastering and guiding of these powers is used up and with it conception of man. Nationalism and bolshevism combined are the cynical retranslation of a high phase of human emancipation into the dull medium of tribal collective instinct—it is the way in which Asiatic history has been going on for ages I suppose.

I heard a long lecture on the historical and political background of the Anglo-German naval agreement,[3] the chief point of which impressed me as being that this was the most unfortunate of atmospheres in which our two countries should arrive at agreements or rather truces. It may be to the good in making another war between us more unlikely and add a certain element of calmness to our relations—but it is a narrow, uninspiring uncreative instrument—considering what essential powers in both our nations could give a solidaric lead to the rest of the world (In the way of sober rational organisation in international affairs).

One should devote one's life to making this possibility manifest. But one cannot do it by settling on the partial stagnation of present circumstances. Don't you agree? Tell me too what you think of the role of St.[4] and G.L.[5] have played and send me the 'Economist' on the result of the Election.

Bless you, fair Shiela—and don't grow too distant!

Love,

A.

¹ I. G. Farben, Frankfurt-on-Main.
² No formal Russo-Chinese agreement was signed until 21 Aug. 1937 (Non-Aggression Pact USSR–Chinese National Government, Nanking). Yet this most likely refers to a decision of the Seventh Congress of the Comintern held in Moscow in July and Aug. 1935. In its Declaration of 1 Aug. the Comintern offered the Nanking Government an alliance with the aim of forming a united front against Japan; this represented a significant shift in policy. See Charles B. McLane, *Soviet Policy and the Chinese Communists* (New York, 1958), pp. 66 ff.
³ By the terms of the Anglo-German Naval Agreement of 18 June 1935 Germany was to have a naval force (including submarines) of not more than thirty-five per cent of that of Great Britain. The agreement constituted a bilateral breach of the terms of the Treaty of Versailles and caused consternation in many European capitals.
⁴ Sir Richard Stafford Cripps (1889–1952), leader of the left wing of the Labour Party; MP 1931–50. Adam met his son John while at Oxford and befriended the whole family. Sir Stafford always kept his faith in Adam.
⁵ George Lansbury (1859–1940), churchman, lecturer, editor; called Britain's No. 1 pacifist; leader of the Labour Party 1931–5; Privy Counsellor.

                                                    Office
                                    Monday, [18th November 1935]

[Dear Shiela,]
    Thank you darling Shiela for your sweet Letter¹ which I am looking forward to reread—it was terribly nice to be handed your British Museum envelope this morning by the postman in Magdalenenstrasse. And the picture postcard is delicious: what delicacy and sweet intimate enjoyment of beauty. I want to ride with you in the moonlight on fine horses and with garments of silk and pearls. Have we both made a mistake a long way back and one not so very far back? It seems so horribly wasteful not to be lovers when the world around us was one for you and me and most most beautiful. It seems so wasteful to wander about with people who are so very much further away than you and yet readier to be near.
    Have I spoilt the possibility of our being together unimpededly by bringing matters to a false issue between us? I think you are right that we shouldn't marry—but couldn't your sweet self other than thrive under my intimate care. I feel and see the dangers to your peace so clearly and you in a way mine that being together can only further our essential progress. Oh, why did we make the rest of the world and thereby ourselves suspicious of us being together? Why did I introduce these heavy binding terms of love and marriage when your womanly nearness was a living delight to me that you did not intend to withdraw on principle.
    Sometimes I think that you are the danger for the spiritual concentration one's work demands, and sometimes darling it seems that I can

only attain it with you near. It makes me very happy to hear of you the way you wrote this time—but it cuts into me to know you moving about in buses and libraries and strange circles so far away that I should be made happy by a mere sheet of paper and a short glimpse of a more lonely mood of yours. Oh, why must you be suspicious and make me feel hard pressed when there is perhaps the only realm of clear joyful love in my present life. There is no mistake in one's life far back unless one repeats it in one's present existence. Not to give trust generously where one could is what blocks the realms of rich and beautiful ripening which haunt our dreams when we failed to embrace them.

[Adam.]

[1] See letter Shiela–Adam, Chelsea, 15 Nov. 1935 and postcard from the British Museum.

Hamburg.
21.11.35.

Shiela Dear,

. . . In my office I spent most of the morning picking out important news for the line[1] of the last few Times issues. Then we went to pay the men of a ship that had just returned from the Black Sea. The First Steward was rather drunk already, or still, and rudely remarked that it was shocking for *three* men to come to bring out to them the little money they received. The other men came into the officers' mess where we paid out the money rather shyly, as if being seen taking money from a black-coated clerk was an indecent act. Some of them were very blond and strong, others pale and hollow. The cook who belonged to the round beaming blond type showed me the place where he keeps all the food nice and cool, and where a mate had managed to bring grapes nice and fresh from Smyrna. He was very proud of the whole ship. They were just unloading figs and there was a lovely sweet smell over the whole busy scene.

It was very nice going through the rough harbour with the motor boat of the company, he made a long way round to show me all the things you don't see so easily otherwise. What makes a place like a factory yard or a harbour so fascinating is, I believe, the enormous, unspeaking and hardly visible human labour which is shouldering it all the time. In the yards you hardly see the tiny dark closed workers hammering away at some place of these vaste bodies of ships and nobody bothers what incredible toil it often is to unload a steamer in the dark or when (as most of the time) there is a hurry. Some of them look quite spent with all the work they have had to do so that they look at you like weary suspicious animals. But that is not the type. That I think is the young very robust and obstinate looking fellow with a dark blue cap and light blue and white blouse and a broad very dirty leather apron. They look very wild and strong and unsurrendering. The man on the boat told me a few things about their inside which pleased and encouraged me. . . .

But you were very nice and sent me that picture card and you are only not nice to be so far away and in different moods so often and so engaged in this distant life.

Love
A.

¹ The Hamburg Levant Line.

Hamburg.
Monday, [25 November 1935]

[Dear Shiela,]

The enclosed I wrote before going to Berlin where I had a very busy and relatively satisfactory three days. . . .

You probably were a little rash in concluding that it was perfectly all right for your being involved into the complexities of my existence—unless of course you take the liberty of withdrawing entirely whenever it becomes a little too 'complex'—there is such a lot more than the personal side (which I too got very weary of turning over and over again). Will you in your work for the Labour Party f.i. keep in sight of the tremendous changes that are taking place outside Europe? Will you realise that the particular brand of socialism in your country is due largely to the fact that it *rests* on rather than challenges your Empire (though it may do the latter in theory)? And if you realise what elements really make the security in which an embryonic amount of international discussion may still proceed—must you not revise some of the socialist views on power and draw rather near to the attitude of the progressive imperialist (to the type of Smuts)? . . .

Now I must stop. I hope you are well and happy.

Love
A.

Darling Adam,

I am very sorry I have not answered your letter for such a long time. It was not entirely because of what you said, and I will try and answer it in spite of your nice helpful letter this morning on which I could 'fall back'.[1]

I don't know which of your letters to answer first, or what of all I have to say to write down. I'm glad your visit to Berlin was not entirely depressing, but you do not tell me exactly what the results of it were and whether you have a job or not and whether or not you will be able to get out of Europe for some time after your exam. I think it would be a very good thing for you to do. My desire to go to China is a little less strong now that I have such a good and interesting job here and I feel it would be wrong to turn my back now. Anyhow China is eaten up by these detestable westernised Japs, so perhaps neither of our desires will be granted. I must send you Peter Fleming's[2] article on the journey he made from Peking to India. Would you like to be an explorer?

The point you make about English Socialism resting on Imperialism is quite right, and I think one should think much more seriously and deeply about politics than I have yet done. Of course in a way I do not think it is necessary for socialism to challenge the British Empire, for this is built in the last resort on the emancipation and equality of the peoples it contains. As you know the greater part of the Empire is made up of Dominions. I have always thought that Dominion status was the ultimate aim for all our colonies, and it is there that the British Empire is so much less objectionable than any other Empire which now exists, and why so many people think it impossible to give back colonies to you, because you believe in the unaltered and unalterable inferiority of all races to one you call Aryan which does not exist. I don't quite know what you mean about security in which international discussion was possible being more compatible with imperialist view a la Smuts than with 'socialist views on power'. I should have thought it was imperialism which was based on power politics and therefore threatened security by keeping a system of international anarchy instead of the international legal system which could result from socialism. However, I think one cannot decide one's politics from abstract thinking and must first have some experience of what the real problems and conflicts are. . . .

Jane[3] . . . you know cannot be treated lightly as you treat so many of your friends. You are hurt that Diana suspects your essential honesty. I think it is because of the lightness and almost irresponsibility of your relations with people ... the letter which you wrote me[4] which you thought would be difficult to answer did shock me a little both because of the almost frivolity of it and because of your going back on what we had said to each other. I do not feel quite like writing about these things at the moment so you must forgive the clumsiness of expression. We could never be lovers both because of the reasons I gave you in Hamburg and because I think such a relationship between us would be to reduce to casualness and impermanence a relationship which I at any rate put higher than that. It is nothing to do with me that you have these relationships so easily and lightheartedly with other people, and I would not condemn it for itself, but it does make me want more to be friends with you than to be lovers. I'm afraid this may hurt you a little and I am very sorry to do so. I think, you see, that today there are many lovers and few friends, because people are materialists and believe only what they see and touch. They have ceased to believe that chastity is a virtue and that there is such a thing as friendship and love where there is no physical expression. It is what you say about nationalism and bolshevism—'the cynical retranslation of a high phase of human emancipation.'[5] Perhaps you will not understand any of this and condemn it. I am very sorry if you will or cannot be friends. I am very sorry that you regard it still as only a second best to lovers 'without the heavy binding terms of love and marriage.'

I'm afraid I have not explained very clearly or well what I want to say to you. I hope it will not hurt you at all. I think it would not do so if you could understand it, nor could you think it harms in any way any 'real and pure joyful love' in your present life.

I'm afraid I have not now said all that I wanted to say, but I cannot go on with this now.

I send you the most beautiful picture I know.[6]

My love always.

Shiela.

[1] See letters Adam–Shiela, Hamburg, Monday, 18 Nov. 1935; Hamburg, 21 Nov. 35; Monday 25 Nov. 1935.

[2] Robert Peter Fleming, author; travelled widely in East Asia as special correspondent of *The Times*, served the war in Norway, Greece, and SEAC.

[3] Jane Rendel.

[4] See letter Adam–Shiela, Monday, 18 Nov. 1935.

[5] See letter Adam–Shiela, Hamburg, 17 Nov. 1935.

[5] Shiela does not remember which picture it was.

Hamburg.
29.11.35.

Dear Shiela,

Since you *were* writing this letter why didn't you say all you had to say. Perhaps you had to write it, but you might have written all in that case. A few things you said I really must answer, others I will not follow up. I do not care to have such letters again.

There is no reason on earth why you should think it necessary to defend either Diana or Jane against me. Of my relations with D. you understand very very little, though the blame for that may rest very largely on me. It was more nearly complete and beautiful than anything I ever had with you, more permanent and selfless. There are powers in her which I have never come across in anyone else before or after and her sympathy in matters that are difficult to convey and her unquestioning loyalty whenever things went at all wrong made her a friend that it is very hard to go without. You know very well that you are not the reason, nor even the cause for its being impossible to carry on this relationship in its previous form. The understood reason was that it took such different shape and value in hers than in my life and that it was endangering her future life and my responsibilities. What you write about that now makes me think that you never really understood before how much was really involved for her and me when we discussed the need for her to put it all on a different footing. Nor need you understand that much about other people's affairs, but if you make them your own by way of giving informations and advice and warnings you ought to understand a little better before you do it in such a hard and aggressive way. I made my position quite clear from the beginning and I have lost very much more than you seem to see.

My real fault with it all was something very different from the 'lightness and almost irresponsibility' you charge me with. The bars to all self expression that I have allowed myself to be handicapped by these last few years made me overload my bonds to those I really cared for and harm them and my own work by over worry. You do not know by experience what years of absence from those you love means. In a curiously objective way you have been witness of the way in which things have gone since I parted with M. And it is painful that someone whose respect and sympathy one would value most should be so much more aware of all that least deserves it. . . .

Regarding my own self, Shiela, after a long walk today I think I understand your reaction a little better. It was very shocking at first—because after the usual tone between us it seemed as distant as the distemper of someone one has bumped into in a crowd and who displays a sudden unexpected anger. If some of the things you say or imply were really true I would be a little ashamed of your not despairing of our friendship once and for all. You say them with very little knowledge of the facts of my existence, and with an extraordinary readiness to imagine the worst. You know, Shiela, that kind of reaction to a person's spontaneous if clumsy expression of the wish to be near the person he loves must have turned many a man into a scoundrel. It has perhaps happend often to you and will in the future.—Remember that almost the worst thing you can do to him is to suggest that this wish of his is unclean or despicable. Or course I should never have written such a letter to you—I don't remember its words now though I am sure they were bad—but you will not have to repeat the lesson of your last to me. And of course I know that when you wrote you were somehow particularly agitated about Diana and that with you that takes the form of forgetting entirely about the other side. Your position towards me was conclusive and clear, there was no need to give moral reasons for rejecting what you had considered less and in conflict with what you already had.

Not very long ago I wrote you a long letter about what justified me in thinking that you might have been the permanent comrade of my life, but I tore it because I feared it might seem naive and pretentious to you. And anyhow it all seems horribly out of place now. You see it was a very clear and definite potentiality for me and since it came to nothing I find it very difficult to find the level on which to go on. I told you that before. Rather than finding you suspecting and criticising me unfairly now, I think we should believe that there was at one time this beautiful (for me beautiful) and strong potentiality and that we then found our ways parting—in the hope perhaps of later on in life when we met again to find that we could be true friends. How can we now when you neither love nor even trust me?

You seem to have an absurdly mistaken view of my relations to other people. The day before I had your letter I said to Siebert what a pity it was to see so many people, so few of which one could like really—the Hamburg burghers are very kindly and after the deserts of Kassel and Berlin often enjoyable and interesting people to meet (in case I should settle here as a lawyer it is even necessary to know a great number of them)—you say he would frown at my social life, he thinks it quite right, and when I said to him that doing too much of it at present was really your fault—he said (without any kind of previous explanation) he knew me well enough to have known that long ago. You see, he is a comrade and not so severe. It is only very rarely now that the sun shines over the Alster—this morning it did and I thought I too could write you a letter to blow away all clumsy clouds.

But I don't seem to have succeeded in doing so. What I really wanted to say, is that at present it would probably be better for both of us not to go on trying, but leaving each other to what work we can do by ourselves and not spoil those things which we shared and hope again to share in a generous and unbewildered way. . . .

May I still believe that there is some truth in those last sentences of (all) your letters to me? How can you in your senses think that I want to reduce it to 'casualness and impermanence' as you suggest?

Love as always

A.

Dec. 3rd [1935]

Dear Adam,

I am sorry you took my letter as you did and think you need not have done so.

About your relations in the past to Diana, and hers to you, I will try not to think any more. All I wanted to say to you was that, now she has the chance of a new sort of life in which you have a smaller part. I wanted to say you must be quite quite sure what you are doing and to make the necessary sacrifice, if you are certain she must live her life without you. If you were not certain I wanted you also to tell her before it was too late and her new efforts were stopped. Why do you not leave Europe and make a new life somewhere with her? You see, now you must do one or the other. Perhaps it is unnecessary to say these things to you, but if you said to Diana the things which you have said to me, if once more you telephoned on Christmas Eve, or if one day you gave her to believe it might have been possible to share your life with you [*should be: her*] if she had not turned away now, you are going to hurt her terribly. All you say about loving her only makes me want to say these things more, just because I know it is hard for you to go without such a faithful and warm friend, and because you must be sure what you are doing, in case it is not necessary to do so. I'm sorry saying these things to you makes you so angry. When I said you were light and irresponsible in your relationships, I did not mean that you do not worry about them and get involved and overloaded with them too; I think those are two sides of the same weakness, and it is [a] weakness most dangerous and hurting to other people. I'm sorry that it hurts you for me to say it to you. It is not because I have no sympathy or respect for you, but rather because of being friends with you and Diana. It is terrible watching you hurt each other. Diana I am very fond of, more so than I have ever been. Perhaps that makes me hard and aggressive, but I do not mean to be, or forget entirely about your side, only she does need support more than you do. I think you need the opposite more. It is your friends' 'unquestioning loyalty' that makes it so hard for you. You should be glad of all my questions! . . .

Finally about me. I'm very sorry if I made you think I thought your wish to be with me unclean and despicable. You know perfectly well I do not, and have never done so. If I rejected it rather more violently than ever before, it was partly because you promised to try and be friends, and your letters make me suspect very much you don't want to be, and perhaps even more because of the things which you said in your letter. You seem to have forgotten what you said, and in your last letter write about having tried to write to me what reasons justified my being the 'permanent comrade of your life.' In the letter which I answered so angrily, you had quite rejected the possibility of my being a 'permanent comrade' and regretted having introduced the 'heavy binding terms of love and marriage.' I think I could not help believing then that what you wanted was something casual and impermanent, and to this, I preferred friendship. It was perhaps silly to introduce moral reasons for preferring it or criticise your relations to other people which have nothing to do with it. The relationship I was thinking of was yours with Ingrid[1] which made the mistake possible about which you told me. I had no right to criticise it. And the 'morals' just happen to be the sort of way of thinking which is natural to me and apparently not to anybody else much and not to you. I do not think being lovers is unclean or despicable. I just do not think it makes people happy or is the best relationship there is. Also I do not think it is the best relationship two people can have unless they love each other exclusively and forever.

Now if you prefer it, we will not go on trying and leave each other to do what work we can do by ourselves, and hope one day we will meet again and not be separated by too wide gulfs of experience, inclination, and feeling. I wanted and still want to be friends with you during this critical part of your life; if you think you can get on better without, then I will leave you, but if ever you are in any trouble or want something I could give you, you have only to ask. Meanwhile God bless you and take care of yourself.

Love always,

S.

[*Postscript omitted*]

---

[1] Ingrid Warburg (now Contessa Spinelli) of the Hamburg bankers' family whom Adam befriended while in Hamburg. She emigrated in 1936 to the United States. Adam saw a great deal of her on his American trip in the winter of 1939.

Hamburg.
18.12.35.

Dear Shiela,

... I am bound ... this time to write you a serious letter—and I shall state as simply as possible what more than once I have turned over in my mind and wished to say to you:

Early in January (perhaps on the 15th or so) I am going off to my camp[1] and after that to a more rigid period of court work in Kassel and then the examinations in Berlin before which there will hardly be a possibility of a break. After that time if no momentous change takes place I shall most likely leave Europe for a longish time.

The months immediately ahead of us will be extremely important both for the decisions which we take or do not take. For me they will be difficult. The attitude I have taken up since my return will be put to a test, the risks and dangers of which I do not fear. But I see a real difficulty in pushing through it all without having one's spirits and one's hopes undone especially since those for whose sake I would consider it most worth while to undergo it in a certain manner, show more shakiness in their belief in me than I have ever experienced in my life. I know that some of your remarks were made in a playful spirit and do not refer to this. But there is a fundamental unclarity in our relationship which most aggravates this difficulty under which I am labouring, besides making me intensely unhappy.

I don't know whether you would consider me sufficiently 'in trouble' to justify my reminding you of saying that whenever this was the case I could ask things of you.[2] And indeed I don't want to put any pressure on you which might further endanger our friendship. But may I on the ground of what I said before ask whether it would be impossible for you to make an effort to meet me in the short space in which we are still free to do so? I must be at my home on Dec 29th— the 80th birthday of my father, on Jan 2–4 I must be in Berlin to help selecting Rhodes Scholars. Would it be possible to meet then?

I know I have made things very difficult for you (and I shall respect this reason for your not coming) regarding the pains of third people,[3] but I think there is this to consider: we have always considered our friendship as bound up with the most important turns we have taken since. I think we are in danger not to treat it as seriously when we make its effect on emotional sides of our lives prohibitive to a clear solidarity when this is called for by the situation. I hope you are not again suspecting me of using big and vague words when I mean a lesser thing. I do want your trust and whole-hearted support in the coming time more, very much more than any kind of emotional comfort or the like. And I don't—judging from your letters—get it from you; you have been partly right in withholding your approval of certain things . . . in others I may be right in thinking that you treated me lightly. All this would fade to unimportance if we could see eye to eye once more about what confronts and endangers our real lives now.

Darling Shiela, does all this seem ponderous and unreal to you? You may see the present situation quite differently and may think it quite unnecessary for me to ask you to come. I shall try to understand that; but I may have to withdraw a bit and let you think badly of me without trying to contradict or persuade you But, Shiela, darling, I would cherish any attack face to face with you and nothing would seem more worth while to me now than to see that you really cared in these attacks.

Give me a short air-mail message soon—

true love
Adam.

---

[1] At the end of Dec. Adam was scheduled to attend for about two months a camp for young lawyers (*Referendarlager*) in Jüterbog, approximately fifty miles south of Berlin, for the purpose of paramilitary training and political indoctrination.

[2] Letter to Shiela–Adam, 3 Dec 1935.

[3] Shiela did consult Goronwy and did not go; see Grant Duff, *The Parting of Ways*. p. 109.

Wales.
29th Dec. 1935.

Dear Adam,

I'm afraid I cannot come to Berlin alone. I am very sorry because I would have liked to see you and have done what was possible to end the confusion of the last few months.

I'm sorry if I have given you the impression that I do not trust you, and so have made the next months seem more difficult for you. I understand very well how you must be feeling now, and how tentatively you look on the future. I am sure you will be all right and in every decision will choose what is best and right, in so far as you are able. I am sorry you are such a long way away. . . It is very nice of you to ask me to come with Goronwy. He thanks you and sends his love. So do I always.

S.

Chelsea.
[*about* 31 December 1935]

Dear Adam,

I am very sorry that I am not now seeing you and that it may perhaps be a long time again before it will be possible. I hope you do not
think I was very wrong to refuse or that I do not mind the false
intrusions and violations of our mutual respect which you say exists.
I do mind them very much and perhaps for that reason doubt that
one visit to Germany under these circumstances is going to remove
all the difficulties. You know and can imagine why I do not like coming to Germany for other reasons as well as for the ones I gave
before. I wish that you could have come here. Would it not be possible? After all, it was here first that we were friends and you are less
of a stranger here and less uprooted than I am in Germany. I cannot
quite account for the very strong antipathy I have for any journey
now. It applies even to small ones here. I would have tried to overcome it but your first letter from Imshausen gave the impression that
going home had made it seem rather ridiculous and accentuated the
differences between us rather than the ties. But I'm sorry if I again
misunderstood you. I'm afraid I do that very often. I am very sorry.
Ever since I came to Hamburg, I have felt you have led me into a
world in which I have no bearings. Please forgive me if my mistakes
hurt you. I hate to do so, but you after all know that one attacks to
defend oneself. And any uncertainty increases both our aggressiveness.

. . . There is on my side also a desire to protect our relationship
from the trivial and conventional but I don't honestly see how that is
to be done without seeing each other often and perhaps even casually
in some place where neither we nor the society around us would be
undergoing any violent upheaval. I do wish we could be in Oxford
again and go for walks and talk about other things but ourselves. I
know one can talk all day long about a relationship and in the evening the thing simply not exist any more because it has nothing to live
on except itself. That's what is wrong with us. Because we talked of
nothing else in Hamburg, because we write of nothing else now. We
must stop it. Perhaps if we had met once again, it would have been
easier to stop. If you think so, do please come here even if it is only
for two days one week-end. If you don't think so we will have to try
and go on without meeting and hope one day we will meet naturally
and often. . . .

Love,
S.

Chelsea.
9.1.36

Darling Adam,
It was rather sad to get your letter tonight when it might have been
so short a time before seeing you—still, it is a stormy night and you
would be tossing terribly on the North Sea. It would have been lovely
to see you again—you see, it is still so true, that I forget what you are
like when you are away and it is as if there were two of you—one to
be with and laugh with and walk with and be happy with—and the
other to quarrel with over interminable blue and white pages—
The thought of being with you has made me see so clearly how
nice you are and how much I like you and long to see you. It would
have been lovely in the New Forest or by the sea—but it will, and
must be lovely again, somewhere and sometime. . . .
Write to me often, always much love, what is Siebert doing?

S.

In the train to Berlin.
10.1.36.

Darling S—
I lost my race by about half an hour, having booked passage and
everything. The man in the camp I telephoned to was very nice, but
he said he really hadn't the authority, and the one who has mightn't
have been so nice. So I decided to go. You will forgive the disturb-
ance I caused. For others than ourselves it may even be better I did
not succeed. Yesterday I went out into the country and stayed there
the night as a transition. The fields were a little bit like England—
hedges and little streams, beech woods sloping to a lake which winds
through woods and large gardens. There is a narrow strip of land and
a timber bridge leading across where I walked last night and saw the
swan glide across smoothly and grand. They are beautiful, aren't
they?
I decided I must look forward to this camp, and almost do now. I
will be out of doors a lot, and I'll like a number of them and learn a
lot. After all, I chose the premises and I must choose the consequences of my present experiment.
In the train I just caught when it was already moving I met a very
nice vegetable dealer who told me all about his life and difficulties
and I told him some of my nicer ones, and we laughed a good deal
together, and next door there is a man with a Zieharmonika[1] playing

'Annemarie... '—do you know the song? It was very popular and reminds me of last summer. Now he plays a tango, but it sounds very rural and sentimental—would you like that? I wonder, but I am sure you would like my green-grocer who just told me that he hadn't yet had the time to have children. He is a Berliner and rather fat and says he has a clever wife. I wish I had too—now I must always be wise entirely by myself and in the end be so wise that I shan't marry at all. That really is it for me—isn't it, Shiela? It would only increase the general misery of the world to have lots of little Trotts of my procreation stalk the world.

I said good-bye to hardly anyone in Hamburg and I think some of the 'patricians' will be shocked.—Now he plays a *very* sentimental song called: Regentropfren, die an dein Fenster klopfen—sie sind ein Gruss von mir etc.[2] The green grocer has just discovered I am writing in a foreign language and asks me with a twinkle in his eye whether I am writing everything I think. No, I answered, perfectly candidly.

The man next door now plays Bavarian dances and a little song: 'Jetzt ging i ans Brunnele, trink aber net . . . '[3] you better look up the rest for yourself (You shan't because you don't understand the dialect).

I must start another page for otherwise he will read all the German words I have written on the first page, and will wonder what curious kind of person I am writing to. He now wants to start talking on catholicism eating a terrific ham sandwich, but I don't want to much.

When you will write to me, Shiela, will you do it via Imshausen, because your hand-writing is so obviously that of a nice girl that they will get rather suspicious of the business journey I absolutely had to undertake before going there.

There will be 150 others (all young lawyers and dentists, I believe) who will come up with me and some of them will look at least as funny as I will in uniform. . . . [4]

Sad, we will never meet 'habitually and sometimes casually', it will always be in societies that undergo upheavals of one sort or another, always in a thick circle of friends or another; always by letter—where we usually do *not* meet but wander astray. How difficult 'international relations' really are, you must have thought rather often lately! They are such a mixture of drama and absurdity . . . but perhaps also full of the child-diseases which precede a vigorous maturity!?

Don't bother about worlds you have no bearings in—it would not be like you and I would not like you to be unlike yourself.

Perhaps, if that pleases you better, you should try and think of me as that 'other extreme' which is sometimes quite useful to balance one's own identity. In fact, I am almost certain I can be useful to you some time later on, whatever happens in the meantime. And I want to be and I want you to be useful to me perhaps. This is a good unsentimental and unmysterious way of putting things to you and perhaps by the time we really should see each other again, the world has changed such a lot that it will be positively romantic to be utilitarian.

It is very difficult to write sense with a melancholic green grocer in front of you—it makes you stop pausing sufficiently between sentences! Tell me how your work goes and what you think of Signor M's future—

I promise to write you a nice postcard in return. . . .

Love till the spring.

A.

1 Accordion.
2 The drops of rain that hit your window pane . . . bring greetings from me, etc.
3 I went to the well, but did not drink.
4 See letter Adam–Shiela, Hamburg, 18 Dec. 1935, n. 1.

Kent.
[*about* 10 Jan. 1936.]

Darling Adam,

Enclosed, I wrote on Monday, found it too silly to send, and now too silly to keep. In future, I've decided, I'm going to write nothing but facts. I'm sure we will then get on very well, and foreign relations will expand into new and undiscovered fields. How are you in your camp, nice, exciting, amusing, stern, or inspiring? It must indeed be a wonderful place. I imagine it on a very high spiritual and a very low physical plane—snow and no fires and hard beds too small for you—with daily hymns to the new freedom and grandeur of the Third Reich. It must be very inspiring. Mediaeval saints know that you only had to be sufficiently uncomfortable to see God—it is only our decadent soft age that has abolished God and discomfort together.

I am staying in a 15th Century house with Peggy. It is very draughty so we sit up the chimney and become very black and hot. Peggy is reading Buddenbrooks and I the autobiography of Nehru.[1] It is very moving. He writes English a little as you do—or rather as you talk it (which is better than how you write it)—He is a very, very good man, and, I think, very spiritual and sensitive. He is, as you may already know—one of the leaders of the Indian Independence Movement, a prominent Congress Leader, and something of a socialist. He is the son of another Pandit Nehru, also a political leader, and formerly a rich and successful lawyer. He was brought up quite a lot by Anglo-Irish tutors, and at the age of 13 was baptised a theosophist by Mrs. Annie Besant. Two years later he was sent to school at Harrow and later at Cambridge. That is as far as I got—but the particular interest he should have for you, apart from his importance in Imperial and Eastern politics—is that Diana and I are acting as his private secretaries when he visits this country next week. Diana because of E.W.[2] who introduced her to the Indian League, I because of Diana, who took me there.

So far, I lord it about the office in the Indian League and say who is and who is not important for the Pandit to meet. I type letters and make telephone calls, and feel very grand and smart. . . . I do think Indians very beautiful, both in face and character. . . .

I am going to a conference tomorrow in which the Labour Party are going to expound how to win an election. Most of the speakers lost their seats. I wonder if the conservative party talks so much or thinks so much. . . .

Much love

S.

[1] Jawaharlal Nehru (1889–1964), follower of Mahatma Gandhi and, with him, one of the leaders of the Indian Independence Movement; President of the Indian National Congress 1924, 1936, 1937, and 1946; Prime Minister and Minister of External Affairs of India 1947–64.

[2] Ellen Wilkinson, Labour politician; one of the few women MPs at that time.

[*early* 1936]

Darling Adam,

Thank you very much for a lovely letter, which makes me like you very much. You write wonderful letters on your type writer in trains, I can barely use mine even under normal conditions. Now I am using it in bed, having just come back from a very nice party of Diana's. I wish you could have been there. . . .

. . . The world seems to me peculiarly wonderful and full of hope to-night. I think I am starting a new life which is going to be wonderful. I feel very good as if I was started all over again at the beginning and all the good out of the past is coming back in the future, all the people I love, all the things I've believed in, the ambitions I've had, all the dogs and cats and the country and horses.

I've been in the country the last two days and it has been like summer and I've felt my heart would break because I have been so happy sometimes—I think the first year after leaving Oxford even the last one there is terrible and full of wicked things, then suddenly one remembers how beautiful and innocent it was and all the bad fall away and it's good again. O I'm talking nonsense. . . .

Now I will try and talk about more matter of fact things. Today I have spent working for the India League and learning to cook. . . .

In the India League, I occupy a very important position because my family were great imperialists and they like to see the youngest generation repent. I think I am going to study imperialism seriously. It is obviously the issue before the labour party and Dalton knows nothing about it and European politics, after all are pretty parochial. Poor Eastern Europe, which last week I was going to adopt, will now have to get on without me and the great Indian masses have become my special care. . . .

Did you ever study English Imperialism or any imperialism for that matter? I read a very good book about India by Robert Byron[1] and have been given a sort of 'Red Paper' called the condition of India. It is obviously a very difficult problem for there are only two possible alternative rulers of India except ourselves (1) the Princes who are rather demoralised and represent the very worst of India and western capitalism and cynicism and (2) the intellectuals and natio-nalists who have adopted this worst of all western inventions—nationalism—which goes horridly with the culture and philosophy of the East. That they have is our fault again for our intolerable behav-iour to them and all this horrible race pride and conceit. Our rule in India, based on race pride and exploitation is carried out by oppression and bullying. It is the horrible truth which only about 1,000 people realise. I heard an Indian say today 'Of the 44,000,000 people in England how many would stand by India' and of course the answer is that 43,999,000 don't know anything about India and that's why it goes on. But how can it be altered and what should be done?

Wasn't it lovely in Oxford? Soon the crocuses will be out and then the cherry blossom and the flowers in Magdalen Garden. O I think it's so beautiful and such a wonderful place and so wonderful to be friends there. I wish we had seen each other more often. I would gladly live all those years again and only ask to do everything I did a little more intensely, not differently. . . .

[Shiela]

[1] Robert Byron, *An Essay on India* (London, 1931).

28.1.36.

Dear Adam,

Thank you for your letter[1] and the two photographs. You look like a condemned convict in both, and the bed looks wonderfully uncomfortable. Have you really no sheets or pillowcases? or do you just have nice striped ones?

You sound very hostile and pleased with your distance from us all! It will certainly be very nice for us when you visit us and our respective husbands and we smile at our troubles of earlier days— 'Two old crows laughed aloud.' The horrible thing about the world is this capacity one learns, to smile at things that once genuinely moved one—at what isn't genuine one can smile now. . . .

At the moment we[2] are working for Jawaharlal Nehru, who is one of the most wonderful men I have ever met—so gentle, patient, and unfaltering. You know he is president of the Indian National Congress. It is such men who would rule India—instead we sent out soldiers and ignorant generals, and wicked old vice-roys, and Beaverbrook young men.

I watched the King's funeral today.[3] Line after line of generals; not even their gay plumes or bright uniforms hid the woodenness of their faces. . . It is not unintentionally that the fighting services are made so grand and associated with all the colour and pageantry that people have in their drab lives. I begin to doubt more and more that this system can be made any better—its very foundations are wrong, all the good in it is perverted to the most worthless ends. People stand all night to see the King's coffin pass by—such is the purpose of privation.

It's silly to be so bitter about the King's funeral which was impressive and gave pleasure to an enormous number of people—but such processions show how firmly the whole thing is entrenched and I begin to wonder if the British are not too corrupt for liberty—or if all Europe isn't. I trust the French a great deal. Have you read Curtius'[4] book yet? It is wonderful.

The Indians are very impressive. When the Prince of Wales went to India, no vulgar curiosity made them go to see what their leaders had boycotted—I suppose it is different since there it is a foreign dominion and here it is thought to be our own army and navy. England is no longer the nation of pacifists that it was when you were here ...

I hope you find what you want in a non-European world—but I expect it's the same the world over, and the only alternatives are a religion which one shares with the people round one, or a world which one makes for oneself alone.

Love,

S.

¹ It must have been a letter, now lost, from camp in Jüterbog.
² Diana and Shiela.
³ Death of King George V, 20 Jan. 1936.
⁴ Ernst Robert Curtius, *The Civilization of France* (New York, 1932).

Jüterbog,

9.2.36.

Darling S.,

. . . Yesterday we had our first day out after four weeks. It was pleasant to walk freely on a pavement, to smoke and drink leisurely. You begin to enjoy the simple things again—which a Sunday at school contained with such luxurious intensity. We drank a very great deal with two young plumbers who seemed to me more intelligent and fresh in their outlook that most people here. The one, called Paul, was very grand explaining to me with extreme subtlety that you must never talk politics in a pub nowadays—he called me 'my little boy' in the end, and to my grief stood me drink after drink (i.e. in turn) which I could not have refused without hurting him deeply. I also had to smoke his tobacco. He earns a guinea a week. His friend Emil was a sarcastic wit who explained the relation of feeling and intellect—he said 'You will have to hurry if you still want to win our hearts.' Personally I seemed to have won them all right, and they mine. I shall meet them again. It is a good thing to find unsentimental friendliness and to witness the world from which I am cut off in the nutshell of one such free evening.

Later on I seemed to have won the admiration of an overcrowded café for dancing well in big boots. I danced many waltzes and tangos. One of my friends found the ground too slippery to remain on his feet and offered to box the ears of one of our superiors who was there in civilian clothes. We had a very gay time . . . I am very happy at the moment—perhaps because of yesterday which has made me feel strongly how necessary people like myself will be in this country— this I realize with no arrogance, but with a glad certainty (I have doubted it painfully and often enough and will do so again to be sure—if only I can keep heart now). Perhaps it is really better to be trusted than to be loved . . . silly sentence. Sometimes, though, I see the barrenness and clearness of winter with a pleasure I didn't know some time ago. And true, the world is very very beautiful. So are you. You trust my sobriety though I've spent all my money in drinks and even had to borrow. I think I shall have to wear spectacles; it doesn't look very nice, but since all my hair is going out it doesn't matter very much. My only comfort about Siebert is that, at present I can imagine it quite a happy thing to be behind gates etc.—Go to the country on Sundays at least, Shiela—send me something nice (perhaps a little pink toothpowder, or a little hair tonic to defeat the queer scent of my queer hat). I am sorry I have nothing more for you at present than such letters and love.

A.

Chelsea.
9.2.36.

Darling Adam,

Thank you very much for your nice letter. . . .

I was in Oxford yesterday. The snowdrops are growing up in Magdalen Garden, soon crocuses, then the summer again—won't it be lovely—if it is possible to look forward to anything with any sincerity. Here people are growing every day more pessimistic. The old vicious circle of strength and security starting again. £3 million on armaments, because somebody else started it and we have to follow or sink God knows if it's not better to sink. I wish I could think clearly about all this—Do you remember how one first started to think about the last war—learned to mock at the world being made safe for democracy, and the rest? Then one began to think again there was something worth fighting against, if not for—and then one sees what one thinks one is fighting is also inside one's own country, one's own heart almost. Can one *fight* for anything good? Isn't fighting itself so hideous that nothing good can come of it? This view has been 'cleaned up' more or less in your country, but it will be remembered everywhere sooner or later. The Indian Nationalists thought that passive resistance and civil disobedience were an unanswerable method of defence against oppression—either from a government or an invader. Well then—but then I remember Mowrer saying in Paris that willingness to fight was the only thing that would keep the peace. I don't know—I hate the whole thing—as much what we would be asked to fight for here, as what you, or the Italians, or the Japanese would be fighting for anywhere else.

I have been very profoundly moved by meeting Nehru. The issue seems to be quite clear—on the one hand, a high standard of living in this country together with a very low standard and exploitation in India, continuing perhaps for another ten or twenty years—or perhaps less in the event of war—then bloodshed. On the other, a recognition of the right of Indian independence, close co-operation with Congress Socialists, simultaneous Socialism in this country and in India, a very much lower standard of living for the upper middle classes here till India had developed as a powerful trading country. Of course the issue is a little absurd—socialism is very very far from this country—far enough from the Labour party, and without Socialism here and in India, we have both very very much to lose—of course, especially us.

However—Nehru is the most wonderful man I have ever met, very gentle, very noble, and very brave. It is really terrible and humiliating that much men are imprisoned in India, perhaps even worse that they are humiliated by our prejudices of race and conquest. Something must be done—I think something is very wrong when women have to take part in politics, but today one cannot stand outside. It is impossible any more to lead a real private life—one has no private life—everything one cares for or believes in is open to be hurt or broken by what happens in the world.

You said if women wanted to take part in politics, they should marry politicians—but somehow marriage itself seems unimportant and meaningless when the world is like this—and it is impossible and wicked not to try and do something directly oneself. I suppose I must be very careful not to continue emotional and over-wrought. Dalton does plenty of convincing me that it is not genius but Socialism which is an infinite capacity for taking pains—so we get hot water for school children and free journeys for applicants for employment—very slowly wealth is redistributed—and what the hell's the point? It is standards of value, not standards of living that are all wrong. Do you know that in the east, men are judged, not by their worldly success, but by the saintliness of their character? The Chinese Exhibition[1] is very soothing. It would be very nice to wake up there in the morning. I will send you some pictures. You will be very happy in the East—but I doubt there is much detachment left in a Japanese-invaded China. Why do you not go to India? You could help the Congress Party, and when India was independent, be a foreign expert, advising them in the law. You would also have the great pleasure of my visiting you next October.

Love, darling Adam,

S.

---

[1] An exhibition in the Royal Academy of Art; Shiela visited it with Nehru.

Feb. 10th 1936.

Darling Adam,

Thank you very much for your letter—you write me such nice ones from Jüterbog. I feel quite reconciled to the seclusion and hardship of your life which makes you think so kindly of me! Your letters are lovely to have and far from annoying or boring me—forgive me the silence of the last two weeks, I was acting, more or less, as Nehru's bodyguard the whole long day.

Last night I visited my god-mother and she told me, had I been a boy, I would have been called Adam. My father is supposed to have thought that was the reason why, contrary to hope, I was a girl! It gave me great pleasure to think of this new bond between us. You are very nice to regret that you have nothing more for me at present than letters and love—you had given me to understand that, as soon as it were possible you would scare me off by not giving me that. So when you go to the East, I will now hope for great spiritual comfort from you while I decay in the West.

Seriously I am very excited by the East. All I read about it, especially what I read of China, gives me a tremendous feeling of moral excitement. Confucianism is the most sympathetic of all religions—or moral teachings—and there seems to me even greater depth and beauty in it than in Christianity, and at no point any conflict between them. I have been reading some lectures by Mr. Cheng,[1] and between what he says and what is said by the English introductions, seems to me to lie all the contrast between East and West: our own terrible spiritual barrenness which makes us ashamed and self-conscious before words and ideas of goodness and righteousness, and their very natural and simple attitude to virtue. I like very much too the 'four secrets of the government of an empire' which were laid down by Se Tzu[2] in the 4th Century B.C. '1) to be faithful to duty and affectionate to the people, 2) to be just and unselfish, 3) to employ only men of merit in the state, 4) to practise economy.'

I think we have a very great deal to learn from the East and I hate very much our attempt to Westernise China and India, and our disregard of how wonderful it would be to Easternise our ways of thinking—how sententious that sounds, but you will understand. I would like to have two whole lives, one to spend all in learning, learning about myself, the world, about virtue and knowledge, and the other, to try and give all this to the world, so it would be a better place. I'm afraid it would take a life-time to grow good, and yet, like you, I feel how necessary it is I should do something . . .

Winter is very beautiful, especially when the weather is hard and

clear. Light is so much more important than warmth—and yet sometimes vague glimpses and memories one has of summer make me terribly sad, as of memories of a country a long way away.

I have a very curious conviction these days that I will die young,
and happily it goes with quite a new understanding of death. There
was time when I would wake up terrified of death—now often I see
death as something very beautiful and desirable. I always thought
one would have to be very unhappy to think that, and yet I am far
from unhappy, tho' perhaps I see the ugliness of the world more
vividly contrasted with its beauty than ever before. . . .

Much love,
Shiela.

<hr>

¹ Mr Cheng could not be identified.
² This is most likely a reference to Hsün-tzu, *fl.* 298–238 BC, considered one of
the two great followers of Confucius.

Chelsea.
29th Feb. 1936.

Darling Adam,
    . . . There's a horrible film on now, written by H. G. Wells, called
'Things to Come.' It begins with war in 1940. The scenes are horrible
and very much what it will be like—would be like, let's still say. By
1960 everybody's reduced to absolute barbarism, and there's a horrible plague called the Wandering Sickness, and people live in caves
and—by 2040, the world's reconstructed on the most up-to-date
technical lines—very horrible it is too—the war part is ghastly. What
is so awful is not knowing one's part in it all. For the present one lives
one's life on the assumption there will be no war.—I wish to God the
Labour Party was in and perhaps there wouldn't be. It can still be
prevented—I wish I knew how. Darling Adam—it seems perhaps
both hysterical and sentimental to say this now—but please don't
let's forget everything. I don't think much of these things now—of
course they come up in my work for Dalton quite a lot. It is very
interesting—but my real work now is to do with India. I will tell you
about it in the morning—even tho' you're not very interested—nor
were two months ago—but now I must go to sleep—

Love,
S.

[*Footnote omitted*]

Tuesday[, 10 March 1936]

Darling Adam,

Your postcard makes me very ashamed and unhappy. It is not that I do not write to you, but that I write and tear up, because of the inadequacy of everything I say . . . I am in rather a turmoil and find it difficult to express myself clearly and simply as one must to friends, and as I particularly want to do to you. It is personal and political—chiefly the latter I think tho' I do not know where politics and personalities divide.

This latest news is ghastly.[1] I have just come from a debate in the House of Commons. The govt. seems to regard war as inevitable—now the object is to win it. It was heart-rending to hear the govt. jeers when Morrison[2] and Cripps said there was only one way out—only one hope for peace—a just and equitable world system based on the sharing of wealth and not the competition system. Of course it's not realism—realism now is just to do with guns—I hate politics—I thought I was a utilitarian, and thought it was to do with walks in the parks, with pleasure and happiness. Politics is utilitarianism—constant and unscrupulous subordination of ends to means—the giving up of every ideal, of every hope because it is not realism—because people 'aren't like that'. For whom also is one responsible beyond oneself? How can it be noble or better to subordinate one's own integrity, one's own horror at war or violence and oppression—to some 'national' or general good. One is torn in bits by the world. Isn't it enough for good and evil to fight each other, without good and good being in conflict. Darling Adam—forgive this—the govt. makes speeches telling one to be calm!

I don't know whether my new work with the India League is just escapism, or whether I am really convinced that the struggle against imperialism is a far greater and better cause than any other which one can adopt. The choice in other affairs on the issue of peace is whether one will support one's country against another—in which I can see no good if one believes neither in the goodness of the one nor the evil of the other—both as a personal and a political problem.

I do this work for the India League—the material conditions are dreary. I work in a very dirty and disorganised office—my fellow workers are very irresponsible and lighthanded students from LSE.[3] The head of it all is an Indian,[4] who is rather impressive, but is terribly ill—physically and psychologically—half my time and all my energies are taken up in supporting him in two spheres–either giving him salvolatiles and trying to make him eat, or urging against suicide and persecution mania—the rest of my time I try to learn about India, raise the worst questions of administrative oppression there in the House of Commons, try and organise meetings, write pamphlets, and reduce chaos to order. . . .

I think at no time can the world have lived so much on its nerves. I wish there were a moral justification for forsaking the damned thing altogether.[5]

Forgive me, darling Adam, for not writing before—and for writing so emotionally now. The House of Commons has horrible effects on me.

Love Always,

S.

[1] On 8 Mar. 1936 Hitler's army marched into the demilitarized Rhineland in violation of the Treaty of Versailles and the Locarno agreements of 1925.

[2] Herbert Stanley Morrison (1888–1965), from 1959 1st Baron Morrison of Lambeth; a leader of the Labour Party; MP intermittently since 1923; Home Secretary and Minister of Home Security in Winston Churchill's War Cabinet; Deputy Prime Minister 1945–51, Secretary of State for Foreign Affairs 1951.

[3] London School of Economics.

[4] Krishna Menon.

[5] The remilitarization of the Rhineland caused Shiela to rethink all her political ideas and objectives.

as from Kassel.

16.3.36.

Dear Shiela,

My trouble is rather that I cannot take very seriously that soulless monster 'Europe' which is agitating you so much. I can and want only to work for the new order of labour which I know will come about whatever our bad fate will be in the near future. I also know that my country has a very essential, if not the most vital contribution to make in that order, whatever its facade is now. To share in this contribution has been the object which I have never quite lost hold of all these years and though it may look like fatalism it makes me certain and tranquil in view of the dangers which shatter people's nerves so much—that certainly makes them no more effective when it comes to really vindicate the position for which they claimed to stand all the time. I think that Cripps is more realistic than he knows himself. In the meantime one must hope the other side will consider the bloody thing too costly for all and themselves. . . .

. . . I am getting ready to go to the East—

Love always

Adam.

This is no contradiction to what I said first: I'll come back a mandarin of the new order—which has already proved itself highly practicable in Mongolia.

Göttingen.
28.3.36.

Darling Shiela,

I've been wanting to ask you to tell me why I make it difficult to write and why you tore up letters. Please tell me—your saying some time ago that I was no cause of confusion or burden made me very glad. But I must obviously behave differently if that is no longer the case. It was very reassuring to remember the confident and happy day on the Baltic Sea, couldn't it at least remain like that?

I would have remained confident and asked no questions, nor ask you to help me in understanding if I had not had a letter of violent accusation from Miriam on your behalf. It makes me think I've carried poison into the very hearts of those I care for, and am the cause for difficulties in their lives, for evil and bitterness.—It mustn't be the case with you, darling Shiela. I gladly accepted the idea that not writing etc was due to your being preoccupied and busy with your own life. I hate to think that something false in me disturbs you and prevents you from being frank. I do not take M's accusations verbally, the facts of my existence have grown too distant for her judgment to be fair. In her view, clearly, I ought to have nothing more to do with either D. or you. (Jane seems somehow to have encouraged her in this.) She argues I am veiling a simple human situation by considerations and wishes that are no longer responsibly connected with it. To crave or give helpful friendship when love fails to be mutual bears, to her, the nature of confusion of motives, a kind of uncleanness. It means—I am not repeating her words but trying to translate them into my own—deflecting people's capacity for the best happiness which they otherwise find for themselves in a fully returned complete love—Perhaps I have thought about this too much to come to a right conclusion, but I simply cannot accept that a) love for a person, even if the return is not in kind, is a wrong or detrimental thing for either, rather than a precious value, and b) that a man and woman, after all, cannot be simple, solidaric comrades who share things whenever their battles coincide, even without fulfilling the dreams of their hearts. (Miriam often argued both points in the same way to me.) If there's the proper emphasis on the latter, there's no danger of dependence or defeat—in fact very much more hope for what happens to D. now, who tells me that she is stronger and happier in every way, and clearly not on the basis of hoping that anything essential will change between her and me in the future. I think it right to have continued giving her the sense of valuing—as of course I do even if I would pretend indifference to it—her comradeship and practical solidarity in the wider developments with which all our lives are bound up. (She writes that your companionship is very dear to her, and though I never enquired—I am sorry, I did hint something about your not writing, in my last letter to her—she tells me how you were, and how nice you were on this or that occasion—once, she said, she wished I could have seen how you were looking—I think we should all be rather proud of her, don't you agree!)

Darling Shiela, forgive my writing you this letter on personal affairs again—but any gloominess between us truly affects my whole life and work rather badly, so that I want your help and reassurance. I dream silly dreams about walking at your side over-excited by seeing you again and unable to explain myself, and you looking at me in a very disturbed way. It is perhaps very foolish, but sometimes you have rather taken the line that there's something false in my whole bearing. Tell me so and I shall try very hard to trace the fault.

Somehow life is tearing me away from all these wonderings at an increasing rate now. But should one's encounters with the open world mean the loss of confidence and intimacy with one's real friends? You used to emphasise that it mustn't be so—but you refuse to tell me of your encounters! I mean this crisis is particularly unsuited for suspending our ties—Is there still a chance of Goronwy and you coming to Germany? My welcome to both of you, if you care to accept it, will be very joyful and glad in spite of this pressure of legal labour which—I forgot—wouldn't hinder you to enjoy the spring in Wilhelmshöhe or wherever you went. I might suggest some things not useless for his Spectator, and if my (probably increased) habits of being a political hermit don't irritate him, I don't think other things would prevent us being friends. I must leave Göttingen for Kassel and I shall live down the valley and you might stay up in Wilhelmshöhe for a few days if you liked to—Easter I must go to Hamburg to see St,[1] who will await oversea confirmation there (unless immediate set-off proves necessary) and to fetch my car—but I have no holiday. Perhaps you would go for one walk with me alone—to tell me that there are a few things in the world which belong to you and me alone, and which are not foul and doubtful, but vigorous and immune to every blow from outside—

Love
A.

[1] Siebert; see letter Adam–Shiela, Hamburg, about 2 Oct 1935, n. 1.

Kent.
9.4.36.

Darling Adam,
   The last three weeks have been rather strange and queer because Goronwy and I have parted, and a break with him is a break with all my life. I have told none but you, my mother, and Christopher,[1] who is an older brother to me. It does not seem necessary to tell them and would be painful, but I would feel dishonest not to tell you—and yet it is very difficult because I do not understand quite what has happened nor what has gone in my life nor what remains. Only at moments I feel an overwhelming and passionate desire for freedom and for a sort of intensity of living which I have long been without and perhaps never known. The sense of infinite possibility is greater even than the sense of great loss, and now, at least, I have nothing to lose but my chains.
   I can't write you a long letter because if I do I will tear it up as I have torn all the rest. I will write to you again soon. Diana is coming here to-morrow and probably we both go to Cornwall next week—I will spend Wednesday in London, so write to me there if there's time.[2] . . .

Much love,
Shiela.

[1] Sir Christopher Cox, former Educational advisor to the Colonial Office, then Ancient History tutor at New College.
[2] There is no answer to this letter among Shiela's papers.

Cornwall.
18.4.36.

Darling Adam,
   Cornwall is more incredibly beautiful than ever. It is dazzlingly clear and the colours indescribably clear and deep. It is difficult not to believe that all one wants is to live for ever with one's friends in such a place. I wonder if we make it impossible ourselves to share these things or whether it is really some inexorable fate or inexorable ideal that keeps one shut out in smoke-ridden towns with hateful companions. Do you think it is no longer possible to live a private life? Sometimes I think it is, because to live one such as one would like to live, would mean to ignore all the things that threaten one now, and live in a world which one had oneself created out of all the best of the past and present—And any moment it could be destroyed by the single word of about five men in Europe.

It seems to me quite clear that it is impossible to do anything which is not very directly connected with the world at the moment. At the same time it is difficult to believe that anything one does will seriously affect the future. Yet I think of the world as made up of a vast number of conflicting tendencies and of it being vitally import- ant to do all one can to strengthen some and destroy others—and that, one must, and can do— and if one is a woman, not only by mar- rying a politician! Do you remember saying that was what women should do? It would, of course, be lovely to fall in love with someone who wanted to do all the things one wanted to do oneself, and who would do it with one and not instead of one—but it doesn't happen, and instead one slowly sacrifices one's personal relations for some ultimate end where all personal relationships will be better and braver and easier than they are now. Nehru said the most fundamen- tal question was the relationship of people to each other—and in so far as one wants to make the world different, one wants to change the sort of relationships that exist now. The feudal relationship was something real and fine, but the post-feudal ones, of one class to another, of one country to another, and one race to another, are both ugly and degrading. The only possible ones now are those of equals, and these are rare and far between. Liberté, egalité, fraternité are still the only things worth fighting for.

Darling Adam—I am sorry I find it so difficult to write to you about impersonal and distant ideas. You said so many things in your letters I wanted to answer and am afraid I may hurt you by not ans- wering. First I assure you that your presence and existence has never been anything of a burden to me[1]—please please believe that. The months since we parted have been terribly difficult and I do think in a sense we have failed to understand each other or have a real relation- ship to each other. You see, I don't think I have ever really believed that you really loved me—but perhaps because we had such a differ- ent idea of what love is, or such a different way of loving. Also, because of the doubts you had yourself, not so much loving me as whether it would have been possible to go on loving me—In a way your not loving me hurts me—but perhaps more than anything, I felt that that week in Hamburg had broken what we had together and had put nothing in its place—or put only the possibility of something which we were neither of us free to work out—neither emotionally nor in time nor in place. So, ever since, I have had a strange feeling both of separation from you yet of ties to you. It was not a burden exactly because somehow I felt that some time, somewhere, we would be together again and would work out something between us, and that I still believe and hope.

Please do not worry about anything till after your exam. It is very important you should do it well and then be able to get away from Europe. I'm sure you should live in the East, and perhaps also in America for a while. All problems now are world problems and must have world solutions.

I have a lot of ideas and intentions. I will tell you about them some time tho' they are not quite clear or settled—or I might as well tell you now. I want to go to India in the autumn for six months or so and study possibly labour organisations or peasant conditions or the national movement, then go to China, Japan and America and study the same thing in each country and try to connect it all together—I want very much to write a book on nationalism in the East,—or is it too ambitious—perhaps you would help me? I shall read about it this summer and learn Hindustani and possibly Russian or Chinese.

I am rather excited by all this—by everything—one wakes up like a dormouse after a long winter and the world is wonderfully beautiful. Here it is quite incredible but even in London, the birds were singing and the trees flowering again. 'Hope springs eternal in the human breast.'

Bless you Adam—forgive my long silences and try and believe it was not faithlessness or indifference but bewilderment and uncertainty, and yet a belief that nothing could change or hurt the possibility of our being friends and very important to each other. Do you believe that too?

Love always,
S.

---

[1] See letter Adam–Shiela, Göttingen, 28 Mar. 1936.

Paris
24th April, 1936

Darling Adam,

Thank you very much for your letter.[1] You are very generous and I think I understand a lot of things after your letter which I did not before, and I am grateful to you for understanding. It is so very difficult to overcome distances of time and place, and I wish I could see you and talk to you, tho' of the alternatives you suggest, I think the second is better, both because, together or alone, we have *got* to find out what shall be our respective 'life-work' and that needs a great deal of hard, clear thinking; and because we have both reached the stage at which, in case of conflict, the romantic must be sacrificed to the moral—as you said, the pleasure or displeasure of God is what really matters to us now. Perhaps even more important is that we do not really know ourselves—or perhaps I should say that only of myself, tho' your letter makes me think you are either changing or finding out things about yourself which you did not know before— for instance, to feel it a sin to fuse romantic and moral endeavour on a lesser plane than that of perfect and returned love is surely a change or discovery in you. To tell you the truth, I am rather bewildered and a little frightened of things now. The one criterion of so many of my actions—caring for Goronwy—being forbidden, I feel reckless and wild and give and accept where I would not have before. It is at once a relief and a pain no longer to calculate—but I do not know what are sincere impulses and what are just filling the emptiness. We could not be happy, or even cover miles of heart-searching when my heart is so bewildered inside. I would rather meet when we are more cer- tain of ourselves and our relation to 'God' and when we know what the battle is we must fight together or alone. I think you will agree even if your little friend[2] does not—her solution is charming and she is certainly a sweet girl.

I am sorry you too have been suffering these things. It is all the pain and excitement of being born—the pain of coming out of the old, warm world and the excitement of the fresh, bright, unknown world into which one is going. Just to-day the first is a little stronger than the second, because I travelled here with Douglas,[3] who has recalled more vividly than ever the frustrations of that old world, and Goronwy and I were long in Paris and I understand the depth of my attachment to him which is perhaps unalterable even if we never come together again. Do you feel like that for Miriam? Time and dis- tance has perhaps made it possible for your other relations not to be coloured by your relation to her—but I feel about other people now—'my heart is too deeply laden ever to burden thine'.

But I have resolved not to think of all this now. The new world is enough to think of—and indeed demands thought, and we both should be grateful that this problem of mixing up ones loves with try- ing to find the way of life which is ultimately right for oneself—is, for the moment, resolved. Love, or perhaps lovers, are insistent and it is perhaps wrong not to accept in the Spring—I don't know—as I say I feel reckless and heedless, and determined to keep the romantic and moral separate from each other where they are incompatible—and where they conflict, to sacrifice the first to the second. I think we both have failed in this way—but I would not call it a sin on either of our parts—where love is not perfect, there is still much good in tender- ness and comradeship, and what you said in your last letter to me, I do very much agree with. There is much truth in Dostoevski's belief that nothing in this world is worth the tears of a child. I'm afraid this letter may seem rather delirious. It seems to me—but you will understand. I have told you a little about the 'new' world in that letter I wrote you from Cornwall.[4] In a way, except for the practical details, it is hardly necessary to explain ourselves, for our problems at the moment are essentially the same. So let's solve them, and at least never fail ourselves if we must fail other people.

Bless you darling Adam—
Shiela.

[1] Letter lost.
[2] As casual acquaintance in whom Adam had confided his 'troubles'.
[3] Douglas Jay.
[4] See letter Shiela–Adam, Cornwall, 18 Apr. 1936.

Paris
26.4.36.

Darling Adam,

Thank you very much for your letter[1] and for your invitation to Göttingen and the Rhineland. It is not from lack of wanting to see you or thinking it unimportant that I cannot come, but just because it would be impossible at this moment for either of us to be very happy or to work anything out even, apart from our happiness and our own lives. The only thing that I have any certainty about is that I want to and can do something worth doing and that is not a personal life. I think I am finding at last what it is and for that reason alone, must be in England this summer. I realise how very different our circumstances and how widely separated we are not only in past experience but in present determination and environment. I think perhaps there is no bridge at this moment from England to Germany and our only hope of understanding and endeavour is to meet on common ground far from either. Perhaps, if either of our plans materialise we will meet in the East and the things which ideally we both care for, may take the same material form. At the moment your fear as you walk to the Law Courts is a little justified. But this, and your finding it difficult to tell me about your youth and the parts of your life outside England, you must accept as part of present and temporary difficulties which could be removed and may be in time. For the moment, time's on our side and patience and determination to get on with our separate lives is what we must have. Don't you agree?

I am sitting in the Tuileries gardens in warm sunshine. The sparrows making love rather absurdly in the arms of the statues and the pigeons picking lethargically at the grass. The trees are all far out and it is summer here tho' in England it is far behind. Paris is extraordinarily lovely to accept like this. It is to the life which I find myself, unhappily, utterly foreign. There is a private detective-like individual studying me from the opposite seat and I am sure we have not one common thought or feeling but then he is peculiarly unpleasant and most Frenchmen have a saving grace of wit which this man lacks.

The elections last night were amusing though not very exciting. Crowds stood outside the newspaper offices where the results were broadcast and reflected onto the buildings opposite. I could not gather which way the vote was going, for though the left seemed to have many gains in numbers, the right seemed in each case of pure election to be elected. Every result set violent arguments going among the crowd, which I found uncomprehendingly funny, though no doubt it was fairly serious.[2]

Mowrer gave me Brand to read. Do you know it? He obviously expected me to. In case you don't, it is a long dramatic poem by Ibsen about a man with the philosophy of All or Nothing. Mowrer thinks I have it too and hoped this would cure me, but so far am I from having it that I found Brand deeply moving and was ashamed of my half way living. Read it if you can get hold of it and have time. It is a very moving history of doubt and moral conflict.

A countryman of yours is elaborately photographing one of the monuments. The detective has gone, so has the sun and I am getting cold. I am better today though still a little chaotic. Paris is not a very healing place though perhaps just for that one should visit it in trouble. It has a remarkable way of destroying one's complacency.

Love

S.

[1] See letter Adam–Shiela, Göttingen, 28 Mar. 1936.
[2] The first ballot of the General Elections took place on Sunday, 26 Apr.; it actually indicated a distinct shift of the French electorate to the Left which was confirmed by the subsequent ballot of 3 May. It led to the formation of the first Popular Front Ministry under Léon Blum.

Kassel.

29.4.36.

Darling Shiela,

Somehow I knew what your letter would contain before I had it.[1] But you should not be bewildered and unhappy, because it's a bad beginning for what you want to do. And what do you mean by giving and accepting where you would not have before? Perhaps it is true that we cannot help each other at the moment, but remember that any time my wish to do so would be very great indeed. And meeting for a little interval might give us both greater certainty of ourselves. You are right to say that my determination not to fuse things any longer is a change, but with you bent on the same we would not endanger each other . . .

No: I fetched a big dictionary to look up what 'heedless' means—and found that you should not be now. I've never had such an unhappy letter from you and you are certainly right that in spring especially it is wrong to be unhappy. No amount of 'clear thinking' will I am afraid in your case alter this state of affairs—as there must be peace and clarity first in which to meditate with purpose. . . .

Spring is very strange and clouded this year—the buds come out in a kind of dull stubborness in spite of there being no sun whatsoever for weeks now and cold and rain almost all the time. My poor father feels that very badly, I think he feels every spring now is probably going to be his last one and the sun on his flowers and trees in the garden he enjoys quite as much as the expectations of . . . You know that I think him fundamentally a very wise man though his sensibilities to the world have decreased with age. Just the other day somebody told me that he had listened to his speeches to the Prussian Diet with greatest admiration, and what pleased me even more is the real gratitude and respect people talk of his experiences with his smaller and bigger municipal and provincial work.

He definitely thinks in terms of 'this' world and another world and when he left the state service in 1919 he made up his mind that having been busy for the first all his life, he was now going to turn away from it definitely and think of other things. Of course he did not succeed in the sense of the age—but there is a profound calm about him and yet a real wisdom about the ways of the world and our country which have made him a very important and very helpful friend to me, especially in these recent years when the tides turned against some of the ideas which he and I cherish—his way out is not to think very highly of the human race anyhow and postulate their having accomplished masters which naturally share his concepts of good government—

But darling, all these things one so much better *talks* about and the more I think of it the better it seems to me that we should meet some time shortly—I shall be very careful with you and leave you to cope with the things you'd better not tell me and promise not to bewilder or frighten you in any way.

The point is one must not refuse to undertake things for fear they may hurt—as long as they are in line with one's ends.

Let us try hard and be brave and honest companions and leave nothing in a fog but face it and share it squarely and be glad of each other whatever happens.

Love and in hope I shall hear soon.
Adam.

[1] See letter Shiela–Adam, Paris, 24 Apr. 1936.

Chelsea.
2.5.36.

Darling Adam,

 . . . I think I thought out a lot of things while I was in Paris, and escaped the mood of that letter I wrote you. I hope so at least; but one escapes easily by oneself, it is the pressure of companions which makes it hard to be single-minded. In spite of Banville[1] I must 'chercher les effets et les causes,' if also with all my heart and love 'la beauté et le printemps divin.' I think both are possible. They must be because both are so strong inside me—stronger than before. For nine weeks, at any rate, I must stay here—a term at the School of Oriental Studies, and nine weeks to discover how I can go round the world. I am determined to go in the autumn. Then shall we meet, or shall we meet the other side of the world? I wish your exam were in June and we could cross the world together—But now to meet in Germany is impossible—both in time and place. The biggest problems we have to work out, we must face alone. I think each would complicate the problems of the other. I admit I could not bring quite to your conditions the sympathetic understanding which you need. I am an alien enemy to it, you see, not one of its children, and I could make it not easier but more difficult for you. Perhaps you would be able to tell me things about your youth and M. and your life outside England. You must one day. But for the moment, if my not knowing, if your not knowing me, if the vast differences between the conditions of our lives, trouble you, we will not write any more. They do not trouble me very much, for I accept them and have a way of being able to shut things off—but if you cannot do that, and if you cannot bear patiently this very imperfect communication we have, we will stop it altogether. We can communicate with picture post-cards, which are a very nice form of communication if our tastes are the same. You can send me a weekly picture of your house—of which I found an enormous number when I was tidying up today. . . .

Bless you, goodnight.
Shiela.

1 'Search for causes and effects'; 'the beauty, the divine spring'; from the poem 'A Adolphe Gaiffe'; Théodore de Banville, *Les Cariatides* (Paris, 1864), p. 286.

Kassel.
8.5.36.

[Dear Shiela,]

Perhaps, Shiela, you were right about time. But to think that you hate this country so much that one cannot see Spring in it together is a little painful. Meeting might have called back to you that being attached to it has nothing to do with the things that it is natural to hate from Paris. These things should not be confused with the fact that you must make up your mind about your imperialism and I about ours. Perhaps I am a little clearer already about mine than you about yours and therefore less committed to mine than you to yours—We'll see when we meet in the Autumn.

My exam is likely to be finished at the beginning of September. I cannot believe that 'that way of being able to shut off things'— Gandhi was 'shut off' when Manchuria was beginning to trouble the world, Manchuria for Abyssinia, and that for Austria, wasn't it?—is a right way for me. It may be for you. However, we are finding our own ways, not each other's, aren't we. . . .

Farewell/love
A.

Chelsea.
11.5.36.

Dear Adam,

I am very sorry if my letters hurt you. I did not mean to, nor should you be hurt by anything I meant. I do not quite understand, but understanding seems to grow less and less with time, and perhaps we die on the day we realise there is no explanation and no under-standing.

We must be grateful for a more beautiful spring than any in our lives and take pain from it, since there is no joy.

Shiela.

Imshausen.
21.5.36.

Darling S

Your letter didn't hurt me, but your not coming made me sort of ill for a time and when I recovered things seemed somehow different, harder and colder and further away. . . .

You didn't hurt my personal or national feelings but a sort of something in between by not seeming to accept any of my faults and difficulties as also part of friendship. On the whole I like your revolting against them but I want you to do it . . . no, do it as you like, because I may have to reserve the same privilege. . . .

Love
A.

Chelsea.
25.5.36.

Adam Darling, thank you very much for the letter you wrote me in Paris.[1] It does indeed explain why you considered it likely we should meet, for it is a very strong and comforting letter, which even now I am very glad of, for in fact, things do not change very quickly. But it did not seem fair to me then, and still does not, to turn to you for strength and comfort, though perhaps for the first time I have felt the need for such turning. My mother used to tell me that love was like that, but with Goronwy I never found it so.[2] I had to be strong for us both, and was not strong enough.

But I have grown up more in the last two months than in the last two years, for all their apparently being in the world and among grown-ups. I am very glad of it, and feel freed of tremendous burdens—of my own childishness, of my own rather conceited earnestness about the world, and of Goronwy's half-resentful dependence on me. I would like to tell you one day about him if I can.

I was, in fact, in Oxford last week-end—and came back last night to find the first letter you wrote me. . . .

But the weekend was nice for I stayed with some countrymen of yours, whom I believe you do not know, but who are very admirable and moving. He especially is all I like most in your people—for you know I do like them very much, and my anger and hatred is only the other side of my liking so much. His name is Rudolf Olden.[3]

. . . India is really a ghastly country—partly in its own nature, but chiefly, I am sure, because of our influence there—We are a people so

anti-pathetic to everything Asiatic that our only object is to keep ourselves so separate and dominant as possible over the real life of the
people. Where our lives touch, we try to change their nature, and the
result is a really horrible vulgarisation of European culture, and
degradation of Indian. I am sure you are right and there is no ultimate difference between men of different races. The companion of
most of my days is a Sikh from the Punjab,[4] and has made nonsense
of many of my preconceived ideas of East and West. I would like to
tell you about him, because he is what I 'specially admire in the
Indian'—gentle, courteous, very sensitive, and somebody to whom
life itself is a pain. He is a writer—rather a good writer in English.
We walk in the parks together and look at the flowers. . . .

Darling Adam—
Shiela.

[1] Letter lost.
[2] Goronwy Rees was an artist with all the wild creativity of his Celtic blood; in
no way a comforting or reassuring character, but one of great charm and intelligence; see Goronwy Rees, *A Bundle of Sensations: Sketches in Autobiography* (New
York, 1960); *A Chapter of Accidents* (New York, 1972).
[3] Rudolf Olden (1885–1940), a liberal German lawyer, writer, and publicist. He
defended the left-wing publicist Carl von Ossietzky in court, was political editor of
the *Berliner Tageblatt* and emigrated in 1933 via Prague and Paris to England where
he resided in Oxford. He wrote biographies on Stresemann, Hindenburg, and one of
the first ones ever on Hitler (*Hitler* (Amsterdam, 1935)). Deported from Britain to
Canada in Sept. 1940 on the steamer 'City of Benares', he was drowned when the
steamer was torpedoed by a German submarine.
[4] Iqbal Singh, (1912–   ) Indian publicist especially concerned with explaining his
country to the outside world. He studied at various universities, including King's College, Cambridge, was an author of many books and contributor to journals like the
Spectator and the *Fortnightly* and is one of the most distinguished friends of Nehru's
still surviving. However at this point Shiela turned her back on her involvement with
India. Her reasons are given in an exchange of letters with Jawaharlal Nehru (Grant
Duff, *The Parting of Ways*, pp. 117 f.) written shortly afterwards, from Prague.

June 9th, 1936.

Darling Adam,
   I really am not hesitating but had quite made up my mind, whatever else I do, to come and see you first. If only it is all right for you, I
long to come and would much rather see you now than in the
Autumn. The autumn may even be there to see you again, but lets
meet now so long as it doesn't disturb your exam. There is no distance or tentativeness in my attitude but only a great desire to see you
and talk about things with you. All that I am afraid of is that you will
find me very bewildered and uncertain of things, and not at all the

heedless confidence I used to have. Like you I have been terribly shocked by the people I love turning away, and all the past weeks have been bad ones from that point of view for me. What shall we do about it all? Your brother[1] and Gornowy are too good to lose in such a world. . . .

Darling Adam, Bless you.

S.

[1] Werner; Adam used to tell Shiela about his arguments with Werner. Goronwy knew Werner from Berlin and much admired him.

Kassel
June 10, 1936.

Darling S.

Will you forgive this overflowing pen of mine?—you must be really frightened by now when you see another of these envelopes waiting for you: though it is more the quantity than their contents which is likely to disturb you.

To-night I thought I might tell you a few technical details which might make 'going Kassel' slighly more attractive for you . . . Your room would be on the fourth, mine on the 1st floor, so you would be very independent and we could have all our meals together—break-fast on a little balcony and supper in my little room. Be nice now and come. . . .

My landlady wants to know when because she wonders about painting your furniture white—I'd rather have the dissonance of colours and have you come earlier. Perhaps you might find it possible to do some good work here and help me to the same—because at present I suffer from such violent distaste with my 'palais de justice' and all that belongs to it because there is no sufficient counterweight. Perform the duties of a friend and be that for once! Forget all my doubtful and aggressive and doubtful remarks and admit that on the whole I have not been as bad as I might have been.

Will you come on Monday, darling S—

A.

3

TOGETHER AND APART IN CENTRAL EUROPE

BETWEEN HESSE AND PRAGUE

7 July 1936–5 March 1937

EDITOR'S NOTE

Shiela was now 23 and Adam almost 27. A new phase had now opened in their friendship. Although emotionally they had drawn closer (see Grant Duff, *The Parting of Ways*, chap. XIII; and the first letters here), politically they were soon to face intense argument. Shiela had returned to her career as foreign correspondent—a career greatly disliked by Adam—and, on Mowrer's advice, taken up the suggestion made by the *Observer* after her reporting of the Saar Plebiscite, to go on their behalf to Prague. Central Europe was now, after the reoccupation of the Rhineland, the focal point of Hitler's foreign policy, and the Sudeten German minority, now largely Nazi in sympathy, his Trojan Horse. Shiela's strong revulsion against them and against Nazi intervention in the Spanish Civil War was to become a great cause of friction between her and Adam. At first, however, the correspondence glows in the light of this happiest of all visits to Imshausen.

7 July 1936

Darling A—
    . . . I am in a hot, full-up, third-class carriage somewhere beyond Eisenach. Two hours away from you can wreak much havoc in my conditions. What can I say that I have not said already or meant when I kissed you? Only perhaps how gladly I feel committed to a special place in your life and how gladly I have committed you to mine. Thank you for these two weeks which have made me strong again—even to face what new pain this may bring.
    Look after yourself and work hard and well—Remember me often and happily and warmly and bless you always because I like you so very much and especially.

Loving
S.

Kassel.
7.7.36.

Darling Shiela,

Ever since you went the atmosphere outside was close and laden with electricity. Now the rain is beating against the windows. There has been a thunderstorm. I hope the same has happened on your way. The guard of your train seemed nice and promised to look after you and the luggage; I hope he did.

The coach couldn't have me this morning and Euler[1] did not turn up in the afternoon. But I am grateful for getting back to it all by myself first. It will not be easy to 'write' again suddenly. You must promise to be patient and I shall make an effort not to let this sort of communication become too unnatural again until we meet again. Also, please carry out your intention to learn my language so it may become natural to communicate in it sometimes.

At lunch I had a talk with a labour service leader,[2] a very nice man that would have interested you—about the growing attitude of the young that go through his hands. It would be difficult to convey what he meant by 'interpreting' him to you. And yet you would have had to admit that his complexities in dealing with the problems that arise in their education are our complexities. These crowded faults and virtues are part and parcel of the European and general impasse. How differently it all filters through the different minds that matter, and yet how fatally bound up with each other they are! perhaps your impression will be that there is not very much time to speculate and try and find passages where emergency bridges ought to be struck now—in the autumn many things may stand out differently and more clearly of external importance to us. Of the rest we cannot, I cannot speak now—you don't even seem quite gone away yet, and it is as if that wide plane is still spreading before us—except that I bless and thank you my darling girl—I had written 'my' and yet you are as free as an eagle, my sweet—

A.

---

[1] Euler could not be identified.
[2] Since May 1936 every male youth had to serve for six months in the *Reichsarbeitsdienst* which involved public projects and was a preliminary to military service. A labour service leader was bound to be a Nazi.

Prague.
9th July, 1936.

Darling Adam,

At moments I wish almost unbearably that you were here—and this is one of them. I am eating my supper on an island and the river is glistening. A brass band is playing lovely gay music rather aggressively and people are dancing under the trees. How much I like pleasure and want to connect it with you! Altogether you have succeeded very much in preventing my running away from you—I am become a most obedient wife. But Prague is really wonderful and I long to show it to you. At sunset it has an almost perfect skyline and there are houses and streets in it almost indescribably beautiful. I love towns built about rivers, and of all architecture Baroque is the most humane and splendid. I would like to visit a thousand new places and all with you. Must we discover all the world first by ourselves? Well let us, if the rest of the world is as desirable as this, it is intrinsically to be discovered whatever way one discovers it.

I live in a kind of Kurfürstendamm,[1] which, like the Kurfürstendamm, grows fascinating and horrible at night—but my room is remote. It has walls of rose-pink Regency silk, except for one of glass. I have a balcony and under me and far away are roofs. I have a blue bathroom all my own, and white painted furniture. I am very happy but I think I shall move and live in the skyline which is so beautiful at sunset. It will mean leaving the hot sausage stalls in the street where I live, the milk bars, and even, darling Adam, the old women selling radishes which remind me of you every fifty yards I walk. What could make me think of you with so much feeling in the perfect skyline?

I am very happy and very fond of you and miss you very much. What a wise man Turgenev was when he made the girl in his story write that the pain of parting was itself a pleasure.[2]

The brass band is a military band which accounts for the aggressiveness. You will have to look out for the Little Entente. Bless you always.

Love,
S.

[1] The well-known Berlin avenue pulsating with life by day and night, leading out of the city in a westward direction towards the lake districts. The street in Prague where Shiela first lived was called Václavské Náměstí.

[2] This general sentiment is common in Turgenev's novels and stories; in particular after his parting from Mme Viardot he mused on recollections of parting.

Prague.
9 July, 1936.

[Dear Adam,]

Thank you for your letter today. It doesn't deserve such a warm letter as I wrote last night, but since I am 'free as an eagle' you shall have it all the same. How nice and plain I look in all the photographs and how handsomely you are looking at me in one. I'm afraid I am a very bad photographer, active or passive, but I will take some beautiful pictures of Prague and send them to you.

I am being very very elegant. I surprise myself at every looking glass and with great pleasure. In fact I am quite the smartest girl in Prague before sundown. After sundown, there are some extraordinarily smart ones with gold faces and feathers in their caps, but I think I am still the smartest respectable girl in Prague. I have just eaten a wonderfully good lunch of goose and strawberries and am on my way to pay my respects to my Legation. The minister[1] has a very bad reputation and is being sent to South America where it matters less. As usual the only man who knows anything about Czechoslovakia is very low down and despised in the Legation. I think neither diplomacy nor journalism are good ways of knowing a country, and yet for all your scorn, journalism is very difficult and I have not yet learnt anything about the country and have only been told what I already know. The difficulty is that all sources of information are official which means that the information, tho' probably reliable and fairly just, is necessarily a little sterile and as Czech policy has not changed for 15 years, it is not surprising there is little new to say about it. I am putting my trust in a Dr. Ripka[2] who is a journalist, but he speaks no English. I will really try to learn German, and I wonder whether to go to the Berlitz School which will be expensive but probably thorough. Till I have a German teacher and a permanent address I shall feel drifting and lost, so I will look for both this afternoon.

. . . Nothing makes one feel so lost in a foreign country as meeting one's countrymen. I have spent the last three hours with one man from the Legation and I felt isolated with him as I have not felt alone. The implication that we are English and those are the Czechs sinks into every word and gesture, and in the end one is quite miserable. He was one of those typical Englishmen—very depressed and yet cynical and joking—and cynical not for some disillusion or misfortune, but by nature—I think it is a lack of vitality, lack of spirit in both senses—and yet he was quite nice and we talked a lot and a long time about all manner of things.

He thinks the Czechs know they are doomed and will be fools if they resist, that the French will not help them, nor will we. He thinks the Poles are sitting on the fence and doing it exceedingly well. They know that Poland will be the battleground of a German-Russian war, and therefore will do their utmost to avoid it; on the other hand a Czech official here believes that peace is certain because of the alliance system, that Poland may go in on the German side but will be a very insecure ally and that Germany has nobody else. The Englishman thought that that wish was father to that thought. I don't know—I don't see how I can possibly find out the position. Nobody will know until the outbreak of war, nor what armed strength nations will have. Apparently there is such a ray as you suggested, but machinery for working it at a distance has to be vast and is very expensive and engines are easily insulated against it. I think I am going to find conversations here sometimes interesting and always unprofitable, and the only things to write about will be possibilities. I think I will have had enough in September. I think I would like the Hungarian job better probably. Budapest is more of a place to live in.

Still Prague is lovely and it is too early to say it is limited. Food grows in the streets and if one lives like a worker, one can live for very little. Elegance, on the other hand, is very, very expensive. I think it is not worth it. The Czechs are simple people and unsnobbish. They have no manners and little grace but seem to be quite sound and good-hearted. It is a virtue that they do not like speaking German; those who can seem to be rather proud of it, but perhaps their manners would be better if I spoke English! Tho' for all that they are quite civil and kind. The streets are very crowded, and being cobbled, very noisy—but away from the crowds and the noise, there are streets of absolute perfection. In the diplomatic quarter there are most wonderful baroque houses. All the Legations are in beautiful houses. The English one is a sort of castle. It even has a ghost and a courtyard. In the streets there are blind men who carry white sticks, and peasants in country clothes selling dolls and embroidery. Women with handkerchiefs round their heads sell the newspapers, or sit on the ground selling big round radishes, some very red like cherries and others white, as you like them. The river is changingly beautiful throughout the day, people bathe in it or row big primitive boats and fish.

In my palace room, my bed is turned down at night, which is a great pleasure to me every evening it happens, and I think I am at home again and my nurse is living here and will come and say good-night and mend my stockings. It is late and I must have some supper and this is a very long letter which you will scarcely have time to read and never to answer. Try and write to me and do not be afraid I will hold you to anything you say now and afterwards regret. I too am beginning to find life a fountain rather than a flowing river. Fountains are lovely while they last so let them at least spring freely and who knows they will not make a river or a sea.

Goodnight, my sweet, bless you.

Shiela.

¹ Sir Joseph Addison.
² Hubert Ripka (1896–1958); Czechoslovak publicist and politician, he worked in the nineteen thirties in Prague for the Brno newspaper *Lidove Noviny* ('The People's News'). After the Munich agreement (29 Sept. 1938) he left Prague to help in the formation of an exile government to which he belonged as Information Minister; in 1945 he returned to Prague and served as Minister for Foreign Trade until the Communist coup in 1948 when he was again exiled. When Shiela went to Prague, Mowrer recommended Ripka to Shiela; he became a major Czech professional contact for Shiela and a friend, much to the displeasure of Adam.

Kassel.
Friday [*most likely* 10 July 1936]

My sweet Shiela—

. . . Parting was in no sense a pleasure I'm afraid, though I too felt gladly committed to a special place in your life. It almost made me ill and I have to concentrate all I can to be able to set my mental engine on the legal track again. I work with others as much as possible and tonight too there will be two colleagues working with me here.—I shall imagine you in the beautiful city you describe and I shall be very much concerned that you really remain the most respectable girl of Prague . . .

It quite healed me to find them¹ on my desk and I shall buy a big nice wooden box for only your letters and one day we will read them together—perhaps when the life of the great couple is going to be written. . . .

You have an extraordinary power over me and I am thankful that you feel it as a 'committment' [*sic*] in a way—I hardly dare telling you all about it. Your being so fair in its use seems to increase it too. . . .

Heaps of love Darling

A.

¹ Shiela's 'nice letters'.

Kassel.
July 10th, 1936.

My Darling Shiela,

    . . . I plead that whatever unrest and wondering may go on in our emotional selves we could be and are of real help and value to one another on our mutual somewhat intricate and yet to a considerable degree common paths. We remind each other that life must be lived simply and bravely and that it can become ordered, even beautiful. We share, I think, the essential ambitions of what man should still be in this present world and we share the smaller gaieties of life.

    Is it damaging to our love—I think decidedly the opposite—that rational considerations are so very much in the foreground? Are our emotional reservations anything but loyalty to our past lives which indeed we should not destroy? There is a very good case for patience in that respect, for I don't think that we have either of us got very far in exploring the circumstances, if perhaps the main trends, of each other's real life. How can we embark on any great decision of being able to integrate the big difference in these circumstances unless we have gained an adequate view of them? You said a little lightly you didn't think I had as yet a life—and your view of this country—which in many respects I share—is such that you cannot but consider a great part of my existence Utopian or even meaningless. Yet it begins to grow more real to me than my personal relationships.

    I want and need you as my friend, darling Shiela—we do not need to worry about anything else at the moment. Let us be strong and unwavering about it. I'd rather march on with nothing but your hand, than lie with you and realise a sudden look of resentment. Yes, we resent each other destroying our past lives. You haven't done justice to mine and my presence very likely reduces the wideness and colouring of yours. But what need we fear when we have a future increasingly in common and can strike towards it without having to abandon anything that is a part of our real self. To fix our eyes on what we can share even now is encouragement and aid in our own separate responsibilities, isn't it? I hope you can agree.

Lots of love,

A.

Prague.
July 11th, 1936.

Darling A,

. . . Today is the sort of day that is gloomy at home but suicidal in
a foreign town. Luckily my room is very pretty and I have bought
some flowers and my big window makes the room light even with the
clouds outside. I treated myself to a large lunch also to keep the
weather out and yielded to the advice of the waiter and ate a very disgusting dish called Cherry Dumpling—that is bad enough but it had
sweet hot cheese sauce over it. Can you imagine anything less suited
to a depressing day. However, since then I have been working in the
Společensky Club[1] (very very smart) and have learnt a very great
deal. Even more important for my happiness, I read a wonderful
article by Masaryk[2] on love of one's country, which was most moving and all that we think. I was specially moved because yesterday I
had a great lecture on British Interests from our Minister here, and I
felt really bruised and hurt by the cynicism of it and by my own
silence towards all that he said. When I did protest that for me it was
not enough to be British because there were other things I believed in
and other things I cared for, he said I was the sort of person who was
ruining England by my anti-patriotism, and that women should
never have anything to do with politics because they introduced sentiment into them. It does not seem to me that politics suffer from lack
of sentiment, but just from the very cynicism that Sir Joseph A.
suffers from himself. We had all this again about the ruling classes
and about Government being a capacity learnt after generations and
not possible to the ordinary man unless he be a genius. What truth is
in it? Is it not again a matter of interest? To the Austro-Czech nobles,
the Czechs govern badly because they pass land laws against the
nobles, but is that bad government? It is true what Lat[t]imore[2] said,
that to understand a country one must know in whose interest it is
governed. This country is governed in the interest of small people.
There is no aristocracy either of land or industry. Then it is important to know whether a man gets on because he is good at his job or
because he is related to somebody else who has got on. . . .

I should not complain of my Minister. He gave me a beautiful
lunch and was nice to me. He lives in a wonderful house and we had
lunch in his garden which looks over the whole of Prague. That was
lovely and he was interesting even if he was provoking. I don't think
diplomats have been the best servants of the League of Nations, and
it may even come out one day that it was they who wrecked it. The
new world will have to be built with new stones.

This is a very long monologue to carry on with you Darling A. I think you should at least send me some picture postcards. I will send you one of Prague. Isn't it very beautiful? I will send you one of the street I live in which you can send on to my nurse, if you will [in your] next letter. I have been careful not to make any derogatory remarks for you to be upset by. I will keep this and hope there will be a letter from you in the morning.

Love always
S.

[1] A semi-official club in Prague frequented mainly by civil servants, writers, and journalists.

[2] Tomáš Garrigue Masaryk (1850–1937), founder and President of Czechoslovakia 1918–37.

[3] Owen Lattimore (1900–　), distinguished American Sinologist.

Kassel.
Sunday [most likely 12 July 1936]

Dear one, talking or writing to you there is always some sort of cloak or veil still that I want to throw off to be quite free to let you hear what I want you to understand. And I don't seem to be able to. You make it a lot easier for me in what you say about the fountain[1] and it isn't really your generosity or seriousness I distrust but my own ways of expression. It isn't even the language entirely though to some extent I always feel that I must change into something different, something more normal, more generally acceptable when I attempt your language. It may be partly due to the fact that I fear (justifiably enough) that the monological part of my life is lived too far apart from others for me to convey it with a hope of immediate understanding—too contrary to other things I do and seem. All this is a direct outcome of having lived essentially alone for many years without even the chance to regenerate and test my ideas in exchange with present and adequate friends. No amount of love can substitute that or create that light of clear open honesty about one's thoughts that a good friend does. And to be without that for so long has certainly damaged or at any rate retarded things that now should be ready to be offered to you my sweet. How can I ask you to respect my past life when I can give you no clear and continuous view of it, when it simply isn't in me to be able to speak unpretentiously and distinctly about the issues that matter to me most. . . .

Do you think that women too have a sort of primary inner purpose for which they must live and to which they must relate their relationships as something decidedly secondary? I don't think that in complete comradeship—as I have once told you before—there can be any distinction between primary and secondary, because the very purpose is common. But is it not that the woman must to some extent recognise the purpose that works in the man and which by the natural partition of their labours later on must have a certain predominance in their life together? Of course she must have her entire sovereignty and independence in *judging* and sizing up that purpose and she will continually share in its elaboration, but must she not to some extent if the thing is to be a success *accept* it? I think the alternative is the couple where she is interested in old age pensions and he in chicken farming or the other way round. What troubles me still more is of course the intrinsic Germanness of the purpose I could offer for our life—however international it may be in its actual application. My visible sympathy for German forms is so small that their invisible presence in the fabric of my life often escapes you. It was a long process before I was anywhere near to relate it to your ways of expressing yourself.

[Adam]

¹ See letter Shiela–Adam, Prague, 9 July 1936, last para.

Prague.
13 July, 1936.

[Dear Adam,]

Thank you, my love, for a beautiful letter.¹ It is a most wonderful, sparkling day, and your letter and the morning sun made my heart want to break with being so happy and yet alone. It is not a pleasure nor a happiness to be parted from you, but yet it is as if all the happiness of being with you lies just outside me in this beautiful sunshine, and I can look at it and know it is there, even when I am all alone. Do you understand that? I think it must be what the Turgenev girl meant one's loving becomes something objective and outside one, which one values and sees as it is itself—but this is all nonsense and if you were here it would not need to be said because it is a beautiful day and we would be wonderfully happy.

Yesterday was a very gloomy day indeed. Sunday is indeed God's wilderness sometimes. The rain tinkled desultorily down my window, the streets were empty and shuttered, everything grey and mournful. I spent all day reading newspapers and trying to understand what this agreement with Austria means.² I have reached such a depth really of international despair and I suspect everything that happens of sinister designs and ominous consequences, and this rather more than most, though the official note here is cheerful and calm. Today I must find out what they really think, but it is difficult and I do not know yet how to do it.

Saturday too was sad and grey, but I think I would not mind if I had a room where I would stay always because I have a lot of work which I like doing after so many years of idleness. I do not like living in a hotel. I do not like porters. There are about eight here and only one nice one. They are all too ready to open doors and hand me my key and my letters and air their bad English—but the maids are nice and talk to me in Czech which is a nice-sounding language. Underneath my hotel I have my best friend in Prague who gives me milk every day and puts extra sugar on my cakes. The cakes are wonderful, large and luscious, like a special sort of fruit.

Darling Adam—you will have not to keep all my letters in a box or I would be ashamed indeed when the great couple came to read them. So you must show discrimination so that we may believe when we read them that all my letters were best letters and all most intelligent and gay. These, for instance, being neither, could be eliminated,—but I will send them to you because I cannot do better now and it says how much and specially I like you.

Best love always,

S.

I'm so glad I have an extraordinary power over you and I hope it will last 60 years and I will always be fair with it so that by the time you are 90, I will make the last week of your life a burden to you, just before we die together, very old and very distinguished.

[1] Letter Adam–Shiela, 10 July 1936.

[2] Reference to the July Agreement (*Juliabkommen*) of 11 July 1936 between Germany and Austria according to which Germany recognized the sovereignty of Austria and each side acknowledged the other's internal developments as a strictly domestic affair. Thus the Austrian chancellor Kurt von Schuschnigg was officially protected against German interference; in turn he had to include in his government some 'nationally oriented' (*national betonte*) personages. The so-called 'German course' which the Austrian government began to pursue partly under Italian pressure—since Italy in its preoccupation with Abyssinia was increasingly dependent on Germany and less interested in the protection of Austria—was subject to differing interpretations in Germany and Austria and offered Austria but a brief respite in its uneven struggle with Nazi Germany.

Imshausen.
16.7.36.

My dear Darling,

It is very nice indeed to feel how very much you have won every-body's heart there—including my father's. And I know it isn't 'for my sake' though that may have started them wanting to like you. It is very good indeed to be in this peaceful environment again, and still more since I feel it is sensitive to your sweet value.

What about this plan?—you learn as much German and 'Europe' as you can till the end of this year, and then go to India to find out what you English are up to in this world while I sail to San Francisco, Japan, and China. During the coming year, then, if heavens are kind we meet in Peking and inhabit the Emperor's summer or winter palace, whatever the season is. I think that's a lovely prospective frame for our present work and it makes me very happy to think of the future like that.—You remember a long and serious talk we had about conditions in this country one afternoon in the park of Wil-helmstal which we ended watching the fat grey fishes in the pool near the castle? I think you understood me then, and if you remember what I said about the difficulties here for one who at one time hated and loved what he belonged to here, and if you still think we can be the 'great couple' we want to be, then all my worries and doubts I am sure will subside. And they for you, I think.

My mother said very nice things about you, and I told her I wished you would marry me far away in China and she said with a smile— (no, I am not sure whether she smiled or not, because it was dark when she was sitting at my bedside, but I believed she smiled)—that it would *not* break her heart.

I am very happy again, and it's all thanks to you. But I must look out not to become too happy—otherwise it will wreck my work. Luckily it is raining and cool, and the house quiet enough.—My sweetheart, I feel that all the roots and juices and strengths of my country here are feeding the love I send to you—bless you always and look after yourself and work well.

Adam.

Prague.
Thursday[, 16 July 1936]

Darling A,

At last, my sweet, a letter from you.[1] It takes so long that way, and in any case does not avoid what we hoped to avoid. It did not matter this time, but there is no point.

I think I understand a little what you say, and wish I could help you more than I do. I know so well what long isolation from friends and from anybody with whom one feels real understanding, is. But the only possible thing for you to do is to make that better is to try and establish a closer and warmer relation between your emotional and your political life and perhaps you cannot do that while you put one so much above the other. Yet I know that it is impossible for you to cease minding far more about the purpose of your life till you are sure what that purpose is or till you can look at it from a little further away. In a way, I think it is only because of your profound distrust of yourself and of that purpose that you feel a conflict between it and loving. I do not blame you in any way for this and understand how it has happened and why it had to happen. But you must want as much to get over that conflict as to do the things which you want to do because only then will you be really satisfied with either. Otherwise you will continue to have relationships which you put secondarily and for which you have not a fundamental respect for yourself in them, because they have nothing to do with the things for which you really care. If you had a really primary relationship the question simply would not arise. What great man ever asks himself which he puts first, his wife or his work? There is no question.

That there should be no question is also very largely due to his wife, for she must bear a very large part of the burden that it should not arise. That is where the question of her inner purpose arises and of that I am not quite sure. There is the doctrine of he for God alone and she for God in him, against which everything within me revolts. On the other hand there is also the fairy story that men and women are souls which have been cut in half and when they love each other they are become whole again,[2] which I like very much. There is also the natural desire of the woman to give all the help she can to the man she loves and in return to be looked after and cared for by him. And the inner purpose of many great women is really to create the man whom they love. It is more natural for women to work indirectly and in a way more humanly. They would like to make the tool and let the tool act. Men want to act directly. So I am not sure that chicken farming for one and social insurance for the other is good. But one cannot really theorise about it all. It depends on the people involved and on the lives which they will lead. And for us, as you say, we do not know well enough what we are or what our lives are.

My sweet, I have to go out to supper, and have been fetched, so I must stop and this is only half written, but it is a long time since I wrote to you so I will post this and try and finish when I come in again. Sweetheart I send you lots of love and wish you were here. I have found a lovely room, very bare, but looking out on beautiful baroque houses all around.

Love always,
S.

Hotel Julis,
Prague.
Friday morning, [17 July 1936]

It is already morning and I have not posted the letter I wrote you and have only just come back. The 'bombe' did not exactly explode but was none the less fairly active. My dinner party took place at a beautiful restaurant on the Moldau with three men, all of whom were married and all of whom for some reason into which I did not enquire because to remind people of their wives seems to me an insult if they love them, left their wives behind. The one[3] . . . is rather unhappy and for reasons to do with his temperament rather than his circumstances. His circumstances I should imagine are happy. He has a French wife and a baby son and at the moment both are away, at least so I believe. I find him very moving as a person. He is a sentimental nationalist but by that you must understand something good rather than bad. I mean a nationalist by feeling rather than by reasons. That is the great difference between new and old nations. In the café they played Slovak folk songs which moved him very much and even moved me but for the reason that I thought that for me and for the English, no such feeling could exist because we were an Empire and no longer an island and so had lost what was real in the love of our country. Now it had become a certain pride in all we had conquered and all we possessed and from that a real national feeling cannot grow. But then they played English or rather Scottish songs and I realised that this article of Masaryk's on Amour de son pays[4] was true also for us. You know that for me Europe is a greater idea than England. You know also that for me Germany means the experiences which I have had there rather than a real appreciation of what Germany means to you. For that reason you are right to be rational in loving me and it may perhaps be the reason why we must, in the end, walk hand in hand and as friends, rather than anything more. And yet there are moments when I have a contempt for this rationalism, but in fairness to you and as blame for myself, I must tell you that those are the moments when I feel most lonely and most afraid, and at such moments one is less than oneself. So we must take care and be patient and not forget that on a human plane where no politics and no questions of nationality enter, we care very much for each other and represent to each other much joy and much strength, and that we both wish, even if it is not possible out of loyalty to ourselves, to be more than that to the other.

Love always

S.

[1] See letter Adam–Shiela, Sunday *most likely* 12 July 1936.
[2] From Plato's 'Symposium'; Aristophanes telling how Zeus split man into two halves wandering about longing for another.
[3] Here Shiela is writing of Hubert Ripka though not mentioning him by name.
[4] Love of one's country; see letter Shiela–Adam, Prague, 11 July 1936.

Prague.
July 17, 1936.

My dear darling,

Thank you for your short happy letter to-day from Imshausen, and I am very happy that your family like me. I like them very much too. It must be lovely there now and I look upon it as a beautiful bay which I have left for a most turbulent sea. I'm afraid its turbulence has penetrated into my letters a little bit but I will try and keep it out and yet also I want you to know what it is like. I'm afraid a fault is coming back which I thought I had outgrown which is, to get terribly excited and especially with admiration, and music—and together they make me quite drunk. Would you mind that? Sometimes it frightens me that you know me so little. If you come to England in September, would you come and stay with my grandmother in the country? You may hate it because nothing could be more insufferable and yet you better see really what all the things which have been round me since I grew up are like and what I am like among them.

Your plan is a lovely one except that I feel so far, far away from India just now and really disturbed about the issue. It is really so very important that the freedom which we have gained over hundreds of years should not be lost, that I begin almost to accept the lack of freedom it means to some people. And yet there must be some solution, by which freedom may advance and not only be defended. They say we are standing with our backs to the wall—Then how can one deliberatly break down that wall, even tho' it be a prison where we have unjustly imprisoned our subjects? Still, India is not very important to you in your plan—The rest is beautiful, tho' rather like a Chinese picture, beautiful and serene but somehow far away from every day. Do you really want to marry me? do not answer that now nor mind me saying the Summer Palace is far away from every day. It must be so till we meet again.

Meanwhile I will try and learn about Europe. I really find this country infinitely interesting and at the same time rather touching. I don't know what it is. To-night I go to Bratislava which is Slovak and was Hungarian and there I will meet a lot of other people. I will write to you from there or from Piešťany where I am staying with some family friends, which I think is a very good thing just at this moment I am a little bit all over the place again, tho' this time from too much and too sudden happiness rather than from those other, former sadder reasons which seem to have passed away having taught me how precarious and fickle happiness is, which I never knew before.

Write to me often such happy and calm letters, love, my sweet.

Shiela.

Prague.
20.7.36.

Darling A,

. . . I am still hoping very much I will get a letter saying you are coming here—I would love it and it would be the very best for me for a great number of important reasons—the biggest being perhaps because—(and it should be me and not you who should be frightened that you do not yet know my faults—and this is perhaps the worst) I am capable of the wildest and stupidest disloyalty thro' simply finding it impossible to remember people I love when they are not there, and thro' finding it quite impossible to co-ordinate my separate selves. So it would be very very good for me if only you could come here and see a little what this life in which you will leave me when you go to China—is like. Then specially I want you to meet the real friends I have made and want you to argue with them because alone, you know, I cannot defend 19th century German romanticism! Those long walks I had with you, my sweet, in Oxford four years ago, have left me only a very poor Hegelian, and when they talk of the opposition of Europe and Germany I cannot answer except that I hope there is none. But it is bad also for my caring for you to be told by university professors that Germany and Europe represent two conflicting ideas—for I care very much for Europe and our national difficulties grow—so I wish I could hear you arguing with them. I said perhaps you would come here and they have invited you for Wednesday supper—or for whenever you come. I wish it were possible. . . .

Bless you . . .

Much love always,

S.

Kassel.

24.7.36.

My fair sweet,

. . . There are so many things I want you to share with me still and to understand. But I know very well that this cannot be done in a rush. Yet there are one or two things I would specially want to talk over with you now. What you say of the relation between emotional and political life is true enough—who else could help better than you. Clearly the root of both these concerns must be in one's own single heart—and it seems as if God sent you to me as my one chance of a true single love.

But perhaps these sayings of the Trott do not seem at all acceptable to you and yet you should know him well enough that there are long stretches in his life where he is neither romantic nor pathetic. . . .

Darling Shiela

A.

29.7.36.

[Dear Shiela,]

. . . As far as I can make out I can be in Dresden by 17.27 (about the same time when your 4.15 will be there)—let the first of us meet the other—if you prefer the later afternoon train I shall of course meet that one too—let Hotel Ruschin, Dresden be our emergency address. . . . [1]

Your threats about disloyalty really scare me. I understand your professor friend hating us, I respect it—but there's no use for the future in this whole source of political reflection and ideologically it is our chief fault to have carried to the extreme what I imagine this honourable and more western folk is more moderately inspired by—but let me come and be defeated by their arguments in September when this rope is no longer around my neck.—Honestly, however, it would ruin the Trott to 'leave you' while going to China himself—in a world that makes the Duff 'wildly disloyal' and progressively hostile.—It will suddenly be too late to do all the great things we must do together. There's but one Duff and one me and of each of them only a measured period of time.

Thank you for your lovely note.
Adam.

[1] Adam was unable to visit Shiela in Prague since he was preparing for his legal (*Assessor*) examinations which were to take place between July and Oct. Instead, Adam made arrangements to meet Shiela in Dresden late in July. For a number of reasons Shiela was two days late for the meeting.

Prague.
15th Aug. 1936.

Darling Adam,
    . . . Prague suddenly seems to me like Oxford did my first term. Suddenly a new living world with things to learn and friends to care for and all in a most beautiful place. My first term was the best. I hope Prague will not decline as term after term declined in Oxford. We met then too, though the first summer term when we walked through the Parks was lovely but then it ended. I miss you very much today. Why do you not write? Come and see me soon. I am very fond of you and want to be in Prague with you while it is still summer. Every new garden I find, and every new place where Prague is beautiful I think of taking you to. You will be able to come, won't you?
    Monday. Now a nice letter from you.[1] Thank you very much. I'm afraid you will often feel angry with Chesterfield because he is profoundly immoral,[2] though sometimes you will find moral value even in his most cynical statements. He will be good for you. It is not enough to judge things only as right or wrong, good and bad. And it becomes less and less enough. The world is too rich and its goodness too varied to fit into calvinistic judgments. I'm afraid I love the world very very much, just in the way Christians were always taught not to love it. It is so beautiful and moving even where it is terrible and wicked. This Spanish thing[3] moves me terribly. Every newspaper is what Malraux[4] says art should be—'an attempt to give man a con-

sciousness of his own hidden greatness.' I hate the killing and suffering even of the side with which I do not sympathise, and it makes me love all the more my baroque streets and the flower markets and the river. . . .

Write to me. My love to your mother.

Love

Z.[5]

[1] Letter Adam–Shiela, Imshausen, 12 Aug. 1936; not reproduced here.

[2] Shiela had given Adam Chesterfield's letters; she had hoped to learn from them both a better prose style and greater worldly wisdom (Philip Dormer Stanhope, 4th Earl, 1694–1773; his *Letters*, addressed to his son, were first published in 1774). In a note to the editor Shiela adds: 'Adam didn't like them and I didn't learn!'

[3] The Spanish Civil War broke out in July 1936.

[4] André Malraux (1901–77), French author, archaeologist, explorer, statesman; active in the Spanish Civil War (*Man's Hope* (New York, 1938)); with French Resistance during the Second World War (pseudonym 'Colonel Berger'); after the war Minister of Information 1945–6 and Minister of Culture 1959–69 under General de Gaulle.

[5] About this time Shiela begins to appear in the correspondence as 'Z' or 'Zámecká', from the street in Prague where Shiela's apartment was located; Zámecká means 'by the castle'.

Kassel.

18.8.36.

Darling S—

. . . It is very sweet of you to want to show me the nice gardens you see, and I certainly want very much to see you in Prague before the winter comes. I know you won't come to Berlin—nor should you really, because it's a bad place for us and everybody. On the other side things will go from bad to worse when you make yourself the mouthpiece of our dear neighbours all over the place, because not only will it not fail to make you hostile to the Trott, but—taking your objectiveness for granted—may perhaps bring on more quickly the Spanish state in all Europe—I don't understand quite how it seems beautiful to you. . . .

Write to me sometimes.

Love

A.

Prague.
18.8.36.

Darling A,
 . . . Spain gets worse every day and your country is by no means
guiltless in it all. German and Italian aeroplanes are reported every
day among the rebels. The English and French answer with pious and
futile work on wording for a neutrality treaty. The world makes one
sick. And the Observer writes an article in which it practically says
that if we cannot win the Olympic Games[1] we had better not go in
for them, and what is the good anyway of having political freedom if
we do not win them. I am sick and angry and should not write to you
now, so I will go out and finish when I come in. I go to Reichenberg[2]
tomorrow. . . .

Love my sweet,
Z.

[*Postscript omitted*]

  [1] The Olympic Games, held in Berlin in Aug. 1936, were used by the Nazis as a
display of the vitality of the new Germany.
  [2] (Liberec); city in the Sudeten area of Czechoslovakia, inhabited by Sudeten Germans.

[*On the train between Prague and Reichenberg*]
19.8.36.

[Dear Adam,]
 . . . The country is full of gay and playful soldiers in railway
trucks. They are having manœuvres—but even playing at war must
be a hot and uncomfortable game when the summer is so beautiful.
Bohemia is a very beautiful country, I am not surprised you want it
but I am afraid you cannot have it. Shall I write a book called Germans and Czechs—historical, political, and psychological?[1] If I don't
become a journalist by Xmas, I shall become a publicist! which
means I shall try and get a research scholarship from Oxford to write
the book.
  Reichenberg. Have now arrived here. The streets are still hung
with flags, tho' thinly compared with your flag days. The only sort of
flag there seems to be is big state ones, which private people would
not afford. I have learnt only about the minority German feelings in
all this—I admire it and find here Saar conditions again[2] and renew
my old sympathies. The people are brave and strong and so far their
situation not nearly as bad. They are very simple people and not very

romantic, but admirable. Why are politically admirable people always ugly? . . .

I am happy. Bless you—

Love

S.

[1] In 1937 Shiela wrote *German and Czech: A Threat to European Peace* (London, 1937), for the New Fabian Research Bureau and in 1938 she wrote, at Penguin Books' request, *Europe and the Czechs* (Harmondsworth, 1938).

[2] Shiela had a great number of introductions in the Sudeten districts especially from anti-Nazi Sudeten Germans like Wenzel Jaksch (1896–1966); he served as deputy in the Czech Parliament 1929–38; Chairman of the Sudeten German Socialist Party 1938; emigrated to England in 1939; re-entered politics in the Federal Republic of Germany.

Reichenberg.

21.8.36.

Darling A,

Your countrymen, even over the frontier, drive me dotty, and I long for you. Now I have seen a deer from my train and I miss you more than ever. How can your country hold two such opposites together, as the stillest and most beautiful country, and the most disordered and almost, if you would not be hurt, ugly-minded people. Just sometimes one meets somebody as still and peaceful as the woods and then there is nobody better in the world—but how many and many one meets who seem to drive all stillness and beauty away. I am depressed—Reichenberg is hateful—it set all my nerves on edge and I decided suddenly to leave. My mother is wonderful and packed up without protesting. Now we are going thro' beautiful country, and she runs from side to side of the carriage like a child and is shocked at my writing and only glancing up—I long to be alone and wish I could walk in the woods we pass and wait for the deer again—darling, I miss you and want so often to talk to you about the things which drive me dotty. It is the whole atmosphere and the sort of intensity which Germans have. It is almost as if they feel rather than think with their minds—perhaps I am writing nonsense and you will say I am being a journalist again. I want really to understand Germany and Europe. I will learn and learn German until I can read your literature and history without faltering—now I still only read newspapers but I learn from them, and learning on a book spoils it and I want to understand at once when I read. Will you think out a plan for me? You will learn how to teach your children.

I have started the Idiot[1] and I long for tomorrow afternoon when we will go into the country, perhaps see the Elbe and stay all Saturday and Sunday. Then to Prague again where there will surely be a letter from you—Now I will read—I ought to try and sort out all the stories I've been told and what they mean and what the solution of the problem is—but I feel so hopeless about it. It is always the same problem. What is the future of Europe? I wish we could solve it together. Alone it unbalances me very much—You are the only bridge I have in this unknown, rather feared, and often hated world. Stay close, whatever happens.

Goodnight, my sweet—

S.

¹ Dostoevsky, *The Idiot.*

Prague.¹

23.8.36.

Darling A,

 . . . I came back here after all yesterday and did not stay in the country. It was wet and rainy and I longed to sleep in my own bed. I stayed one night in Bodenbach² and saw one of the people I should have seen on my way home from Dresden. It turned out that it was better after all to have seen them now than earlier. I recovered a little bit from my Reichenberg depression and met a sensible man in Bodenbach who cheered me up a little bit. I'm afraid I find the problem disagreeable and study it against my will—especially now when I want to read about the French Revolution and pre-war history. But I will try and be very patient and objective. You would be pleased (fairly) with the message I sent the Observer, though I was not very pleased with it. Recordable facts are against me, but the real principles which are at stake support me.

 I don't know what you mean by saying that I will bring on the Spanish state³ all over Europe if I do what I want to do. Remember who started the Spanish War. Are we just to stand still and let them win over the rest of Europe, because if we do not let them, they will commit the same sort of atrocities here?

 I deny absolutely that any of the neighbours of Germany are a danger to her. Everyone is ready for peace and for the construction of some sort of European system. The only things they are not ready for are bilateral pacts which leave a very strong spider talking to a very weak fly. In the realm of spiders and flies, England is still the largest spider, though we don't seem to know it, and I think it is our job to look after the flies. That is what I am trying to do and is very remote from Spain. If it brings on the Spanish state in all Europe, it is the fault of the spiders.

I asked Nehru once whether revolutions always meant dictatorship and oppression. He said his sort did not mean it unless the other side appealed to violence, then he would have to answer with violence. There will always be violence in politics. I think we learnt slowly in Europe, though we often forgot, and we got as far as the liberal democracies of England and France. We might have got further only those who lost some of their power and those who were impatient to get hold of the power still denied them, turned to using violence on their own account, and now we are in danger of losing everything.

I don't want to be made hostile to you, and am not mad because I am not a spectator and you an actor, as you believe. We are both spectators and actors at the same time and not so very much divided. If I were ever to become only a spectator, I would not watch this particular play, there are nicer ones to watch, wiser and more peaceful. I would have children and live in the country somewhere very remote and read books and bathe and have a farm.

The Idiot moves me more and more. Dostoievski's love of children is very very touching. The Russians are incredible and make life seem all of infinite beauty and splendour. The girl is wonderful and so is the Idiot. I wish she had married him in the first place. . . .

Love
Z.

[1] Answer to letter Adam–Shiela, Kassel, 18 Aug. 1936.
[2] Bordertown between Germany and Czechoslovakia; now Podmokly.
[3] See letter Shiela–Adam, Prague, 18 Aug. 1936.

Kassel.[1]
24.8.36.

My darling Duff,

Thank you for your letter from the train. My God, how often I think they are dotty, and how true it is that their number is very many, and how much more awful it is to be dependent on them for something you must have from them. But this dottiness is something very serious that must be dealt with and cannot be dealt with by the lid theory[2] which I am afraid you subconsciously followed by running away from them. These psychological incompatibilities which are so painful between you and me (in the singular) will—if they are not dealt with rationally—no doubt stew up to the same kind of plural incompatibility that our fathers did not prevent, and left to us in the shape of a messy deteriorated Europe.

The point is, sweet, we cannot stay close whatever happens,[3] because if that happens again all Duff–Trott coalitions are going to be torn asunder. . . .

How right you are about the Russians! The Idiot perhaps more than any other book (except perhaps Hölderlin's Hyperion, and Hegel's Philosophy of State) has made my outlook for what it is worth.

We do really admire the same things, but all our secondary habits are as different as can be. Both our habitual lives are not so good—not what they might be.

I never told you that you prevented me from killing a beautiful stag in the Trottenwald the other day. I sat there watching a vast slope with yellow dry grass up and down, bending though in the middle that I couldn't look further than 20 metres to the opposite fringe of the wood. Later on in the evening I happened to read a letter of yours when I suddenly heard footsteps and saw a stag before me. I couldn't move, and dropped your letter, which made him turn and move back to the pines. I saw him again later, but too far away. You would have loved his superb solemn movements. . . .

. . . Stop making me love you when you aren't willing to answer for it. We must be very proud but we must also have care for each other. Think a little and you will find out what it means. I love ducks well, but I love the young growing swan we saw together when you were here still better—the swans altogether which are so awkward when they walk on land.[4]

Goodnight darling Duff.

Your Trott.

[1] Answer to letters Shiela–Adam, Prague, 18 Aug. 1936; 19 Aug. 1936 and Reichenberg, 21 Aug. 1936.

[2] The 'lid theory', originally Mowrer's, was advanced by Shiela to Adam since the time of remilitarization of the Rhineland (7 Mar. 1936); it implied a kind of containment policy of the Western powers towards Germany. Adam saw it, however, as a threat because it reminded him of the humiliating Versailles Treaty; he envisaged a general European settlement rather than an Anglo-French peace.

[3] In case of war.

[4] Shiela and Adam often watched the ducks and swans in the parks Adam took her to in July and they were inspired to draw analogies between them and their own characters and their relations to each other.

Prague—Karlsbad.
26.8.36.

Darling Adam,

You don't deserve a letter—your country does nothing but infuriate me, and yet it's a most wonderful day, the country is noble and sweeping, and we have just left a station where the peasants were dancing on the platform—so I am very gay now too, after four days of half-depression. Even your hateful militarism cannot take the light out of the sun or the colour from the country—who now is producing a Spanish state all over Europe?[1] German foreign policy is becoming ingenious—blessed indeed are the simple-minded, but I'm sure God himself knew limits. Still, politics, you say, divide us, so divided we be—I will tell you about the corn sheaves which lean against each other in the fields, and the hops which, in this country are as dignified as forests, and the hills far away which I suppose your splendid millionaire army will march over, singing, one day, because of the poor oppressed Germans and the wicked Bolsheviks. They too make me sick with this buffooning trial[2]—I am beginning to believe in no one but myself . . . I believe very much I was born to save the world some way, and perhaps solving the G.P. is the way.[3] And the solution, dear A, is making you somehow citizens of Europe because at the moment you have no manners for society and should be excluded till you learnt some. Has Chesterfield been translated into German? Will you be angry? . . .

Yes—I am feeling decidedly cross after all—your last letter about Spain made me angry[4]—(lovely sparkling river below me—am fond of you really and the sun is shining) and today's news has finished it off.[5] . . .

Karlsbad.

Darling sweet, Karlsbad is wonderful and I am profoundly pro-Trott—please let's come here when we both have white hair (yours a wig), when we have had lives of infinite beauty and splendour, and we will walk very slowly through the woods till we sit where I am sitting now and see the plain full of people whom our noble and splendid lives have made happy—This is an absurd place—all that it should be for Turgenev girls—absurd 19th century flamboyant hotel architecture, white painted chairs and tables everywhere, trees with red berries on them, and pine woods and hills. I am very happy and wish you were here. . . .

Karlsbad is beautiful but it covers appalling poverty—people are hungry and ill with hunger. Your people, as they are called, are not oppressed politically, but are in a ghastly state of poverty, and the fault not a small part of yours. I don't know why anti-social economic policies are not stopped—the Czechs cannot support the broken export industries that we support. The unemployed . . . are discontent so you can imagine the bitterness here and what it leads to. All the blame is put on the national issue and there is only an international economic way out. Don't find me cross. In myself I am happy and friendly and fond of the Trott.

Love
S.

[1] Cf. letter Adam–Shiela, Kassel, 18 Aug. 1936; also letter Shiela–Adam, Prague, 23 Aug. 1936.
[2] Reference to one of the great show trials in Russia against the 'Old Bolsheviks', most likely the one against Grigori E. Zinoviev, Lev Kamenev, and others; see Robert Conquest, *The Great Terror: Stalin's Purge of the Thirties* (New York, 1968), pp. 82 ff.
[3] German problem.
[4] The letter is missing.
[5] Most likely the reports in *The Times* of 25 and 26 Aug. about Hitler's decree extending the period of compulsory military service in the German armed forces from one year to two years.

Karlsbad.
27.8.36.

[Dear Adam,]
    . . . We will have to be very very best friends in Europe to put up with some of the things that happen, and worse—that we will each do. . . .

Z.

Herrnskretschen.
Saturday 29 August, 1936.

Darling Trott,
    This time I really have run away and am in a lovely lovely place on the Elbe—just where it becomes German. I send you a picture of the village because I'm sure you will approve of my being here. I have not seen the Elbe to-day because the banks are high and the sun doesn't shine there till late in the morning, so I came up this valley. At one

point you can walk no further and must take a boat through black sunless water and high grey cliffs. It is very beautiful and very still. Now I have climbed up one of the cliffs and am in the sun and the stream rustles below, a long way down.

When I was sitting by the stream lower down a boy came and sat beside me. I was very cold to him and said I wanted to be alone but he would not go away. He thought I was German and when I said I was not, he took it for granted I was Czech and I let him. When he went away (we quarrelled all the time) he said he knew I had a Deutsche Seele[1] (and had lost it only through bad education) and for all I said—wished me well as a deutsches Mädchen[2] (because I have blue eyes). I was rather petulant because I wanted to be alone—and my German collapsed altogether—even to understanding what he said. It all ended by him addressing me as a woman (and therefore Göttlicher[3] than a man) and wishing me a nice husband. They are certainly dotty but I agree the lid theory is no good and I have no other and perhaps there is no other possible for the moment. I argued once with Mowrer your way and he answered: 'If a man stands at your door with a pistol and says "I want what you have and if I cannot have it, I will kill you" you do not give it him and go away to think what is the cause and what is the cure of crime. You call in the police.' When a nice, unfanatical German boy says to me. 'England is finished. France is going under. Jews, Christianity and communism are the three united enemies of Europe. The German race alone is ehrlich[4] and must rule, I wonder if it is not time to count my soldiers. I agree, darling Adam, the lid is not the way out but one thing is absolutely certain—the only way out is for Europeans to know what they mean by Europe, to know how Europe is threatened now and to be ready to die for what they believe and what they want to make. And being ready to die is the lid theory. If we do not believe as intensely in ourselves, as you believe, then it is true—we are finished. We must believe, and believing, it is not a lid but a barricade that we must make and not a barricade against Germany (that not because Europe without Germany would be a Europe with a cancer growing in it) but a barricade against the real threats to the Europe one believes in. The boy was right. The Jews, Christianity and communism are united and they are the Europe I believe in. And by communism, I do not mean the Russian grimace but Christianity. From Christianity and from the Greeks and Romans, all our civilisation descends. We cannot now turn aside and believe in Race and Nature about which this boy spoke. It is terribly terribly difficult because one does not only wish to preserve but to create as well. Mowrer said we were standing with out backs to the wall and could not afford to risk

the wall falling by changing the stones in it and yet perhaps it will fall
if we do not change the stones—but which stones?

Your letter of Monday was sent to Bodenbach where I found it
yesterday. I realize that the incompatibilities between us are serious
and between the plural us, terribly so, and perhaps my wish to stay
close whatever happens is vain and even wrong, if you ask me not to
make you love me. If you ask it, I will stop. About the duck and the
swan I do not understand. It means something to me but I think not
what you meant it to mean. Either one is a duck or one is a swan—
even the ugly duckling was a swan all the time[5]—perhaps he would
not have been brave enough to grow up and then would have died
believing himself and believed by others—a duck. So one must be
brave. I will try, dear Trott, and you need not love me any more. I
will answer for the bit the best friends in Europe must love each other
and I will try—and defend the D–T coalition and the Europe–Germany one too. I think we care a very great deal for the same things. Is
it dangerous for our own caring for each other to treat our hopes and
our doubts as the miniatures of the greater question? Duff–Trott:
Europe–Germany do not match at all. I perhaps psychologically my
part and you yours—but you intellectually and spiritually are my
part as well as yours.

When the German boy, thinking me Czech, said 'England is finished' I felt nationalist for the first time in my life. Is that healthy or
unhealthy? I have always believed more in something we can all
share and hate this dividing up and shutting out. I wonder how many
people came from the Olympic Games fervent nationalists? and
whether the world will be better for it. England is beautiful. Nowhere
is the countryside so gentle and sweet and English poetry is
unequalled. Must we then build aeroplanes and guns and go to war
and die because we are not 'healthy' any more? The British Empire
may grow smaller because the Indians too are proud and independent, because negroes wish to be free. Is England finished because she
has taught her subjects what freedom and democracy are? If Germany has her colonies back, there will be a revolt of all coloured
peoples if we have taught them anything. Italy, Germany and Japan
alone are the healthy nations they say because they have not 'finished' a stage of development we should be ashamed not to have left
behind. Darling Adam, your German boy made me angry indeed.
Who has told your countrymen they are ehrlich—ehrlich—I can't
even spell the word—that every one of them tells one how ehrlich
ehrlich they are. The English are smug and complacent but it is
hardly a quality the Germans need to copy.

Now I have made myself very very cross and I am hungry too and far from home. The bees are very happy in the heather and the air is full of hot summer sounds and smells. It is undisturbed on my hill and no one passes on the road below me. It is sad we cannot pass our spare time together. When will you visit me? I will come back to the German frontier with you and we will stay here? When do you go to Berlin? And how long for? Tell me what you will do.

LOVE

Z.

[Postscript omitted]

  [1] A German soul.
  [2] A German girl.
  [3] More Divine.
  [4] Honourable, honest.
  [5] 'The Ugly Duckling' by Hans Christian Andersen was a favourite fairy-tale of Shiela's childhood.

Tuesday 1 Sept. [1936]

Darling A,

You are good and nice to write me such warm letters when I write you such cross ones. Thank you very much. It made my home coming much nicer, for otherwise I didn't think much of it and still do not think very much of it. I feel very revolted by this journalism. The Observer is most tendentious about what I write, granted I write tendentiously too but I like my own tendencies better than theirs. The heading of my latest effort is Striking Power of the Czech Army—as if the wretched people could stike anything at all. And I wrote an absolute knock-out for Henlein[1] which they have ignored. They want me to write all about Russian aerodromes and communist dangers as if they were your countrymen. I want to run away and live a private life.

Your letter was very nice—may you perhaps go on loving me a little bit however hard I try not to make you? I did not mean you personally having no manners for society, you have nice ones and would make beautiful society like the Prince imagined the Epanchins'[2] party was like. I meant that Europe cannot any more be made up of melodramatic acts and lies and bigger and bigger armies and bigger and bigger lies; no I don't even mean that quite. I meant that there must be some sort of international order whether it be law or convention or justice or well-wishing, and every act since the war seems to have destroyed even the semblance of law that was there before it.

And in the last four years, one country has most of the blame. Things are really disgraceful. I don't think good people exist any more in the world and life is ugly. Now I am being cross again. I had lunch with some English and that always makes me cross because they complain and grumble, because they have foul manners and are snobs. I don't want to be cross. I want to be back in Herrnskretschen.

It was so lovely there. Yesterday was perhaps loveliest of all. Everyone said it was a bad day and an unfriendly day and how awful the weather was, but it was so lovely. A giant noble wind and giant clouds, everything on a very big scale, the sun very bright when it shone, the rain very hard when it fell, and the sky wide like it sometimes seems. I walked up a winding road and found a Churchyard which was very peaceful and the grave stones were very moving. I found a lovely wide hay field and sheltered in a hay cock and a man came along and did not think to turn me away and there seemed so many things to think of. The Idiot moves me very much. He is a most beautiful character. Do you think Dostoievski was himself like that? He was epileptic wasn't he? I don't understand Aglaya?[3] Do you like her? I admire the other wild mad woman more. Aglaya seems to do nothing but laugh and sulk and is not at all generous. Why does everyone love her? I wish I could write just one book like that about the people I have known. I want them to live forever.

You could teach me manners more than I teach you. I know I must have bad ones or people would not be so rude with me. I would gladly teach you anything I could but I don't think I have anything to teach. Perhaps happiness a little but it doesn't seem teachable. . . .

Love
S.

[1] Konrad Henlein (1898–1945), leader of the Sudeten German Party; he became a tool of Adolf Hitler in the dismemberment of Czechoslovakia. This passage was deliberately ambiguous because of Nazi censorship; Shiela's 'knock out' in fact was *against* Henlein.

[2] From Dostoevsky's novel *The Idiot*; Prince Lef Nicolaievich Myshkin, General Epanchin, his wife, and daughter Aglaya.

[3] Ibid.

Imshausen.
4.9.36.

Darling S,

How good that you wrote this second letter on top of the 'cross' one, which bewildered and frightened me a little . . . and also made me hate this insufferable habit of journalism to pick up 'impressions of everyday life,' and elaborate on that substance an equally unbalanced and painful wrath by which nothing but the general confusion is furthered. . . .

Of course, neither of us have very much right to be complacent about our respective countries, though in some specific aspects we have, and you to a large extent in the political aspect which gives you an unfair advantage because it is mostly that aspect one refers to when comparing countries. (I admit though that I considered ourselves even there in a relative advantage as long as we were in no more danger of teaching the coloured comrades what you are teaching them.) The real point surely is that there is no good in comparing countries in that way and to listen anxiously to the sentiments of vulgar Saxonians, because that, and I'm afraid most journalists' habits of thinking and feeling end with counting one's soldiers and not only counting them. . .

Bless you dear darling

Love
A.

Prague.
5.9.36.

Darling Adam,

You have not written for a long time. I hope there is nothing wrong. . . .

The air is full of birds. I think they must be on their way South. I wish you could have come here before summer is over. It is nearly over now. I am going to Bratislava for the conference of the Little Entente[1] next Friday. I think it will be very gay, like a party. The sessions are in private so I don't see what other reasons journalists go there for but to enjoy themselves. That is why I am going anyway, tho' I hope also to learn about Yugoslavia, Roumania from the Y and R journalists, and to make some friends. I can then visit in Belgrade and Bucharest. . . .

I would like to go into the country this weekend and instead have to think very seriously about the Little Entente. I know it all so well. Their policy has not changed for 15 years, and anyway, in the end, they have no policy—they can only pray that the great powers will not endanger them, and it is rather a pathetic prayer now—I can't solve the German problem. No doubt the lid is no good, but supposing Germany wishes to expand—territorial expansion is impossible because the world is not a vacuum—economic expansion with Schacht's present policy[2] means political dependence. It is the Zollverein[3] again. So then the question comes, which is better, to allow or oppose the expansion—the one means war, the other means the end of European civilisation, which has developed along Christian, individualistic ways. War is ghastly and terrible for the individual suffering it means: but the other is suicide for the individual. Do I talk nonsense? I do not know, you see, I do not understand your country or your countrymen, but they seem to be denying all the good as well as the evil Europe has made. Italy is worse, of course, but Italy has so far been only her own grave and the Abyssinians! Russia never represented Europe at all, and therefore, I think, is no danger for Europe. My German is much better—this winter I will try and make it quite perfect, and will read your books. I must learn a few words of Czech too, for sometimes it is very difficult. . . .

Love,

S.

---

[1] The Little Entente (Czechoslovakia, Yugoslavia, Romania) was formed in 1920–1; its original purpose was to forestall a resurgence of Hungary; it became in the course of the nineteen twenties a tool of French foreign policy aimed at maintaining the European status quo.

[2] Hjalmar Schacht (1877–1970), German financier; helped Hitler to power; served under the Nazis as Minister of Economics (1934–7); President of the Reichsbank (1933–9); Minister without Portfolio (1937–43). He developed German trade through bartering agreements with Balkan and Near Eastern countries and financed German rearmament. He became increasingly disillusioned with National Socialism, turned to the Resistance through which he was connected with Adam. Arrested after the plot against Hitler in July 1944.

[3] Shiela in fact had in mind the Customs Union (Zollunion) which was launched by Germany and Austria in Mar. 1931. It was vigorously opposed by France and its satellites as an infringement of Austrian independence and a new threat of German dominance of Central Europe. The International Court at The Hague, to which the matter was finally referred, handed down a verdict against the project.

1. Imshausen. *Courtesy of the von Trott family*

2. An aerial view of High Elms (the Lubbocks' country house) 1926

3. Shiela Grant Duff

4. Adam von Trott zu Solz

5. The wooden cross, erected near by the Trott family seat and looking out on the surrounding Hessian hills, carries at its base the following inscription: 'Adam von Trott zu Solz. Executed with his friends in the struggle against the despoiler of our country. Pray for them, take their example to heart.'
Courtesy of the von Trott family

Zamecka.
[*about* 10 September 36]

Well—well—well—I didn't think it was as bad as all that, and I still believe you're unreasonably put out by my Herrnskretschen letter. . . .

Now . . . you must answer back, because I am very seriously disturbed by the problem and want to solve it.

First of all, about journalism—this new attack—(you need only put 'foreign' in front of it to be perfectly at one with the leading thinkers of your countrymen.) The 'insufferable habit of journalism to pick up impressions of everyday life and elaborate . . . an unbalanced wrath'—what do you mean? If you mean I was wrong to find *all* Saxons disagreeable because I found some so—well and good, but that is a personal and not a professional mistake. If you meant it wrong to find out the problem of the German minority by talking exclusively to beggars and waiters, you're quite right again—but you seemed to be condemning the only possible method of journalism, which is to study problems in general, by facts and figures and treaties and policies, and then to see the actual conditions to which all those apply. I admit that I 'elaborate on that substance an equally painful and unbalanced wrath, by which nothing but the general confusion is furthered,' but that is a matter of my own temperament, rather than of journalism, and your accusation should have been personal instead of assuring me that it was not. The truth is that I don't move along the same lines as your countrymen, and when I come against them, they rub me up and anger me. But when I write, I try to remember that. In any case, my paper is now directed by Lord Lothian,[1] and I am sure he remembers it. This is all off the main point, which is that your attitude to journalism I find vulgar and unthinking and it infuriates me—there! By this onslaught you need not be bewildered or frightened, for if it is unjustified you can prove that it is, and if it is justified you can mend your opinions.

Now, I will attack you for not going on with the problem at all, and instead saying (something also very silly) that it is no good comparing countries politically—no, you can't be as silly as that—your English went very much to bits. Writing for the pleasure of the postman[2] has a shocking effect on style—and style being the man (we used to write essays at school on that subject[3]) what will all the men be like soon? In fact, I see you don't say anything at all on my problem, so I shall drop the subject and just tell you the concrete form it has these days.

The Little Entente is based on the maintenance of the status quo in

Europe. She is the stabilising power, Germany and the Rome Powers are the dynamic. The problem is what sort of power is this dynamic power? And how can it be either directed into other channels than territorial aggrandisement, which means war? or should it be stopped altogether? It is a perfectly concrete political problem which journalists and politicians are called on to solve. The only difference between a journalist thinking about these things and an ordinary man, is that the journalist thinks out loud, and it is his duty to think more deeply and more concretely than other people. What do you say to that?

But my hand is aching and I have quarrelled enough. It is not quarrelling, darling A, really, but I do beseech you to be determined and firm. When I am hysterical and stupid, the thing is to say so, and not be distressed, and above all you must realise that I am in deadly earnest about all this and it is important for us too. . . .

Love then
Shiela.

¹ Lord Lothian, one of the chief advocates of the appeasement policy, had joined the Editorial Board of the *Observer*.

² The censor.

³ 'Le style est l'homme même' (the style is the man himself): Comte de Buffon (1707–88), *Discours sur le Style*, on admission to the French Academy, 1753.

Bellers
Hessen.
7.9.36.

My darling Duff,

. . . I feel there's a danger of war breaking out between us, and that my last letter wasn't much good in making you stop counting your soldiers. In the meantime, you will be pleased to hear, I have dismissed mine for pleasanter occupations: celebrate the end of harvest with beer and dancing, dig potatoes, chase deer, read books, and listen to the high autumnal winds—which are so unaware of this restlessness they pass. You are letting this Europe grow on you too much, and it will devour all your unspoilt pleasure if you aren't careful. I wondered whether you would have considered me an awful barbarian at that village feast when you danced and drank to the morning and laughed about the funny drunks.

But really I was very sad thinking that all the time so many things are obstructing us, and that I can't do much about them, and hate the filthy mess of politics being so hard on you.

I respect and understand very well the need of being alone adequately—I feel it myself. And also I know its close connection with the best things that have gone before in our lives. To find one's own peace one must remain true to them, and not urge on them new things which make the old 'seem nonsense' as you once put it.

We are not doing that darling. But we are being very impatient with each other and we mustn't be any longer.

What will happen with Spain? I haven't seen the news for a number of days—but it looked very sinister when I saw them last.

I am staying with Heini[1] in his hut now—somehow he is even sadder—it's partly to do with his having to leave this place and do his labour and military service. He has been reading about the Greeks, and them themselves, and has not been bothered by the things that threaten us.

But darling Duff, there's no escaping them one way or other—one must endeavour to accept these difficulties in and around one—there's no paradise to retreat to anywhere. Neither this place nor China are paradises. Have you gone to Vienna, and do you still plan to come to Berlin? Please do—if I don't see you it will become more and more difficult to disentangle the big lump of things which I shall not feel well before I have shared it out with you. I shall be very good about you wanting your peace from me. I am ashamed of having been interfering and arrogant, and I think that my last letter must have seemed so too. Could you not have a little more confidence in my love for you—both being good even if my letters are bad? Don't decide in the end we are both too different and difficult that it is a strain to continue. We are, I think, both children of a yet unborn civilisation, but its and our hope should be that it must be born if this present one is not going to be destroyed. And if it's going to be destroyed, darling, let us love each other well in the meantime—we will bear it all with more dignity then—but should we not remain a little more hopeful in the face of it all still? We aren't yet used up, are we? And the sooner you get away from that journalism the less you will be.

Write to me my sweet—and I will do all the better for us—don't be cross anymore.

Love
A.

[Postscript omitted]

[1] Adam's younger brother Hans Heinrich Siegfried (1918–). known as Heinrich or 'Heini'.

Imshausen.
14.9.36.

Darling Zamecka,

. . . Sorry to write distressed letters—I promise that I won't do it any more, and the matter about the individual and Europe, to which you are perfectly right to refer, is a deadly one, and equally bad for all of us. But there must be a way out of the 'world-civil-war' that is threatening to break out, with either side of which we are profoundly out of sympathy—as Werner puts it in one of his letters . . . I never could speak very well while I swam, I get water into my nose. Only when I imagine I'm a swan I can talk and chatter while floating about. But I am not a swan, I am a heavy fat sea lion with a lot of bestial resource though the water is running all over my nose and eyes—I dive deeply and reappear with a sigh of strength and satisfaction. Thank you for the nice picture of ducks and swans—it makes the ducks look altogether better and tougher, and the swans complacent and self-satisfied. . . .

Love and five kisses
A.

[*Postscript omitted*]

Vienna.
17.9.36.

Darling A,

. . . Vienna is lovely but most lovely is to live in a home and to be woken up in the morning by a little girl and to be given presents by her—life is very gentle and sweet like that.[1] And the sun shines very bright and hard now autumn is coming, and makes me feel strong and full of endeavour. I tried to answer your letter in Bratislava[2] and did answer it, but my answer was angry and hard and undeserved. I mind you wanting me to be free of politics and journalism, tho' when I come into private lives I understand what you mean—but I do not want to be free of it. It is more important to me than anything in my private life, even tho' that is happier and richer perhaps than ever before. You do not understand when you condemn my life, for it is not condemnable. I am learning more than ever before and not only from newspapers and superficially. I am trying to learn seriously and fundamentally about the world, about politics and people, languages, towns and books, and I feel a great release from the bonds of the last years, and a greater certainty and wholeness inside. . . .

I slept a long time and then read Marcus Aurelius,[3] whose principles I am a little in need of, and whom I find severe and necessary. When I go back to Prague I shall work really hard, and also have German and Czech lessons. You will disapprove of the latter, but wrongly. I am going to understand Central Europe, and a Slav language is necessary, and Germans and Slavs and Western democracies are all part of Europe. I like the Czechs more and more and prefer them to their partners of the Little Entente, tho' I understand why they appeal little to the imagination as people. But I find the English attitude to Central Europeans on the one hand, and the Germans and Austrians on the other—one of self indulgence. Vienna is much more luxurious than Prague, and German policy now makes Englishmen feel very important there . . . I am sorry you will not think about the German problem with me. . . .

Love always—
Shiela.

[1] This was Connie, daughter of Muriel Gardiner, an American who studied medicine and trained for psychoanalysis in Vienna and became actively involved in the Austrian socialist underground. Shiela stayed with her repeatedly when in Vienna.

[2] Shiela had been attending the Conference of the Little Entente there.

[3] Marcus Aurelius (121–80 AD), Roman Emperor (161–80 AD) and stoic philosopher, author of the *Meditations*.

Prague.
[*about* 24 September] 1936.

Darling A,

. . . I am afraid you are upset and finding it very hard to work. I wish I could help you, but do not think seeing you now was the best way of helping you—or perhaps that was selfishness. People can help one, but in the end one can only save oneself by oneself. It is hard and painful sometimes, but has to be done. When people are kind and gentle one can afford to be more severe with oneself. That is what I find here.

I wrote to Nehru a rather apologetic letter, asking him not to think I had deserted him, and had a very nice letter back[1] saying that his work is only part of political work and he does that rather than anything else because he fits in there better than anywhere else, but if I find I fit in better somewhere else, I am right to do it. He thinks also it is more important to stop war than anything else, and says he does not think any good can come, even for India, from a world catastrophe. I was thinking of an imperialist war being the chance for the colonial people, but he does not seem to agree. He is a very admirable man. But I think he has doubts, which will make him a less great political leader for being a much greater man. I think he is one of the best people I have ever met. I wish he were a European and I could work with him to save Europe. . . .

S.

¹ For the texts of Shiela's letter and Nehru's answer see Grant Duff, *The Parting of Ways*, pp. 117 f.

27.9.36.

Darling,
    . . . What you say about Nehru makes me like you very much, though it is vicious apparently to have done entirely with the Trott as European co-operator. But perhaps you are right: to us both Europe gives only problems, and bloody ones I know, and they haunt us and don't let us be what God meant us to be. Human greatness is the only thing that can really surmount national boundaries—you see it in art and thought and great action. I think you have the most spontaneous admiration for greatness I have ever found in a person. I think you are probably right about Nehru. . . .

always love
A.

EDITOR'S NOTE

Late in October 1936 Adam visited Shiela in Prague; upon his request he met Otto Strasser, one of the chief dissidents from the Nazi Party who had moved into exile in Prague in 1933. He and his brother Gregor (who was murdered by the Nazis during the purge of 30 June 1934) had been leaders of the left wing of the Nazi Party in the nineteen twenties stressing the 'socialist' premisses of National Socialism. Otto Strasser was expelled from the Party in 1930 and founded a splinter party, the Union of Revolutionary National Socialists, known as 'Black Front'. Adam was attracted by Otto Strasser's emphasis on socialism and by his plans to work towards a revolutionary German government that was eventually to negotiate with the Western powers; see Grant Duff, *The Parting of Ways* p. 147. This meeting is particularly interesting in the light of Adam's essay 'Nationalism and Internationalism' (1934), Trott Archive, in which he projected the realization of his socialist objectives within the framework of a 'rational and constructive order of national and international society'; these thoughts were not far removed from those of Otto Strasser.

Prague.
1.11.36.

Darling Adam,

I have read all my papers, eaten my supper, done everything immediate that I ought to have done, and 9 o'clock is striking. You are still on your long journey, and lest I fall asleep tonight while you lose your way, and seem to fail you again, I will write you a letter.

You are right to reproach me and I am very sorry that I do not help you or give you any impression that I am near and strong and solidaric. Yet it is not true, nor that I underestimate you. I admire you very much, and especially lately, and if you win through this crisis[1] alone, you will be glad in the end that you are able to do it; and I am nearer than you think.

I am very sorry you have gone away. It was too short, and only now am I beginning to remember a thousand things I wanted to ask and know about. When I am away from my friends I freeze up and melt only very slowly back into their lives. I am very much contained in all the forms and facts of my daily life. I'm sorry it makes me such a bad friend.

Our walk in Prague was very nice, and it was lovely to see one day of Autumn. This stout grey rain is chilling, and this afternoon I began to be depressed for the first time for so long—tho' I slept and I worked and now I feel better—Now you are four hours beyond Leipzig, perhaps I can write one more letter and go to bed.

Look after yourself and write to me very fully about what decisions you make, about Imshausen and the woods—perhaps it is still autumn—and about all those timeless, restless processes which go on in your head.

Much love
Shiela.

[1] The condition of Germany and the difficulty of finding a place and work for Adam in it.

Prague.
2.11.36.

Darling Adam,

I miss you very much today. There are so many things I want to talk to you about, and so many things left unsaid. I feel almost as if I had woken up and found you gone rather than let you go with my eyes open. I was as bad a companion to you as I feared I would be, and you must forgive me and trust it will not always be so. I wish very much we could share an impersonal life together for a while—perhaps in Berlin it will be possible if we meet people together, then we can talk about them and what they say, and so see things as not being part of your life or my life, but as life going on round us.

Today has been very wet and cold. I wasted the morning in a car with the English, a car which never found the way, so we just sat in it. It was quite comfortable. This afternoon I had coffee with Barbara,[1] who was pleased with you. You had pleased Neill[2] most by telling him what your brother had said to us about him. Barbara did not ask much about you. I told her that for you she represented a tradition which you cared for very much, and she sighed and protested a little as if the tradition no longer lived. I said it was very important she should influence Neill rather than Neill her, and she accepted it a little unwillingly. When I said I was not really fit to judge it, she said, Yes, you know a lot. . . .

Now I must read my Sunday paper. It is very very long. Mussolini seems to have made another insolent speech. I want to read history books and do more work. My face is burning; I like wet walks on the outskirts of town and country—so many wet walks in Oxford.

I feel very solidaric to you and contrite for my absence from your side. We will save the world between us. You give me great hope and great ambition. I believe profoundly in you and admire you very much, and approve what you have done in the last three years.— Only it is difficult to say, and even now seems crude and unnecessary—but without, you do not believe it—

Bless you, Lots of love,
Shiela.

[1] Code-name for Wenzel Jaksch; see letter Shiela–Adam, 19 Aug. 1936 n. 2.
[2] Code-name for Otto Strasser.

Imshausen.
Nov. 3. 1936.

Sweet Shiela,

Before I got your letter, on my two walks—one alone and one with Monika who is staying with her boy—I thought of writing you these things: that my visit with you was very good for me and I thanked you for it—and that only when I remembered how terribly beautiful you were when you danced in your dark silk dress with Ripka and leaning back, smiled at him, I felt as if the burning wax of a candle was being spilt inside me... that I was happy to remember you saying that you would like to walk with me in these fields here—that when I stopped to tie the laces of my shoes and smelt the peculiarly winterly smell of the wet and smeary ground, and saw the dead yellow grass; all that was more part of me than any philosophy in the world, and that that was quite easy for you to understand—also the Imshausen always looks rather decrepit in many ways in the winter as all the houses of the poor gentry do—that speaking to the boys on the field was lovely and fresh, and that when I descended to Solz from the hills the village band was playing 'Ein Jäger aus Kurpfalz'...¹ (do you remember it? I sang it to you in the Weser valley one afternoon when we stopped the car because it was raining too hard?)—and that I am pleased my sister has a lovely fat little boy, like an old Chinese who likes nothing better than grandsons. And last night I wrote a letter to your mother (I hope she doesn't mind being pursued by so many) as I wasn't sure how right it was to write to you at the time.

And now your very nice letter came and I am happy, and when you ask me to tell you all my troubles I must think hard, and I find I have none, except those we all share more or less consciously—only with me they are conscious in a positive and simple way. I think, you know, good old Neill was very important for me to meet, for whatever his detail qualities are, his will is determined and he will not make mistakes out of fear, though perhaps out of lack of thought. I am thankful to you for being my link to him. Do not tell Ripka anything about it, and tell me if you had to. From England I have had no answer yet—somehow I think the travelling fund will not prove as accessible as I thought. I think I will leave on Friday and be in Frankfurt till Monday, then go to London. On the 15th I will go to Oxford and perhaps stay a week, then go back to London and stay as long as I think profitable and possible. At a pinch I can delay my entrance into that Institute² till after Dec. 1 and you know I am not missed anywhere over here when I happen to be absent.

I bought an interesting novel on the way back—Rebecca West's

'The Thinking Reed'[3]—she must be a very intelligent woman and I am looking forward to meeting her. I told you I made her acquaintance in Hamburg when she asked me to come and see her when I am in London. She prefaced her book by a quotation from Pascal's Pensées: 'Man is but a reed, the most feeble thing in nature; but he is a thinking reed. The entire universe need not arm itself to crush him. A vapour, a drop of water suffices to kill him. But if the universe were to crush him, man would still be more noble than that which killed him, because he knows that he dies and the advantage which the universe has over him; the universe knows nothing of this.'—it was a comfort to read this praise of man's thinking capacity, and Mrs. West's wise and delicate, though at times sightly affected application of it, when I had had such a severe lesson all my thinking was wrong. But in that I think you are right; that it may prove better for me and my friends to win through this crisis by myself. To a large extent it is not their crisis too—to some extent it is, and they, I think, realise it. I don't think it is exactly 'help' I was asking from my friends. But I am thankful in the end when they hate me to be too humble when I ask what I want from them, because it is a sort of fraud making them and me forget that in the end I must and will do without it.—You and I are very queer creatures together—you are right: not as far away as we think, but strangely unmelted. When the bigger glaciers melt there's a big torrent, you know, and as long as the vineyards and villages down the valley are not guarded and built it may be God's wisdom not to let them melt . . . Give my love to Adrienne[4] and Barbara and, darling, you look after yourself and don't mind the grey rain.

Love and write again.

A.

[1]   A German folk-song.
[2]   In Oct. Adam had an interview with Ernst von Simson, a former State Secretary in the Foreign Office and a member of the Supervisory Board of I.G. Farben on entering its legal department. Von Simson advised against it since the personnel policy of the company was by no means free from political considerations. Instead he urged Adam to join the Institute of International Law under Professor Viktor Bruns; Clarita von Trott, 'Materialsammlung', p. 82; Sykes *Loyalty*, p. 176; Malone 'Adam von Trott', p. 170.
[3]   Rebecca West, *The Thinking Reed* (New York, 1936); the quote is from Blaise Pascal, *Pensées*, no. 347 (London, 1908), p. 97.
[4]   Adrienne Borovicka, wife of Prof. Jan Borovicka, historian at the University of Bratislava.

Imshausen.
4.11.36.

Bless you darling,

. . . You are quite right when you think me damn incoherent and young at times, but the point is: I know that too most of the time, and women are not there to state faults, but to help mending them. Now, suddenly, you seem to be willing to do that, and suggest that all your criticism is embraced in a certain belief or trust in the Trott— I think that is very nice, and it will make our friendship flourish. I think it can obviously be at its strongest and best only when we are together—one of the good things about you is that you contain your-self so well in your daily 'forms and facts'—and when one is apart, loyalty to person tends to be loyalty to certain ideas or ways of life, and that is not necessarily a come-down. . . .

The world around us will be important all right when we meet in towns—which will be where we meet before I leave—and our self-importance will be deflated all right by all the battle that means. To think you are solidaric strengthens me a lot—and you must not even become treacherous when I begin to make all my mistakes . . .

Another good walk this afternoon . . . —and a very winterly wood and field. I heard the wild hawks cry way over the tree tops. I love the dusk of winter nights, and the cunning shine in a peasant's eye, whose talk to me may mean 'more land' to him—an extension of the map in his mind. . . .

Bless you sweet,

Love
A.

[*Postscript omitted*]

Prague.
Nov. 9. 1936.

Darling A,

. . . I went to an armistice service yesterday and was rather moved, for all the disagreements I had with the preacher. I wonder if your brother is not right, and that Christianity is impossible. I have got to a point where I can go no further. It seems quite certain that all Christians must condemn war—and I have always believed it a wick-edness of the Christian church that it blessed the fighting troops—on the other side it seems to me equally certain that if one is not pre-pared to fight, the world is given over to the devil. Is it just the sophistry of patriotism that makes one believe one must fight for goodness' sake? All the really noble things of history were not wars, but movements like the Renaissance, scholars and artists who translated the Bible, and the Greeks and Romans who built cities and palaces and monasteries—I do not understand it at all. Perhaps you will one day, and perhaps I would if I were not so worthless. . . .

Love
Shiela.

[*Postscript omitted*]

65 Eccleston Sq.
London.
Tuesday [10?] Nov. 1936.

Darling S,

. . . Before I left Frankfurt the chief legal director of the chemical concern, whose son wants to become a Rhodes Scholar gave me a princely lunch. They have a monster building of bright sandy stone with thousands of large glass windows, millions of busy clerks like ants crawling about it, and—evidently in order to flatter me and show his importance—he discussed the legal aspects of setting up a huge plant for the manufacture of artificial rubber, with fabulous sums of money. But he is a thorough crook, and when he glanced at me with his dead fishlike eyes, I felt he must know I knew it. No chin at all, and flat ears like a fiend. He said he had lunched with Schacht two days before (that's the sort of company, young man, you are presently sitting down for a meal with) and Schacht had been very cheerful about the new defeat he had inflicted on Ley's 'bolshevik' tendencies.[1] He had said to L: why, you may as well go to the war ministry and tell them to hand over to you command of the army— that is what handing over Industry to the Arbeitsfront would amount to. Ley had promised from now on to stick to his agreement with Schacht, but 'of course, being a bolshi, he didn't consider any agreement with the bourgeois as binding.' Some weeks ago matters had got so far that Schacht had forbidden his officials to have any dealings with Ley and friends, etc., etc. . . .

All the people in the boat train, mainly dark and cunning men like yours and Ripka's Rumanian poet friend, seemed to whisper numbers and multiplications to themselves, and there was a girl who looked ghastly with a feather green hat, and a badly painted turned down mouth. There was a nice sailor on the boat, with a noble English face, and most young men are nice. There was also a girl who had a nice knowing Jewish kind of smile in the train. But altogether England seems to me rather terrifying just yet, and I will write to you again when it is less so. Write, otherwise it will get more and more difficult not to scratch out again everything important and it is such trouble to make it unreadable too.

Love
A.

[1] In the setting of the Nazi establishment Hjalmar Schacht was distinctly an outsider. Originally considered to have played the part of an economic dictator, he stood for sound economic principles. He was challenged above all by Robert Ley, leader of the *Deutsche Arbeitsfront*, the Nazi monolithic labour organization, who pushed ambitious labour policies, and by Hermann Göring, who subordinated sound economic principles to the prerogatives of armament and the war economy. Schacht was on the whole successful in blocking Ley. But after the institution of the Four-year Plan in 1936 his influence was certainly on the wane and Göring's on the increase. In Nov. 1937 he resigned as Minister of Economics to be replaced by Walter Funk.

London.
Nov. 12th. 1936.

My dear Shiela,

I had been with Goronwy all evening when I found your letter waiting for me. I think I understand why you must get rather distressed by all that is going on, and I hate not to be there to comfort you and cheer you up. I rather needed you in the same function over here when I find it very difficult to find my feet this time. I feel very much the stranger and I constantly find myself saying things that I don't really want to say at all. Everybody seems so hasty and unsettled—but perhaps that is only something wrong with oneself.

You are not so interested in all this perhaps—but want to know about G. We haven't talked to each other sufficiently for me to be able to answer all the questions—at any rate not the main questions you put.—I liked him very much, as always, and enjoyed his company very much indeed, perhaps feeling a little that in the end he must find that I am too different, and different in a way making it hard to be a good companion for him. But that evening I think we liked each other well enough. He said a lot of things about you—but not all—as I didn't either—but he said he liked and admired you more than anybody else in the world, that he enjoyed being in cafés with nobody more than with you, that you could be a very good journalist one day if only you worked hard enough (he seemed to think one ought to be in England to really become a good English journalist), that he was very glad you were so happy in Prague, and that he would love to come and see you there, but didn't quite see how it could be done. . . . He evidently is *very* fond of you—but I must see him again, and perhaps he can tell me more. He said very decidedly that you must marry an Englishman, perhaps one of the good army type, a good deal older than you, rich, and who would treat your idealisms as a whim, and who adored you. He thought you were a little bit apt to be carried away by people who flattered you (it had never occurred to the Trott), and G. was very pleased when I told him you thought he knew you completely. He said you were in danger of just caring for qualities (highmindedness, bravery, goodness, etc), not for the people themselves, and that perhaps made you a little cruel at times. He said you were the most fascinating character he had ever met. . . .

I don't know whether there's much about the Trott I want to talk about at the moment, except that I very much enjoyed meeting your mother. I think from what you told me about her—Goronwy said she was the nicest person he knew—I was more able to appreciate her fineness . . . And though her activities and responsibilities are very admirable, there are obviously too many of them, and I quite see you cannot live there undisturbedly. She was very sweet taking me to the Armistice silence at Westminster Abbey, and saying afterwards how glad she was to have me there too, and we must prevent it all happening again.—We galloped down the street together—I think she runs almost better than you do—to be in time (of course we were late).

I felt there was a gloomy inertia in the Armistice crowd as if resolved to fight for nothing more at all. I knew England during the great economic depression, you know, and it was very different then. There is something very good and reassuring in your English faces, and you know I love and admire your country for it, but there's also an expression of being fatally bound up with some system which is daily proving itself wrong, and yet cannot be altered—is it capitalism, economic imperialism? Everywhere the right-minded people are reduced to ineffectiveness, here they can express themselves freely, but they seem diffuse and without any conception of that and how one must concentrate on getting actual power to assert justice internally and internationally. I shall make an effort to see what your officers are like, and your conservatives. I met Moira Lynd, and the Rendels,[1] and Goronwy's editor,[2] and G. and I talked a lot about the attitude of this country towards a potential European war. But all that isn't enough to go on, and all I say are just my first impressions, and it is quite wrong to be depressed by them.

My days with you at Prague, are very important to me, Shiela, and we are trying to do the same thing in the end. We must both go on without anxiety and it will encourage the other. . . .

Accept my true love, dear girl,

Adam.

---

[1] Moira Lynd, A. M. (Sandy) and his sister Jane Rendel; friends of Shiela's.
[2] Henry Wilson Harris, editor of the *Spectator*.

[Prague]
[*about* 12] Nov. 1936.

[Dear Adam,]

. . . Yesterday I talked with a very nice, misguided boy. That is the terrible thing in national socialism. It is a real offence against the Holy Spirit, for it uses goodness to make evil. He was a student, quite intelligent, full of a desire to serve a noble cause, to be honest and good—a fervent follower of Spengler[1] and Houston Chamberlain[2]—whom rather ironically he called Austin Chamberlain.[3] It is really a battle of ideas rather than anything, and what makes me really on the other side is being deeply moved by the history of the Renaissance when I was 16 years old. Reading about the revolt of scholars and poets against the restrictions and scholasticism of the Church, which did not recognise the value of the individual, was the greatest intellectual influence of my life and the basis of my hatred of national socialism and communism. They won in the end against much greater odds than us. Perhaps we are on a falling wave, but we can do something and shall do it.

But you must answer this letter with facts about all you do, and not with what you think about this. I want to know everything. I like your objective circumstances letters very much. You describe things and people very well. I remember the time I stayed with you before going to Salzburg you told me about such a lot of people whom I then felt I knew very well.

How is Werner and what is happening to him? I hope I will see him again, and that he will still be in Berlin when I come or that we will one day be in the same place. How is Heini too and your father and mother? You told me nothing about your Imshausen decisions. Did you make some, and what were they?

Ask my mother to send you to see Sir Neill Malcolm.[4] He is a great expert on China, helped arrange the Chinese Exhibition,[5] and is the adopted father of Wheeler Bennett.[6] Tawney[7] must also know him, but we know him very very well. He is my brother's god-father, tho' they do not have a very spiritual relation to each other. I hear you went to lunch with my brother and sister. Did you like them? She is very very nice, and he one of the best people I know. There is the same sort of unworldliness and goodness in him that my mother has. Do you get on well with my mother? She is very fond of you and was very moved to spend armistice day with you. I wish I had been with you too. There is no armistice day here. I went to Church the Sunday before and the preacher said perhaps it was the last time we would celebrate armistice day. . . .

Love my sweet
Shiela

[1] Oswald Spengler (1880–1936). German cultural philosopher; author of *Der Untergang des Abendlandes*, 2 vols. (Munich, 1918, 1922), an elaborate historical construct according to which 'cultures' inevitably go the way of rise and decline, turning into 'civilizations'. After the First World War Spengler tried to translate his theories into practice and adopted as a publicist a fiercely nationalistic stance. Though himself disapproving of Nazism he in many ways prepared the ground for National Socialism.

[2] Houston Stewart Chamberlain (1855–1927), English cultural philosopher; author of *Die Grundlagen des XIX Jahrhunderts*, 2 vols. (Munich, 1899) in which he developed a racial philosophy; he was Richard Wagner's son-in-law.

[3] Sir Joseph Austen Chamberlain (1863–1937), British Secretary of State for Foreign Affairs 1924–9; awarded the Nobel Peace Prize in 1925 after signing the Locarno Treaties.

[4] Major General Sir Neill Malcolm (1869–1953); League of Nations High Commissioner for Refugees 1936–8.

[5] See letter Shiela–Adam, Chelsea, 9 Feb. 1936, no. 1.

[6] John W. Wheeler-Bennett (1902–75); from 1959 Sir John. During the Second World War he served as member of the staff of the British Library of Information in New York 1939–40; Assistant Director of the British Press Service 1940–1; Special Assistant to the Director General of the British Information Service in the United States 1941–2; Head of the New York Office, British Political Warfare Mission in the United States 1942–4; British Foreign Office, European Adviser to the Political Intelligence Department 1944; Assistant Director General 1945. Most likely Adam had first met Wheeler-Bennett in Sept. 1935 when visiting, with Shiela, Count Bernstorff in Schloss Stintenburg; see Editor's note preceding Chap. 2 and letter Shiela–Adam 15 Oct 1935. During Adam's American visit in the winter of 1939 they were to become closely associated. Wheeler-Bennett attended the Conference of the Institute of Pacific Relations in Virginia Beach with Adam (18 Nov.–2 Dec. 1939). He was intimately connected with the formulation of Adam's foreign policy memorandum of Nov. 1939 to the State Department, and the one of 28 Dec. 1939 to David Astor; see 'Adam von Trott und das State Department' and 'Trott und die Aussenpolitik des Widerstandes', *Vierteljahrshefte für Zeitgeschichte* 7 (July, 1959), 318–32, *passim* and 12 (July, 1964), 300–23, *passim*. In the course of the war, however, Wheeler-Bennett turned against his erstwhile friend and advised the Foreign Office to exercise caution with him; see also John W. Wheeler-Bennett, *The Nemesis of Power: The German Army in Politics 1918–1945* (London, 1954).

[7] R. H. Tawney (1880–1962), leading member of the Labour Party since its early

years. After lecturing at Glasgow and Oxford Universities, appointed Prof. of Economic History at London University (1931–49); author of *Religion and the Rise of Capitalism* (London, 1926). Adam had met him first during his visit to England in May 1935 and admired him greatly.

Saturday 14th Nov. 1936.

Darling A,
    ... I wonder if what you say is true, and people feel themselves chained to our inevitable and bad system, and are prepared to fight for nothing. It is a terrible posture, and I also had that impression a bit, but I am sure it is übergangsomething[1] and those honest faces mean something fundamentally healthy and strong in England, which the intellectuals wholly misrepresent and neglect.

But I like the Czechs who will fight for something, and who are new and young and vigorous, and want to be, even if they fail to be Europeans. I know you think I overestimate Ripka's Europeanness, but I find something essentially hopeful and touching in his concern and desire to be European.

I must post this or you will not get it. It is a little disjointed and in bits—but go to Berlin soon, and I may come.

Love
S.

[1] transitional matter.

London.
16.11.36.

Dear Darling,
    Thank you for your bundle of notes. I liked to have them very much. There isn't much time to write a lot, but the enclosed note is not quite good enough. Oxford in the end was very nice, and I really am rather at home there. I stayed with the Warden in All Souls,[1] and both nights I ended by talking to Shaiah and a nice new Fellow called Hampshire[2] till about 2 a.m. ....

Well, to fill out the few gaps. My Imshausen and family decision was that I will go to China if possible. The possibility depends now on a decision of the Rhodes trustees, whom I have asked to spend my 'third year' at Peking. I spoke with Lothian this morning, and on the whole he seemed very friendly and reasonably favourable, though it's a board of people who really decide the matter. I told him that the

Czechs considered him the person who advocated giving them away to the Germans—we had a long and interesting talk about the matter which I may tell you about when we meet. . . .

I think I cannot be John the Baptist[3] for you—it is simply not true that I am not good enough to lace your shoes, and also I cannot be your suffering slaving knight in waiting, nor can I be one of your 'flatterers' although I have a genuine inclination to flatter you, altogether I cannot just have a post or be a key. You must think that over. . . .

Lots of love my dear from your old Trott.

[*Postscript omitted*]

---

[1] William George Stewart Adams, economist, Warden of All Souls 1933–45.

[2] Stuart Newton Hampshire (1914–   ); from 1979 Sir Stuart; philosopher; Fellow of All Souls, Lecturer in Philosophy at Oxford, 1936–40; Warden of Wadham College 1970–84.

[3] This was a chaffing reply to an earlier letter of Shiela's to Adam, from Prague, of early or mid-Nov. 1936 in which, anticipating a visit to Berlin, she wrote: 'Go soon to Berlin and prepare a feast for me, at least you are to be a sort of political John the Baptist, if you don't mind, because I have decided to save the world.'

Prague.
19.11.36.

Dear Adam,

What a distasteful place you make out England to be. You write me the chilliest letters, tell me the chilliest things about everybody, and generally give me as little taste to go there as my other friends when they write. I think it is time you left it and became John the Baptist—no nonsense about that. . . .

I'm sorry the Oxford man didn't materialise—or I gather he did not as it now depends on the Rhodes Trust. I hope it will be all right. I want you to go to China very much. I was accosted in the street by a countryman of yours today. When I rejected his advances, he asked why I had no zusammengehorigkeitsgefuhl.[1] Why does contact with each other's countries make us hostile to each other? And yet we both sympathise with the complaints of the other. I think the truth about England is that it is in a stage of transition and has suffered a terrible lack of direction during the last years. When necessity arises—it has already arisen, but when it is a matter of life and death, English nerves will recover, and you will see there is lots of vitality and essential caring for something left in England. Intellectuals in all countries are supposed to be the weakest, most frightened and least vital part of the community. I do not quite agree, but among the African tribes it looks like that. . . .

I don't know why you protest against not being good enough to lace up my shoes. Surely John the Baptist was good enough wasn't he, or didn't they wear shoes? . . .

Write to me again. John the Baptist or not, I think I will probably come to Berlin. . . .

Good night horrid beast.

Love, in spite of it all.

S.

¹ Shiela's version of *Zusammengehörigkeitsgefühl* meaning something like 'community spirit'.

Yarmouth.
25.11.36.

Darling Zamecka,

It wasn't that I was cold and trying to find warmer words, when I wrote [the] letter that angered you so—but sick, exhausted, and somewhat bewildered by what I come across here. You must have a little more staying power with the Trott, because otherwise a whole world, or at least a continent of difficulties, collapses on us. We mustn't only have a sense of pride about ourselves, but of each other, even if either of us behaves badly or unsatisfactorily at times—as I think we both do. . . .

There were days when I was feeling very happy in your country, and I am glad I came and I am sure they will stick in my memory more than these other ones. I shall tell you all about the things I did and the people I saw. I think I agree with what you say about the Übergang and England finding herself again—only at present I think she is taking a very cynical line about Europe. . . .

But you are a good girl, and I am very proud of you and think—besides perhaps Tawney (and even him I wouldn't except quite)—that you are the only English person who doesn't in some way or other convey to me a streak of slackness. Never mind, you go on offending my countrymen, and I won't mind either. . . .

I am staying with a Lord Percy in a very remote part of Norfolk, which is fortunate because I have been asked for a written statement about going to China, and I sit long times in a room with large windows on the ground floor and can't think what to write—because (at the moment) I'd much rather stay and save Europe with you, and even if that is a self deception, as the Lord is trying hard to convince me, I'd much rather have this illusion with you and let the rest go hang. But I must try, you tell me, to go to China . . . —I wish you would write this China statement, it is for a board of thick headed old gentlemen who think that Peiping doesn't lie within Rhodes' will. Bless you Zamecka, and don't let me down, or despair of the Trott's use to you. I quite see it's no use subduing our memories by a rush of duties and engagements, you mustn't do it either, and I'll be your John if you'll let me baptise you.

Love
A.

Nov. 27th, 1936.

Darling Duff,
    . . . I was told today that I can have the grant for China. So that is settled. . . .
    . . . I shall get any amount of splendid introductions, starting from Roosevelt and several Chinese cabinet ministers, to Chinese intellectuals and commercial attachés in Tokyo etc.
    It is very hard to go away from Europe and we must think it all out very carefully. . . .
    We will be very careful and gentle and strong with each other this time. In a way I have always known that you love G. and like me very much.—Well. Let us be very honest and simple. Anything may happen around us—there is no guarantee of return to reason, even here where one should expect it most. It may all just slide downwards. But there's no justification in all that for us who care for each other, not to be brave and clear in our friendship while we haven't been brought down by the brutes yet.

Love and joy,
Adam.

Prague.
beginning Dec. 1936.

Darling A,
    I am very very glad to hear all is well with China, and you are very very smart with your Chinese professors and Roosevelt. Is it very hard to go away from Europe? We will think it all out very carefully, but I am sure it is right to go.
    I am coming to Berlin on Monday 7th Dec. I'm sorry it seems so

far away, but it will give you all the more time to be John the Baptist. . . .

We will be gentle, strong, and honest with each other if we can. In these days the abyss between man and man seems to have widened for me, and I feel we are all quite quite alone, and cannot do much for each other except in superficial daily life. And that is a frail deceptive bridge. We must not only be honest to each other, but we must believe each other too. . . .

No there is not just a slow slide downwards. You are wrong about England. I cannot believe that they are all slack and that there are no constant and unchanging values. Remember after the Napoleonic wars England was like that—a fen of stagnant waters, they called it then, but Shelley was also writing then 'To defy power which seems omnipotent,' and that is all we have to do and we will do it. We will sort out all the things you heard and said, and see what is true and significant. . . .

Love, and do not think hardly of all the slack desires expressed in this letter. I have great longing for a life of infinite beauty and splendour, and the first I need is physical beauty and material splendour, then moral, and I have lots of the rest of splendour and beauty already in my life. I like my life very much, only want a comfortable week while my flat stands so empty and unwelcoming.

Love,
Z.

. . . Monday. After all full of beauty and splendour—went riding very early in the morning, and snow on the trees. Will you come to Zürs for Xmas? I am going there 21st Dec for a week to ski. Please come, answer.

Prague.
20.12.36.[1]

Darling A,

Thank you for your letter. It was a little frightening and desolate to come back from Vienna and find no word from you. In a world which one finds more and more populated by people mostly second rate, it is terrible to think one must part from those whom one values because one cannot find the means of being loyal and generous friends. I am glad it is not so, though I understand you have to bear most of the burden of it, and are more loyal and generous than I am.

I am glad your house is being put so well and capably in order. I'm sure it will also have some effect in saving Chiang Kai Shek. I don't

understand what is happening there, but send you what the scanda-
lous 'Week'² says about it. It doesn't make it much clearer for me
though perhaps it will for you. I'm too confused and ignorant of
European politics to have thoughts to spare for the extreme orient. I
trust you to inform me when time arises.

I learnt a lot about Europe from listening to Mowrer's conversations with people, though unfortunately little has stayed in my
memory. One of the disadvantages of being a girl is that men prefer
personal conversations to impersonal ones with one, and at the
moment I am mostly interested in [the] latter. Still, it was very nice
and encouraging to meet Mowrer again, and meet one more friend
whom I am quite sure is first rate. I'm afraid it is a little snobbish to
talk in such terms, and I remember being rebuked for it when I was a
child, but I think sooner or later one must judge people or become
slack and unscrupulous. We agreed. I wish you knew Mowrer. He
makes all the virtues more splendid, and life seem nobler and death
seem nobler than any other man can do.

I went to Vienna by mistake though I did not regret it. Yet Vienna
is perhaps the most depressing of all the unhappy Central European
towns. It is really like a grave, the remnants of something beautiful
and gay decaying in a mould of misery and rottenness. The last
morning I went to the Spanish Riding School, and watched the beautiful Rubenesque Arab horses, and spoke with a groom who had
served the Kaiser, and whose father had served the Kaiser. Then I met
a French governess in the street, who was frightened to cross the
street alone, and when I helped her, told me a pitiable story of slow
deterioration and begged for money. I went on to the Daumier exhibition, and saw the incredible cartoons of Louis Philippe, and all the
ugliness of life in picture after picture. What do such exposures sig-
nify, when today they are of less historical interest than of immediate
topical accuracy.

It is late. I have spent most of the evening with Ripka and a Russian emigré, who believes the real threat to the world is the danger of
the hegemony of women. If I had not liked Ripka before I would like
him now. I think their attitude to women is a very good test of the
value of men. I think no great man has ever despised women
honestly. I grew very angry and was even rude to the Russian. Afterwards we went to a café together and talked about pacifist and absolute values. I found myself saying that the only absolute values are
those inside oneself. I had never thought of it before, but it seems to
me very simple truth, and one which accounts at once for the terrible
relativism of the world we live in, and the constant desire for absolute values which we all have. . . .

Much love to yourself, and a very happy Christmas. So many Christmas trees here and in Vienna.

Love
Shiela.

[1] Shiela did visit Adam in Berlin where they stayed with his friend Wilfrid Israel (see letter Shiela–Adam, Potštejn, Dec. 1936, n. 3). By mistake she had to make her return trip to Prague via Vienna.
[2] The *Week*, a radical news-sheet edited by Claud Cockburn. It was widely read in the corridors of power since it was as well-informed as it was amusing.

Potštejn.
16.12.36.

Darling Sweet,

You write me such nice letters, and I like you. I wish you were here. I've started many letters to you, but I felt your absence so profound I could not finish them or tell you about the funny nice things and people here. Now Jane[1] has come here from Prague, where she arrived yesterday in an empty flat—and she has brought me a letter from you and a very sweet book. Thank you a lot, darling Trott. I am so glad you do not have to put me out of your mind, but have protective feelings for me. Continue, and the thought of them will keep me safe while you are in China. I am sure it was because you wished so well for me that I have had such a pleasant calm Christmas.

I have a new friend. She is 40 like all my new friends, but I think she is much better than the others. She is Countess Dobrzemsky,[2] whom I am staying with. She reminds me a little of my sister Lulu because she has the same kindliness—but she is more tolerant and knows about the world, about people and books and places. What I like best about her is that she is good. So few people are good any more. I remember at school we used to ask each other a very silly question—'would you rather be good or clever?' I think most people have decided to be clever. It's no use at all. Some of the things she says astonish me. They are so simple and obvious and yet seem quite lost and smothered by all the cleverness which goes on. O you would be very pleased by my being here. So calm and peaceful, only reading, eating, sleeping, walking. I have been reading about the Emperor Charles of Austria, about an English girl who travelled barefoot and alone in the Carpathians in 1890—and I feel brave to think of doing it now! There is a wild and rocky river which flows through gaunt and sunless woods—there is snow on the hills, and over all, huge wet clouds. The house is 18th century—long and low and most exquisitely proportioned. The stones tanned with two centuries, and the iron gates quite green. Oh, how I would like a life forever like this—but then I have all the thoughts that I have written in the enclosed. There are so many things to think out. . . .

Later. Full of fierce arguments this evening with four very high-up barons, and me declaring in very bad German about how to rule properly—and Jane and I being put down as reactionaries, but all being very friendly and nice because, after all, we are all barons really and understood those things. It's all absurd. I want to have a private life in an 18th century house with a garden and books to read and grown-up friends.

Goodnight, my sweet, and write to me soon in Prague and tell me about *your* Christmas. I like Wilfrid[3] very much and am glad I know him too, and grateful. I really am most grateful to an Almighty God, who just sometimes lets me meet good and brave people, just sometimes lets me see the stony rivers and wooded hills, and just sometimes lets me remember that life is also gentle, kindly and quite private.

Sleep well, Love always,

Shiela.

[1]　Jane Rendel, Shiela's friend.
[2]　Née Széchényi.
[3]　Wilfrid Israel, friend of Adam's; owner of a large Berlin store. A Jew, he was protected by a British passport and stayed in Berlin helping other Jews to emigrate. Shiela and Adam stayed with him in Berlin in Dec. 1936. He eventually left for London in May 1939 and met a premature death when he was shot down in a passenger plane over the Bay of Biscay while returning to England from a secret mission to Portugal where he was trying to arrange the rescue of Jewish refugees through Vichy France; see Naomi Shepherd, *Wilfrid Israel: German Jewry's Secret Ambassador* (London, 1984).

Imshausen,

Jan. 7. 1937.

Dear Sweet,

Let's both take a little more time over this letter—you, not to read it in a hurry when you rather want to go on to something else, and I, not to write to catch the next post which leaves in about an hour's time, for I have only just come. For really there ought to be a lot to say by now.

My writing so little, or rather not all since you left, was of course an attempt to establish a principle for me, but I cannot say that it is much good just yet. I was righter when I said we must not be heavy and deliberate about what life is doing to us anyhow. But when your

darling answer to my Xmas stuff came, I somehow hadn't the heart
to write cheerfully and as I should write to you, darling. So I let the
principle cramp me again and then I wrote that silly letter to Prague[1]
which you probably got before leaving P and were made sick by it,
and it was and is all very unsatisfactory. The real point, sweet, of
course, is that I find parting damn difficult at the moment, and parting with you has somehow—perhaps exaggeratedly—come to mean
parting with most of what seem positive, joyful, and right in my life;
that taken away spreads a sort of doom and defeat over the rest. You
see, sweet, after all, it does not take so very much to reduce the Trott
to quite a miserable wretch, and I am rather sorry to refer to him like
that, for very likely he will appear worse company in that capacity to
you than those who surround you now. No—let's not be suspicious
of each other . . . also darling, although you are by far the most difficult, you are not the only one I find very hard to leave behind under
these appalling outside prospects. My father, the family, Heini,
Werner, who have a sort of claim on one that I don't feel I am fulfilling. You know a little the instinct in a gloomy situation to entrench
oneself in one's most immediate loyalties and given ties, one's great
and justified uncertainty about the future in general makes one's first
reaction a defence, if desperate, of what is nearest to one . . . .

. . . Yesterday night I spent in the most extraordinary castle I ever
was in, near Ansbach. In the Middle Ages it used to belong to the
Hohenzollerns,[2] and was never conquered in the 30 years war—
unlike humble Solz which was burned to ashes—and now it belongs
to the man who has filled it with Chinese vases and pictures—a
slightly bogus performance. Good God, I spent the most uncomfortable night of my life in that vast medieval room they gave me and
never attempted to heat. Two broad renaissance beds with roofs over
them you know, walls two feet thick, and big Chinese jugs and
basins. My belly was sick, too, and when I got into those cold damp
bedclothes I think I really would have preferred to die than to face a
whole night which I knew would have to be interrupted by long
walks through gloomy winding corridors, and stairs with the wind
blowing right through them, blowing out one's candle and banging
the very doors one would have shut quietly. But towards morning, I
had a dream which started badly but ended very nicely. I found a
man's thumb cut off, with a black nail, very red and quite warm still,
bound into my handkerchief. I threw it away and then I saw Miriam
and then I saw you and we were all three walking arm in arm down a
sunny walk and laughing. The old man was really very nice to me
and in the morning drove me to the station again through furious
rain. . . .

I want to laugh with you very much, and want to see the sun and stop being heavy, and if we must part or perish, do it in a good frame worthy of the better Duff and Trott tradition. Do you think you would trust me and—in a quite different way—yourself, to give each other the farewell we deserve?

At present I am going on with the duty of parting with dutiful stubbornness and not any kind of joy. Tell me what you think of my going through England again. Somehow I feel my place there has got all wrong—I'd like to explain that to you—there's something slightly indecent nowadays in pretending the 'good European' abroad—but the 'nobody should travel' rule will not stop a thing—considering where we are by now. Perhaps we have been over-anxious all of us these last few months, danger really ought to make us good humoured than the opposite. And you and I of all people have really failed in their place to keep a clear and unafraid readiness to understand and assist mutually, which surely is necessary for a peaceful state of things to win through all this madness. If we don't stick to it, it won't be there any more in the next generation at all . . .

Bless you, and true love,

A.

¹ Letter lost.
² The electoral family of Brandenburg since 1417, royal family of Prussia since 1701, imperial family of Germany 1871–1918.

Hofgastein.
12.1.37.

Darling A,

Thank you for your letter which I will try and answer carefully and well for you, tho' I do not know quite what to say. You must not feel that parting with me is parting with all that seems joyful and right in your life, for you will soon find that is not true, and then again you will be worried. On a littler scale, it felt like that to leave England this time and it is the only time I have ever cried to go away or felt so sure of not returning—and yet now, even if I never did return, I would not regret the last six months. I think, to go away even from the people one loves best is the only thing that can save and heal one sometimes, and I think you are in need of that saving. So you must try and be glad now, remembering that gladness will come. I know it is a terrible wrench. If you feel your family has a claim on you which you are not fulfilling, try and talk to them and see what it really is. If it is true, it should not be hard to find what it is and perhaps you can fulfil it before you go, or even in going. At any rate you should face it squarely, even if you cannot fulfil it.

As for us, there is a long future ahead and many summers and winters which will be a pleasure to live in. Living here alone now . . . and in a white room looking over to the white mountains where the sun is shining, I feel more certain of recurring happiness than ever before. The elements are so very simple, one should not find it hard to be happy even in a gloomy situation. Fears of the future are silly things to be made unhappy by. Do you think we could have a holiday together in the snow before you leave? I think it would be lovely and every week the sun grows warmer and brighter. I think it would fit you very well for your journey and tasks in America and you would remember what it is to be hopeful and content again. . . .

My love to you and be happy and glad. Remember that 'hope springs eternal in the human breast'. I wish I could send you the sunshine and the snow which makes me so certain of it.

Shiela.

Imshausen.
[about 15] Jan. 1937.

Darling S,

Yes, let's meet when Berlin is over and all definite and determined. It would have been nice to be with you in your snow and with the brown brave ones you like. But I couldn't go away from here just yet. I am transacting exchanges of land for the family, and had to get over being sad and sick by myself. Though I am suspicious of my surroundings to some extent for their uncritical feudalism, I think on the whole it has been good and wholesome to have been here. It has convinced me and reassured me about the necessity of going away, and as you say, to leave those I love best. I have nothing to offer them now, and should meet with them as new people. I think I am sufficiently tough again to go through with what has to be done. I don't trust myself to be sufficiently tough yet to go to a chalet with you and not want to part as we parted in Kassel.

I find it very difficult still to write to you, and sometimes I regret violently that I can't write to you in my native tongue, which would seem artificial communication now. I find when I have things to tell you that I know you know about, yet perhaps don't know that they trouble me, I find I get long-winded and involved and I tear up the letter. I find I am rather critical of the way in which we have spent our last few times together, as untrue to the previous ambitions of our friendship, which were both more joyful and more stern.

And I find it very difficult to co-ordinate you with my work in the near future—another proof perhaps that one must part with those one loves best. I find I can go along happily and shape things and courses, and then a phrase or touch in your letter, sweet, will upset it all at once. It is my fault, not yours, and if we met now, it would be me again who would prevent us from being 'joyful and stern.' You are very generous when you forget all about this and say you will have a happy week with me, but when we meet you will most probably again find that I am not good enough yet to be happy with. The curious and humiliating thing was those times you found this in a sense I thought you were right, because the real thing for you would be a man whom you could love passionately and (yes!) obediently, and that again could only be a man with a full and devoted life—the young men of good promise and a bit of stuff here and there to 'admire' cannot reassure your uncertainties.

But hang it all, I am good enough to be your equal and sovereign friend, and our parting shall be free and strong. . . .

I am sending you a charming Chinese novel in German. But I would like you also to read Kleist's 'Penthesilea'[1]—promise. That's what you might have been like if you weren't English! Now you must read it to clear up this offence. Are you and I really proof that England and Germany can only have trade agreements and never a complete alliance? If that is really so I must say I have had a profound lesson in diplomacy. We are very bad at communicating in abstract terms (so a girl and boy should be), we are bad at fixing our respective currencies to a common standard, we are quite good at bartering niceties, and I think we are quite good at preserving a long-term credit as the basis of it all.

Be a good girl and write me a long letter about what you thought when you read this silly letter, and send me your telephone number because I am sure not to find the card on which you put it down when I want to telephone.

Bless you,

T.

---

[1] Heinrich von Kleist, '*Penthesilea*' (1808): a drama dealing with the love of the Queen of the Amazons for Achilles.

Berlin.
Feb. 5, 1937.

Dear Sweet,

Thank you for your letters and your sweet card last night, which made coming home late happier, and going to bed sort of lovelier—you are very nice to like me very much, and let all go hang, and I wish I could give you all the happiness too that you wish me. Is happiness really like summer? I wonder. It is, I always try to think, not something in itself, but something that just happens, along with the right way of living, thinking, and feeling. I am not very far away from that somehow these days—but it's slightly Chesterfieldian, and dead on the side where life's real springs flow. . . .

I no longer think, S. sweet, that parting with you means parting with all the things that are right and happy—I think I shall now find my way to them alone. But darling, I think nothing has changed in the feeling, and in that you are the only one who moves me really. Your handwriting your words, our memories—I mean the good ones—have an effect on me like nothing else, and when we meet I know I shall want you very much and that it will seem absurd to part—and that I shall be a bore for you again, and all the rest of it. I resent the idea of your being lonely and unprotected sometimes now, and in the sway of influences which are really not what you should and will eventually be.—In the last week or two I have rather pushed back these thoughts and have minded my own business, and on the whole I think I could get almost anything I wanted in this place if I applied myself—I think you have slightly underestimated that always. After five or ten years drudgery in some carefully chosen starting point, one really could do things. And that, after all, is what one wants most of all. But before that I must tidy up the Trott's head, heart, and soul, and for that I must go to Peking and become very wise and ponderous. I will come back bald and changed, and you will like me less—but then perhaps it will be the time for our great European alliance, and without even the handicap of being the slightly dubious character I seem to be for you now. But hang it all, sweet, let's be brave masters of the present when we meet, and there are so many unideological, unprinciplelike, good and happy things we can share, and which will make us joyful and strong in the times when all the oceans will live between us. . . . I love you, sweet—but don't mind or be frightened, because I have now built this terrific cage for my future, so your independence is not threatened. But I love every damn bit of you, and you will have a hell of a time meeting your

Trott.

EDITOR'S NOTE

The following letter taken by Shiela's mother to Imshausen, announcing Shiela's departure for Paris rather than to see Adam. Their meeting was postponed because in Feb. 1937 Shiela undertook a mission to Spain for the *Chicago Daily News* (Mowrer) and indirectly for the Spanish Government. She was asked to investigate alleged massacres committed by Franco's troops in Málaga and also to collect evidence on Franco's fortifications of the Málaga harbour. It was hoped that information obtained by her might sway the Non-Intervention Committee of the Powers which was formed in Sept. 1936 and met in London. Shiela's secondary task was to help (or at least bring news about) Arthur Koestler, then of the *News Chronicle*, who had been kept in Franco's jail for several months, much of the time under sentence of death. The episode remained without appreciable results or consequences. Koestler was later exchanged for the wife of a Nationalist pilot; see Shiela Grant Duff, 'A Very Brief Visit', in Philip Toynbee (ed.), *The Distant Drum: Reflections on the Spanish Civil War* (New York, 1976), pp. 76–86; Grant Duff, *The Parting of Ways*, pp. 148 ff., and Hugh Thomas, *The Spanish Civil War* (New York, 1961), p. 373.

Feb. 1937

Darling A,

My mother does not know it is Spain and perhaps would not mind but I did not tell her. I'm afraid you will be very upset when you get this but please do not be and please be very understanding how it feels suddenly to be presented with such a proposition. I had a telegram from a former employer in Paris saying would I undertake important work for ten days and wire immediately. I telephoned and could say nothing except that it was to go to Spain. I said I would go. I will come back through Paris. Could you meet me there about the 24th on your way to England? I must be here on the 1st. I'm afraid you can only wire acceptance or refusal to Paris—Chicago Daily News. . . .

Love always
Z.

1937.[1]

Darling A,

. . . Bless you. Duff–Trott will be all the finer for sacrifices made on its behalf. I am rather amazed by all this and having tossed one night over it, I am not sure whether it is all a nightmare or a good dream, or a good or bad reality. Anyway I must stick to it and hope it will do the world good as well as my profession. Anyway I think Mowrer is to be trusted and it is not a wild goose chase nor means I will be raped by Moors nor shot for treason, though what the hell it does mean, heaven alone knows. I'm afraid I'm expectant and excited though have been so severe to all my English friends who wanted to go. It means rather making money out of other people's pain and yet the snow lies bright on the ground and I can't feel anything wholly bad. So don't be angry with me.

Love
S.

[1] Letter sent to Leipzig and forwarded thence to Imshausen, posted at Eger from train Prague–Paris *en route* for the Spanish Civil War.

Nuremberg.[1]
13.2.37.

Darling A,

. . . There is something strange and recognisable about your country which I rather like. I do not understand how frontiers can change people so. You know lately I have come to think of a lot of things more as you do and even to understand your complaints against journalists. (But it is not necessary and I will go on being one, and try and have a different attitude of mind.) It is an attitude of mind which they and people who read them have—even my mother has it a little—somehow one has to be a philosopher or artist or just a good person to solve problems or even have the right to look at them. . . .

Oh I wish terribly I was in Leipzig now, that we could spend the evening together and in Prague next week. It all seems a nightmare. I had longed for the week and this is dotty. There somehow seemed no choice. Bless you and write to me. How silly you sad in Leipzig and me sad in a train.

Love
S.

[1] Posted from train to Paris *en route* for the Spanish Civil War.

EDITOR'S NOTE

The following letter was left by Adam in the hotel in Paris where Shiela and Adam were to meet.

Imshausen.
18.2.37.

Dear Z,

This must be only a short note—I have tried to write at length, but think it better to say the things, not write them, and this morning there was your card, which makes it seem more likely we will meet than the luxury train note. I shall leave here tomorrow (Friday) night—stay at Frankfurt (Carlton Hotel) till Sat morning—meet my brother Heini whom I don't want to put off again, and start for Paris in the evening and arrive at 7:55 on Sunday morning. I will go to the hotel to which this is addressed and hope to find some message—though preferably you. You've trained me to be a pessimist though.

Your mother's visit here went very well. It was a little ironic to take her over the snowy hills in brilliant sunshine last Sunday, when we had planned to be in the hills.—But the wheels of world history[1] have grandly superseded that. I felt a bit numb and reduced at first, but tough and gay within myself, and no lame duck for your charming little mother.—It is sad enough to think that your alliance to a world I neither like or understand will inevitably grow closer and closer and reduce ours. No more metaphysics or friendship—there's been enough of that in this Europe which I am glad to leave. I hope you had a good time. Sorry I can't come to Prague.

Love,
A.

[1] The events in Spain.

EDITOR'S NOTE

Shiela returned from Spain, arriving in Paris on 24 Feb. where she met Adam who had waited for three days for her. Possibly in irritation he asked Shiela how she knew which side in the Civil War was in the right (Shiela Grant Duff, *Fünf Jahre bis zum Krieg,*

1934–1939. Eine Engländerin im Widerstand gegen Hitler (Munich, 1978), pp. 217 f.). The following day they travelled together to London whence Adam proceeded to Oxford. Shiela left for Prague on 1 Mar.

1.3.37.

Darling A,

It seems so very final getting off the boat and returning to the depth of Europe—that I must write. . . .

Bless you, dear Trott—I am pleased with you, and think you not in such need of blessing as you and I have been during the last year and a half. We are getting stronger to deal with this hard world, and we will be happy and good allies.

I thank you for all you have done for me, and it was very much, for without your encouragement and kindness, I don't think I could have been brave, and one has to be jolly brave—

The boat's engines are stopping, and we are in the dark harbour. I feel a little like going into a dark jungle, and you across the open sea—but we will cut the European trees down, and make it a fine place to live.

Love always,

S.

4 St. James's Square
S.W.1
March 5. [1937]

My sweet,

Thank you for your note. Don't have the final feeling. Europe is not the world and the world must belong to us and support our bond as Europe did. You are splendid and brave and I shall try to be the same. In all this haste and turmoil here your memory has stood out clearly and unperturbed as something very special and very precious to me. We will not lose each other. We will not be captured by the fatal round of things.

Bless you, I wanted to ring you tonight but I don't feel we can talk like that. I shall write to you from the boat. I am just packing up. Your country has been very kind to me. I am glad you belong to it and yet so free and so strong to be away.

Well, Duff, the rush and sweep of the big waves of your Atlantic will soon lie between us. But it's all right, I too am pleased and content in you and I know there's nothing fatal or final to divide us.

Love always,
Adam.

4

THE NEW AND THE OLD WORLDS
ACROSS THE ATLANTIC
Beginning of March 1937–7 July 1937

EDITOR'S NOTE

The period from March to July 1937 (Adam was almost 28 and
Shiela turned 24 in May) found Adam and Shiela separated by the
Atlantic Ocean. Adam was travelling in America, first visiting his
relatives along the East coast and meeting, partly through his Rhodes
connections, all kinds of interesting people in Washington and
Boston. He then made his way via Ottawa, Toronto, and Chicago to
California where he met up again with his old friend Miriam and
stayed with Julie Braun-Vogelstein. Meanwhile Shiela was in Prague
writing for the *Observer* and getting deeply involved in the problems
of Czechoslovakia. But she resigned from the *Observer* over disagreements with the editor's policies. The worsening crisis over central Europe made Shiela increasingly aware of the need of engaging
herself in the combat against the menace from Nazi Germany.

[*beginning of* March 1937]

[Dear Shiela,]
  The first day it was impossible to write—because (I'm afraid the
first and the only one of the lot) I felt as sick as could be. Now that
the sea has become really rough I seem to be one of the few remaining
cheerful ones, eat enormously—a melon for every meal!—and am
having a lot of fun. How you would love your open Atlantic. It is so
varying and manifold in its colour, depth, and motion—and sometimes far away, almost beyond the horizon, you see a patch of golden
sunrays on the water. Yesterday and the day before there were long
times without any clouds at all, and we stayed on the highest up deck
and slept in the sun. My table was very wary of me in the beginning,
suspecting me to be haughty. Now I think I can twist them round my
thumb. My left-hand neighbour is an extraordinary man—an engin-
eer who has specialised building libraries, and has done so for most
of the academic institutions you and I know. He has also done it for

the Vatican, and told me all the dirty stories (they aren't dirty at all really) that he told the Pope, who once was librarian, and therefore showed a special interest in the job he was performing for them. He also told me of a cardinal who—borrowing an ordinary suit from him—went to see Josephine Baker with him one evening in Paris. Do you think that is a true story? He is a good boy, though, and has worked his way up from plate washing in the Astoria Hotel to his present job of £1300 a year. He said I could do some real good in the world if I kept in touch with the under-dog! Introducing him to a diplomat friend I have in the first class, he said to me he thought 'that was a shit of a man'—grown up like a protected industry. When I refused a cigar from him the first evening, he said would I rather have the money? He has been an American citizen now for seven years, and has spent five of them representing his firm in London. I never saw anybody so little of a snob as this ruffian, I have to look out to keep on my feet in talking with him. But we like each other, he has shown me pictures of his wife and asked me to his house. And we have big contests of who can eat more at meals, and sometimes he and sometimes I win. I am afraid we are rather shocking to other people. Yesterday he was feeling sick and I triumphant.

The brass band of the ship is playing about two yards from where I am sitting and blowing at full speed, and I try to write to their time, but it is very difficult.

It was very good you took me to your house that last evening, and that we walked together in the morning. It sort of seemed to give me a start in the world.—And it is not a jungle into which you are returning, is it? I can't see how a serious person can be so stupid as to think you a spy—do you think your correspondence with a young German may have something to do with it, specially when after opening it, it must have proved highly unintelligible to the general reader? The brass band is really getting too bad. Remembering that I played in one for almost five years at school, I understand what happened to my wits. Thank God they've stopped.

England was quite different this time and much pleasanter. In Oxford I met a lot of Chinese, including their Ambassador, whom I saw again in London. I also saw Halifax,[1] whom I had so much wanted to meet, but hardly had a word with him. He seems in many ways the person one should try and become like. On that Saturday evening I met a remarkable man called Sir John Hope Simpson,[2] who rescued some few million people's lives with flood relief in the Yangtze valley—he told me all about it, and what one must do to get great masses of people working together. He also did famine relief in India, and settled over a million families in the Balkans. I liked him very much. I saw Maurice Bowra[3] on Sunday morning, and we had a very friendly parting. Same with Shaiah, although he had the cheek to say that I was now 'worming my way in with all the crook-humanists of the world.' He is a nice but not a very loyal friend to us, you know. I told him that you were being very successful indeed, and making big strides. I think you are in a very good strategic position with all your English friends—one higher up, as it were, in daring and worldly experience—and if one day you launched out with something really good, you would be on top of them all, which I would enjoy a lot.

I'm sorry our time in Paris wasn't a little longer. I was very much aware of the sinister familiarity everything had for you, but I am sure a few more days with enterprise and sunshine would have banned those ghosts. I have been writing you a pretty useless letter, darling—but I feel very much between two worlds, and though you are still near, somehow I feel our nearness will have to be different from what it was. I have always thought that since last summer, but did not find the way—perhaps it leads around the world. Huh, it will be strange to think of you across continents—but perhaps it is right and good for both of us. Love always, my dear, A.

(Later.)

I dare say, sweet, the style of our letters to each other will have to change somewhat in the future—them taking such a long time to reach. We will have to take the 'longer view' of things, and make an effort to convey what is really essential in what happens to us. You are very present still, and I think of you with a bright gladness. There's no one like you to me. . . .

You know the ocean is really immense. Today after constant flight through it without seeing a thing—the gulls dropped back three days ago—we saw the first boat, a coast guard they said. Somehow it is a very wintry ocean to look at, irresponsive as bare fields are at first sight in winter, and the boat is too big to bring one really near it. But it is very much the great world, solemn and without human beings shaping it at all, or rather like what one imagined as a child the world before God started creating it.

But you know the fundamental feel one has about the world outside will be very much the same wherever one goes, and it will be even a good lesson to find that little clouds form the same sort of shapes in China as they do over our valleys at home, and that people only make different things out of the same substance. And even in the middle of Europe, horizons can be wide, and the sky inexhaustibly deep. I know you are jolly brave, and that therefore what life is really all about will not be denied to you. Perhaps your future is still fuller of unknown things, and mine more like a challenge to shape more definitely the things one has known to come up again and again demanding to be mastered.

Somehow I don't think I have done at all well these last years . . .

Tell me please of the development of European affairs. Goronwy too promised to write about them. He was very pessimistic. . . .

Perhaps there will be some quiet time soon to write to you again. This boat is really Europe still, and from tomorrow the world may really begin to seem a bit different. Must stop now.

Love, my sweet.

Just had a radiotelegram that Hasso and half of the Br. household[4] is sick, but that they want me to spend the first evening there.—I don't think I can go very well, because of the cousins I am staying with.[5] We are now a few hours from New York, and the ship is again surrounded by lots of gulls. Last night there was a nice dance—all very simple genuine people. Nicer to be with them perhaps than my smart cousins. I noticed with the Astors how very great riches transform all practical laws of life. But they were very friendly and kind to me, and I really liked Lady Astor for all her wiry liveliness—she said the last day 'I am sorry the little Trott is leaving,' and I am about twice as big as she is, and I told her so—she gave me a letter to Charlie Chaplin, and money to buy riding boots and a trench coat which she thought I ought to have when I went to the Virginian horse farm of my cousin. I wish you were coming there with me—as it is I shall soon concentrate on the severe and serious side of it all, and you too must be very successful and solid, and when we meet again we will be, and it will be grand.

[1] Edward, 1st Earl of Halifax (1881–1959); MP 1910–25; Under-Secretary for Colonies 1921–2; President of Board of Education 1922–5; Minister of Agriculture 1924–5; Viceroy of India 1926–31; President of Board of Education 1932–5; Secretary of State for War 1935; Lord Privy Seal 1935–7; Leader of the House of Lords 1935–8, 1940; Lord President of the Council 1937–8; Secretary of State for Foreign Affairs 1938–40; and British Ambassador in Washington 1941–6.

[2] Sir John Hope Simpson (1868–1961); Director General, National Flood Relief Commission, China 1931–5.

[3] (Cecil) Maurice Bowra (1898–1971), from 1951 Sir Maurice; Fellow and Tutor Wadham College 1922–38; Warden of Wadham College 1938–70; Professor of Poetry, Oxford University 1946–51; Vice-Chancellor of the University 1951–4. A renowned classicist and literary critic, Bowra was one of the most colourful figures at Oxford after the First World War; one of the so-called 'Oxford wits'. He belonged to the circle of friends and acquaintances of Shiela's and Adam's while they were at Oxford. Now Bowra 'suddenly turned up' at Imshausen. Adam in a note to Diana described him as 'very nearly a real friend', Hopkinson, 'Memoir', p. 70. For Adam's dramatic final encounter with Bowra, in June 1939, see Editor's note preceding letter Adam–Shiela, Cliveden, 19 June 1939.

⁴ Julie Braun-Vogelstein (1883–1971); widow of the German socialist Heinrich Braun; a wealthy Jewish lady of strong personality and wide interests. She was a prolific author of books, especially in the fields of art history and biography. Adam met her in the winter of 1934–5 through his friends Hasso von Seebach and J. P. Mayer, joining them in protecting her and her niece Hertha against Nazi harassments. A relationship of mutual confidence developed between them, and while Adam initially featured as her protector, in subsequent years she became a mother figure and patron to him. She emigrated to the United States with her niece and Hasso von Seebach, eventually renting a property in Carmel, California. Adam spent much of the second leg of his American journey (starting 7 May 1937) in the Braun household, living in a garden house overlooking the Pacific Ocean. Adam and Mrs Braun-Vogelstein were to meet again and for the last time during his second visit to the United States in 1939–40; see Julie Braun-Vogelstein's autobiography *Was niemals stirbt* (Stuttgart, 1966); Malone, *Adam von Trott zu Solz: The Road to Conspiracy against Hitler*, thesis (Austin, Texas, 1980), pp. 402 ff.

⁵ Dr William and Louise Schieffelin. He was a cousin of Adam's mother and, like her, a direct descendant of John Jay.

Washington.
[*about* 26 March 1937]

My dearest,

Distance makes one think, doesn't it? But if it's to help you and me, we must not allow it to sentimentalise a thing, and I have therefore not sent a letter off to you which I wrote some few days ago.

My very kind host,¹ whom I met only twice and for a very few minutes, has put me up in a beautiful 18th century house up on a hill in Georgetown, the oldest part of Washington, with a serene view over this beautifully laid out place. The house is very much like those English houses which envelop one at once with a sort of gentle and rational peacefulness—a splendid contrast to ruthless gigantic New York. The bookshelves are full of Pascal, Thomas, and history, and the old Viennese butler was the only person in the house. There was a charming Dominican Father, my host's brother, with whom I had a very nice dinner, after which I brought him to the station, because he is going to see his sister in Buffalo—fantastic. The governmental buildings—the Capitol floodlit—were magnificent on my way home. The Treasury with Hamilton's statue, I liked best. He was a close friend of my great great grandfather,² and I saw one of the most famous original portraits of his in the Jay's old country home, which I visited the day before yesterday—also a lovely place, with Shetland ponies and horses and dogs, and revolutionary memories all over— all the big men stayed there—since it was two days coach ride from New York, old Jay must have been quite a person. His bookshelves were interesting, French politics and literature, classics and Biblical stuff, and immeasurable parliamentary minutes. I am sure you would have liked his atmosphere. A cousin showed me round it all, and when we came to the little farm house where Jay had lived before building the bigger one, there was a dog fight, and she so badly bitten that I had to take her to the county hospital and go back to New York by myself. That evening I dined with a lot of Republicans and one 'brains-trustee' (Taussig)[3] for them to pounce on—it was interesting and I tried to back Roosevelt v. Wall St. I think they are at quite a turn in their internal politics and social relations. I hope to learn a lot in this place—have been given very varied and interesting letters. I made a mistake reading all the names to my host in N.Y. the other day, because he is somewhat at the top of the opposite faction. He is in with the big business world, though himself a kind humble Catholic lawyer now. When I was trying not to trespass on his time when I first met him—there was a queue of business waiting—he said: now you stop and sit down quietly because I would seriously like to help you. Then he sent me to the President of the second biggest bank of the world—across Wall Street where his office is—to give me introductions to China. What I shall do with them all, I don't know. I really need somebody to stimulate some tough practical ambition which I haven't got but ought to have. Sweet Shiela, how much better we would do many of these things together—I often think of that. Next time I go round the world I'll know how to do it and take you with me—yes? You know, America so far is not a beautiful land, full of litter, decrepit slummy houses, and as rough and untidy as can be outside the cities. But this town makes one feel wide and generous, and there is a natural dignity about it which I have sensed in no other capital yet . . . . I hope to hear from you soon. You don't seem far away and I am glad and truly fond of you. Bless you darling.

Love always,
A.

[1] Dr Schieffelin.

[2] John Jay (1745–1829), first Chief Justice of the United States.

[3] Francis William Taussig (1859–1940), political economist; Professor at Harvard University 1892–1935; New Dealer.

Bartolomejska 1,
Prague I,
May 2nd 37.

Darling A,

Thank you for a charming white Ethiopian cat and for a breath of high-minded American life.[1] Your letters open infinite vistas of noble generous life and I long to make friends with your American cousins, play with their dogs, ride their horses and have an 18th century life. Mine is dreadfully 20th Century. I have a sort of hit and miss journalistic success and some wispy new acquaintanceships and a life of complete anarchy. I like the sound of yours much better.

. . . Perhaps one should always be unhappy in the spring, for then one experiences it all. One sees the cherry blossom and the sunshine and the chestnut leaves and the swallows all the more sharply for seeing them alone and wanting terribly to give them all to an empty space—and one feels the whole of happiness and unhappiness at the same time. Spring in Prague is so beautiful. It is full of fruit trees and swallows and blackbirds and the sun is so warm and bright. . . .

I will write you a better letter from the country, one you should have from your best friend. I am very proud of that position.

Much love
S./Z.

[1] On a postcard from the Boston Museum of Fine Arts.

Washington.
28.3.37.

Dear Duff,

This would be a place for you—so full of politics, and yet human and ridiculous and also strong and with a sweep both into history and into all sorts of bogus future imagery.

. . . Saturday I lunched with a he-man of a journalist, the editor of the Washington Post,[1] good fatherly friend he might be. He walks down the street like a ranch-owner, broad-stepped as though the place belonged to him. That afternoon I had an almost two hours talk with Frances Perkins, Secretary of State for Labour.[2] We completely charmed each other, I thought—anyhow she me, and she seemed to go on talking quite willingly—on sit-down strikes, religion, and that politics are only such a small part of life—she was very nice. A big, warm, stable perceptive mind she brings to play on things—I thought that's what I should like to make you more like, though, darling, you are better stuff than she, and a rather handsome young Scotch lady. Do you not write to the Trott any more?

Afterwards I went to a lovely middle West film, and enjoyed myself in a semi-German drunk cafeteria—I like the lot of coloured boys and girls—their chatter and laughter is like sprinkling clear water in the sun. Today I lunched with a philosopher, and saw water-falls in the afternoon. Tomorrow I see the great senators Lafollette and Wagner[3]—altogether lots of experience worthy of a good journalist to write up, but the only really good one I know is too far away to do it.

Bless you, and write sweet,

Always love,

T.

[1] Felix M. Morley (1894–), former Rhodes Scholar; editor of the *Washington Post* (1933–40) with whom Adam became friends. Morley kept his faith in Adam throughout.

[2] Frances Perkins (1882–1965), United States Secretary of Labour, 1933–45; first woman to serve in a United States cabinet.

[3] Robert M. LaFollette, jun. (1895–1953), a member of the well-known Wisconsin political dynasty; United States Senator for the Progressive (later Republican) Party 1925–47. Robert F. Wagner (1877–1953), Senator from New York (Democrat); sponsored labour measures initiating collective bargaining.

New York.
18.4.37.

My darling Zamecka,

I wrote you a long long letter in reply to yours but I did not send it. I had to educate myself to a more reasonable philosophy of life again—and now I think I have succeeded to some extent. . . .

But you remain a sweet, resourceful friend over the distance, and all the brave and cheerful part of your letter I liked enormously. I read it to a charming young cousin of mine and she admired you a lot. She is the only person I have told a little about you, and her I am sure you would like. I stayed with them in the country last weekend and they have a house in the middle of the woods, and six dogs, and three horses on which we galloped through the country which reminded me of the setting in the early American films we saw in Europe. That's how some of my cousins live—they have a house in New York and go out for weekends. They are all over 6 feet tall, and really very charming and innocent and quite intelligent. Others are in business, and very eager 'patricians'—i.e. very much one of the '800 families' running all sort of useful and useless enterprises, functions,

balls, and charities. The old uncle himself is charming, and though a
'republican' and belonging to the Episcopalian church, quite a 'radical' and friend of my present host, who is perhaps the best known
sponsor of the underdog in this country. He too is a friend of your
Nehru, and knows all the Oriental revolutionists. He cannot enter
England for more than three days—I think because of that com-
promising friendship with N. . . .

On the whole, I dislike New York, but like Americans. . . .

Washington I really like very much as a place. I want to take you
there, to stay in lovely 18th century Dumbarton House, which
belongs to wild Bill Donovan, the Irish colonel who stood for Governor of New York because he knew all his old soldiers would vote for
him, and who sent his boy around the world in a sailing boat without
an engine to become a man.' And I would take you to see Mount
Vernon, Washington's country house five miles down the Potomac
River, laid out in graceful revolutionary style, full of independence
and nobility, and to General Lee's home on the hill over Washington,
with a picture of my great grandmother in his dining room. And I
would take you to see Secretary Stimson,² who lives in a wonderful
house, and who is a wise and beautiful old man who was most
encouraging about China.

And we would see Senators and Representatives, and as many
clever journalists as you like, and sight seers and squirrels in the President's garden, and Negro cafes and about 20 friends. You would
like it very much. And I think New York too would excite you more
than it does me—yesterday I met an editor of the New Yorker, and
thought him dull. Lin Yutang, the Chinese literary star (read 'My
Country and My People'³—very good in its way) was far nicer and
also tremendously encouraging about China. Everybody is hoping
that Japan is giving out, and the whole weight of sympathy is on the
Chinese side—except for some commercial quarters interested in
Japanese prosperity.

My friend Eberhard⁴ from Leipzig is arriving in New York May
20th, and will join me in California—that means starting serious
work, and at the moment I am confident about the outcome. When
you see the 'rest of the world'—come out to China via India, and
then we'll divide the empires between us. Remain my best friend—I
don't even want to add 'in Europe'—and write me lots about yourself
and your life,

Bless you,

A.

¹ Colonel (later General) William Donovan (1883–1959) (called 'Wild Bill'

Donovan), with whom Adam stayed; became head of the Office of the Coordinator of Information in 1941, and, in 1942, head of the Office of Strategic Services (OSS).
  ² Henry L. Stimson (1867–1950), American statesman; Secretary of State, 1927–9; Secretary of War, 1929–33, 1940–4.
  ³ Yutang Lin, *My Country and My People* (New York, 1935).
  ⁴ Prof. Wolfram Eberhard, sinologist and friend of Adam's whom Adam met through Prof. Gustav Ecke (see letter Adam–Shiela, California, *about* 10 May 1937, n. 8). Eberhard (who was about to emigrate from Germany) and Adam decided to meet in California. In fact Eberhard arrived early in June in Carmel where he tutored Adam in Chinese; Julie Braun-Vogelstein decided to finance his trip to China so that he might be of assistance to Adam.

Potštejn
7.5.37.

Darling A,
  Here I am, again tucked up in bed with a hot drink before I go to sleep, and I think it must be a form of casting off the winter and becoming fresh and strong again. The Spring is so beautiful in the country. Bohemia is a vast orchard of flowering cherry trees, and the grass seems greener and richer than the grass has ever been. It seems one's sense of pleasure is quickened every year, and every summer day is more full of pleasure than any summer day has ever been. I think it must be that summer's days were always shared with other people, and so the emotions one had which were nothing to do with the day, covered it up. Now I share it with nobody, I see only it, and it is lovely. I think when one grows up one learns to be happy for things which have no personal relation to one. Egocentricity takes a new and easier form. Sometimes I think I am learning to be happy on so little, and then again it is so much that I have.
  I want to learn to understand and forgive everything. I remember Douglas saying 'Tout comprendre, c'est tout pardonner,' took no account of sin—but I think it does, for even sin, whatever it is, must be forgiven 70 times 7. This country, which is so full of political hatred, is curing me of all fanaticism and all hatred. I cannot hate even the agents of your regime, or even justify any deceiving of them. I am making friends with two of them, and I understand how they think and work, and however much one may disagree, to hate is to misunderstand immediately.
  I have written quite a lot of the pamphlet I am doing for the N.F.R.B.¹ on the relations between Germany and Czechoslovakia. If they publish it I will send it to you, and you must criticise it very severely because you know more than I do, the motives of German

foreign policy. When I read what Hitler has written, I get excited and believe in all the publicist attacks—and then when I talk to the nicest of your countrymen and they reassure me, I believe them too! How does one evolve judgment from credulity? I suspect most people's judgments are a priori, and are really prejudices—and yet to have no a priori standards is the sort of anarchism I live by. Perhaps writers should be anarchists, then readers must think for themselves, and not just adopt from credulity and reject from prejudice.

What a dull letter this is being for you—you write me such nice letters tho' so few. All letters should be descriptive, and your descriptions are especially nice. I cannot describe so well. I am staying with the nice woman Jane and I stayed with for Xmas.[2] She is a woman of great generosity and a sort of simple understanding which sometimes is clouded by her upbringing. She was born in Hungary and brought up with a thousand servants to wait hand and foot on her. Two years after she married and a few weeks after her son was born, her husband was killed in the war. She was left wholly unfitted for looking after even herself, still less a child and an estate and a house. She has a sort of lady housekeeper, the widow of a Polish officer, who looks after her and the house. She also is nice but has no understanding tho' greater judgment. She is a most terrific snob and an anglo-phil. But I like her and feel she knows more about the world I live in than the others. The son and I ignore each other. He is tall, rather handsome, though his face is too sensual and at moments too half-witted to be altogether pleasing. Just now and again, when he smiles genuinely, it is even a beautiful face. He has nice manners and bad ideas, and understands nothing at all. He is good and just to his servants but does not understand when a man of the servant class revolts from bitterness and from a sort of despairing inferiority. The Bohemian nobility appear to be more useless than any other nobility in the world. When we passed the boys playing football on the green, I decided there must be no nobility any more. They make life poorer, not richer, now. And a useless nobility is a contradiction in terms. I wonder what the new aristocracy of semi-officials will be like in your country when the new system settles down a bit. I'm afraid it will be no good because I see no sort of aristocracy in a state which demands that all should be sacrificed to the state which is the highest good and above criticism. The duty is to serve not to sacrifice—a few years of sacrifice and there is no more to give. Why do you and I prefer the 18th century to the world we live in? I wish you were an 18th century American. I wish I could visit your America but I do not see how I can. I see no way to move from Prague, and am afraid it means I shall spend another dark winter there. Perhaps I shall work hard and earn money and reputation enough to set me free. I am determined never to leave Prague except as an advance—now it will still be a retreat.

If you meet a job worthy of the Duff in America, send her a telegram. It is half-way to China—but it must be an advance, and I fear it cannot be said to be that where it does not depend on my small Prague reputation. The only person who knows about my reputation is Wilson Harris.[3] In Prague I am thought never to do any work and to know nothing!

Love,

S.

---

[1] New Fabian Research Bureau.

[2] Countess Dobrzemsky; see letter Shiela–Adam, Potštejn, 26 Dec. 1936.

[3] The editor of the *Spectator* (see letter Adam–Shiela, London, 12 Nov. 1936, n. 2) for which Shiela wrote regular (but in those days unsigned) articles.

Ottawa.

30.4.37.

Darling Duff,

Your letters take very long, and with you as with myself, the weight of daily dealings outweighs the capacity to convey a summary of one's doings . . . If I had known more definitely before, I could probably have done a great deal for you in the American Newspaper world. I know one of the owners of the New York Times quite well, and could have met several of their editors if I had wanted to, and yesterday—before your letter came—I met the editors of the two most important papers here. Your return from Prague must not be a retreat, but I feel that another winter might be very trying. We must think about it. If you want to understand your own country, you should probably take up the Empire and its problems, and India to which you have such special access. Won't you start out there this winter, and go on to the East after that? I would think of it seriously, because I am sure that even your capacity of independent travelling will decrease if you don't attempt it on this bigger scale soon. Before then, you ought to finish some definite piece of work in line with what you have done these last years—even if 'Europe' remains an open question in it. You must be disciplined about that a little, otherwise a part of you that is important will remain unsatisfied and unhappy, and you will feel that your efforts and sacrifices have not led up to the proper thing which they still might if only you put in this little extra effort to clarity and order. I am very glad you are wondering of [*sic*] what place German foreign policy really ought to have in Europe, it seems much more constructive to admit that some place there must be than just to go off into a tirade about the present one. You will probably soon see a little book about this by H. F. Armstrong 'We or They'[1] and you will admire it very much at first, and then you will wonder about the constructive value of this whole position. Liberal-democracy!—all very well, but what about its application, what about the grievances which have made for its defeat in the countries where it has been defeated?

I have made some very good friends in the United States, and am very glad I went there. Harvard was very nice, and—largely owing to the Frankfurters—very welcoming and homely.[2] I met a wonderful old Italian there, and saw some lovely pictures. Montreal is an extraordinary city, three quarters French, and one quarter British—the first all in slums, the latter in granite business houses. Ottawa is provincial and charming—this palatial house is situated in a noble park with large trees that rustle at night and kept with all royal ceremonies to remind people of the idea. My hosts[3] are very charming to me, and I have long, extremely instructive talks with him about the world and Canada in particular. Today we went for a nine miles walk, and tonight I'm leaving for Toronto, tomorrow night for Chicago. End of next week I shall be in California—you are so far away Duff, and I am sure, with your passion for present and immediate things I am little more than a name with a number of different question marks to you. I am sorry I cannot be with you in Spring—you are beautiful and free and strong and genuine, and most people are none of these things, and don't stir one to be oneself and brave at it. Will we all be destroyed or recede into our various pasts? The sun is warm and powerful today, and where you are it's probably midnight, and you are sleeping your sound cat-like sleep, from which you can awake to such hostility. Bless you—I shall write again, and you write to me.

Love always,

A.

---

[1] Hamilton Fish Armstrong, *'We or They'; Two Worlds in Conflict* (New York, 1936).

[2] Felix Frankfurter (1882–1965), Associate Justice, United States Supreme Court 1939–63. Adam had a letter of introduction to him from Isaiah Berlin. The meeting was a happy one, except that Mrs Frankfurter had some misgivings; she found Adam 'too darn good looking'; Sykes, *Loyalty*, p. 187 f. By contrast, Adam's subsequent visit to Justice Frankfurter in the winter of 1939 was disastrous. Frankfurter had been warned by his friend C. M. Bowra, who suspected Adam of political duplicity.

[3] John Buchan, Lord Tweedsmuir (1875–1940), Governor General of Canada.

Prague.
19.5.37.

Dear Trott,

Thank you for your nice letter from Ottawa.[1] You have a very grand time with all your conversations with statesmen. I'm afraid I cannot do the same thing—which is what visiting India should be. Even in Europe, the hardest struggle of all is to win the right even, to enquire into political things. In India, where girls go only for pleasure, I would not have that right yet. It is strange that what is regarded as admirable and necessary in a man is still regarded with suspicion, amusement, or boredom in a girl. In order to do anything serious, one must first prove one is serious, and I have not done that yet. I think it is what you mean when you say I must first finish some definite piece of work to do with what I have done these last years. What do you think it should be? I would rather like to lecture, or work with Miss Headlam-Morley in Oxford.[2] I agree that winter might be very trying, and I do not like the thought of it, except that my room is a refuge that even London does not possess. I shall finish this pamphlet about Germany and Czechoslovakia this week, and see what people think of it. I'm afraid it will be neither original nor serious—in that it will contain nothing that most people do not know already, and will be superficial, but it will not be only anti-Nazi. There is a man in the Legation here whom I talk to, but I cannot make out quite whether he is being serious or whether he is deliberately playing with me in some way. If they print the pamphlet, I will send it to you, and you must tell me what you think. You are more helpful than any other friend I have, and are, I think, the only one who has any idea of what I want to do in the world. . . .

I would rather go to America than India. I still am not strong enough to go to India alone. Is there any means of continuing the sort of enquiries I care about now in America, and be given enough help to live there? You have made me want very much to see America and make American friends. I hope to find there freedom from all the prejudices and habits which clog Europe. Hadow[3] thinks the only hope for the world is tradition, and he is right that it is something good, but wrong in that it has failed to make a new world and has let us be faced with the present one. I met some Labour M.P.s here, and Attlee,[4] but they are too locally minded . . . I'm sure there is a way out. . . .

Much love always,
S.

---

[1] See letter Adam–Shiela, Ottawa, 30 Apr. 1937.

² One of Shiela's tutors at Oxford; Montague Burton Professor of International Relations at the university 1948–71.
³ Robert Hadow, Counsellor and head of the Chancery in the British Legation in Prague. See Grant Duff, *Fünf Jahre*, p. 169.
⁴ Clement Richard Attlee, 1st Earl, Viscount Prestwood (1883–1967), leading Labour politician; Labour MP 1922–55; Deputy Prime Minister 1942–5; Prime Minister 1945–51.

as from California.
[*about* 10] May 1937.

Dear Duff,

I spent three most interesting days in Chicago, which I would have very much liked you to share with me. It really is a wild and fascinating place. Social forces as we only just suspect them behind the scene of our society work with complete shamelessness, and are referred to with cynical realism and mostly with little more than a shrug of the shoulder. I suppose slaughtering so many animals every day gives a place a brutal quality—but it isn't just that at all. The worst gangsters I am sure are smooth and sweet and sentimental to their children and beasts—it is only that 'concepts' like law, government, police, do not mean a thing to them except perhaps disguise for some particularly clever form of racketeering. I am sure you would have liked the atmosphere! There was a bar with 55 women employees, all with a 'college' education, to entertain the guests with gambling, singing, and drinking—I picked up two rather sweet middle-western girls (no college education) who were in town on business (selling advertisements of sorts) for a few days only, and took them to the coloured districts, where they knew of a really astonishing place: Negro men dressed as women, and performing wild and exotic dances alone and in groups. Really beautiful creatures in build and even in features. The place packed with a discriminating coloured public hurling dollar bills at their favourite singers and dancers. They are wonderful, these negroes—so uninhibited and gentle, full of natural vitality and yet very vulnerable to our type of civilisation. They all have an expression of passionate suffering somehow, I mean the finer ones have. They can give you the loveliest melting smile when they feel you mean well. Some of the dancers were very proud and moving, I thought. The two middle western girls were very pleased with my liking their coloured countrymen so much, and though it was difficult to entertain them both, we had a very pleasant time, and parted at some station at two in the morning. Their subway stations in Chicago are all wooden and primitive, and the trains run terrifically fast, and people and children walk over the unprotected rails, and the sheds that form ticket offices right near the centre of the town sway like branches in the wind when these terrific trains stampede along them. It's all very grim and wild, but in the entire 'let go' spirit, extremely human and real and livening. The real Americans still seem to know that life is wild and unexpected and adventurous when it is real, and not a mosaic of concepts, all named and labelled and calculable as some of us think. Washington may become a focus one day, but it is very far from here.

For almost two days now I have been racing through these wide spaces. You have probably read or heard them described so often that you will be bored by my telling you how different they are from the spaces we know.

I sent a pair of white mocassins to your English address from Montreal and hope you will get them all right—I liked the feeling that for a short while at least there was no tariff barrier between us. Next time I will be in British territory will be your settlement in Shanghai where I shall probably be in Sept.

You would have laughed very much if you had seen me in the royal household of your governor general in Ottawa.[1] I bowed dutifully whenever they came in or out of a door, led by a (rather nice) young naval officer shouting: THEIR EXCELLENCIES! There was another aide de camp who belongs to your father's regiment,[2] and who knew your brother Neill—'an excellent soldier he would have made' he said about him. Himself he was a charming apple-cheeked, smiling, uncertain youngster who agreed with most things I said, and shaking his head ponderously, would repeat: 'You know, I believe you Germans are in many ways not unlike ourselves.' But he wasn't at all arrogant, and enjoyed court life like an 18th century page. I liked him too. But best of all I liked the 'Comptroller of the Household' a heavy beautiful big colonel with a blond moustache and the most British physiognomy I have ever seen. Whenever he said something very difficult, like how far away some spot on the mountain was, or who was coming to dinner, he had to shut his eyes and lean his head back on his strong neck. We took a great mutual liking for each other, I think. His girl told me he had said to her: I don't usually like His Exc's guests but. . . He believes in spending his holidays alone in the wilds with only an Indian guide, shooting bear and fishing. It was only later that I suspected that 'alone' meant also a very nice girl whom he took with another girl to dance with me on my last night of my stay. These Canadian girls are very nice. (The whole country would rather suit you.) They combine an American directness and vitality with some of your good English qualities, and there's no pretentiousness and no heaviness. The colonel's girl is in the coalmining business, and promised me fabulous profits if I entrusted my spare money to her. She also would come to China as a secretary. She knew all my red friends in Canada, and put personal greetings on the back of my letters of introduction to Toronto. There I met another very good group of people, and very much regretted having only one day with them. My chief friend in Ottawa, David Lewis, who was president of the Union during your last year at Oxford, is now Secretary of the Canadian Labour Party, the C.C.F.[3] He was very nice and clear and firm, but overworked and slightly discouraged by their lack of funds and leaders. This labour battle in North America, you know, is an immense and complex, slow-moving thing and different from the kind of social advances we have witnessed. It is more elementary, less doctrinaire, more massive, and yet more personal too. There will probably be a great deal of violence before they are through, and what exactly 'being through' means in their intentions, nobody really knows. Lewis,[4] the CIO leader, thinks it all right to use Communist organisers to get his people together, yet he himself cannot even be called a socialist, though people say he is 'moving towards' being one, whatever that may mean. Actually, he probably loves power, and is going for it the best way he can gather it best—he used to be a reactionary union boss before, and occupies a suite in the Mayfair Hotel, and loves being photographed in a broad brimmed hat and a big cigar, and pushes forward his chin like a dictator—'America's biggest 'sit-downer' stands up' the news headline runs, if he happens to stand in the picture.

I am now going on an 'Indian detour' off the train, and shall tell you about it when I come back.

I took some pictures and will send them to you if they come out, but I doubt it. We saw a church in the Indian village, built by the Spanish Jesuits 400 years ago, with a broad white clay foundation like a fortress, and two elegantly pointed spires like a Russian church. We saw a little Indian baby in its cradle—being a flat bed hung up on four pieces of string at the roof of the house. The Catholic father who showed me the church, an old German Jesuit with blue eyes, said they let the Indians combine their old rites with Christianity—so they pray dancing in the churches, and bury without a coffin, and have their secret clan rites, and legends about evil spirits, which they keep out by painting their doors and windows blue. Small white houses of baked mud, and only women and children about the place trying to be photographed for money, or selling pottery. Their land is communely owned by themselves, they don't vote, nor pay taxes, and are virtually independent of the New Mexican Government, which they consider foreign. This state is as much Spanish as it is American, and both languages are in official use. It was extraordinary to step out into full summer vegetation, when only four days ago or a little while longer I had walked on the wintery Canadian hills. . . .

The summer will help a great deal—perhaps you can have a horse in the country where your matron friend lives, and participate for part of the week at least in the serenity of her life. To work hard, as you and I always want to, one must have peace, which you can only get some such ways which combine meditation and human companionship. Please don't think I am falling back into my old patronising ways—but you see, all this is what I very much need and want myself, and now at long last feel that I will eventually get—in China at the latest. These last years have, I think, frozen me inside to an extent which can only be gradually thawed up, but some crusts have already fallen off, and I am much freer and opener to the world than I was.

If I were you I would plan very carefully to have another home in the country near Prague, go there a good part of the week, and so arrange it that you feel free, peaceful, and protected enough that you can write that summary pamphlet of yours about which you have never told me, or some other coherent bigger piece of work—do it as well as you possibly can, and get some paper to send you to India, or if they won't do it, go on your own and offer to send them stuff. That would give you something definite and big to look forward to and would spur your present efforts. I wouldn't stay another winter in Prague, and would do everything before the autumn to ensure that your departure is no retreat. But don't attack too ambitious a task, like writing a book on German foreign policy yet. You will have to know a good deal about that anyhow to make that pamphlet a good one. You too must learn not constantly to want to overstep your limitations and be frustrated by doing so. You must, I think, make up your mind whether your salvation is to lie in the way of adventure— in which you should let all I said go hang—or in the way of solid work and achievement, in which case you must not follow up everything that thrills and excites you at first sight. You must have the courage to let that alone for a while, and trust that when you come out at the other end of your concentration on work, you will still be able to enjoy life as you do now. Inside your work, I don't think it is a matter of constantly weighing against each other the ideas of wanting to reform the world, or the life of 'infinite splendour and beauty'— because whichever one you will ultimately choose as your own—they both involve in your position of freedom and independence a tough concentration and continuous effort. You may think that I for one am hopelessly committed to the Christianising side and that I do not understand the terms one has to make with the devil to get the things you want to have. I think there you are wrong, both about yourself and about me. If you want to be your special self and develop it to a full personality, I am certain you cannot ever do it by playing the devil's journalistic game cleverly, because a) it commits you to all sorts of inferior practices which would deteriorate that self, and b) you are not clever enough for it. Dorothy Thompson,[5] the most popular and really rather clever and witty American journalist took a strong line against Roosevelt in the last campaign. When a friend of hers and R's wrote to her, taking her to task on the grounds of the things she usually stands for, and asking why she did it, she replied: 'Dear Mr... I cannot tell you how much your letter has troubled me, but you know you have to write certain things to live.' She claims to be one of the leading liberal influences in the country, she is married to Sinclair Lewis[6] who must be a wealthy man. I couldn't quite admire her after hearing this, though I had done so before in a way.

Yet I still agree with you that to learn about people and politics, to see the world and develop oneself, journalism may be a better tool than anything else at the moment, and I also think that within its frame you can do some substantial work, and I think you should stick to it, but have no illusions about the 'beauty and splendour' it can offer to a person like yourself in the end. I think I am probably carrying owls to Athens[7] and you will be quite bored by this long letter.

At lunch on the train I met a Catholic priest who had lived in the interior of China for five years through famine, revolution, banditry, and all—he was very humble about it, and is on his way back there. He said he had friends in his locality whom he would trust like his American relatives, and that since he had no wife, people would come and tell him things they would tell no-one for fear they would travel around. He gave the coloured waiter a 20 cent tip, and the boy came up to him at the end of the meal and said to him Father, wouldn't you like a little more hot tea before you go away? and he took him by his hand very simply and grinningly said no thank you. He invited me to his friary in Los Angeles, and hoped he might come to Fu Yen University in Peiping, where my friend Ecke,[8] in whose house I am going to stay is a professor.

Bless you, Duff, and write to me fully one Sunday in the country. Don't take Europe over seriously, even if we have to die there, it's a small place—I'll try and tell you as much as I can of the great big world beyond it as I go along.

Love always from your true
Trott.

[1] See letter Adam–Shiela, Ottawa, 30 Apr. 1937.

[2] The Black Watch.

[3] Canadian Commonwealth Federation.

[4] John Llewellyn Lewis (1880–1969), President of the United Mine Workers of America 1920–60, and the Congress of Industrial Organizations (CIO) 1935–40.

[5] Dorothy Thompson (1894–1961), one of the most powerful and prestigious American journalists; columnist for the New York *Herald Tribune* 1936–41, she came out for Roosevelt in Oct. 1940.

[6] Sinclair Lewis (1885–1953).

[7] A German version of 'carrying coals to Newcastle'.

[8] Gustav Ecke, an old and close friend of Adam's who had been leader of the youth group (the *Nibelungenbund*, part of the so-called German Youth Movement) to which Adam belonged as a boy. He left Germany for China in 1923 and eventually became a teacher at Peking University.

Prague.

21.5.37.

Darling Trott,

Thank you very much for your long letter from the train.[1] It excited me very much, as all your letters do with that new wide world. I loved the description of Chicago and the Negroes, uninhibited and gentle and full of natural vitality. The only one I have ever known was Padmore[2] the Communist, and he was beautiful like a leopard. But I do not understand how you knew all about the gangsters in Chicago. Do they walk about the street and stop and talk, or who were your friends? You have a wonderful time and meet wonderful people. I wish I were meeting them too, though perhaps I would not see them so well as you describe them. I see the Comptroller of the Household, and would like to talk to the priest.

I wish too that I were a Catholic and could have a Father Confessor. I am much in need of a peaceful, thoughtful life, and somehow cannot give it to myself. Perhaps it is too early yet to rest, and I must go on with this racket, or perhaps in the summer I could find a nunnery. I do not know. I do not know what to do and your advice is abstract, and I do not understand it quite. What are the idées fixes I have about myself? I think I do not know what I am like. I suspect I do not seem very nice to people because they do not wish to see me, on the other hand I think I am nicer than I used to be when I was younger. I think I have learnt what unhappiness is and I never knew before. I think it makes people gentle and kind and forget themselves. I am only unhappy for moments because always comes back a suggestion of infinite beauty and splendour. I'm afraid I want that more than work. Ultimately all I want is to understand, to love good people, and to be something. In so far as I want to reform the world, it is only to make that possible for myself and for other people. To reform all the time is to lose the very thing one looks for. . . .

Pilks[3] gave me the poems of Manley Hopkins, and they are most beautiful and moving. This one is called 'A Nun takes the Veil' and I read it so often before your letter came and you suggested a nunnery for me!

> I have desired to go
>   Where Springs not fail,
> To fields where flies no sharp and sided hail
>   And a few lilies blow.
> And I have asked to be
>   Where no storms come,
> Where the green swell is in the haven dumb,
>   And out of the swing of the sea.[4]

Go on telling me so much about the world,

Much love,

S.

Several days last week I met and talked with Henlein party men. I liked their clean nice faces and idealism. I met Jaksch,[5] and said was there no way out of political fighting, could one not understand and live in peace with each other when people were nice. He said, No, one must hate one's enemies, and be proud and know them when one saw them, not like Lansbury[6] shake hands with the murderer of a thousand socialists. He said I must be a good sozialistin.[7] I asked a Hungarian why one had to hate the political opposition. He said it was because the country was raw and had no tradition of honourable opposition. One could only be friends with one's political enemies if one believed they were honest. What is it all about?

[1] See Adam–Shiela, as from California, *about* 10 May 1937.
[2] George P. Padmore.
[3] Arnold Pilkington, a friend of Shiela's.
[4] Gerard Manley Hopkins, 'Heaven-Haven. A Nun takes the veil', W. H. Gardner (ed.), *Poems and Prose of Gerard Manley Hopkins* (Harmondsworth, 1970), p. 5.
[5] See letter Shiela–Adam, 19 Aug. 1936, n. 2.
[6] See letter Adam–Shiela, Hamburg, 17 Nov. 1935, n. 5.
[7] Socialist.

Los Angeles.
[*about* 18] May 1937.

Wicked Duff,
   . . . I love California. You never saw such a country. It's all sun
and blue skies, and unheard of palm trees along modern traffic roads,
and through clear unveiled sunlight all day long it's cool and easy,
and the houses are white washed as they are in Italy, but they are
clean and big and modern at the same time. I am told that Los
Angeles is now the most corrupt town in the States, and big business
just solidly aligned with the 'elements of vice and gambling,' but
Nature seems to defeat even such blatant misuse—at any rate on the
surface. You ought to be very grateful to me for writing this letter in
my hotel room in the early evening, because I want to go into the
streets of the city for the night, and to enquire into these elements of
vice and gambling, and watch the Mexicans dance and the ships in
the harbour in the *Pacific* Ocean! . . .
   I met M.[1] for the last weekend and I think I need not fail her, and
it makes me very happy. She was very apprehensive and frightened
too, but we had a peaceful and strong quiet time together in these
wild hills, which I imagine Greece must be like. Rugged rocks, and
yet deep dark greens in the valleys, hot yellow sands in between, and
wonderful colours and smells. It is the kind of landscape you know,
which sustains a strong presence, and makes you think that no more
important experiences than your own have gone on in it before, as
we must always feel must have in Europe. . . .
   The maid just came in and within half a minute she had told me
the major facts of her life—nice elderly lady—that sort of thing
happens here you see. Her husband graduated from 'Oxford Medical
College' whatever that may mean, her daughter, born for journalism
(!) contributing stories for the 'Child Life Magazine' when she was
twelve, is now 21, editor of the society journal . . . and goes to college at the same time—she herself went to college (a most important
phase in any self-respecting American's life) for two years after she
was married. I said 'Your daughter must be very smart to do all that
and she must have inherited some of her smartness from you'—
which made her grin all over her nice row of artificial teeth. She
returned the compliment by saying that she got a nice class of visitors
on her floor, and only very rarely 'toughs' and they came to every
hotel after all, but here they did not last.
   Tomorrow I shall see both Upton Sinclair and Ch. Chaplin, I hope.
S. has already rung me up, and Ch is going to be 'fixed' for me
because my letter from Lady Astor alone may not have sufficient pull.

Usually I get the run of a place after the third day, but this time I have to go away on Thursday, because my dollars are giving out, and it is time that I withdraw from intellectual America to the country places, both to find out what they are like, and to recuperate a more contemplative mood and save money. Already I made the younger diplomats of the Consulate in New York lend me part of their foreign currency income.

You remember you promised me that under no circumstances you were going to be a War Correspondent—I realise that you wouldn't not do it just for the sake of keeping a promise to me, but I hope you will stick to what made you give it easily. Life is very strange and full of possibilities, but once you have hardened yourself to the ghastly industry of news in war, I am sure you would be hardened to the other side too.

Tell me about the beautiful Bohemian countryside in summer—how closely knit fields and woods and hills are in Europe. You know, going through the deserts and snow mountains behind glowing fields of cactus trees and rocky sand, one knows that one day one will be terribly homesick to see those things you can see every day when you choose to leave your Prague. People think less of distances here—they don't mind a week-end three hundred miles away—they are masterly, but somehow, I find, not foolish and contemptuous of their land around here. Nothing is more depressing than to look out of your train windows in the east, or to go beyond the suburbs of a city. Here you can see your green rocks behind the traffic lights on the horizon.

This afternoon I saw one of the film studios in Hollywood; I wasn't very much interested, except for the fact that part of the workers out there are on strike, and the place was carrying on in defiance of them—I was shown round by a dull office person, who apparently had instructions not to talk about these things. He professed to be more ignorant than in his senses he can have been. But there was a very visible sort of strike cloud over the whole place. I wish I could take you out with me tonight, it would be very happy and comradely, you would like it and not find me a bore. I am very happy, and you are the person to whom I most wanted to tell it. I hope you are too, Duff!? Would you not tell me? Don't feel you must give me up if you want to be an independent person. That's morbid, you see—I'm quite sure. Don't be morbid, you are by very nature the opposite, obviously.

If I go on now I will write a lot of dull nonsense—nor have I any right to make personal remarks, have I? We parted very much as separate persons, and you left me in the wilderness to pick my berries wherever I found them, nor were you very much interested where it was that I did.

I met Sally Goodwin, a dancing girl, last night, who has been in Europe four times, and makes her living now by making five cents out of very ten which every dance partner has to pay the proprietor of the place where she and about 30 other girls wait in one row on one side of a big hall to be engaged by the patrons (college boys, drunks, sight seers, travelling merchants etc) who sit on a long wooden bench at the other end of the hall. She was by far the most successful in attracting partners, with her beautiful figure, good looks, and intelligent and nice to talk to. She saves all her money to travel, and is going to Hawaii this summer, we may meet again.—I also went to a burlesque show—unique and indescribable American attraction!—which went on till about 12.30, and then I wandered in what they call the 'red light district', saw all sorts of queer faces and people, fighting amongst them with a lot of crowd and no policemen at all, and ended up in an all night cinema, where the downs and outs seem to go for sleep for 5 cents. A long, black, tunnel-like place with five seats on each side of a broad corridor in the middle. Old broken men, crumpled Asiatic tramps, oily round Mexican faces with big round yellow hats, blond tired-out boys, grey melancholic observers, and from time to time the academic looking cashier walking up and down the corridor with white trousers and a flashlight, to see whether anyone had fallen off his seat or was bothering his neighbour. Almost everyone had his little parcel of things with him, and there was an awful stink in the place. I stayed a little over an hour, and then went home a little disappointed. It's very much a southern city, you know—in summer it must be really tropical. If I can stand the heat, I think I am going to like the tropics very much indeed. . . .

In Chicago on the green university lawns I saw a girl walking in front of me with a big head of golden hair, and your way of moving and throwing it back, and of waving to friends, and of carrying a lot of books under your arm. It was a happy sunny day, and I thought how brilliantly fortunate it is in one's life to love people like you. It is very painless and happy just now, though the whole world is between us.

Now I really am going to stop and see museums and people instead of writing to you.

Love
A.

Write to me too.

---

[1] The ostensible purpose of Adam's visit to the West Coast was to stay with his

friend Julie Braun-Vogelstein in Carmel (see letter Adam–Shiela, *beginning of* Mar. 1937). There he was to join the Sinologist Dr Wolfram Eberhard with whom he planned to take up studies of the Far East and who was to accompany him on his projected visit to China. But the ultimate purpose of Adam's sojourn in California was to see his old friend Miriam Dyer-Bennet again. Since Eberhard's arrival was delayed, Adam had enough time on his hands to devote himself to Miriam. After a first meeting in Carmel, the two moved for a number of days to Taft, a town in the mountains of the Coastal Range north-west of Los Angeles. The meeting was, as Adam attested, a happy one, though not without overtones of sadness or without forebodings of the inevitable parting; see Clarita von Trott, 'Materialsammlung', p. 101; Sykes, *Loyalty*, p. 190; also letter Adam–Shiela, San Francisco, 30 June 1937, n. 2.

Prague.
30.5.37.

Darling Adam,

Thank you for your long nice letter from Los Angeles.[1] . . . You are a good nice boy, and I am very glad of you. You know now I made no morbid decisions not to write to you, tho' I'm afraid the letters themselves may have been morbid. I feel better now, and have recovered myself in a wild swoop of telling Garvin[2] what I think of him for presenting Central Europe to your country and resigning from the paper. It is an immense liberation, and I ride in the early mornings again. I ride to the country outside Prague, and the fields are deep and luxuriant, and come up to the woods like English fields. There is mustard and corn and hay, and we galloped through a field where the grass came up to my toes and made a lovely cool sound against the horse's legs. I think I would already be homesick if I lived among cactus trees and rocky sand. All my patriotic feelings are bound up with fields and woods and meadows. I think that is why I cannot understand and ultimately resent ideas of Volksgemein-schaft.[3] I can understand a French man loving La France, and you loving your home, but not loving the King, who is ugly, or a lot of people whom I don't know. . . .

What am I going to do? I have no further reason for being here, and no more secret funds, and yet I do not want to leave before the summer is over. England offers no pleasures, and in October I will return and work at what? I shall ask Mowrer if he can get me onto an American paper, or find out about Canadian ones. I would prefer first to go to Canada I think. When do you leave America for China? I thought of leaving Europe after Christmas. I would like to see my friends a little more. . . . I might also try to get something very smart like a Rockefeller—and try and write a book about nationalities in

America, so that we can do something with all these awful nations here, and especially in South Eastern Europe. I'm afraid in the pamphlet I did not attack National Socialism as hard as I could. I really hate it, and all the more that National Socialists are nearly always fine upstanding young men, and obviously very innocent and stupid. A Henlein deputy is going to explain Soldaten...⁴ to me next week, because I protested that your countrymen were so military. I hate armies and all views of life as a Kampf.⁵ You'd think Germany were situated in the Arctic Circle, and infested with bears and whales and storms and ice-blocks and natural phenomena of a peculiarly violent kind. What's wrong with you?

> Au corps sous la tombe enfermée, que reste-t-il?
> D'avoir aimé pendant deux ou trois mois de Mai.⁶

I think your countrymen must learn to take life lightly. The armed fist never alighted with special care on the really touching and gentle things of life. Perhaps my father could have taught me about soldiers and why they are all right—I don't think the Henlein deputy will do anything but excite me further.

Arnold Toynbee⁷ is here. Do you know him? I know him very slightly and it was he who suggested my present life. I think the English liberals are not tough enough for this arctic life, and Toynbee believes the Germans are wickedly suppressed. He seemed rather surprised when I said the Henlein party was Nazi, and answered 'But they say they are not.' I have had long conversations with a man in your legation here who explains to me what you want. I gather it really is the unity of all Germans, politically, if not territorially, and German domination of Central Europe. I am thinking of all these things very much because of the pamphlet. I would love to forget this part of the world in America. I will not be a War Correspondent, and hope there will be no war.

But I wanted to write to you about the early morning sunshine, and about the soft acacia trees which brush our faces when we ride through them, about the lake we waded through and the summer country. It really is so beautiful that when I see it, I think nothing else matters, and when my horse gallops through the long grass I am wholly and completely happy. I wish you were here and we could share all the summer pleasures together. I would love to dance with you on islands in the Vltava,⁸ and lie all day reading in those deep green fields. I wish summer were eternal. 'I would go where Springs not fail'⁹ but it is no longer a nunnery because I feel happy again in a slightly convalescent way. I have discovered a wholly new friendship—it is with Adrienne's little girl who is 15 years old and very wise and quick. It is an enormous pleasure and I would love my daughter very much—I thought I would only love my sons.

Bless you dear Trott, and go on writing me nice letters.

Love always,

S.

[1] See letter Adam–Shiela, Los Angeles, *about* 18 May 1937.

[2] J. L. Garvin; editor-in-chief of the *Observer*, one of the chief advocates of the appeasement policy.

[3] Folk community; National Socialist image of a racially pure and harmonious community.

[4] Soldiers.

[5] Struggle.

[6] Au corps sous la tombe enfermé, / Que reste-t-il? D'avoir aimé / Pendant deux ou trois mois de mai. From the poem 'A Adolphe Gaiffe'; Théodore de Banville, *Les Cariatides* (Paris, 1864), p. 286.

[7] See letter Shiela–Adam, Chelsea, 11 Oct. 1934, n. 1.

[8] Vltava (Moldau), the river which flows through Prague.

[9] See letter Shiela–Adam, Prague, 21 May 1937.

California.
May 29th, 1937.

My Darling Duff,

. . . My life has suddenly changed entirely. After coming up from Taft—I inhabit a small very nice building near the Braun's house, with a big studio-like room, in the midst of all my books, and with a view to the glorious Pacific . . . The waves are of a peculiar glacier-like colour, changing from deep blue through all shades of green into immaculate white, foaming in the brilliant sun and washing the sloping sands with an eager and elegant swing. There are also rocks on which I sometimes sit and observe seals which bend their supple shining bodies to the rhythm of the waves, and almost, it always seems, get smashed against the sharp needles of rock that stick out, but artfully reappear on the other side of the threatening wave every time. You see it is very happy and good to be here, and rest from all this new world, and get strong for the ancient one I am about to visit now.

My companion, Dr. Eberhard, will join me next week, and then we will start to work seriously on the route and the content of my forthcoming discoveries—he will occupy this room, which is big enough for both of us to spread our books and maps and things, and I shall move into another little house which I have just rented for three weeks. Then we shall move up to San Francisco and Berkeley and pay a diligent farewell to pacific America. So you see I am just on the brink of changing from a bogus into a serious traveller. Very soon, too, darling, it will be nearer for you to write to me via Siberia which will mark an important stage in the Duff–Trott relationship which I think will be infinitely enriched by all these treasures of the wide world.

I am sorry you didn't tell me earlier about your wish to have a job in the States—in the East I might have been able to do something about it. But on the whole I think that India is more important, and also 'half-way to China'—those words had a warm glad echo, did they ring a little uncertain—in fact, India being oriental, it's more than half way—America is 'Western', very tryingly so in many ways, not so much while you travel, but when you try and settle down amongst them, and you would probably not profit essentially. You have their virtues already, except for their naive kindly sincerity (like me you are much too European and wicked for that!)—but you have what I like most in them, an almost beast-like naturalness combined with a quick and subtle capacity to react. How do you like that?

· ... Neither you nor me want to commit ourselves—we want to explore and be free, and while doing so we sympathise very much with what we individually make of the world and ourselves. I think we are up against much the same difficulties in doing so too— because people who do not really commit themselves do not really mature, though they can grow harder, smarter, more flexible, they do not really put on weight as persons that matter. People matter only in so far as they commit themselves to things bigger than themselves. But there are people—and I trust that you and I belong to them— who are in themselves committed to quite a substantial bloc of things, but are not entirely sure which they include and which they exclude, and are careful and not rash in deciding and finding out in themselves which are which. Perhaps you and I do not matter very much to the world, but our being friends is based on the fact that we potentially do matter, and that's why it's an important part of our existence, and a noble and exclusive part. I am glad you are proud of it too. I hope I am again not being too German and explicit. But I thought you'd be glad to see that I'm not involved in a silly fantastic romantic sort of way in your absent charms, but that I consider you a real close friend. My discoveries shall be yours and yours mine, and I shall tell you all about things too that I don't want to write about now.

You must not think that your letters become boring to me when you start worrying out in them what it is that makes a judgment true and not a credulous or a prejudiced one. You see that kind of a thing, and you can turn where you will—if you're serious about what you are telling the world, it is that way that philosophy (so much despised by you) comes back again—that kind of thing I always thought you were not able to see through to, and therefore could never be a really convincing publicist. You *must* have some philosophy of life and politics, and with you—as with all lively active characters—it is one which you will want to share with your friends, or rather, will want to select your real friends by. Forming and discarding friends as you do—you have a comparatively good capacity for both, certainly considerable for a Briton—is probably the way to arrive at your philosophy of life. It will not be a 'system', but an extremely sharpened instinct for 'right' human qualities, their relative order, importance, and origins. It is the kind of knowledge which is supremely necessary for the writer, politician, wife you may become later—it isn't at all 'anarchic' if you really remain fair and observant, and are not carried away by flattery and excitement. Try and describe to me a little more, Duff—I am interested in the people you like, objectively. It pleases me to hear you say that I would 'approve' of this or that man of whom you apparently have a good opinion, and I liked the sound of the married 50 years old Russian who had a 'world in his memory.' I have not a moment's doubt that you recognise the important qualities in a man, and are not on the whole taken in by the bogus ones, but do you 'store' these experiences as you should? I think your being *so* observant and sensitive to the true things of nature, the blossoms, spring, skies, chestnut leaves and animals of the world, should not let it be emptied for you by letting the human figures which you experience become unreal phantoms, not having them in your actual presence any more. I think that's a criminal waste, and something that you ought to work against—or are you meant to collect material just for some other artful person who might really make use of it, and master it and mature it *for* you. I can so well understand your saying that you felt just on the brink of the life you really want. I think you have all the elements and just fail to put them together so that the thing might look and feel whole to you. You have the 'simple things' that even a war couldn't take away from you: the green fields, books, animals, and you also have access to human beings, the relation to which after all are the most important possession you have. But *your* person, *your* enjoyment of it all seems more important to you often than seeing them in their objective relations, their actual states of mind, their objective place in the world, their qualities as they work out for good and evil—so once you would be really concerned with this you would be in the middle of all those complexities and problems, which, as matters of your own personal preference or moral conscience, are just bewildering and insoluble. One day you will consider Nobility a very relieving value, the next day when you see a football match, you decide that there must be no more nobility—this day you want a life of infinite beauty and splendour, and tomorrow you want to reform it, and feel badly that you and I cannot do it, or indeed any one of your friends. The only way I think not to become really nihilistic or journalistic about it all is to be objectively and not selfishly concerned in one's immediate relations with the world, and be intelligently interested in the characters which attract and deserve your attention, and relate them to the aspects of the world which you can wholeheartedly accept and enjoy, the green fields, books and animals. I am writing you a very German letter indeed, am I not—it's all a play on the words objective and subjective, isn't it. Every 'scheme' of work is largely a play of words, and it's only with working at it that the world and its relieving lack of system pours in.

I have only now read Tawney's 'Religion and the Rise of Capitalism'[1]—if you haven't yet read it, do. It's not long, and gives a lot of historical body to things one has tried often enough to think out in the void. He doesn't quite come off either, somehow, but he is very strong and integer as far as his theme carries him. Won't you perhaps send me the 'Poacher'?[2] Why don't you write a *novel* about the Czech–German problem, and bring in all the inside knowledge you have gained and are gaining of characters. Try to meet a man called Friedrich Stampfer,[3] as I am told the finest type of old German socialist, bring him greetings from Frau Braun, to whom he is devoted. She may send him a letter through you, in which case his name will not be mentioned again, nor hers. You may like him a lot, let him tell you his story.

My love, sweet Duff—don't change too much, but take my wise advice, and give me yours. I'll bow to all your criticisms.

Bless you,

A.

[1] See letter Shiela–Adam, Prague, *about* 12 Nov. 1936, n. 7.

[2] H. E. Bates, *The Poacher* (London, 1935).

[3] Friedrich Stampfer (1874–1957), German Social Democratic politician and publicist; member of the German Reichstag, editor-in-chief of *Vorwärts*; in 1933 emigrated to Prague and in 1940 to the United States where he was active in exile politics.

Prague.
2.6.37.

Darling Trott,
 . . . I wish you were here to talk about the future with. At first I became very depressed to think I was starting again where I started in 1934, 1935, 1936, but I think it is better this time because I have got on a little further. I believe the pamphlet is really rather good, and if they accept it I will send it to you. You will think it awfully pro-Czech, which it is—not because I like them very much, but because for the moment I think they are right. If only your country meant other things than it does today, I would not be so pro-Czech. They are also not my idea of Europe, but they are better than Nazis. I think I shall probably stay here in June, July, and part of August, then go slowly home, perhaps to your sister, mother, and Salzburg, and possibly France. In September I shall try and get round a lot of people in England so that I can earn some money and see a lot of America and Americans. When do you leave there? You have excited me very much with America . . . .
 Dear Trott—you are a good friend and cheer me very much—it's funny how life bumps up and down for no apparent reason. Now it's up, and I shall make wonderful plans—stay in America so I can see you before you go to China. Then I will stay there while you level the roads in China, and then visit you there?
 Good idea?
 I am lying on my back wanting to be sick.

Love
S.

Carmel.
3.6.37.

Darling Zamecka,
 Yes, we've had lovely days together,[1] in woods and near rivers and deer—and we are best friends and can most certainly tell each other what pains our mind. . . .
 I think you have made an admirable job of this year—Garvin or no Garvin—and that on top of it all we have made our friendship survive as we have makes me very proud and glad indeed. You know, a person like yourself, who isn't composed of partial fires is bound, in her heart of hearts, to love what you call an 'image' (it is really a person—as opposed to things which one can be merely 'aesthetic'

about!)—otherwise she would either cool down or burn up. Hope must spring eternal or one would cease to live, but one can dissociate it from the particular person without letting it degenerate into mere appreciation—can one not? Your sympathy for the many persons you meet seems so floating, casual, and easily changing at times— that I think you might well invest in them a little of the fire which you devote too exclusively to one image (and a few satellite saints!) and on the other hand to the world at large. . . .

And yesterday too, when I walked back from the beach thinking of what you had written to me, I felt convinced that people's loves and hopes, hatreds, fears—indeed their *personal* side—which you could, if only you would, penetrate with your sympathy and understand- ing—would be the adequate clue to your comprehending and repre- senting the political scene. The large trends and ideas would enter easily enough, because you feel how it feels in people to care for an idea, a cause. And the realism of it all could be there—the way you can see policeman, soldiers, bankers, barons! You know what love, ambition, cruelty, generosity, are all about, and you're too proud to just sit down and be unhappy about your own self and story. That's why you came to Prague, and that you've made a home there for yourself to return to in peace is a magnificent achievement to your credit. The struggles of this year may pay to making you an indepen- dently creative person, and to be one that carries weight objectively, I mean beyond her individual intercourse with people. I think it would not be right to make the routine of journalism your final aim, but the kind of personal imaginative yet realistic presentation of things which you get in a novel. Go about it with all the passion for a wider world which has so far prevented you from falling in love with any single person—for I still don't believe that you have, darling. Write a better novel than Goronwy's, and use as your setting the semi- Russian background against which you have recently lived, and out of which the persons you are experiencing are carved, and in which every major issue that haunts the European mind is, as it were, perso- nified in one way or other. You have the country background of your shepherds and nobles, and to some extent of your Trott, and you have the charm and corruption of the old European town, and you have the warring of loves and ambition, and sense of justice and of power warring inside your own room. So far neither pole has attracted you strongly enough, but between and around these focuses you should be able to evolve an objective picture which could truth- fully absorb your own full person.—You see, even your letters to me might be considered something of this sort. You *can* write, and things ring very true and come very near objectivity sometimes. But your changes of subjective angle happen too easily, because you know I have both sides too, and know that you have them, and you can turn without fearing disintegrating effects. And you remain in suspense, you get no further. If the warring sides were embodied in characters, names, lives, passions outside yourself, life would expand towards greater, more objective strength and perhaps conviction. To write without any angle, leaving that to the newspaper reader, surely is no solution—in fact you will never write well that way. Read good novels—the Russians and not your own—*not* the modern ones, they are so self-conscious and vain. I know a bit about them, but I think you'd agree with this suspicion!?—and arrange your own scheme and then start on your own chapters right away: not allow yourself to be discouraged, and rewrite them seven times. Let me be your critic, and tell no one else in the world about it. In nine months time, surprise the world with an A1 novel and come to the Orient, to find me bearded and bald but also grimly set on my own purpose in life. You're right, to help pressing the good stuff out of which Germans are made into better directions! That's my job—and perhaps I am a little further on regarding 'exactly how' than you've given me credit. In me too, dear Duff, you will have to get a little more objectively interested before you can be a really useful friend—you are now, but you could still be more so.

To understand the disrupted German spirit, read some of Nietzsche too like your Sudetendeutscher[2]—N. is good, in parts most noble and encouraging stuff too, but I believe we will have to fight him tooth and nail. Yes, write to me often too.

Love always,

A.

[1] Reference to Adam's and Miriam's stay in Taft (see letter Adam–Shiela, Los Angeles *about* 18 May 1937, n. 1).
[2] Reference to a Sudeten German student whom Shiela had met at an inn in Slovakia in May; letter Shiela–Adam, 16 May 1937, not included here.

Prague.
15.6.37.

Darling A,

I agree with all the criticisms you make of me, and yet come to a different conclusion as to what I must do. You are right that I must choose once and for all whether to have a life of subjective beauty and splendour, or whether I am going to try and do something worth-while and work seriously. To go round the world and visit you in China is a life of beauty and splendour. To work seriously is to stay in Central Europe. It is neither beautiful or splendid, and today when the choice was put clearly before me, I wanted to cry, and I felt great bitterness against the world, which, over and over again, demands courage of one, and demands that one should live a stern dutiful life without so many things which make life splendid and beautiful—worst of all, without friendship and love. I am very isolated here, and am deeply distrusted which makes me act stupidly and provocatively. I make anti-Czech jokes to the Czechs and anti-German jokes to the Germans, and both think what much worse jokes I must make when they are not there to hear them. But none of that is really important—only perhaps more reason to go on with it till I come through to the other side and force them to trust me.

My reasons for staying here are these. If I stay here now I can, by means of wire pulling, become correspondent of a respectable English paper. I know more about Central Europe, oddly enough, than most English people—even the well-informed ones, and if I stayed here another year and worked hard on a self-respecting job which demanded that I should work, I would certainly learn a great deal. I would learn Russian as well, and visit Russia, and I would really learn about your country. The wires which are now to be pulled will never be there again if now I retreat. I leave one more thing in the middle uncompleted, bury one more talent and dig up the next. I'm afraid I must stay. As . . . Diana says too of unpleasant conclusions, they are good for the character. My danger is always superficiality, which others would mend for me by giving me work, and perhaps it would really be cowardly to run away from these people whom I feel quite clearly are my enemies—journalists, Czechs, diplomats, all of them, but I'm afraid the thought of running away had made me very relieved, and I have behaved with yet greater finger snapping than ever, which is a mistake and has made it harder. I wonder why it is that it is always your countrymen who are nice to me, and chiefly my own who are not?

If you very much disapprove, you must write to me quickly, but I think you cannot disapprove if you want me to be serious and work, and least of all if you want me to be a political ally, for I am learning so many things that would be useful to you, and my vanity is growing nice and small, and the value of good people is rising very big in my eyes through the sad lack of them.

Now I will answer your nice long letter which came this morning. Somehow in California you seem nearer again, perhaps it is because you are settled in one place, and an aeroplane flies to you. I like the picture of you walking on the shores of the Pacific very much, and find it easy to address. I feel rather jealous of my letters that they can also be carried along the Pacific shores while I stay at home. My typewriter has so much greater powers of travel than I have.

You know me very well when you suggest I should write a novel about these problems here, for it is what has been vaguely in my head all the time, and what I would most like to do if I could, but I seriously doubt that I can. I'm afraid you credit me with too much sympathy and understanding. I can enter into people's ideas but not into their lives, and the novel must be about their lives—but perhaps I could learn to do that. I think the only way probably is to take a certain character, and study him very carefully and build it around him. I have one in mind, but the only hope of doing it is to make friends with him, and I do not know if that will happen. He is a countryman of yours from this country, and is supposed to be the brain behind the movement here.[1] I doubt it a little, or else believe the brain to be very small. But I do not know whether I should make a Czech or a German the chief person, or whether I could make it a novel with two heroes, and show how the conflict stands between them. I will think a lot about it and see if it is possible. I'm afraid I write novels very badly—I often try, and I always make the same mistake, which is to say how the people think instead of making that clear from what they do and say. You know, that would keep me here too, because I cannot write it in another atmosphere, or I would not believe such things possible as happen here, and I would make it unreal—and I cannot write it in one summer which will take me from place to place. . . .

It is very late and I must go to bed. The routine of journalism is not my final aim, but I think to succeed at that, on a good paper, is the only way to succeed at something else—even the novel, still more some vague political object. I want a wider world of personal experience, but the political world here is very wide, and perhaps I can only get to the first by going deeply into the second. I can think of no work which I would prefer to a job here such as that which seems to be offered. I can think of no town gentler and kinder to live in, but I can think of friends and companions which here are missing, of a gaiety and charm of life which here is heavy and grim—but that I could and should have by reading and writing and imagining. I want to learn about the world as it was, not only as it is and as we shall make it.

Thank you for being a good friend always. You are very good to write me such letters. You must tell me more about yourself and the way before you, about your work and what troubles you. I hope your man has arrived[2] and you are not disappointed in him or in your subject. Thank you for your cuttings of how Americans see England.

They were very revealing. I wish I saw American papers. Are there any good monthlies or quarterlies I could take regularly. I believe I can get Foreign Affairs[3] here.

Love dear Trott,

Z.

¹ Karl Hermann Frank, from 1937 deputy leader of Henlein's Sudeten German Party (Sudetendeutsche Partei : SdP); after 1939 State Secretary and from 1943 Reich Minister for the Reich Protectorate for Bohemia and Moravia; responsible for the brutal Nazi policies in Czechoslovakia.
² Wolfram Eberhard.
³ Meaning the quarterly, *Foreign Affairs*.

Prague.

27.6.37.

Darling A,

. . . Tonight I am going to Budapest. It is exciting to go to a new world and talk about new things, or the old ones with new people. I think I will learn a lot, and I hope to find people very noble and grand in Hungary. I am more moved by finding people noble and grand when I disagree with them than by almost anything else. I spent the evening with some Henlein people here, and though they are not noble we had a sort of moral ground of understanding based on our opposition. If I make friends a little bit more with one of them, I will write a book about him. I want to write it very much, but am afraid I cannot translate the life I look at into a book. Even my pamphlet, which was facts and theories was a failure. I believe though that it is better than they say. I will rewrite it in July or August and give it to somebody else if they do not want to publish it. I wrote an article this week which attacked your country rather. I will send it to you when I get it. I rather hope it is not signed or they will close the frontiers to me, and somehow at the moment I inspire confidence in your compatriots. I wonder why. I suppose it is my fine Germanic appearance— we fought a lot about Germanentum[1] with the Henleinists. They are very uneducated and odd, but quite nice as people. . . .

. . . We will laugh again all right, and turn this chaos into a real Europe. When I talk with your compatriots, I feel it really is defying power which seems omnipotent, but we will be Titans and try it, and we do not fail if we try. Europe is certainly in a very very bad state, and war is touch and go now. A week ago it was frightful—a Saturday, a bright full moon hanging over Europe, Tuchachevski[2] scarcely dead, Blum[3] crashing, the German Government demanding intervention in Spain because of the Leipzig,[4] and threatening punitive measures against Czechoslovakia because of Weigel.[5] My mother tucked me up in bed and went back to her hotel, and I really wondered if bombs would not fall on the bridge between us before morning. It is a little better now, but I think the world will explode or not before Xmas—which is really why I do not want to leave here now and explore a new world. I am too much involved in the old. If it is broken, and I am still alive I will try and see what the unbroken half has to offer us for a new life. It is not England's place primarily to behave as a European power. If we have to do it, it is because the strongest European power is unaware of any interests other than its own, or of any goodness or peace. I will go by the sea in summer and read history and see how such a nation has grown up in Europe. . . .

Love,
S.

[1] Germandom.

[2] Michael N. Tukhachevsky (1893–1937), Soviet Marshal. On 12 June 1937 he and seven of the highest-ranking generals were executed after a secret court martial in Russia. They were accused of conspiring with 'an unfriendly state', presumably Germany. The Nazi secret service (Reinhard Heydrich) was instrumental in furnishing information implicating Tukhachevsky; the information was channelled to the Russians via the unwitting Eduard Beneš, the President of Czechoslovakia. The Nazis thus hoped to weaken the Russian military establishment.

[3] The Popular Front Government of Léon Blum, in power since 5 June 1936, resigned on 19 June 1937 over the Senate's refusal to grant the government emergency fiscal powers.

[4] Attacks against the German patrol cruiser in Spanish waters on 15 June and again on 18 June 1937 created a diplomatic incident. As a result Germany and Italy withdrew from the naval patrol conducted by the Non-Intervention Committee.

[5] Bruno Weigel, a German who had worked in a Czech gas mask factory until accused of espionage and arrested late in 1935. Weigel claimed to have been tortured by the Czechoslovak police. He was released and returned to Germany. The Weigel case served the German government to stage a diplomatic offensive against Czechoslovakia, starting with the airing of the case in the *Völkischer Beobachter* of 18 June 1937. It was on this occasion that Ripka asked Shiela if she knew no powerful people in England who could alert opinion as to the dangers of German–Czech relations; see Grant Duff, *The Parting of Ways*, p. 156 and succeeding chapter on relations with Winston Churchill.

Prague.
28.6.37.

Darling Trott,

Your country is behaving quite atrociously, and I am more than ever decided to stay here and defeat its games. The last week has been very excited, and for the first time since I have been here I felt the danger of war was really very very great. I know it has been great before and it still is very great. The Czechs are such fools and your people so deliberately unscrupulous that I am shocked, and wish to make a formal protest to you.

I am on good terms with your people here and absolutely astounded by their mixture of naivete and bad faith. The Weig[e]l case, which you probably will have read about months before you read this, was another shocking example of how diplomacy is now carried on by your countrymen. I think you must hurry up and gain influence and importance, or the name of your country will be too black for even a Trott to whiten.

It all shows that one cannot live a good life without believing in God or standards of right or wrong above all national and political standards. If the good of one's country is all one has to serve, then there is no dishonesty, no cruelty, no treachery which one may not commit, and that is what is happening to your people. In a while it will happen to us too, and we will be fighting for power and domination with the weapons of deceit and brutality.

I'm afraid you will not appreciate my decision to stay here, but it is, for the moment, quite made up. I think the fate of this country will be decided in the next six months, and I feel I want to stay by it till then. It is perhaps rather foolish and conceited to think I can do anything about its fate, but I know a lot, and I am trusted by certain people, and am the only English journalist. I shall go home at the beginning of July, and try all I can to be made correspondent of the Times, the Daily Telegraph, or the Manchester Guardian—the first, of course, if I can, but I doubt it. . . .

I am going to Budapest for a few days at the end of the week, and then here, and then home via Paris. I hope to be in London in July, and perhaps somewhere by the sea in August. I long for the sea, and for wind and salt in the air. In Sept. if I have a job I will come back here—go to Bucharest for the Little Entente, and then work very hard and steadily. I somehow feel Europe's cracking will put an end to it—when I am free from it I will go round the world and visit the Trott in China—by which time I want him to have found Buddha, or Confucius or Mohammed, or Jesus Christ, and teach me about Him.

I hate the relativity and chaos of all our standards. I am longing for a summer holiday, very quiet and long somewhere, to read lots of books and be with real friends again—but I don't know how it will be arranged and quite who the 'real' friends are. . . .

No letter for a long time—time you wrote again. When do you leave America? Write to me and believe I am right to stay here. Mowrer said he would have nothing further to do with me if I could not prove once that I could go through with things.

Much love,

S.

San Francisco,

30.6.37.

Darling S,

Thank you for two beautiful long letters which I shall only be able to answer adequately when I am alone again on the sea—by a string of rather unfortunate misunderstandings, my passage has been arranged for me from England to start from Los Angeles on July 17th.[1] It will be nice to go on a little English freighter all by myself, but I shan't get to Manila before Aug. 9th, and thence via Hong Kong to Shanghai before Aug. 17th. That will cut us off for a while.

When you get this you will probably have decided about taking up that more promising paper connection—it is a very serious decision, but from what you say in your second letter, I believe it will be a right decision. Even as far as Duff–Trott is concerned, the sharp knife method is probably better than the elastic bond tying one, and the choice of hard labour more adequate than that of the infinite beauty and splendour of travel and meeting across the Oceans. My darling Zamecka—no one supplies for me the joy and beauty that a friendly nearness to you means to me; but you and I won't marry I believe, and since we won't, we have no right to urge what we want immediately from each other. In fact, we had to part, and both determine to work hard at separate tasks. Your brave choice to stay on and work in Central Europe is really a second step to that parting of ways, and our vague prospect of revisiting each other in the Orient was, as you say, only possible on the basis that somehow or other our work would meet there. That would not justify your giving up what you believe your work is for the prospect of travel and adventure. But the far world has seemed a whole shade greyer to me now that the likelihood of suddenly meeting with you in it has suddenly vanished—we will meet again then as hard allies, hardened if we succeed through an objective working contact with the world as it really is, and strengthened in our mutual self-respect. Good God, I do not think much of myself at the moment, not really advancing with my respective task, and failing humanly in what I came out here to remedy.[2] I shall try and explain it to you from the boat—you will respect my not being able to write much about it now. You know how these things have been troubling me, and I do not think that you will withdraw from such failure, if it turns out to be that in the end. I know what you mean when you speak of isolation. And loving you is still some comfort, though I can not get at it now.

The European situation accounts for our nervous condition, darling Z—how a few peaceful days in my woods would cure you. How removed and yet how near I am to what troubles you—if all this doesn't tear us to pieces, we will come out stronger, wiser. But it's true, people like you and myself should have some stronger anchor in themselves, that all those who mix up their personal unsettledness with the political upset that looms over Europe, and in a different and less international way over this country—yes sometimes it is better for the character to be unhappy, but not in the confused and bewildered kind of a way that people nowadays tend to be unhappy.—One should perceive sharply all the time *what* fate, what limitations make one's condition what it is, and perhaps we are both nearer to that than we were a few years ago. . . .

Bless you always, my sweet,

Love,
T.

---

[1] Since Sir Stafford Cripps paid for the ticket, the reservation was made from England; thus Adam had to travel the Southern Pacific route instead of joining Eberhard on the way to Shanghai via Japan.

[2] The reference is to Adam's relation to Miriam.

July 3rd 1937.

[Dear Adam,]

Now I am back in Prague again.

I stopped in Bratislava and talked to the leaders of the Hungarian minority. The chief leader is awful, and ended all my illusions as to the noble Hungarian soul. He talked to me a lot about it, and about honour and justice and nobility, and I grew very impatient and even rude. Then luckily another man came in and I talked to him instead. We talked on a lower plane. I have a profound suspicion of anyone who mentions honour as a political motive. It is always the motive for the meanest and most oppressive acts.

Europe is an awful mess, and the dangers of war greater than ever. Mussolini wrote an article in which he openly said, we must have war now before England is strong, and your own country seems to be of the same opinion. Japan and Russia also look like war. Please do not go to China till you are well and till the situation is clearer. We really must do something if war does not break out next year. I think we must all work very hard to build up some sort of idea or possible system which would make Europe whole after the war. You must meet all your countrymen wherever you go, and try to find out who can be trusted as a European and who not. Now when I go back to England I want to find which of mine are good and which not. I keep hearing that young conservatives are good, but I cannot think who they are. Bill Astor is supposed to be good. I feel the only thing which will withstand the horror of the next year is some sort of personal integrity and private affection. If England and Germany should fight, I feel that caring for you is a very important part of all I must do in the circumstances. I am glad to have Hungarian friends, and wish I had Italian and American.

I am going to Paris this week and then to London, and in August I want to go somewhere by the sea and read history and biography and perhaps some Russian novels or French. I do not know how to write a novel and doubt I could do it, so much must come in. . . .

Write to me in London, and I will write again—but where? You will be leaving America soon.

[Shiela.]

San Francisco
July 5th 11 am 1937.

my sweet Zamecka,
here I am sitting in one of this cities [*sic*] crowded streets in a car—too tired to look up the people I have letters to in my pocket, too tired to look at the beautiful colourful sights of this place: exhausted from within and without. You will understand why I didn't want to write to you during the process which has brought me to this state of mind. And I hope you will find it possible to sustain confidence that I shall deal with all this eventually.

I am sailing—as I told you—on July 17th from San Pedro (MS Maron) and get to Manila August 9—right through the tropics. I am looking forward to this solitude on the waters and hope you will manage to keep things quiet in Europe that long. Otherwise I may be taken prisoner of war in Hongkong (where I get August 13th) and write to you with an English stamp for years. . . .

[Adam]

Prague–Paris.
7.7.37.

Darling Adam,

Travelling through your country makes me want to write to you, tho' no letter for a long time, and the last rather depressed. I hope you are better. Do not be ill, or go away till you are better, and are sure the Japs won't make war on the Russians.

Your country is beautiful, and I want to say I am sorry if I have hurt your feelings in the way I have written about your country. When peace is so precarious I find it difficult not to get into an ally–enemy mentality. I wage such a long, hard battle with you in everything I write and say, that I forget your Germany which is different, and which is pictured in my mind by woods on summer evenings, with little deer standing by them. I wish you did not kill them and like to kill them, they are the most beautiful and gentle of animals, and it proves that sin and hate are really the foundations of our character that we kill them. I went to lunch with some Bohemian nobles, and walked through their rooms and passages made ugly with antlers, and really disliked them for it. You will not take this very seriously? But I think it is serious. Just as half the pleasure of killing a deer comes from it being so beautiful and gentle, so half the attraction of war is killing people who are young and good and guiltless.

So I am going through your country again, and wondering how we can be good Europeans. I think it is time to be, and we must work to that end. Everywhere is the same cry, how can we make a Europe, and we must do so. It is not enough to wait for external pressure, we must make it from internal and not external necessity. We need ideas, and you, who are not in Europe, must see more clearly than us what Europe is, and what are the ideas which could make it a whole, and be stronger than nationalism. I think in ten years we must decide things in Europe for ourselves. It sounds rather pretentious, but I feel strangely and dutifully ambitious. We must do something, and therefore we can. . . .

Now I must look out of the window. Bless you. I will perhaps add something in Paris. I go for four days.

Love
S.

5

'A TERRIFIC CURTAIN . . .'

TO AND FROM THE FAR EAST

16 July 1937–10 November 1938

EDITOR'S NOTE

The Far Eastern journey took Adam into a world not only of Confucian serenity but also of the Sino-Japanese conflict. Meanwhile Shiela, going backwards and forwards between London and Central Europe, strove to alert British opinion to the imminent dangers of Nazi aggression. It was shortly after Adam's departure for the United States that Shiela established contact with Winston Churchill, and she had just returned to Prague from a trip through Yugoslavia, Rumania, and Hungary when Hitler invaded Austria. At that time Adam was in Japan and Shiela left for Vienna; at the time of the Munich Conference in September 1938, when Czechoslovakia was unceremoniously truncated, he was in Tsingtao, while she was in the thick of the struggle over appeasement in London. With the distance in space came also a distance in thought which the correspondence was not able to bridge.

Adam's decision to return to Europe late in October 1938 was prompted by the news of the death of his father. He was then 29, Shiela 25.

Los Angeles,
July 16th 1937.

My dear Zamecka,

You deserve a much better farewell letter than this one probably will be: I am just about to sail from San Pedro[1] and have not much time to write all there is to write about . . . I feel that a terrific curtain is going to fall when I have crossed the Pacific—over the first act of my life and that all sorts of completely new characters, scenery, problems will mark the second and it will have much less of the lyrical or, if you like melodramatic quality of the first, and will yet carry on a particular theme that the first has only indicated and will be greyer, harder and more silent.

I am glad you are out of Central Europe for a while: you were becoming distinctly nationalistic, whereas the thing called for from you is not the falling back on nationalism and hypocritical virtues of your blessed government but on some firm and constructive vision of a cooperative and ordered international future by the standards of which you judge and criticise the present lack of one. This may sound like utterances from the man in the moon—but I am sure they are nearer the truth than your back to the wall attitude. You haven't any right to denounce the policies of a country which is rather blindly and—I certainly admit—rather viciously groping for some economic outlet from the assumed moral superiority of a nation which has all she wants and has got it and maintains it with methods which are in many respects as blind and vicious. Surely you are not going to stand on it being a matter of degrees? I'm afraid that I feel utterly despondent to the kind of battleground you seem prepared to take sides on. In many respects I feel that the internal development of Germany—if only the European peace can be kept—bears more promise in its potential social and economic working out and more honest and substantial bearing on a cooperative international future than the 'powers' that have let Spain and Abyssinia happen. The Americans hate dictators—but you go around and ask them what they think of your foreign policy! they are rightly disgusted with both sides. What are *we* going to do? Give up our ideals, grown as a remedy to the post-war muddle, our commonsense rationalism about internal and foreign politics and plunge into the same kind of parochial emotionalism that agitates both sides? If it comes to the blow-up we shall probably have to die anyway   why get all mixed up in it first and not realise in cold blood what it all means and then stoically disregard the growing chaos and work as if our work were already part of that rational alternative of the probable future, because that alternative is what we consider worth living for?

I know I have fallen short of this very much in the past. I have been insane the way I have let personal things mess up my life more than once. I have learnt a good deal, I hope, in the 'first act'—why, you should be glad that many of these things are constitutionally spared for you! You have less right than even I have to be hysterical—

I have bought myself a hat in which I look—they say—like a Cuban coffee planter and I shall be a whole month on the sea—God bless it—and when I arrive on the other side all people will look very different and have beautiful slanting eyes and I shall love them.

I wonder if you will have written to me in Manila—quite like you not to have done, you witch! No, you are a charming and brave ally in the 2nd act too!?

Anyhow I am glad the moist British seas will calm you down a bit and you will join me in the good stoic philosophy!

Both the European and the Asiatic horizons look indeed black as I am embarking—but I shall know by Manila what has happened and won't go into the trap of Hong Kong if you have started your holy war against me and my Hessian boys—bless you my sweet.

A.

Be careful with letters to China. I'll send you addresses as soon as possible. How was Budapest? Did you see the crown glow on the castle in the setting sun? Do you know our poet Nicolaus Lenau?[2]

---

[1] Adam embarked on the following day on the MS Maron.
[2] Nicolaus Lenau (pseudonym for Niembsch Edler von Strehlenau, 1802–50), German lyric poet.

London.
July 22nd, 1937.

Darling Adam,

. . . On Saturday I went to lunch with Winston Churchill, which is nearer the thing. I have not been convinced sufficiently to hate Conservatism, and somehow there are only two political possibilities—revolution and conservatism. If one hasn't the faith that my French friend[1] has—that the world can be transformed into one of good and noble people—then one must be a conservative of all that is at present good and noble. That does not mean belonging to a Conservative Party—but only understanding history and what we have inherited and what we must change and what preserve. . . .

Love, my sweet, and hold tight to being friends. I am resisting the expansion of your country to the teeth in SE Europe. Perhaps I will enclose the greatest attack. I have written another about Hungary this week.[2] Tell me what you think. I believe we must make your explosion an internal one by building a Chinese wall, or we will have war.

Bless you, be brave and strong and handsome. Sleep and eat a lot, and breathe big chunks of Pacific air.

Much love,
S.

---

[1] A Swiss Communist boy called François Jaeggy. He later became one of Switzerland's distinguished psychiatrists.
[2] Shiela was now writing unsigned articles not only for the *Spectator* but also for *Time and Tide*. She regularly sent Adam copies of her newspaper articles.

Chinese Sea.
11.8.37.

Darling Duff,

I feel badly out of touch with you. It is my fault, I know, for having written you bad letters, and for having acted, felt, thought like someone off his head for the last two months. If we could be together just one afternoon I am sure you would understand and forgive—but now, I am afraid, you are going to condemn and doubt too much. There will have to pass some time still before I can write to you at all satisfactorily, because I know you do not like a laboured understanding, and attempts to analyse pains and problems too much. And in that I agree with you. I had plenty of both, and since war in China[1] will be the next thing—there seems plenty ahead too. I should like to imagine the eagle eye following me, but I feel there are too many clouds between me and it.

The long voyage over the ocean was itself beautiful—the solitude of the seas, the nights which I sometimes watched from the top of the mast, the sunsets and early dawns (though of them I saw less because in this heat one usually sleeps better towards morning), the calm steady movement of the ship, all this ought to have pacified internal upsets—it did often, and whenever it did, all the old things in Europe seemed near and warm. But most of the time, they seem threatened, uncertain, and likely to be shattered by some event that I can neither avert nor see ahead.

I wanted to write to you about my country, and how I see it, and how it must continue to be the ground of my own efforts—how these cannot affect the present phase, and how it was our duty to remain intact for whatever came after it; but it wasn't somehow the thing to write to you about at the present moment.

America—and especially California with all its grandeur and beauty—was hard to digest. I wonder what you will make of it all when you come there. The Americans are in many ways a mixture of English and German, and raise that question of our mutual relation in a peculiarly vivid and almost haunting way. They have your language, and to a large extent your political institutions, but they really have our social immaturity, our violence and formlessness of feeling, though also something of what we call Gemüt, a kind of sensing the world by an imaginative sensitive mind, and some sort of sincerity, which your more sophisticated attitude has tended to pervert. But they are also as wild as neither you nor we, primitive, cruel and coarse.

On this ship there were four Americans—three of them left in

Manila—a film producer, a whiskey merchant, a hotel owner and a young clerk. Unfortunately there was nothing to stop them from dominating the ship by their noise, but on the whole it was good natured noise, and though it annoyed me a lot, and really got the better of me, it also taught me a great deal about myself, the English, and the Americans. The ship, you know, is a British freighter, and we have our meals with the captain and officers, and the conversation between them and the passengers (one of them believed me a spy— the whiskey merchant), the jokes and stories they enjoyed, the jealousies who has the bigger and better ships, 'America rules the world' said the hotel keeper, and England would have been defeated in the war had not America stepped in, and the captain remarking on the general secondrateness of everything American. They are all terribly nationalistic, except perhaps for the film and whiskey man, who felt, as Jews, on a particular defensive of their own. It wasn't very fortunate, but most instructive company. I'm afraid in the end—the first time this has happened to me—they all (I mean the passengers) considered me their enemy, levelling all kinds of charges against my suspicious and vicious character—I felt much as you must have done at times in Prague when all the guttersnipes turned on you, and even lost my humour at times to the extent of wishing you were there holding my hand and telling me I was a good boy after all. I am not at all sure that I am—and besides, you don't really want me to be, and want me to become hard and vicious and not too ready to trust and be trusted by everyone.

In Manila I would have liked very much to take you around—you would have loved it. And you seem to be the only person with whom I haven't felt continuously unhappy going round with. I would have taken you to the cock-fight where crowds of seeming south sea islanders (the Filipinos are a beautiful race, with elements of the Spanish, Malay, Mongol, and South Seas in them) stand wildly gesticulating round a caged in cockpit where two birds fight each other till one dies or runs away—giving the crowds a chance to win or lose fortunes on their champion. An extraordinary scene which I did not really like, but which seemed to bring out a wild, utterly strange world to me—the Orient, both exciting and soothing. Life is crowded and swift for them, and yet when you look at them closely they seem neither rushed nor worried, but solemnly absorbed in the little things they happen to be doing. You go around in the streets in tiny coaches pulled by the Filipino pony which is like a Liliputian horse. The coachman usually a small boy talking [to] and challenging his little horse incessantly—if you start talking with him, the horse simply stops.

Or I would have taken you dancing in the St. Anna Cabaret, which is famed for having the largest dance floor in the whole Orient, certainly bigger than any I have ever seen before. I talked and danced with the Filipino girls there, they are very nice to look at. On one of them I called the next afternoon at her house, which was a little wooden cabin on four poles over a swamp in which a black pig and her four little children were snorting about. There were four little children in the house too, of whom she said they were her brothers and sisters, although they called her 'Ma'—she was very strange and exotic without the paint and dress-up of the Cabaret, and at first it was difficult to talk. The room was all dark brown wood, and the walls mostly windows, with little squares of shell instead of glass. Outside you could see the tropical swamp, the palm trees, all the things that suggest this combination of warm moist fertile nature with extreme human squalor—the small wooden shacks crowding round dirty patches of earth, and then again beautiful tropical flowers, with strange smells, and huge trees and long green grass. She told me her life story which was pathetic. Coming from a rich family—her father being president of some town—she had always had plenty, and was brought up in some convent of Catholic Sisters, of whom there are very many in the Philippines, and though she had to pray every morning at five, she said she was allowed to play afterwards and had nothing to worry about. But she ran away when she was 14 and went to the Cabaret, which seems to be some kind of slavery, because the girls are not allowed to go anywhere else, and whenever they go home before 3 a.m they have to pay a fine, and whenever they displease some customer they are locked up in a dark room. Her family took the attitude that she had disgraced their name, and that none of her brothers or sisters were allowed to be sociable with her. By then she seemed to have forgotten that she had told me that the kids around the room were her brothers and sisters... Her one brother had become a senator, she showed me his picture, and whenever she was in a very bad way, she'd go to him. A year ago, her father had died and not forgiven her, and he had always been specially fond of her, and now her mother would come to her once in the year for two or three days and would 'help her with her housework'—she said 'you have no idea how hard I have to work' getting the clothes, food, house ready for the kids, and spending all night at the Cabaret. She was pathetically touched by my not seeming to want anything out of her. Sometimes she smiled like a child, and sometimes she had the broken look of a hunted animal. She told me how her neighbours despised her for going to the Cabaret—'it isn't as in your countries' she said. Every Sunday she goes to Mass at five in the morning, and she goes to confession every month, and the priest 'accepts everything'. And by praying she said she could often make herself not be mean. When I said the oldest of the little boys, whom I liked, looked at me angrily, she asked me 'do you blame him?'—but she was very glad I had come out all the way to see her, because she lived way outside the town. You will probably find this rather a sentimental story—for a few moments she seemed like a companion. Have you companions, Duff? Is your English summer what it should be? Are your old friends pleasing or hurting you? . . .

It is hell to convey anything in letters, and in the next few months it may be difficult to get the mail from where I shall be. It was impossible even in Manila to find out how important this North Chinese conflict is going to be. Yours and the American fleet have moved to Shanghai, and the Japanese (let's call them 'barons' in our letters—none of my letters lately have ever arrived in Peiping, or at any rate not at my friend's place!) are clearing out of the upper Yangtze. In Hong Kong, where we shall arrive tomorrow, I shall not know a soul, because I never planned to get there. But I shall certainly find someone intelligent to explain the situation to me. It's all like a big adventure now, and I shall get my first lesson in individual smallness face to face with a big break-up—there are good sides to such an experience; but if I could have had it in my own way, I would have preferred scholarly cloisteredness at the moment, such as was promised me in Peking. Very probably I shall not tell any of my friends where I am going, because there will be all sorts of stories anyhow—you must keep your trust in the Trott in spite of all the damn foolishness he has displayed of late and of old. I want please to find you still friendly and open and near, whenever I come back, and from my side you can be sure of that, and that whatever in the world you will do, you will remain one of the eye witnesses that I want to have called on when the most final accounts are settled. Hell, so many people are interfering with our lives, to so many we have to give half answers, and so many we have to fail that way— we must not allow each other to fail that way too.—Mean anything? Are you very much in England at this moment? You seem damn far away, and I more almost than ever faced with a heap of scrap and disjointed ends around me—but the thought of you is cheerful, and makes me see it more as a heap of building material than as the turmoil it really is. It will take you a good deal of friendly patience to see it that way too at the moment, I dare say— but you will, won't you?

Love always,

A.

Would you like to know about California? It was a hard shake—but perhaps good for that very reason—I am glad I went, because it clarified me, and it removed bitterness. I am not very wise.[2]

[1] On 7 July the Japanese opened a new phase of conquest in China precipitating a clash with Chinese troops at Lukouchiao near Peking.

[2] 'California'—a reference to relations with Miriam.

London.
29.7.37.

Darling Adam,

I hope this will reach you safely in Hongkong. I do not like you approaching a Sino-Japanese war through piratical seas. What can you do and what will you do? It is appalling how the world seems cracking up like a huge Volcanic region, thousands of dead in China, hundreds of thousands in Spain, air crashes, train crashes, mining disasters, crime, disease. A spirit of violence is really prowling the earth. . . . The Times writes of the smell of dead bodies by Madrid, and there seems a terrible coincidence between the metaphysical and the material world. I don't think I have ever in my life been so directly apprehensive of chaos and disorder. It seems to spread from my own life, from the lives of my friends, to the outer world, to the edge of Japan and the edge of Russia. I think I must really try and order myself or one will go mad.

I am going to my grandmother this weekend and then to Scotland with Jane. I hope to one quiet lovely place by the sea and to stay there all the time. I have an incredible longing for peace and quiet, and a life so simple that the order of it is clearly perceptible. Then I might read and even start to write something. If only I could understand and keep hold of the variety of things and people I meet and deal with, I feel I could write a real book—or if only I could write the book, I could understand their life—rather pretentious that, but I feel in need of blessing of some sort. . . .

Thank you for your Los Angeles and San Pedro[1] letters. Your criticisms are quite right, but your country holds the key—we want a new international order, but your revolution is making conservatives of us. The international order you suggest is worse than the one present. I must fall back on the 'nationalism and hypocritical virtues of my blessed government' because we are fighting for our lives and I presume that our lives must be saved before our morals can be improved—for a very virtuous corpse is valueless. I cannot argue these points any more. It is like physical weariness—one simply cannot walk a mile further or stand up any longer except by sheer will power, and that is rather the decision I have taken. You are falling back on a quite indefensible position when you say that France and England have 'let Abyssinia happen'—but I agree, while taking a hard and stoical decision to resist a certain policy to the death, one must work out a rational and possible future. I find Eden[2] weak and crazy when he says we cannot decide what we will do in a certain situation until that situation arises. I think the so-called 'instincts' that English statesmen ruled by was a very clear perceptiveness of our purpose—now we have lost it, and 'instinct' is a very muddled conception of how to get out of bad situations—so naturally we can't decide things any more. I do not ordinarily refuse to think of problems any more—only today because I have a bad cold and feel absolutely physically and morally exhausted. It will be lovely to go away. Think of me on the shores of the Atlantic when you touch the Atlantic–Pacific continent. I wish you lived in the same town to build up an ordered and sensible society to live in. I feel other people in other centuries had their religion, their morals, their society built for them, and we must build it all for ourselves. Let's build one better than ever has been before.

Much love, look after yourself, and write me long long letters about the people you meet, and the things you think.

Much love always,
Shiela.

---

[1] See letter Adam–Shiela, Los Angeles, 16 July 1937; a letter from San Pedro could not be found.
[2] Anthony Eden KG MC (1897–1977), from 1962 Earl of Avon; Conservative MP 1923–57; Minister for League of Nations Affairs 1935; Secretary of State for Foreign Affairs 1935–8; for Dominion Affairs 1939–40; for War 1940; and for Foreign Affairs 1940–5 and 1951–5; Prime Minister 1955–7.

Hong Kong.[1]
[n.d.]

[Dear Shiela,]

Got your letter and am very glad that you are going to Scotland with Jane. Give her my love. I have written to her, haven't the money left to send it airmail. One must deal with chaos inside first and then with the world ... think it all over in your solitude—solitude helps. I don't know what I am going to do tomorrow (Shanghai is flooded by Japanese ships and troops and I may stay here for a week). But I really am calm and unchaotic now. Gosh, how I wish to have you here tonight in this strange looking place.

Take and keep my love, Darling.

A.

---

[1] The ship reached Hongkong on 12 Aug.

Hong Kong.
20.8.37.

Darling Duff,

I should like to write you long interesting letters, but it does not seem easy at the moment. My ship, as you may have seen in the papers, was commandeered for troop transport north, so there was no question of getting to Shanghai. I stayed here, went up to Canton, and now have to decide what further chances remain for Eberhard and me—he's still in Japan. I think I shall ask him to come down and try everything possible to get into the interior and leave Japan for later. All mail and money went to Shanghai, and at first it was difficult to get a cent of credit down here. With a few days more I hope that can be cleared up.

China is amazing. The soldiers of Kwantung look like children, but one of our Generals who was returning from leave in Java to Nanking told me the central govt. troops are good stuff. Peasant boys, quick in uptake, brave and loyal. I also met a Chinese general—an American or Canadian gunman originally, they say—who conveyed a little what is in the Chinese fighting spirit this time. And Yesterday I spoke to someone who had just come down from Shanghai—it must be hell. You don't know these Oriental streets—crammed with destitute human beings even at normal times, but like a desperate hive now. Some of the Chinese girls are extremely beautiful—I haven't made their acquaintance yet—they wear thin long dresses with a slit down at the side—most becoming. They look sweet-tempered and innocent like children of paradise. The place itself is quite beautiful too—only tropically hot at this time and mostly overcome with low grey clouds, dripping with dew over the thick green undergrowth of the hill at the foot of which the Chinese quarters are huddled together. I live half way up the hill very unromantically in a German-kept boarding house—rather luckily clean—there's a bad cholera epidemic which will probably be intensified by the refugees crowding in from Shanghai.

I have met some English people . . . —yesterday night there was a party at which I'm afraid rather immorally in these times we drank rather a lot and listened to stories about the interior. I long to get there away from here. But my resources and Eberhard must be cleared up first. Unfortunately I have not a single powerful address in the south of China, all my letters being for Nanking, Peking, and Shanghai. In Japan I would have facilities for inside observation. But somehow I cannot make myself go there at this juncture. You are very right in what you say about the present state of the world, and we do agree and must not quarrel over national govts. etc. I am very glad you could go up to Scotland. I know it will be lonely sometimes and that Jane will not always have been a help perhaps—but the sun and the wild grass and the sea and the cliffs will. I wish we could talk one whole day—yes, I too wish we could be in the same town, and build a society of decent relationships around us. Sometimes I tempt myself with thoughts of emigrating into the wilds, and let these bloody continents go to hell, since I cannot stop them on this course. But must we not grit our teeth for what comes *after* that hell? One must learn to sink and preserve our real desires beneath these awful changing currents of events, and believe they will stand out strong and clear when the tide turns. In a way, it is just arrogant egotism to be a moralist about the present—and to be a moralist on the side of 'lesser evils' is certainly a most corrupting affair. It is only after being sure of one's fundamental desires and convictions and commitments, that one may safely compromise with the faute de mieux. One deteriorates through half-hearted identification with half approved causes and persons. I have done a lot of that, and a lot of the wisdom I hold forth I have never applied sufficiently to myself. I realise that by this I have often made life more difficult to my friends. . . .

I think you see the ultimately desirable relationship between your and my country on a rather irrational and momentary background, which, justified perhaps by the powers that reign now, allows of no calm and constructive vision of Europe which is necessary to our insides even if Europe actually goes bust. To be a stoic is to have a calm strong realisation of values and proportions go on inside even if outside they're shattered. I need to be helped to be a stoic too, and it is your duty not to let yourself be defeated in this endeavour. If you're in London, you might be of immense help if you could get me (perhaps through P. F.[1]) some South Chinese introductions which could be forwarded. If all possibilities of travel out here fall flat, I may decide on a wholesale change of subject and go to South Africa, and visit Humphrey House[2] on the way in India. Will you please write me his address and perhaps in the case I do make that decision, get me one or two letters to India and Africa as well. But that will only take place if I really cannot penetrate here. If I can I shall probably be rather cut off in the way of mails, so write soon with air mail after you get this. Answer carefully darling—all Shanghai mail I'm afraid, will have been lost.

Love always,
Adam.

[1] Peter Fleming; see letter Shiela–Adam *about* 26 Nov. 1935.

[2] Humphrey House (1908–55); friend of Shiela's and Adam's from Oxford where he was Fellow and Lecturer in English Literature at Wadham. In 1936 he became Professor of English Literature at Presidency College in Calcutta and in 1937 Senior Lecturer at the University of Calcutta. He returned to England on the outbreak of war as a trooper, becoming Senior Lecturer in English Literature at Oxford after the war.

Canton, China.
31.8.37.

Darling Zamecka,

It was very nice suddenly to get your Manila letter in Hong Kong.[1] Manila, you know, is not in the West Indies, and how was it—you thought—I was making my trip towards China by way of West Indies? You see, you really must travel more!

You say you long to hear, sweet—and you tell me a lot of your life, and how difficult it is not to doubt everybody. You make very high demands, but it is right, and general tolerance really implies much less respect. The East makes you wordy or entirely silent.

I left Hong Kong, because for many reasons this was a better base to explore possibilities from. Eberhard has in the meantime come from Japan,[2] and he's staying in a rather dirty brick building in one room with me now. I wish it were you instead. No, not really, because last night we had our first air raid, and being wakened by bombs is not so nice with people one really cares for. Tonight they are expecting another raid, and the Chinese planes have been humming way up in the air all day. Actually they brought down two Jap bombers early this morning. It was a beautiful sight seeing three of the attackers disappear into the dawning sun with a silhouette of a pagoda looming up sharply on the horizon, the bamboo hedges of our garden in the foreground, and all the incredible wealth of unheard of tropical flowers and bushes. It is terribly hot and moist, and now at night the crickets are loud enough to burst your ears, while little salamanders are walking up and down the fly net which protects the porch on which I am writing to you. This afternoon I walked through neighbouring fields and villages. At every corner you see soldiers with mounted bayonets, and even coolies with guns. Everybody is terribly excited, and half Canton is evacuated. How the life on the Pearl River—of which you may have heard—would delight you. Hundreds and hundreds of sampans, little wooden boats with a tow-like matted roof, rowed by women, standing up in their black silk garments, very often with a little baby tied to their backs. Women seem to do all the hard work on the river—you see them carry loads of freight, and handle the heaviest poles and rudders and things. And yet some of them have the tender, sunburnt, peasantlike loveliness which is so delightful in women. They always look at one very thoughtfully, and sometimes they smile, showing delicate rows of white teeth, and I smile back. I like it best when I am quite alone with them all, and nothing at all reminds me that I am an onlooking outsider—they have a sensitive polite way of making you feel that your strangeness is perfectly all right. Even the toughest rickshaw coolie you can win with a brotherly sort of smile—(very wrong policy, Eberhard insists, who shouts at them in German). You must be firm at the same time, otherwise they get the better of you right away and really despise you. But they seem to take life very much like children, with a defenceless kind of trust, coupled to tremendous greed for the things that can be had immediately and with (this I am not certain of) a look of great potential loyalty to things they'd really love. They say that when these crowds get frightened, they become entirely unaccountable, and may run, or shoot you down out of mere confusion.

I shall try to get in some calmer province, but if Germany should side with Japan, we can no longer risk it. Hell, it would be a shame. China is very beautiful—the hills and river quite incredible. I came up here Sunday night, and had a camp bed fixed on the deck, and saw the moon and then the sun rise, and then the early work of peasants and fishermen, and the glorious slow moving junks—housing as it seems, a whole village and its belongings. It is damn hard to give up the north and Peking, but it would have been awful to be there under the Japanese auspices.—It will probably work out, that if we get out of these bombardments all right, we'll travel through Kwangsi, go back to Hong Kong from where Eberhard will reimbark for Europe, and I for Japan, India, and South Africa, if I make the Rhodes Trustees see my point. I am sure you will.

Yes, hold tight to being friends too. We care for the same things enormously, even if unfortunately not quite enough for each other.— I know Winston Churchill is nearer the thing, but isn't he a war monger? And isn't the 'lid' theory as unsound as it ever was? Your intended 'internal explosion' will blow the lid up—a cynically conservative attitude cannot take it on to educate the explosive forces, a paternal, or better, fraternal conservatism might. Don't make yourself a wire in a cynical game of Central European power politics. Much as I believe in the 'long hours alone' in your own home, I hate both the idea of your getting too lonely, and too bound up with politics there. Darling Duff, you're a brave and a good and extremely lovable woman, don't get bitterly and peacelessly involved in a conflict, which must—if you are to remain yourself—be outside your reach.—My morals may be an extremely selfish one, to withhold entirely at the moment, let the bloody turmoil work itself out, not spending myself on any one side of it now, but be true to what one wants to stand for oneself with one's friends, and ready to work for its coming through when we do really get involved.

The Chinese woman has come to tell me where to go when the bombing starts again—it's in the basement where all the servants live. One is really involved all the time. Perhaps I belong to a fatalistic dying race, because the bombs don't seem to mean anything ultimate at all—perhaps the chance of escape is too big still. I'd hate to hear of bombs falling on Prague. Will you really go back there, darling? Bless you, and continue to write to me and be a loyal friend to your

Trott.

[1] See letter Shiela–Adam, London, 22 July 1937.
[2] He had joined Adam in Hong Kong on 26 Aug.

September 4th. [1937]

Darling Trott,
Your Hongkong letters are a great relief for, tho' written long before, they arrive reasuringly after typhoons and bombardments. For heaven's sake be careful. Do nothing stupid or violent for the sake of immediate escape from long-term troubles and perplexities. Be very wise, very calm. Do not go near cholera, or eat or drink anything whose previous history is not known to you. Do not try to go into the interior unless Eberhard is quite certain it is possible. It sounds wild and insane to me, but he must know and be responsible. I think it is a good idea to go to India or S. Africa—except that Humphrey is no longer in the former and I do not know if the latter is very comfortable in Anglo-German relations. I would approve the former tho' seriously and not as a visit to the viceroy. I would get you introductions to Indians. Your smarter friends had better do it to the British. You could call on my name when you get there, because I believe streets are named after us.[1] I'm afraid I cannot get

introductions to South China as I am not in London, but my sister Lulu who married Robert Boyle, knows people in the Loyal Regiment which is stationed at Shanghai. Robert is in West Africa. I will ask her and add names at the bottom. I will enquire vaguely about S. Africa and India but frankly I do not like the first. I think of it as a boring colony where all natural art and culture is dead, and appalling Anglo-Boer society imposed. I think the problems there are not even interesting—only disagreeable—oppression of the natives, national and racial snobbishness of the most kleinbürger[2] sort. Go rather to Malay or Indo-China or Burma to Tibet in a monastery under the mountains—or if you want white men go to New Zealand or Australia or one of the Pacific English-speaking countries. I am very very sorry your Chinese plan is interrupted. It shows one cannot go emigrating into wilds and letting continents go to hell because they send us there instead. My theory of politics is that they are a necessary evil one must interfere with in order to stop it interfering with oneself . . .

Paris is wonderful. I have never stepped into such an air of gaiety and pleasure. I did nothing specially gay, but seemed to breathe it from the absurd sights and sounds of the Exhibition, and the pictures are superb. I have never been so touched or pleased by pictures—in the evenings I walked about the darkening streets which were sad as Utrillo.[3] I suddenly became aware of a sad and pitiable world which I had long since forgotten. It is on that we build our pleasure and our happiness I am frightened sometimes that I have had so much and have so much. It seems it must cease—something must happen, all my pains cannot turn to pleasures, my distastes deepen into sources of comfort—yet they do. I wish I believed in a God to thank. But I suppose a great typhoon will come and sweep it all away—but I have had it now, and if I die I would still think one glorious hour of crowded life is worth an age without a name, and die happy like Charles James Fox.[4] But it is all personal happiness, founded on no certain rock of faith in another world or confidence in this. We must build it up, make it tolerable and good. If we cannot stop the continents going to hell, we must at least, as you say, help to make what comes after. I think the age of continents is beginning and that of nations ending—let's hope to God anyway. I want to be a European—not English or French or German—vaguely that is my interest in Central Europe. In itself I almost hate it and cannot bear the thought of being submerged by it, so must give it the virtues of Western Europe. One must never never despise Western Europe. It may be effete and decadent but it is the flower of Europe and must remain the ideal. But we must make it strong without hurting or changing it. It is not accepting the 'lesser evils'—yet I understand what you mean—yet somehow one must change the evil in it and strengthen all that is good. It is so good—one must die for it even if it means dying for my self-seeking relations in the city and yours on the land. One can avoid deterioration through half-hearted identification with half-approved causes and persons by seeing clearly what one approves and what not, and if one must fight with the disapproval, never hide one's disapproval. Bless you. Be strong, stoical and decided, and if you change your address, plans, or are in trouble, telegraph me in London at once.

S.

¹ Shiela's great-grandfather, Captain James Grant Duff served in the Bombay Grenadiers; was Resident in Satara, and wrote a three-volume History of the Mahrattas; her grandfather, Sir Mountstuart Grant Duff was Governor of Madras.
² Petty bourgeois.
³ Maurice Utrillo, French painter.
⁴ Charles James Fox (1749–1807), a liberal English statesman; his last words were that he died happy; George Macaulay Trevelyan, *British History in the Nineteenth Century*, 9th ed., (London, 1930), p. 116. The preceding clause is from Sir Walter Scott.

London.
Sept. 10th 1937.

Darling Sweet,

It was lovely to get your Canton letter tonight,¹ and I feel warm and near you—but really so far, and bombs have been dropping around you the whole 17 days between your writing and my reading. Please, please be careful. I don't want to lose you. You must be there too to build Europe, for if I build it alone I will build a prison and make a penal system, and only you can prevent me, by showing me they are not all mad or wicked. But you are right and I must not get bitterly involved in all this. I am not really so bitterly involved as before. I care awfully, but sometimes it all seems a mad dangerous game, in which one only has to be braver than everyone else and dare them out, and I get excited instead of religiously wanting to save the world. There is no saving. I can't save myself or Diana or Goronwy, so why did I suppose I could save crowds? I hate political good works. Only a little of life is political, and we try and make it all political. It is waste and wicked. The wet autumn trees are so beautiful.

Yesterday I walked thro' the park. It was a wet Sunday and it was growing dark. I walked about among the crowds at Marble Arch listening to the speeches. I think it is the most terrible and pathetic sight in the whole world. People cold and shivering, starved in mind and heart and body, people mad about God or Sin or the ruling class or something, standing close to each other, all so ugly and inhuman and pathetic. It frightened me very much, and it too made me realise that politics is a game played by a few well-fed, idle people, it has nothing to do with this misery. Their misery is not poverty only, but being only half alive, and their minds tortured and deformed. I have been reading a book about a Rhodesian Negro. With their magic they try to make people happy—a witch doctor is there to cure evil luck and unhappiness. It was by a psychoanalyst, and it seemed to me that they were both after the same thing, and almost in the same way— primitive magic and psychoanalysis. If you go to S. Africa, I will send you the book—but I do not approve altogether your going there. Go to the Conrad places[2] in the Pacific—but I wish you would leave China. We see pictures of it burning, and scattered with corpses. I wish you would leave it. Your letter frightens me, tho' in a way I sup- pose it is something to be there and see these things, people dying, people afraid, but be very careful, and come home soon. It sounds most beautiful, I wish I were with you. I don't think we would mind the bombs. I would rather die with someone I cared for than someone I didn't. . . .

I am rather depressed today. The news from Canton was terrible. I wanted to send you an Eagle cable[3] to leave China, but felt that death was so much a matter of chance in China that it might even occasion your death by making you choose a certain road on a certain day, on which a bomb might fall, but please, darling Adam, leave China as soon as possible, and send me a cable to say where you are going, and that you are safe. You must write regularly to your mother too because she gets very anxious—I wish we could meet again. I would like to go to sleep for a few years till all this noise in the world were over. . . .

I wonder what you will do, and how you feel. I long to have letters from you from China. Any news. I cannot let myself think of the possibility of you being killed, and if you never came back, I would never believe you were dead—but please darling sweet, come back, and do not die. Please be careful, and write often. I am in great need of you, and you must not die. Please leave China soon. I wish we could meet on the Pacific somewhere, and discuss your future, but I'm sure you will decide it very well for yourself, and that it will be a very grand and fine one.

Take care of yourself. Think of me a lot, and the eagle[3] will look after you but you must come back soon so I can have it again to look after me. Bless you, be happy and strong and safe.

Your loving Zamecka.

[1] See letter Adam–Shiela, Canton, China, 31 Aug. 1937.
[2] Joseph Conrad.
[3] Reference to an eagle on a picture postcard which Adam had sent to Shiela. Adam had proposed to Shiela a watchword between them, 'the order of the golden eagle', if either should desperately need the other.

On the Kwei River—
September 21st [1937][1]

Dear Duff,

I wonder how your stay in Scotland was. When I get back to Hongkong—it seems difficult enough—I hope to find a lot of news from you. How nice if you were here to just tell them me, because I am interested in more than you usually put in your letters.

On the whole we've been out of luck here, but a more detailed account of that I shall write later and send you a copy of. The land and people however are fascinating and beautiful. We have been on a sampan now for five days and will be for another two. You must imagine a middle size wooden boat—looking as a Chinese writer put it 'like an upturned eggshell with a roof over it'—in which we dwell under the matroofed middle part while two men row in front and one man at the back. There is also the wife of the man at the back—he's the owner of the boat—and two very nice little daughters and all that on a bottom of wood of probably less than 20 square metres. It's like

FIG. 1. Adam's and Wolfram Eberhard's Journey to Kwangsi Province, September 1937

travelling in a gipsy cart only that they are much cleaner and entirely adapted to the river which they never leave. I think I told you already how much I like these boat people. They are supposed to be the most ignorant and lowest race and class around here and knowing this may add to their extreme modesty. The little girls do nothing but stare at us all day and try to bring things when we appear to be wanting something—it's an experience which is entirely out of the ordinary for them as few Europeans travel round here. The mother cooks our meal on a space of 3 square feet and it tastes quite nice once it's ready.

The River is very beautiful indeed—I had bad luck with my camera but still hope that some of the pictures may be saved. It is a very great shame that we couldn't stay on, because the last town we were in was in every way suited to a longer stay.[2] A former imperial office had attracted a good deal of life and art to that place which is situated in a wilderness of fantastic hills such as one might expect on the less believable looking Chinese drawings, rising from a flat plain in almost vertical steepness to rugged heights—wood and rock forming grotesque patterns. We passed one of them which is supposed to suggest 28 horses in different positions on the surface of the weathered rock and while you are wondering you feel the strange symbolic [sic] that these people attach to things natural and the charm of such procedure as opposed to ours which abstracts meaning into a concept rather than an image. In a shop I saw a lovely galloping young horse painted in black and white by a modern artist which I very much wanted to buy for you but which wasn't on sale at all—the horse I believe always conveys vigour, youth, joy to the Chinese but in a way that he need not *think* these terms and remember that horses are always symbolic of this as we would. A bamboo branch will suggest loyalty, steadfastness, and a pair of wild ducks—love. Coming up to Kweilin by bus I was suddenly struck by the enchanting magic of the Chinese rural landscape, suggesting a peaceful placidity such as I have never seen it before. The green here verges into blue and the opaque streamlets running through and filling up the rice fields and the sudden changes into rugged mountainous country, and above all the amazing colours of the sky towards dusk make it a world one will surely never forget and which I am sure must be the inspiration of a lot that is great in this country. I shall have to leave it after only having touched its fringes, and without having made a single real friend among the Chinese. But of their ways I have seen a good deal, travelled in their way of travelling, eaten their food, stayed at close quarters with them and seen them march to war—which looks very different from our way of doing all these things. Just now the little girl is offering me a queer onion like fruit which neither I nor my Sinologue friend has ever heard of—it tastes like sweet peas. You cannot get very far without the language though and in the language you cannot get very far within one year—so perhaps providence with this bloody war has really spared me an impossible attempt. You know that it was my chief wish to have some time for quietly working out things, for which purpose my friends in Peking suggested a good environment and that in so far China as a subject had been secondary. It would have been a wonderful background—the scholars are really the aristocrats in this setting—but I have no right to be thrown out of gear by this adversity which is China's, the world's not mine in particular—actually I am a lot luckier than hundreds of foreigners in these parts at the moment. I don't think that I should stay for too long a time in India on my way to some other place to settle down in for a while, because India even in winter must be very hot and tropical a climate which does not agree with me in the long run. That's why the north of Kwangsi was so nice because we passed into cooler and more bracing spheres—even in Hongkong which indeed is tropical all right—people seem either toughs or washouts. I met two nice girls there, one English and one half American, but although we went swimming and to the films we didn't find each other absorbingly interesting. As a matter of fact, Duff, I think I must give a very bad impression to any nice girl at the moment. I am sure they must think that I am pretty foul. You must be careful to remember that I am going bald very rapidly and that my remaining hair on both sides is turning grey. Do you think it's some disease or the general depression of human affairs that we have to live through or my particular personal misfortune[?] You don't know my capacity for heavy melancholy and I think I must look out if I am not to return to that kind of gloom which in certain respects possessed me before I met M[3] and you.

My friend's presence—he was in California with us part of the time—reminds me of those still incomprehensible weeks which I understand so little in their real significance that I cannot even say whether they were a failure or not. They certainly were in the pursuit of happiness on both sides, but it wasn't that which made me go. I wanted to be clear and that I seem to have become. Life seems very empty at times.

I very much wonder whether you will be going back to Prague or not. It must seem a big sort of decision at the moment. But I think we would do well to make up our minds to the fact that as to exterior planning our decisions cannot reach very far at the moment and that the same may happen to your solitude in Prague that happened to my hoped for one in Peking. At present I am still at a loss to find a work-able path into the future, most roads seem blocked and yet it is too easy to complain of the state of the world when it is one's own power to adjust and scheme that is lacking. It doesn't do to be eaten up by doubts and wonderings—right or wrong is strangely mixed up in all possible courses and it is not so much a matter of choice but of carv-ing out in practice the maximum of right in any one of them and while one isn't concerned in doing that one surely should increase one's powers by gratefully accepting what beauty and joy one can yet perceive. Nietzsche says: Since ever man was he has too little rejoiced. This only, brothers, is our original sin! And when we learn better to rejoice we best forget how to hurt others and to contrive pain. I think you rather agree with this philosophy.

As to actual courses later on, it seems to me that I should stick to Germany and help to work out things there. I could become a univer-sity teacher, or I could still enter the diplomatic service. But it seems that both would inevitably bring back the impasse of all these last years and that some job on the legal side of industry is where I should try and grind myself through. The job will probably be 100% hell and not a mixture as the other two would be. But as a person I would remain intact and independent.—Well, Duff, here's another of your 'half-finished' friends for you! I know I am and I am grateful to you for being apparently still willing to go on with some patience and confidence being my friend still. Sometimes I think that it must be truly a big strain for you, but sometimes I don't.—I wish you were drifting down this lovely river with us. The banks are now full of wood—a rather rare phenomenon for China and from time to time we pass those junks which are pulled up by man power, either towed from the bank or worked with a rope that is fastened some far way off and which about ten people wind on to a vertical roll in front of the ship giving the most frightful squeaking noise or pushed forward by coolies with large poles on the sides of the deck; they have a weird song not entirely unlike that of the Volga boatmen. Life is terribly hard for them. Sometimes you see five figures bowing deep with the tow-rope round their shoulders on the river bank moving inch by inch while the ship is passing up one of the many rapids through which we are drifting and bouncing downwards with considerable speed.

Did you get a letter I wrote to you from Canton?[4] Communica-tions were severed soon after we left and some of the mail to me will probably have got lost too. It's a very dramatic spot really.

In Liuchow I bought you a ring which really consists of four rings which it is very difficult to fit into each other so that one can put it on. Probably I will have lost it before I come back and probably you will not like it anyway. If I had had a little more money I could have bought lovely things in Kweilin which has one very good antique shop.

Back in Hong Kong,
September 27

We passed the Japanese warship unmolested below Wuchow and arrived in this safe but difficult place—I am leaving for Japan before next airmail—found one very nice letter from you about Paris and a little about Scotland. My people seem to have been overanxious—I am glad you would not be that anyhow. I may get into North China via Japan, but not for a long time. Thank you very much for offering your help about India—I only know Humayn Kabir[5] with whom I walked up the Themse[6] when I first saw you—near [the] Trout Inn.[7] I hate to leave China—but not HK. I'll write you a better letter soon.

Much love.
Adam.

[1] In spite of warnings from Chinese, German consular, and Rhodes Trust authorities, Adam and Eberhard proceeded with a three-weeks' visit to Kwangsi province, leaving Hong Kong on 27 Aug. for Canton, and leaving Canton on 4 Sept. for the North. Their route took them on river boats along the Hsi River to Wuchow, along the Hsün River to Nanning, and by bus to Liuchow. The next stop was Kueilin (Kweilin) the capital of the province. This letter was written during the last leg of the journey which, starting on 16 Sept. took the two travellers along the Keui (Kwei) River on a sampan back to Wuchow, and from there to Hong Kong where they arrived on 24 Sept. Adam subsequently wrote a report on the trip: 'A Trip to Kwangsi in September 1937' (a German version is entitled 'Streifzug durch die Provinz Kuang-hsi'); Trott Archive. After this expedition Adam and Eberhard parted company since the latter, partly because of the unsettled conditions in China, chose to take up an invitation to teach at Ankara University.

[2] Kueilin (Kweilin).

[3] Miriam Dyer-Bennet.

[4] See letter Adam–Shiela, Canton, China, 31 Aug. 1937.

[5] An old friend whom Adam first met when spending Hilary term (mid-January–mid-March) of 1929 at Mansfield College, Oxford. They met again during Adam's first year as Rhodes Scholar in 1931–2, when both were students at Balliol.

[6] German for Thames.

[7] Near Oxford, at Godstow.

[Ashridge Park,]
[*about* 5] Oct. 1937.

Darling Trott,

My letters to you must be piling up in the vaults of the Shanghai bank. I wish you would write to me. Banks should give interest and my deposit is getting very large in the Shanghai bank. I can't ask you in every letter where and how you are. I suppose I must assume you are safe and in Hong Kong, or you will not answer my questions. Come home. Why need you stay in China? If you would go to America I would meet you. It is so long ago, and I am much in need of my best friend in Europe. I am slowly demoralising. Ambition has gone, and Innocence is closing up its eyes.[1] Do you know the poem? It is very beautiful.

I am in the Conservative Bonar Law College[2]—if that isn't demoralising, what is? My last shred of honour—Douglas' Case for Socialism[3] is in my suitcase. I walk about with a miserable expression of scorn on my face, which doesn't cut any ice with me. The hall of the house is like a cathedral. Old women sit about in it reading books with Boots Library[4] tickets hanging out of them. I am slightly amused, slightly bored, and very much look forward to going to bed. I have a cold and fever. I think if I could be it alone in Switzerland, I would like to be seriously ill. I feel it would kill all the poison in me and the world, and we could start again.

I have got past the stage of being upset by anything that happens anywhere, but have an awful feeling that if only the worst would happen I could deal with it. It is this senseless waiting about which is so hard to bear. I have a lovely time, and yet, o yet—something's wrong, and the glory has indeed passed from the earth. My friends are changed. There is no innocence or kindness left. Everybody is very nice—just like that. All reduced to a dull and sensible grey.

I shouldn't be writing this to you—but a nice cheerful letter about how beautiful the autumn is, how happy the world, how hopeful and good. So it would be if you were not in China. . . .

My pamphlet is really quite good, and sound people like G. P. Gooch and Seton-Watson think it all right.[5] I think I might be allowed to write a book on the Little Entente on the strength of it, and it would be a good thing to do. I would meet all the crooks of Central Europe, and learn what we are to do with it when the question arises. The time before it does so is getting smaller and smaller. Perhaps I am ambitious after all. It's all a matter of self-control, which I lack terribly, and so all my energy is wasted in gestures of pity and despair, in sudden and unpersevering interest. You were wrong to doubt the value of Ripka's influence over me. He steadied me up and encouraged me to be serious and hard working. Here I am up and down all the time and accomplish very very little. I meet quite a lot of people and that is fun, but I can't get away from myself.

The cathedral is filled with girls in silk frocks, and men quite as dreary as the socialists.

Continued later. It is a most wonderful beautiful day. Breakfast on the lawns of English country houses is very beautiful. It is really complete peace and sunshine, and I shouldn't write you such gloomy letters. Ashridge Park is a fantastic place, with bedrooms which Queen Elizabeth slept in, and therefore lots of turrets. The people here are very odd and a real proof that the backbone of England is conservative. They must have been a greater despair to the radicals of the 19th century than to the communists of the 20th, for a change in their manners, religious conviction, or moral belief must have seemed a far more difficult job than their uprooting from conservative politics. If the one happens, then I suppose the other can, though they look very solidly placed to me. The library is full of books on socialism, and the Daily Herald[6] is on sale at the hall. That's the way to do it. It's regarded [as] so fantastic and absurd that anyone should be persuaded by books that books have free access. A bell has sounded now and they have all gone to pray. I can't pray, and certainly not among conservative lower middle classes—and besides, the day is so beautiful, and if I could believe in God, I would put him on a green lawn where the autumn leaves had fallen, and the sun shone.

When my friend Bienstock[7] came to stay, we talked a little about God, and rightly he said to me, life is without dignity or purpose if one does not believe in God—perhaps it is why I am unhappy—I have no other reason to be—only the waywardness of all things—it is really quite funny and pleasant at Ashridge. Chelsea provides a number of budding conservative young men. Last night we listened to Harold Nicolson[8] on the Foreign Office, a very good, interesting lecture. Everybody was obviously expecting it to be just funny, and so laughed where it wasn't meant to be funny, and not when it was. He attacked your friend Brick and Drop[9] very forcefully and met with complete silence.

Love me, write to me—be safe and well.

Zamecka.

[1] Michael Drayton (1563–1631), 'The Parting': Since there's no help, come let us kiss and part / Nay, I have done, you get no more of me; / And I am glad, yea, glad with all my heart, / That thus so cleanly I myself can free. / Shake hands for ever, cancel all our vows, / And when we meet at any time again, / Be it not seen in either of our brows / That we one jot of former love retain. / Now at the last gasp of Love's

latest breath, / When, his pulse failing, Passion speechless lies / When Faith is kneeling by his bed of death, / And Innocence is closing up his eyes / Now if thou wouldst, when all have given him over / From death to life thou might'st him yet recover; In Sir Arthur Quiller-Couch (ed.), *The Oxford Book of English Verse 1250–1918* (Oxford, 1939), p. 167.

  ² A political institute at Ashridge Park sponsored by the Conservative Party. They were debating British foreign policy and Shiela wanted to know what their position was. She met David Hopkinson there and introduced him to Diana.

  ³ Douglas Jay, *The Socialist Case* (London, 1937).

  ⁴ A lending library.

  ⁵ George Peabody Gooch (1873–1968), a historian of Germany; Honorary Fellow of Trinity College, Cambridge; editor of the *Contemporary Review*, for which Shiela started writing in 1937; Robert Seton-Watson (1879–1951), expert on Central European and Balkan history; Masaryk Prof. at the University of London 1922–45; Prof. of Czechoslovak Studies 1945–9.

  ⁶ A Labour newspaper.

  ⁷ Prof. Gregory Bienstock, a Russian Menshevik friend of Shiela's from Prague.

  ⁸ Harold Nicolson (1886–1968), from 1953 Sir Harold; diplomat, politician, author. Served in British delegation to the Paris Peace Conference; National Labour MP 1935–45.

  ⁹ Joachim von Ribbentrop (1893–1946), Hitler Germany's Ambassador to the Court of St James's from Aug. 1936 and Foreign Minister from Feb. 1938.

London.
11.10.37.

Darling Trott,

It was lovely to have your letter this morning, and I'm afraid the news that you were leaving China (have left indeed), though you looked upon it sadly, was the best I could have wanted—except that you were coming home, or somewhere within reach. China sounds most beautiful, and I am glad you will remember it, as I remember Spain, as a beautiful country where the people are noble and generous—but China must be more beautiful, and the Chinese sound gentler and kinder than the Spaniards. I wish I had been on your sampan with you, and seen those hills and plains. Your travels sound a little sad and forlorn, and I wish I was with you, because together we would find much pleasure in fundamentally savage places like Hong Kong . . . .

Your quotation from Nietzsche is very moving,[1] and it is the attitude I would like to have, but find so hard. I am very intolerant, and a thousand things I condemn a priori. I met a wonderful man—at least listened to him but did not speak, who had been Bishop of Johannesburg, and his gentleness and tolerance was a wiser lesson than I have been taught for long past. Tolerance is so often tolerance of evil, and his was only of good, of pity for misunderstanding, and even, in a good way, understanding of evil. I am still sure that tout comprendre should be tout pardonner, though in practice it is so hard to forgive. He had a beautiful childish face, and a kind smile. Was very much against people like Herzog and Pirow[2] in South Africa. I didn't feel any more in favour of your going there after hearing what the problems of the place are, and how difficult it is for good men. Wouldn't it be lovely to go to a country where good men were in the majority. Even here, where standards of public honour are fairly high, I find a shamelessness and selfishness past all belief even in people's professions. I am staying with my grandmother in the country, and the house is full of city chaps, friends of my uncle. They most sincerely believe that the only aim of our foreign policy should be to keep stocks and shares high and steady in the city, and that any other aim is mischievous and fatal. They condemn our foreign policy for being 'aggressive' when heaven knows the world waits on us making any positive gesture at all. The Times reports that the conversations concerning the shooting of our ambassador are proceeding with 'cordiality' in your part of the world.[3] I begin to sympathise almost with the bombardment of Almeria after that.[4] O heavens, how can one find sanity and kindness in this world of international discord. Where is the faith of our Oxford days? . . .

[Shiela.]

[1] See letter Adam–Shiela, on the Kwei River, 21 Sept. 1937.
[2] General James Barry Munnik Hertzog (1866–1942), founder of the Afrikaner Nationalist Party; Prime Minister of the Union of South Africa 1924–39. O. Pirow; Minister of Railways, and Harbours and Defence of the Union of South Africa 1937.
[3] On 26 Aug. 1937 His Majesty's Ambassador to China, Sir Hugh Knatchbull-Hugessen, was wounded following a machine-gun and bomb attack by Japanese planes on his car which was travelling from Shanghai to Nanking. The incident was closed on 22 Sept.
[4] The bombardment, during the Spanish Civil War, of Almería (near Málaga) by the Nationalists 3–7 Feb. 1937.

Tientsin.[1]
[20 October 1937]

Dear sweet,
    I seem to have arrived in yet another still more beautiful continent. The air is clear and autumnal and the sun shines brightly all day from a vast immaculate sky. The north is fascinating—quite different in this very part with no government at the moment, but wonderfully substantial and dignified. Maybe I am wrong—but it is very good to really get away from . . . Hongkong, I meant to say. For I was interrupted and am now actually in *Peking*.

It still seems impossible and unreal, but it is without doubt the best thing that has happened to me for a long time. I don't know where to begin telling you about it all, but I must if you are to understand all the new strange and magnificent things that enter into my life. Darling Zamecka you will be rather envious I fear though if you've gone to Paris instead of Prague all is well and you are living in the other great city of the world.

My friend[2] met me at the station with his two princely servants one of whom is looking after me now in a gentle and dignified manner and they brought me to this house which we are inhabiting together. It is a mixture of palace and peasant quarter outside the inner city and surrounded by trees.

next morning

I made my first round of visits yesterday. It is all very strange. The huge imperial city with a dead life. The Europeans seem like dwarfs in it all—persevering tenaciously with their petty habits from home. But we live so far out that I shall see little of them. My host is a very peculiar man—a little like a magician. Our household will not be very easy. Imagine yourself being suddenly surrounded by huge cold calmness, ancient and solemn, looking down on you, as it were, and waiting with an ironic smile which turn you're going to take next. The deadness and forlorn beauty of it all is bewitching and one feels like a fool outfooled.[3]

  [1] City in the province of Hopei.
  [2] Gustav Ecke. See letter Adam–Shiela as from California, about 10 May 1937, n. 8. Adam stayed with him for about a year while making excursions to Japan, Korea, Manchuria, and the interior of China.
  [3] The rest of his letter is missing.

Peking,
Oct. 21st, 1937.

Darling sweet,
    . . . The second page had to be torn for its inappropriate mention of topics—Let our correspondence remain as European as possible. Your papers can actually tell you more what is happening on a large scale out here than I can. And what is happening to me on a small scale—it seems very much and very important—is extremely difficult to convey in its beginning stages. Everything is quaint and intriguing, and one day you will have to see it all for yourself. I think of you very often when I sense this penetrating spirit of superior calm and serenity. It is just what we all lack, and the equanimity of people living at

the fringe of economic disaster all the time, their bright, tranquil gaiety, is lovely and reassuring. So far I am most grateful to have found a really peaceful haven for the time being, and in my host a friend of unusual size and intellectual generosity. Perhaps the inner Trott is being given its chance now, and you will notice the changes later which you have been waiting for. I am being taught lessons which can no longer be learnt at home, and I have a beautiful room and writing desk, and nothing but natural sounds and exquisitely balanced human constructions around me. It is now entirely my fault if I can make nothing of the i. T.[1]

And what are you doing, my dear? Remember that in everything you do I am deeply concerned. Try and be tranquil too, and fix your eyes on the serene and permanent side of our Europe. I hope you have gone to Paris and not the other place. But if you have, I admire you for it. It is difficult not to know where you are—and still more to think that you might be lonely. The eagle wants to look after you, and he can fly over all clouds of depression and over all chasms of terror on this bloody new world. I am not forgetting that world—it is present even here all right. Send me the drafts of what you write, I mean the scraps of preliminary attempts which otherwise go into the waste paper basket.—You would very much approve of all my new friends, they seem like the elite of the world to me at present, although they're all of distinctly west European origin so far. I am going to take French lessons from a White Russian former diplomat probably, or from a Chinese girl who was brought up in Paris. I shall be neither social nor flirtatious, and am meeting 'old China hands' in preference to the legation quarter where Gerry Young[2] has risen to some prominence and treats me with friendliest hospitality.—Our home is our castle though—it is run on the slow and dignified style of imperial Peking, with even the children of the servants playing their part in the same. Actually it is not an aesthetic spleen, but an ingenious design to rescue a calm retreat for thought and work. You and I know that this is a hard secret, and I will take advantage of this for both of us. Let me hear from you soon, my sweet.

Lovingly,

A.

[1] 'Inner Trott'.
[2] George Peregrine Young, friend of Adam's and Shiela's from their Oxford days. Adam met him again early in 1935 when Young was Third Secretary at the British Embassy in Berlin.

London.
25.10.37.

Darling Trott,

I hope you are liking Japan. I'm afraid it cannot be the time of year for cherry blossom, but all the same, perhaps it is very beautiful. I hope you are happy. You have written me such depressed letters since you left Europe. I hoped you would cheer up when you got beyond our reach. I'm afraid California made that difficult. Please cheer up now. In order to be happy at all one must have a sort of blind optimism that the cycles in which the physical world moves are somehow related to the cycles of returning happiness. There is so much pleasure in the physical world. Yesterday I went and looked at it by the sea, and I think nothing so beautiful, wild, and strong, as the winter sea, and I wish I lived by it, or could always go to it. Instead I return to land-locked Central Europe, where not even the sea wind penetrates, but there will be snow and winds from the mountains, and they will be fresh.

. . . Prague feels again like a home I return to, or rather a wide world I go back into with some relief, from the coils of my well-loved friends. But next time I shall come back more gladly because of new things to do and new people to be friends with. I have become a very dutiful daughter to my family, and take an odd sort of pleasure from living among my relations.

Last weekend there was a party for all the workers on the estate at High Elms, and for the family, because of the birth of the new heir[1] (my cousin John is disinherited). It was a very shaming performance and a mockery of feudal relations, but very much a tract for the times. Feudalism is dead in England, and on the broken relations of master and servant must be built something more honourable and equal from man to man. The present relations are sordid and ugly. The butler is a fine handsome ex-soldier, and serves the family favourites with the servility required of him. My sister says he will knife us all if ever there is a revolution in the country. Unpleasant as that would be, it would only be the other side of empty servility. . . .

[Shiela]

[1] Eric Reginald Lubbock, (1928–), Liberal MP for Orpington 1962–70, now 4th Lord Avebury.

Peking.
Oct. 1, 1937.[1]

Darling Zamecka,

I've just come back from Yenching, a university outside this city, where I was staying for two days with M. Jablonsky, a Polish baron who is interested in Chinese languages and customs. This did not prevent us from getting onto the subject of Eastern Europe in the end, and I was stunned by my ignorance. I wished you had been there—I often wish that. After a period of peace and relaxation, all the old problems come back to one with renewed violence, and grab and shake one, and leave one exhausted. George Taylor,[2] of whom I may have told you in England—a very good student of Chinese politics and history—has just come out here to teach at Yenching, and gave me a very gloomy picture of Europe. He thinks your govt is definitely bent on lining up with the Fascist powers, using internal anti-fascist feeling in England as a whip for more occasional threats. Letting Spain bleed herself white he considers a deliberate policy on your side, also the reducing of France to a second-rate power, and of keeping her there—all motivated by the fact that class interest with you (only partially identical with imperial interest) is overruling national interest, and a stabilisation of the present class principles only hoped for from the fascist regimes. They are supposed to form, he thinks, a cordon sanitaire around Russia. Any bluff from the English side of using Russia as a lever against Germany would always be called.

I think this may be an over-simplified view, but there's a good deal of the crude logic of big property owners in high politics at the moment—and many whom one wouldn't have expected to do so seem to rely on their crude motives to keep the peace of Europe. It may be a very sinister peace, but still better than the opposite. What will happen in Central Europe though?

I long to know where you are. If you have written to me, your letters must have got stuck in Hongkong or Tokyo. It seems to me that we are both in rather an isolated period of transition, but I should like at least to know the externals of your present life. Is it all excited and Parisian, or is it Slavonic and solitary again, or are you nestling in England after all. You mustn't let me down entirely, for when I come back to Europe I shall be very much in need of a friend like you to teach me again to breathe that atmosphere. I think I shall try hard to go to Paris as a period of transition and for finally learning French. I don't think I shall bring much back in the way of Chinese studies, but I hope a clearer head and a calmer hand. At present my head is stuffed with a cold, and I feel a bit cut off from you in Europe.

Let me hear from you soon. Don't think I am sinking away in silk cushions. I am very much part of the same universe as you. I hope all is well with you.

Always love,
A.

¹ Adam made an obvious error in the dating of this letter. The correct date is most likely 1 Nov. 1937.

² George E. Taylor, an orientalist whom Adam had met in Nov. 1936 at Chatham House. Trott saw a great deal of Taylor while in Peking; see Malone, *Adam von Trott*, (diss.) p. 510.

Train, Paris to Prague.
2.11.37.

Darling A,

Writing to you is becoming quite an occupation for journeys—but never before for such a long journey as this, and it is more to distract me from a slow death by suffocation and combustion than because I have anything nice to say. I was in Paris for three days and Brussels for one since I last wrote. Paris has lost all its terrors for me and I like it enormously and feel at home—so much at home that I trail round the streets on ineffectual practical missions . . .

I spent a certain amount of time with my late employer,¹ and admire him as intensely and deeply as ever. I meant to learn all the political secrets of Europe from him, but instead we talked about God and immortality and our purpose in the world. He has extraordinary clear and simple beliefs and ideals which I envy—I have developed so lazy a habit of mind that I scarcely think any more, and tho' I am reading Pascal and feel among those he condemns in the first few chapters, it is as yet impossible to change my ways. Even Notre Dame no longer gives me a sense of God or eternity, and eternal spaces no longer frighten me because I no longer know what they are like. The world has become horribly 'quotidien'² and the only things which stretch beyond are love and friendship and politics, and all these are declining in value—perhaps not friendship—for my friends I care more than anything in the world, tho' I should not. They tell me, in order to serve a political cause, or even to do one's work well and honourably, one must put certain ideas above personal interest—personal interests and friendship are so often interchangeable, and every time I choose a public rather than a private loyalty, I feel ashamed—one of the strongest influences I have come under lately has been Hadow's.³ We disagree so profoundly and yet with such respect for each other, that somehow even disagreement honours us. He teaches me a more human view of politics, a more simple idea of honour—tho' my late employer thinks the trouble in Prague may be of his making because he didn't want me there. I am sure he didn't want me there, but also sure he would never have done anything to make it harder. He was about the only diplomat who was friendly and kind. I wish I didn't have a thousand lives—and only one of each with each of my friends—or perhaps I should be glad of such variety.

I had another talkative taxi-driver who wanted to take me [on] a free tour of Paris in his motor car. He was very inquisitive and had a decided penchant for intimacy—which is so extraordinarily unpleasant with strangers. Luckily the latter seems to be confined to taxi-drivers taking one to the station.

I think I shall stay in Prague till near Christmas, and perhaps go somewhere in the mountains for most of December and January, and start work at the end of January. I am rather looking forward to studying again, reading history books and biographies, and learning systematically. There are a thousand books I want to read.

Write to me and tell me your plans. I want awfully to go to America.

Love always,
S.

1 Mowrer.
2 Ordinary.
3 See letter Shiela–Adam, Prague, 19 May 1933, n. 3.

Peking.
6.11.37.

My Dear Zamecka,
I miss your letters very much—although I think it may be a good thing not to depend on letters rather than on common thoughts, of which I am sure we have many. There are a great many things which I should like to discuss with you, though. One of them is my relations with the local Germans here. I am afraid, although I have been here only about 20 days, I have a bad reputation with them. They think me baronial and conceited and perhaps politically undesirable. I am afraid my disappearing hair adds to the appearance of stand-offishness (I'll keep my hat on when we meet again!)—The Americans here have been told about certain deprecating remarks which I made in the wrong company about their country, and they dislike me. And to

your countrymen I have said a little too boastfully that I don't wish to be invited, and the world fashion of being anti-German adds to it all, so that all in all I am very much out of favour with European Peking. But all this must sound surprisingly petty to you, and it is, and doesn't really matter. But you used to tell me about your little feuds in Prague, and we must both learn to be wise and determined about these matters—otherwise they bite and weaken one.

My love for Chinese Peking is still growing, and is, I think right and profitable. In many ways, it is truly like being transplanted into a mediaeval cosmos with mediaeval myths, and a strong natural simplicity which presents to one the issues of mind and soul in a much more differentiated and fine form than our harried and brutalised social system. All these are mere words in a letter, but like a fairy garden in reality, which tempts one to enter more and more deeply. Do you disapprove?

I read an article by Wheeler-Bennett[1] today in some American quarterly, on European Possibilities—well written but very gloomy. Yet, what he calls the 'miracle of peace' seems the only working hypothesis on which one can go on at all. It is rather defeatist to call European peace a miracle—he says the next two years are going to be the most critical in the history of Europe. But I cannot see what substantial appeasement can grow out of the mere fact of your having completed your re-armament. Unsound Machiavellianism will not keep Europe together. Perhaps the last war destroyed what used to keep Europe essentially together in spite of its many nations and states, and perhaps it is merely romantic to hope for another actual . . . [2]

[1] Wheeler-Bennett, 'European Possibilities', *Virginia Quarterly*, 13, no. 4 (Autumn 1937), 481–500; the 'miracle of peace' was an alternative to: (*a*) a show-down between the two rival groups; (*b*) giving Germany a free hand in the East; (*c*) a Russo-German *rapprochement*. The author envisaged a chance for peace if the gap between German and British rearmament could be narrowed. 'A war postponed may be a war avoided' (p. 500); cf. letter Shiela–Adam, Prague, about 12 Nov. 1936, n. 6.

[2] The rest of the letter is missing.

22 Nov. 1937.

Darling Trott,

Thank you for your letter[1] this morning. . . .

I don't know what to think of your George Taylor, and only hope he is wrong in his criticism of the government. If he is right, it means once and for all that one cannot go with those people, and yet you know, property owners and landed property owners did stand for something once—for ideas and books, and certain forms of life which were pleasant if no more. Compromises are so difficult. How can one oppose them where they are wrong, and yet not destroy the good things they stand for? They are such blind fools. The only hope is that France shall be the leader of European civilisation in all the parts of it that matter. If we reduce her to a third-class power, we will be led in the arts by the boors and buffoons of your and my country. I think when these things are happening at home, one must be there. The pretensions of it!

You ask about Central Europe. The English opinion here is that things are moving pretty fast, that the Czechs will give the Germans autonomy, and then, in my opinion, your game is almost won. My people don't think so, but I think they blind themselves out of snobbish dislike of the Czechs. My Czech friends do not confirm this. On the contrary, they say that Czech opinion has hardened against Henlein, and that all parties now see that there is nothing to be done. Henlein has apparently hardened too, and today would not come into the government if they asked him because he is out for autonomy. I persist in thinking it a foreign and not an internal problem, and one which is as much dependent on us as on any others. We have to make up our minds what we can allow you and what not. If you want what we cannot allow, there will be war. That I presume was the purpose of Halifax[2] in Berlin. Heaven knows the result. The Evening Standard published a story that you would bargain colonies against a free hand in Europe. You denied it hotly. It was said to come from Italy, with the aim of making agreement impossible. The Czechs treated it with scorn, in which I envy their sang froid more than their understanding, because I think they are quite capable of it at home. Nobody cares much for this place except a few very unrepresentative people on the left with no influence.

Delbos[3] comes to Central Europe next week on a sort of Barthou[4] journey to fix up the French allies.[5] I suspect it is a hopeless case. I do not know who is winning the race at the actual moment, but in the long run I suppose you are. I don't know why the French risk an open defeat unless they are fairly confident. It is something that the Poles and Yugoslavs even receive them. I may possibly do the whole journey if some paper may want it. I hope they will, for professional reasons, and they won't for private ones, because I want to get out of this world for the moment . . .

I will send you the Spectator[6] with an article by me in it. It is what the Czechs say, but the latest information goes the other way, and the talk I had with Hodža[7] made me suspect that things were going the other way. They are bringing the whole matter into the limelight now, and that, I suspect, is the beginning of the end.

Bless you, sweet, be happy. I will not let you down entirely, as you say, but look forward very much to your coming to Europe. I will be a nice West European friend for you again, and shake off my East European manners. I look forward very much to you coming home and we will have a lovely time. When will it be? I hope you have a happy Xmas. If you came home, via America in the late summer, I might meet you half way, and we could stay with your American cousins that have the dogs and horses.

Much love to you always.

S.

---

[1] See letter Adam–Shiela, Peking, 1 Nov. 1937.

[2] Viscount Halifax paid an official visit to Berlin between 17 and 22 Nov.; on 19 Nov. he had a five-hour talk with Hitler in Berchtesgaden; on 20 Nov. he saw Göring; no official communiqués were issued.

[3] Yvon Delbos (1885–1956); as Foreign Minister (1936–8) he forced through the Non-Intervention principle during the Spanish Civil War.

[4] Louis Barthou (1862–9 Oct. 1934), French Foreign Minister 1934; assassinated with King Alexander of Yugoslavia in Marseilles by a Croat extremist; see letter Shiela–Adam, Chelsea, 15 Oct. 1934.

[5] After the First World War France had to reconstruct its Eastern system of alliances by becoming the chief patron of the Little Entente. Also, France concluded in connection with the Locarno Treaties (Oct. 1925) a Treaty of Mutual Assistance with Poland and Czechoslovakia, in case of a German attack. The French system of alliances, however, did not hold fast in the face of the Nazi threat.

[6] 'Czechoslovakia's Germans', 'From a Special Correspondent', *Spectator*, 19 Nov. 1937.

[7] Milan Hodža (1878–1944), Czechoslovak politician; Prime Minister 1935–8; advocate of Danubian Federation.

Peking.
3.1.38.

Darling Duff,

What is happening to our letters? I have not heard of you more than once since I came here in October, and for some weeks now I too have failed to write. I do not know where you are or how you are. . . .

The last three years in Germany my friendships seemed the most real part of my existence, it was very natural to relate most things to them, and amongst them you know you were the most important. But something has changed since I was in California, and I am beginning to find myself—not only outwardly—in a different universe. . . .

I read quite a lot, and work—but not as calmly and undisturbedly as I should. First, because I haven't quite the presence of mind to turn from Europe entirely for a while (my silence is part of that attempt) and secondly because, as always, I get involved in other people's lives and upset my peace by them. You are so far away, Duff, and I don't know what you will make of the things I write to you—but you are so sweet and candid to me that I think you should extend your sympathetic confidence even to my instabilities which I think are much worse than yours—because they sometimes shake me like a plum tree—prematurely and violently so that all the half ripe plums fall off, and even some leaves, so I look decrepit for a whole season. In other words, I want you to be friends with the plum tree quite apart from its plums. . . .

Hell, there are 500 reasons why it must be difficult to carry on a normal correspondence from this realm to yours. But I *want* to 'hold tight to being friends' as you once put it, and I send you all this long-winded letter and some scraps, not because I think it is a very spirited contribution to this friendship, about which I care a very great deal, but as a document of my existence that you may make the use of that you please. I know that we would remain substantially loyal even without 'documents' like this—but I want it from you too, because it is so easy to lose the fresh vision of the friend one cares for in the rushing and distant crowd of indifferent people.

Love—and write darling—

always your
Trott.

London.
[21 Jan.] 1938

Darling Adam,
   . . . Now I have had a long letter from you—rather sad and worried. Do not be. Our friendship goes on without letters, tho' I much like to have them and to write them. If I write little, it is because I often start and make an incomplete picture which I do not want to send—but I will write more often, and if you can write to me, I will like it more than long silences, tho' I am not afraid of them. . . .
   Bless you—be Bloody, Bold, Resolute, not only to Macbeth's purposes, but just to snap your fingers at the world, at any damn European community, or extra-European crisis.

Love
Shiela.

Peking.
Jan. 26th, 1938.

Darling Duff,
   Thank you for your letter—I cannot quite explain why we should find it difficult to write, but I too have done a bit of 'tearing up.' But the Trott has not really changed, and couldn't ever be chilly as far as you are concerned. But our worlds are very far apart at present—and I am very far from mastering my side, and rather than conveying it inadequately, I feel I must keep quiet for a while. I don't seem to be able to write to anyone at all except my people—and to them I don't write often. This, I know, has rather a selfish side, but I don't seem to be able to help it. The letters I actually write after an effort seem utterly ridiculous.
   Possibly you will have to let me try and get 'unattached' too—I appreciate the true value of it, I think, and you are right to say that it goes together with essential faithfulness to one's friends. I wrote in my last letter . . . that I think you are extremely loyal. It is perhaps your most outstanding quality—though I realise too that it is a source of possible dangers, as it narrows your possibility of happiness sometimes. But that is very much to your credit, sweet, and, I am sure, will make you triumph gloriously over the wear and tear of that 'wide plain' into which you are 'winding' after beautiful and solitary Prague. (I am ashamed when I compare my accounts to your vivid and real descriptions of what you have experienced.) But I wish

somebody would take you out of that journalism. You will frown again and perhaps smile a little bitterly. Hell, I know we have not much 'pick and choose' for ploughing through some tolerable place in our world.—This sounds grim for you and me though.

> Peking,
> 28.1.1938.

[Dear Shiela,]
 . . . We are both in a distinctly privileged position and for many reasons not subject to the fate of surrender which most people are suffering.

You know here one is outside that vicious circle of glamour, excitement and depression which one gets entangled in in our big cities—but there is no ready answer for what makes the people here superior to it. The decayed culture of China still lives in their heart, and it has a calm and big character. But I don't want to tear up this letter again. . . .

I gave a lecture to the German Club on 'Anglo-German Relations since 1871' and told them that whereas we had an authoritarian patriotism you had a spontaneous though subconsciously imperialistic one and while Bismarck knew how to handle this profound difficulty his successors muddled it into a hopeless sequence of bluff counter bluff and that we both must not behave like that again.

Darling, I should like to come back soon and give you—as you once let me—the protection and sense of purpose which my clumsy Germanic soul has always wanted to give you. But I must not come back before I am not different and can do something. Now I feel that every day brings me nearer to that—at home I would probably find the opposite. Perhaps I am wrong, but as long as it appears so to me I must stay and work it out.

> True love always,
> A.

> Czechoslovakia.
> 10th Feb. 1938.

Darling Trott,
 I'm sending you by this same post a copy of Time and Tide, which has a painful and apposite little story about letter writing, an article by me[1] about the League (which you will probably disapprove of, but tell me), and an article on Germany by Norman Angell[2] which I

think is good. The events in your country in the last week[3] are very stirring and now there are rumours of revolts in the garrisons. I cannot take them very seriously, but perhaps we will learn more. Those chiefly concerned are on the Polish border—You will know all about it long before you get this, so it is silly of me to tell you. People here are very frightened and think it means a sharpening of policy against them, and I have a suspicion that strong precautionary measures have been taken akin to mobilisation. Personally I see no very great need for anxiety—if anything I feel rather hopeful, but that is because I am pessimistic by nature, and believe your country to be united behind its leader and prepared for a radical foreign policy in any case. The loss of certain of your generals and their moderating influence does not make the war more certain, whereas it may affect the outcome. . . .

Much love,

S.

[1] 'League and Axis', 'From a Correspondent'; *Time and Tide*, 19 (5 Feb. 1938), 153 f; the article amounts to a plea for the League to assert its coercive powers against the aggressions of the Berlin-Rome-Tokyo Axis.

[2] Norman Angell, 'A Monthly Interpretation of Foreign Affairs; The Englishman Replies'; ibid., 167–72.

[3] On 4 Feb. 1938 Hitler reorganized the military and diplomatic command. Field Marshal Werner von Blomberg, Minister of War and Supreme Commander of the Armed Forces, and General Werner von Fritsch, Supreme Commander of the Army, were replaced by Generals Wilhelm Keitel and Walther von Brauchitsch. Constantin von Neurath was replaced by Joachim von Ribbentrop as Foreign Minister. The changes in the military command were brought about by Hitler by means of personal charges against the generals; Blomberg had become vulnerable through his marriage to a one-time registered prostitute; Fritsch was framed on false charges of homosexuality. Though Fritsch was later rehabilitated by a military court, the so-called Blomberg–Fritsch crisis left the army humiliated and degraded and allowed Hitler to carry out his strategy of conquest, starting with the annexation of Austria (11 Mar. 1938) without interference from the generals (and for that matter the Foreign Office).

Bucharest.

28.2.38.

Darling Adam,

. . . I am having a very funny time, hobnobbing at meal times with fictitious princes, standing with my toes on a red carpet as the Fourth Estate, which the King had graciously allowed to witness the Inauguration of the Constitution (which successfully deprives the Fourth State of all Liberty) and talking in over-decorated oppressive rooms with irate politicians. It will be fun to tell my grandchildren how I assisted, in one country after another, at the suicide of democracy. I shall tell them how pleased and self-congratulatory everybody was at having lost their freedom. . . .

Now I'm in the Prime Minister's antechamber. There are 8 P.Ms.[1] in the government and even my rather minor one has a very superior antechamber. A heavy carved ceiling with a picture on it, and book cases and old leather bound books. The Roumanian civilisation makes an impression of the kind French 18th century houses must have made—or would make now. Everything very splendid and rich, but built on corruption and a remarkable absence of hygiene or cleanliness. Curiously enough the barbaric Serbs are much cleaner, and somehow one feels there is a stone floor to the house—here it feels like a marsh, very warm, soft, comfortable, and pleasant like a mud bath. I told that to a Hungarian diplomat who was delighted. We made great friends. He also is a new kind of person. He has the features of a nobleman in an 18th century portrait, incredibly fine and delicate. He has white hair and small white hands. First I called on him on the recommendation of my Minister. Then we sat next to each other in the Legation. I had a lovely time in Bucharest. Everybody spoilt and flattered me, and at the same time I worked very hard and well and learnt an enormous amount. I am collecting hommes de confiance[2] in each country. I now have one each in the Little Entente states and Hungary. I am a little bit frightened at how well my work is going—at the same time very pleased and excited. It makes one feel very proud to work well, and I do work quite well now. I hope England, where I shall spend all the summer, will not upset it. I shall perhaps plan a book on Great Britain and Central Europe. I am about the only English person who believes G.B. has interests in Central Europe. I want to see who is right and study it very carefully and historically. It will be the history of the German Empire too which I should learn.

The exciting thing about my journeys is a sense of an international society one belongs to, which is based in every country on common convictions, aims and hopes—and fears. It makes one think Europe must be a whole one day.

The sky is burning, which is very exciting. I am going through Transylvania in a train, and it seems they have natural gas in the earth and there is a huge crater where it pours out in flames. It is night, so it is very impressive. O I do love life so much and have such a lovely time—even tho' the night is approaching and all the places in the carriage full up so I can't lie down and sleep—and I danced till 4 a.m. There is a wonderful tango called Violetta. I wish you were here and we could dance it. I love dancing more than anything in the world—except sunshine. I am in a very happy frame of mind. Are you too? You should be. One has to learn to find it inside and then quite insignificant things please one outside. What a lot of preaching I've done in letters to you. Please don't keep them. They read so priggish. I am so dirty—and in Romanian trains there is no encouragement to cleanliness. I think I shall go and eat to make up for it. Love old Trott. Lord Halifax and I are quoted together in Czech newspapers!

[Shiela]

¹ Meaning, evidently, deputy Prime Ministers.
² Contacts.

Beppu,
March 15. [1938]¹

Darling Zamecka,
   Don't you get my letters? Yours from the Bohemian hills are so angry. Time, space and developments hold us apart very sternly, don't they? Are you still in the Balkans? It is very difficult to write at present but never mind, one must learn to stand by oneself these days. I have left Peking for a while and plunged into another extraordinary solitude. This little port is charming and for days I have seen no western face and chat daily with people and girls in no language at all. While I write this a little geisha is sitting at my feet watching this small scribble with fascination (she's left now); their relations to one are strictly sisterly however. Of course I am not 'content', Duff, though it is a good thing my people think I am, Don't be hostile to my being in the East. It is not a facile escapism. And nothing, on careful consideration, makes my presence indispensable anywhere else. I think you must agree.
   I went to the summit to-day (Mt. Aso picture on pc.). It's the largest volcano in the world. Thick white sulphurous clouds bursting up from hell in revolt it seemed with the sunshine from above and the clean cold wind which finally disposed of them. People go up there to pray for their boys and soldiers at the front. I saw a lovely girl there. She seemed very frightened and concerned. It may seem strange to you that while the face of Europe is being changed I should idle in this wilderness. I infinitely prefer it to humiliating inactivity at home, and to cut loose and free from all attachments that are not essential

and independent of periodical reassurances makes me better inside. The eagle relation[2] seems very important still though I am not sure it is not in your way in some respects. It was in mine for years, but isn't any more I think. It seems clear that the eagles have to live and die on separate peaks though they may come and fly over to each other at times and keep a watchful eye in the meantime not to let the other get lost in the chasms that separate them. Do you agree? You never refer to this question of mine. But darling you are a she-bird and should remember in this one respect I am no good to you. I have drilled this into my plan of life now and I think you will find this has made me a better and more useful friend later on. But the transition remained difficult and equivocal.

I don't know quite how long I am going to stay in the East. I have started to work seriously on their political philosophy and the collection of this material may take longer than my intended stay. So far it seems probable that I shall sail in October, pass through India and possibly stay awhile in Turkey on my way home. The question is financial more than anything else but my chief concern is the book I want to bring.

I parted on good terms with all my Peking friends including Jeanne[3] of whom I told you but I had to part and am very glad of my solitude here.

To learn to be alone is the best we can do these days.

Bless you, always love
Adam.

March 18th

Hearing in Kobe and Kyoto of all that is passing in Europe,[4] I wish you were in the States already. Maybe when this gets to you it will be too late darling to remind you of your promise not to continue your trade when the thing starts but perhaps you are good and remember it and stop on your own accord. Go to America. Remember how long life is and that all that really matters should come after 30, 40 even 60! Be good darling and don't go hysterical as I quite see one might. I'll give you a few good names in USA but don't expect too much of that country anyway. Do you think you could face India—you will see how little England really is in Europe and how equally wicked we all are—the world is like that all over—but to keep the kernel of it sweet, one must not despair or be afraid.

Love to you
A.

[1] This letter from Japan was written on five Japanese postcards.
[2] See letter Shiela–Adam, London, 10 Sept. 1937, n. 3.

³ A French girl with whom Adam had become friends in Peking.
⁴ This is clearly a reference to the 'Anschluss' of 11 Mar. 1938 when Hitler annexed Austria. By the terms of the Treaties of Versailles and St Germain, union between Germany and Austria had been explicitly banned. After Hitler seized power in Germany the Nazi pressure upon Austria increased, leading to the occupation of Austria by the German army. Thus Hitler took the first step in his policy of aggression which was followed by the destruction of Czechoslovakia (1938–9) and which culminated in the outbreak of the Second World War in Sept. 1939.

March 20th, 1938, as from London.[1]

Darling Adam,
    It is difficult to write to you—after these days in Europe,[2] specially since I am sure that from China they appear just and long over due. I do not know how I can explain to you that now war has become a certainty and that there is no turning back on either side. It will seem so just to you that that which the social democrats desired[3] should now be achieved, that it was so right of them to desire it, so justified now to achieve it. How can I explain to you in these circumstances that to desire it was a betrayal of the European idea, that the means by which it has been achieved has plunged Europe into the gloom of knowing at last that war is inevitable, that we fight on the old dreary plane of imperialist interests on the one hand, of a war to end war, of a war to make democracy safe on the other. Did they who bled to death in the mud of Flanders think that they were fighting only that their children should grow up and fight the same battle? It is true, too horribly true, and for the first time since January '35[4] the cold despairing determination which has been growing every day broke down into tears. I visited your legation here and was talked to in a tone of incredible brutality, a tone new to your countrymen, which shows not an added bitterness but a growing contempt for every restraint. 'We cannot, of course, expect England and France to be pleased to discover that they did not, after all, win the war,' he said, and when I said how horrible were the arrests and suicides in Vienna, he answered Wir lachen nur darüber.[5] O Adam darling, one feels horribly, horribly betrayed. Why was one brought up to believe the war a horrible crime if all that was important about it was who won it. I have written something about it which I will send you if they publish it. It still seems to me unbelievable that one can publish thoughts which one really thinks, that one can say out loud things which have always been private. I used to think it would be terrible to do such a thing, but now I feel as if one is in court being judged,

and that one must defend oneself and the things one cares for before all the world or they will be condemned forever.

I went to Vienna last Saturday. It was the 12th, the day the troops were marching in. The police had already arrived and the town was intoxicated with excitement. Lorries rushed through the streets carrying boys with rifles on their backs, with revolvers at their hips, black prison vans, hospital vans, police cars, and then came the troops, tanks, field guns, anti-aircraft guns. It was the nearest thing yet to war. Dimly I remember the armistice, the marching of our tired soldiers through Whitehall. Then people were mad with relief that war was over. Thank God I do not remember them being mad with joy that war had begun, but this was how it seemed in Vienna. It is, of course, the bloodless taking of an immensely important strategic position, just as the Rhine was, and your people should be glad that it was bloodless so far as the opposition was concerned. It has not been bloodless since. Central Europe has become the scene of a man hunt. In fear, all countries are shutting their frontiers so that the hunted are like rabbits in a warren, nets on all the holes and ferrets sent in. You will not understand. You were born a German and now it seems that our generation must learn to hate each other as the last generation learnt. To what purpose? To no purpose at all, if either of our governments were asked. Your Government has plans only for Deutschtum,[6] for which it takes a Lothian to enthuse, mine has plans not even for a Britanientum.[7] How desperately one needs a Christ with a plan for humanity—or even a Christ with a plan for Europe. Instead we turn with a sort of blind faith to Winston and Lloyd George, because they won the war, and think that the next must also be won. Let them win it, but for heaven's sake, let us make the peace.

I can hear you thinking out loud 'How hysterical she is' and blaming the Czechs for my behaviour. I assure you they are calm, so calm that I almost doubt that they know what has happened. If Beneš[8] ruled England or France, I assure you that the world would have been different and better—but we will quarrel again over that. If Schuschnigg[9] is a mortal enemy, I tremble to think what Beneš is once he is in your hands. How you wish I had never had anything to do with Czechoslovakia, with politics, with journalism, with personal ambitions of such a martial character. I remember Mowrer writing me a letter years ago saying I did not realise the blessings of a pokey life. Well, now I do, and now it's too late. I go home some time this week, and will try my best to have a pokey summer. Already I find the sun shines brighter and more warmly, the birds sing more touchingly, the flowers have more colour, but I cannot love people more. People and politics are too closely intermixed for one's

relations to them to be unsullied—or perhaps I shall love them more.
I don't know. There's a beautiful Clare poem, I cannot remember it
very well, but it is somehow like this

> I long for fields where man has never trod,
> Where women never smiled nor wept,
> There to be with my redeemer, God,
> And sleep as I in childhood sweetly slept,
> Untroubling and untroubled where I lie,
> Below the earth, above the vaulted sky.[10]

I find the physical world of ever increasing beauty, and long for this
summer in England and in the country. Bless you, and forgive an
unhappy letter. If only at the peace we can be the best friends in Europe, perhaps we can still save the things which 3000 years have given
to Europe. How pretentious that looks!

Bless you.

S.

[1] Written from Prague on Shiela's return from Vienna.

[2] The annexation of Austria by Germany on 11 Mar. 1938. On Saturday, the day
of the 'Anschluss', Shiela spent a long evening with Muriel Gardiner (see letter
Shiela–Adam, Vienna, 17 Sept. 36, n. 1), hearing all of her anxieties about the fate of
her socialist friends; see Muriel Gardiner, *Code Name Mary: Memoirs of an American Woman in the Austrian Underground* (New Haven and London, 1983), p. 95.

[3] Adam had voted during the Weimar period for the Social Democratic Party.
The Social Democrats all along had been strongly advocating the Anschluss as long
as it meant a union between democratic—and preferably socialist—Germany and
Austria. Naturally the Anschluss was performed by Hitler on very different terms
which the Socialists, long outlawed in Germany, were bound to resent. Shiela's
remarks suggested to Adam that his feelings about the Anschluss might be ambiva-
lent, which indeed at first they were; see letter Adam–Shiela, Shanghai, 6 Oct. 1938.

[4] A reference to the Saar plebiscite, which Shiela covered as a journalist; see
Chap. 1.

[5] 'We just laugh them off'; the person in question was Herr von Chamier, Shiela's
contact man at the Legation.

[6] Germandom.

[7] An ironical adjustment of Britainnia to the 'Germandom' concept.

[8] Eduard Beneš (1884–1948), Czechoslovak Foreign Minister 1918–35; succeed-
ing Tomáš Garrigue Masaryk as President of Czechoslovakia 1935–8; headed the
Czech government-in-exile during the Second World War; President of the Second
Czechoslovak Republic 1945–8; resigned from the Presidency in 1948 after the
Communist coup.

[9] Kurt von Schuschnigg (1897–1977), Austrian statesman; Federal Minister of
Justice 1932–4; Minister of Education 1934. He took over as Federal Chancellor
after the murder of Dollfuss by the Nazis on 25 July 1934; jailed after the Anschluss
in Mar. 1938.

[10] John Clare (1793–1864), 'Written in Northampton County Asylum': I long
for scenes where man has never trod— / For scenes where woman never smiled or

wept— / There to abide with my Creator, God, / And sleep as I in Childhood sweetly slept, / Full of high thoughts, unborn. So let me lie,— / The grass below; above the vaulted sky. Sir Arthur Quiller-Couch (ed.), *The Oxford Book of English Verse 1250–1918* (Oxford, 1939), p. 735.

Chelsea
April 2 1938

Darling Adam,

I feel I must write quickly after my last letter but I have little more cheerful to say. Opinion here is hardening except in the Government which is ruled by all your friends—Lothian, Lady Astor. Low[1] calls them the Shiver Sisters and they are attacked everywhere but nevertheless are very powerful and have great influence. . . .

Chamberlain is said to have told the Trade Unions we will be at war with you in September so please stay where you are or go to America. I don't want to fight you but am determined nevertheless that we have to win this war. The English say it doesn't matter who wins.—There is no victory in war—but your chaps think it does matter, so I perforce have to too. . . .

. . . I remember walking across the Parks with Miss Grier[2] the day after the Austrian February revolution[3] and she denying it was partly our fault. We are still making good the wrongs done to democrats and defeated enemies and now you are dictatorial and victorious. I cannot get away from the subject with you and yet, yet, the world is so infinitely beautiful. No word from Wilfrid[4] nor from your family for years—nor from you. Write soon. Love me

Shiela.

[1] David Alexander Cecil Low (1891–1963); from 1962 Sir David; cartoonist with Lord Beaverbrook's *Evening Standard* 1927–1950. His witty graphic warnings about Nazi aggression and British appeasement policy attracted much attention during the years before the outbreak of the Second World War.

[2] Lynda Grier (1880–1967), Principal of Lady Margaret Hall.

[3] See letter Shiela–Adam, *beginning of* Mar. 1934, n. 1.

[4] See letter Shiela–Adam, Potštejn, 26 Dec. 36, n. 3.

Yumoto Nikko
Japan.
1.4.38.

Darling Shiela,

This is the first letter of which I can have a reasonable certainty that it will ever reach you—it will go by the way of your Embassy in Tokyo, and will not, I hope, be looked into by a hundred jealous eyes. I think that some of my previous letters must have been repressed because people thought our particular jargon a code for sinister exchanges—your (very few) little notes sound as if you did not hear from me at all.

How much one lives outside our present day world at Peking came back to me in this country which—with all its rural charm—is probably the most trim technical civilisation on earth—all the more so as its present victim is a people that one cannot help loving and admiring. It is the battle in the sense of town against country again and there can be little doubt that as far as actual battle is concerned, the more mechanised and the more concentrated (and both the Japanese certainly are) are bound to win. But for a long view of the future, there is more than one danger of ultimate defeat lurking in these victories. Even the most intelligent and experienced observers of the whole situation cannot give any forecast of what may happen—but one can certainly study the forces at work in these quarters better than ever before. Your country, under the heaviest sacrifices of 'face' and capital is playing a double game, supplying both sides, awaiting their mutual weakening, and mapping out a more definite sphere of unimpeded interest in the south. The more immediate dangers for your interests' possessions there seem to have blown over and the temper of Japan more tuned to the city of London than it has for some time. This may be somewhat below the military surface of the country yet, but must, I think, win—though it may take the direction of America. It may not, however, mean that the return of both your governments' interest will make for a shortening of this cruel conflict.

Everything is more and more closely connected with what is happening in Europe. In Peking yes, but here it is not possible not to think of the daily position at home. I wonder where you were when we took Austria. You will probably have to revise a good number of your premises—though your experiences of the countries concerned will be specially valuable for digesting these new developments. How very much I should like to have one talk with you now! About so many things!

It was very nice getting a cheerful letter from Rumania[1] the day before yesterday. You seem to stick to your style very well, and one day you will probably be a European celebrity in the stop press. I admire you for your guts and pertinacity, and I know well enough what hardships external and otherwise that sort of gypsy life involves. You are brave and bright and deserve to be liked by so many people, which is the basis of your success.

I am damn tired of travelling and eating in restaurants and with strangers all the time. Japan, after all I have seen on the continent, is almost too much. I think I have had a good chance to see some of its roots these few weeks—but it is a constant strain, and a pleasure only in the country which is lovely on a small sort of scale (as people always say). . . .

Before leaving Tokyo I received a telegram from Lord Lothian saying that he had cabled the balance of my scholarship to Peking (much less than I thought there still was) and that an addition was impossible. I had not expected the latter, but this may affect my return plans. I long to be back in Europe—I long to see my friends and to have people of my own kind around. On this island for the first time I have been really seized by homesickness—but how can I just follow it? At present I bring nothing back that could justify my long absence and I must if I want to get a university job. One's future is badly blocked in on all sides isn't it? I cannot even really wish for a university job—nor probably have a chance to get one. It would be the most rational approach to the given situation.—I could very probably get that legal job in industry I once told you about, but I want that only as the last resort. . . . I am afraid China has made me rather less than more able to fit in anywhere.

You will probably find your hopeful friend Trott turn into a complete Don Quixote while you will go from strength to strength as a European publicist. That is really what we should all be instead of nibbling away at our private misfortunes.

You are right, my sweet, one must be right inside and then one can enjoy the smaller outside things. . . . Bless you, and don't get lost to your old Trott.

[1] See letter Shiela–Adam, Bucharest, 28 Feb. 1938.

Kent.
April 24th 1938.

Darling Adam,

  . . . Altogether this place is looking so beautiful, so green, that I am very very happy. I only wish you were here. I wish you would come home, tho' perhaps it is as well you have been away through this year of hard-headed, hard-hearted ambition. I'm afraid the first year, when you helped me so much, gave you pain often. Have you grown stronger and more determined through these last years too? I want you to be happy. They say it hasn't changed very much to be a professor at a university, and I think you would be happiest doing that, and that it would be the most worth while. I wish you could spend a year or two first at a French university. I fear France is declining and you are the heir. You must know what it is like not only to rule Europe, but to make a European civilisation.

  I am writing the second chapter of my book,[1] which is about Bismarck and the Kaiser, Hegel and the generals. German history is rather exciting. Do you know that Lagarde[2] said 'Prussia has not enough body for her soul; Austria has no soul for her ample body.' So now we will see what the Prussian soul will make of its ample body. History should give grandeur to politics.

  Bless you, sweet. I like you very much. Like me—let's always be friends. Bless you and a big kiss.

S.

[1] *Europe and the Czechs* (Harmondsworth, 1938); see letter Shiela–Adam on the train between Prague and Reichenberg, 19 Aug. 1936, n. 1.
[2] Paul de Lagarde (pseudonym for Paul Anton Bötticher (1827–91)), German linguist and nationalist publicist.

London.
9.5.38.

Sweet Trott,

  Thank you for a nice long real letter of the first of April (what an awful long time ago) sent from Tokyo. It was very good to have, tho' I am always a little distressed by the sad tone of your letters. I'm afraid it is the shadow of California, and of the last years still. You do not seem to be able to escape and recover your gay grand self of Oxford. You will one day, because you are more innately grand and gay than anyone I know, and I always laugh when I think how you walk about like a prince. One finds one's old self in the end, and you will be happy again. It is a little hard even to be in quite such princely surroundings as Oxford and the buttercup fields in summer, but it must happen again. When one is brave inside, the whole world is gay, and one only needs sunshine to be happy. Please be happy, sweet.

. . . You need hard work, and it is that that keeps me alive now. I would be very unhappy if I stopped to feel Europe's heart beating more and more wildly and irregularly around me, so instead I work and resolve grim death to save Europe. We will. There is so much beauty and wisdom in it that cannot die. Do you not feel, there in the East, that Europe is a whole, and that it is something at its best, so good and beautiful? I do like it very much, and more and more as it grows wickeder and wickeder. I'm afraid I'm a combative nature, and care more for the things I must fight for.

Your letter about Japan was very very interesting. I am surprised that you emphasise the mechanical aspect so much. I suppose it is after China. I regard the East as so little mechanical, it must be very frightening if it is. I'm glad the Japanese are likable. Have you read La Battaille yet?[1]

. . . When I've finished my book, I shall retire to my house in the country, and if, as they say, we are in for twenty years of reaction, I shall become a historian and have a horse. I should like a husband too, but faute de mieux, I shall have my friends to stay—very often. I will make a circle of civilisation in the farm-yard—I look forward to the future very much. I have even deceived myself into a wicked frame of mind. Either there is war, and then we die for our principles, or there is peace and reaction, and we retire and cultivate our gardens. So I am happy either way, and happy in the present. O happiness, how grateful I am for it. I wish I could give it to you. I should when you gave it to me. What will you do? You only say you have less money than you hoped. Do not hurry home to Europe. It is not the place for you. Soon the issues will be clear and you can decide accordingly. Till then you must treat yourself as a slave you are training to be a free man, be very stern, disciplined, but permit yourself every real pleasure, because that is what our Europe is—the countryside, music, poetry. Take care of yourself, and believe your Duff is very faithful and affectionate, and expects a very grand princely Don Quixote to return.

Much love always,
Shiela.

P.S. You should get regular work soon. Best would be if you would get a job in an American or German University. If you could teach people, your own ideas would grow clearer.

---

[1] See letter Shiela–Adam, Bath, early July 1934.

Peking
June 4 1938

My darling Duff,

I know this time I was very bad about writing. There was even a certain amount of hostility in my silence at first, because by becoming aggressive, I felt you had abandoned being a good European. Although in your letters from Bohemia I can understand and swallow you being aggressive, it is very difficult to do so when there is the pathos of an excitedly successful modern English publicist added to it. In contrast to your Bohemian ones, your first English letters were definitely not written by a 'good European'. As soon however as you got into the country again your tone was genuine and sweet. I am no great publicist and must be very humble with the advice I venture to give to one—but this is surely a contrast which you must look out for if you want to remain true to your style. Sweet Zamecka, I love your style and your being concerned about certain things in the way you are and I think we agree much more than you sometimes think and you must not mind, perhaps, my feeling hostile as I don't really mind you being aggressive. We should think, still, a little more about avoiding the catastrophe by constructive means and attitudes than building strategic positions for the event of its happening. If it does, all is up anyway. Your concentration on the Central European issue with an ideology of uncritical democratic liberalism will I fear make you less and less capable of seeing the really world wide problem of making Europe into a source of order and constructive lead on a large scale once more—because no other continent can do this. We certainly are *one* still and most of what our orators and your publicists produce runs against actual fact and necessary trend of Europe's relation to the world.

I am preparing at the moment a report on my journey through Japan, Korea and Manchuria which has opened my eyes to many things I did not so far realise. Before however I can claim to have an objective picture of the whole far eastern scene I must try and get to Hankow and Ch'unking and I shall do so before my return. I saw a number of interesting and intelligent people coming from there, so I can more or less take account of what passes there in what I say on things up here. But as you realize in talking to people who never actually went to Rumania, the 'feel' of the place (is that what publicists call it) is most important. . . .

Peking is incredibly beautiful now. When you climb the 'coalhill' near the palace the vast town at your feet is all hidden by the fresh green of trees—the lakes, the temples are luxuriously beautiful. But I am being very thin and puritan and working and writing very few letters.

Love always, my good Duff

T.

[*Postscript omitted*]

London.
23 June, 38.

Darling Trott,
. . . It is strange that politically you should find my Bohemian letters better than my English ones. It is because there, democracy is really vigorous and brave and my friends serious about politics. Here, I suspect it is a game of self-advancement and I hate it. They don't believe in anything—that is what is so terrible—and when I say that Liberty is worth fighting for and an idea worth more than any other the world fights and dies for to-day, they say that is high faluting. I think it is and I know what liberty is because the loss of any of it makes me rage. They ask what is the liberty of a coalminer or of an unemployed man. It is greater than a King's. Which does not mean he should not have more but it means he has a lot to lose and to keep it he should be taught to be ready to fight and if necessary even to die. I am aggressive and the conservatives and diplomats say I am a warmonger because I say some things are worth dying for and to defend the country of my late adoption, is one of them. My people are cowards and they cannot think straight.

I have a new friend like that. . . . I am rather fond of him though we quarrel every time we meet. We reproach each other a great deal and never agree. I don't really know why I like him. The week-end we all but had war,[1] he was staying with me at High Elms. It was extraordinarily beautiful and the country so green and sheltering and rich. We walked in the fields and the woods and I was leaving for Prague and then he was recalled and it felt as if he were a young man leaving for the war from the house all the young men of my family left in the last war. It was very moving and he is very much of a young Englishman to be killed. But you see they will die because those who weren't killed in the last war were too cowardly to build a new world, because they have muddled and betrayed. Because the others were brave and died, they said, nobody must ever die again. Instead they should have said 'what did they die for? Now we will be faithful to that.' Now Europe is dying, European civilisation challenged and they say 'if only it can die quietly'. . . .

I am a good European but Europe cannot be evolved from certain things. They have to be destroyed utterly—not the people but the ideas and some of the people. I want you to be a great political philosopher and find new ideas, above all to destroy Hegel once and for ever, to go back to the Greeks.

My book is terribly aggressive and I have written some things about the G. mentality which you will not like but I am so convinced that it is anti-European and must change absolutely.

Bless you and come home soon. Perhaps I shall live in the country from now on, have a brindle spaniel and a horse.

Love, sweet

S.

[1] Reference to the events surrounding the weekend of 21–22 May 1938. Municipal elections were scheduled for 22 May in Czechoslovakia. In answer to reports of German troops movements the Czech Defence Minister called one class of reservists and certain specialized units to the colours. However, the elections passed by quietly, thanks to the restraint of the Czech officials and the population, including the Sudeten Germans, and the war of nerves was called off; see Grant Duff, *The Parting of Ways*, pp. 169 f.

Peking.

3.7.38.

Shiela My sweet,

I haven't heard for ages nor have I written. Nothing important has kept me from doing so except perhaps that all letters are so inadequate and that the best goes without saying. You have not been absent from my thoughts. But I think you have become a more detached and unsentimental onlooker in my life and that many things present to it are very distant to you. You know I have never really begun telling you about the East and what it is to live here. Perhaps it will be easier when we meet again and we can talk. At present the beauty of it all is almost painful because I know that it must pass from me so soon now and that it will then probably remain a mere memory for ever.

The last month I have been busy writing various reports and statements, partly to clarify my own mind about many things I saw and heard on my journey to Japan and partly to get into touch again with some people in Berlin and London and finally—because I wanted, however ineffectively, to state what I think would be a real way out of this awful mess in the East.

As I told you in my last letter, the European situation, the fierceness of hate and fright, has somehow passed from my immediate consciousness and I see, out here, all the Western nations embroiled in a common fate which will gradually overtake them if they do not come to their senses. I still think they might—since the alternative will be more and more costly—and I also think that Anglo-German cooperation in some shape or other is the only key. As peoples we will certainly never love each other—even as individuals I sometimes doubt how near we really get to understanding. But I think we might have that close and subtle relation that one has to an opponent in fencing—with occasional common visions and passions in other fields.

How charmed you would be by many sides of China—their human, gay, affectionate nature, their sombre and imperial buildings and the sensuous countryside. Sometimes I have come home at night, driven or rather pulled by a gentle barefooted coolie through the wide deserted street leading north from the Palace, or with my bicycle ride through the moist and hot summer fields with their many groves and their ups and downs. It's a completely new kind of solitude I enjoy away from all and everybody and of which I know it is passing as fast as a dream. (How funny you should suggest I was suffering from unhappy love affairs—I have none at all neither happy nor unhappy and strangely enough don't miss them at all.)

The day after to-morrow I am going up into Shansi to a place called Taihsien[1] where I may stay a few weeks if it is possible. Early in September I shall start home, stop in Shanghai, Hongkong, Hanoi, go up to Yunnan, down to Indo-China, Saigon, Angkor, Bangkok, Singapore from there possibly a trip to Borneo—Ceylon and then (instead of taking in India which would become too much) go straight through to Port Said and by train up through Palestine and Syria to Ankara where I shall stay another month with Eberhard to work up some Chinese stuff and return home through the Balkans. Perhaps I could catch the Duff even on one of her official passages and take her to dance instead of writing messages to the anxious English. How heavy and oriental I will be and how sweet and gentle and grown up you'll be, please.

Bless you and be good and don't write an outrageous book.

Love
Adam.

[1] City in the province of Shansi.

Peking,
July 20, 1938[1]

Dear Shiela,

It has been on my mind for some time to write to you more fully than it has hitherto seemed possible during this last year. There is so much to say, really, that it is very hard to know how to begin and put in on a piece of paper. Even when I was with you, remember, I was a good deal more tonguetied than was good to get clear about certain fundamentals which matter a good deal in both our lives. That was, I think, due to the fact that I made the mistake to try and reach with you a degree of emotional intimacy which would then make it easier to communicate to you my real thoughts. And that mistake was simply due to the fact that I was in love with you. Had that been mutual all might have been well and good. But probably your instinct was right to resist that temptation. Neither of our characters makes it possible to base a permanent relation on mere emotional attachment. Mine to you foolishly hindered me to work out clearly what held us together beyond that. I think it was to a large extent the unfortunate state in which I was placed in other respects which made me incapable to be clearer and more constructive in my contribution to what we vaguely wished to become the 'best friendship in Europe.'

If this part of our relation is to be permanent we must not remain vague and romantic about it. Although you are not very explicit in the views you hold in your letters I cannot fail to realise in all you say and print in papers a tendency with which I increasingly disagree. It would be makebelief [sic] to doubt that this must one day seriously affect our friendship. When I was with you in Europe I would not have this true because my love for you held me spellbound and I hoped it would gradually defeat what stood between us. Perhaps you underestimated this when occasionally you reproached me for not being more explicit in my attitude to you about these things.—And, certainly, I *was* unclear about some political issues which for you never even had to be a problem at all. And in my home country I *had* to be on the defensive before I could hope to reach a clear attitude of my own to all these new complexities. Had it been possible for you to love me you might have helped me to work that out. Since you didn't it was certainly right for you to follow out your own idiosyncrasies.

Oh hell, how difficult are all these comments and explanations—it is only that I think we have the duty to know how far we can go together and where our ways part. You see, in a sense they did when you went to Prague and decided to be a journalist. After the time when you were comparatively nearest, I mean in Kassel,[2] you immediately fell for those people to whom even what is best and potentially worthy of imitation in us is an object of profound suspicion and hate. I do not blame you, Shiela darling, because many of their partly professed and partly honest beliefs are so similar to your own that it must have seemed to you more important to follow them than my vexed and incongruous position. It was all the more natural that you followed their ideas and distrust even more the chances of too strong an emotional relation to me. It took me a damn long time and distance to really see this and I see it without bitterness. Even then when—perhaps weakly—I felt in the worst plight at home and need of you, when I waited in Dresden,[3] I did not feel bitter, because it was too immediately painful.—In all the time following we did not really solve the contradictions.—Could my attitude to you have been unemotional and based on a rational consideration of all the difficulties opposed to a common life together all might have been well.

My attachment to you as an honest and free person is much the same and I have no doubt, if we met, I might fall in love again. As it is I am in love with no one and feel very much in need to get very clear in my relations to the few who seem important from this distance. I am afraid that when I come back and we should not fall in love— though we will be cheerful companions whenever we meet—our 'means and ends' in Europe will profoundly disagree. It is good that this should be very clear beforehand and not obscured by emotional excitement.

I have never hesitated to tell you how I hated your ambition to make a name for yourself in journalism. You have, to a slight extent, taken this objection of mine seriously, but mainly you have put it back to obsolete prejudice and treated it lightly because you knew very well that my affection was stronger than my disapproval.

I believe that in your own life you want 'liberty and truth' more than anything else and that your 'rage' about oppression and dishonesty is quite genuine and heartfelt. But I do not believe that in judgment (or hard work which it requires) you are capable to apply these principles fairly to the conditions under which they must operate on the 'other side.' I think very few people indeed are capable of that—but any occupation with current events which fails to reach such fundamental detachment and fairness is bound to be swayed by collective prejudice and the uncritical interests inertly entrenched in it. That's why I think a person like you with your impulsiveness and your strong personal ambition—however sincere your beliefs may be—is bound in journalism to become a prey of forces which you cannot control. There is quite enough of cynicism and of sheer love of high life in you to bridge over the first few conflicts which must be traversed—though ultimately you could not be cynical or corrupt.

Mme. Tabouis' book[4] which I have just been reading also is not corrupt or cynical—but I think it is hopelessly shallow in its premises and irresponsible in its conclusions. As a person she is probably charming and one might well fall in love with her etc. but as a judge of the complex European situation and its future possibilities and as an inspirer of right principles she will count for very little in a few years. I hope your book will be better than hers.

Your former employer wrote an article[5] about Canton which you may have seen. It is another example of what I mean. It is no doubt well written (I saw it in a translation) but again hopelessly shallow and without a hint of the real power that is moving China's resistance. I do not mean foreign powers for them he may have deliberately left out, but what he calls the 'solid foundation of a Chinese national state.' Just big words inflated by a sense of righteousness about the personal preferences he happened to have formed. Perhaps my attitude to him and Ripka is still a bit coloured by my former resentment that it was they who took you away from me.—But really I do feel that a fellow like Mowrer with his great talent and sense of justice ought to stick to his home country to try and establish the rudiments of liberty and justice. My friend Roger Baldwin[5] who is the head of the civil liberties union was put in prison and hounded like a public enemy on other occasions because he insisted on the reality rather than highflown quotations of human rights, liberty and justice. If M. was only compelled to read the every day *local* columns side by side with the idealistic comments and denunciations he writes about Europe, he might be a little humbler about the good he is doing to the world. America—in all a young and wonderful country with a foundation of right and a wide range of possibilities is full of oppression and injustice and his home town leads the way in that. Is it not sometimes just as much an untruth to be silent about certain things as to state them incorrectly? I am sure you will agree that this is true of a lot of the high phraseology used by your Central European friends.

The more I have seen of conditions in the rest of the world, America, *your* position in the Pacific, the whole attitude of Western powers here, the more I feel sick about that whole *spirit* of denunciation against Germany. If it came from God, it were sufficiently justified, no doubt. But from you—who are committing the same sins every minute of the day in some part of the world which you prefer not to know—such denunciation raises an awful feeling which I hope you will not minimise when you denounce the 'German mentality'.

Oh, darling Duff, I am afraid we should have a sound fierce quarrel before we could really be friends. And at the moment, I fear, you will be so excited about being an author of a book inspired by M[owrer]'s and R[ipka]'s and T[abouis]'s that it will completely silence the small pangs of conscience the old Trott could raise in you and you will probably be as unfair to him as to his countrymen— There is no hope that the present alignment of European forces will ever lead to a constructive peace. The effort to consolidate it and deepen the cleavage seems to me a bad service to Europe and to the world.

Perhaps those who object to involve the democracies in fight have a sounder instinct for the fact that their only spiritual certainty rests on the denunciation of an opponent whom they neither know nor try to understand and that solving the true cause of their own inertia and unfulfilled application of liberty and justice to *their* given conditions would be more progressive than a merely verbal proclamation of these values in international politics—which should really also be based on a responsible adjustment to given material conditions. I agree with Samuel's article in the 'XIX Century'[7]—but I resent and consider as utterly hopeless and damaging the highhanded denunciation of a people which contains just as many hard-working and responsible 'Europeans' which have been defeated and silenced by economic desperatism and not least by the leading spirit of Europe wanting to perpetuate Germany's defeat in 1918.

As long as it is not possible for you to consider all that happened in Germany a *European* phenomenon and responsibility, no step further can be made. If on the other hand you try to hedge in Germany morally and materially the explosion is bound to happen and destroy what foundations of a Europe in our sense may still be left.

Perhaps I am too much out of touch with what is happening in Europe every day now—but this is certainly how we look at it here and Peking as you know consists of a most cosmopolitan community hardly biased in Germany's favour.

I have just been up in Shansi and Suiyuan,[8] lovely but miserably unhappy countries. I saw the upper reaches of the Yellow River, 'China's Sorrow' and the Mongols and Turks which up there intermix with the Chinese. I wish fate had permitted your having come with me there and—as I did in Paotow[9] approach under a clear evening sky the far outlying pale brown mudwalls of that city which made it look like a fairy castle in 'Arabian Nights.' It is so far from the heat and petty bitterness of European family quarrels, so solemn, eternally oriental though held under martial law and only ten miles from enemy territory. We were welcomed hospitably by an old Chinese merchant and another very scholastic but rather beautiful young dealer who offered me his girl for the night. I made her acquaintance, she came from Suiyuan province while he had all the culture of the old capital. I did not sleep with her but she was nice and her little sister sang Chinese songs to us. In the streets Mongol soldiers were galloping on their little horses, and bought their things in the bazar-like open shops where donkies were tied to poles as in the Bible. Later I made the acquaintance of a charming old Mongol prince and his lady and heard all the ideas which they inherited from Jenghis Khan. The great issues of the present international situation meet most vitally in that region we travelled through—Japanese, Mongol, Chinese, Russian, Western influences fighting it out on the back of the peasant who mostly turns bandit or starves or survives in more sheltered areas after his own fashion.

Life is wide and honest and passionate out there and one cannot quite see oneself fitting back into all the petty entanglements of our beloved continent. Returning to Peking I found letters from Imshausen indicating that all is going wrong there and your nice letter with its cracking humanitarian whip,[10] occasional affectionate touches and I hope—after all—a sort of stubborn medieval loyalty and modern solidarity with

Your
Trott.

[1] The original of this letter is missing.

[2] The meeting in late June–early July 1936; see Grant Duff, *The Parting of Ways*, chap. XIII.

[3] This is a reference to the meeting between Adam and Shiela in late July 1936 in Dresden when Adam, because of various complications, had to wait two days before Shiela arrived from Prague; see letter Adam–Shiela, 29 July 1936, n. 1.

[4] Mme Geneviève R. Tabouis (1892–); French litératrice and publicist; foreign news editor of *L'Œuvre* from 1932; she has been called 'the Cassandra columnist of France' for her pessimistic forecasts; wrote *Blackmail or War?* (Harmondsworth, 1938); fled to the United States in 1940.

[5] Mowrer in the Chicago *Daily News*; Mowrer subsequently published a book on the subject, *Mowrer in China* (Harmondsworth, 1938).

[6] Roger Baldwin (1884–1981), director of the Civil Liberties Union 1917–50. Adam met him through Sir Stafford Cripps.

[7] Herbert Louis Samuel, 'The Choice Before Us', *The Nineteenth Century and After*, 123 (June 1938), 641–55. Herbert Louis Samuel, 1st Viscount (1870–1963), British liberal politician. He disapproved of Neville Chamberlain's conduct of affairs; proposed a different version of appeasement which would have involved British rearmament short of division of Europe into two blocs, refusal of guarantees to any state (notably Czechoslovakia), negotiations over former German colonies.

[8] Provinces in north-western China.

[9] City in the province of Suiyuan.

[10] See letter Shiela–Adam, London, 23 June 1938.

Peking 10.8.1938[1]

Darling Duff,

I hope my letters lately have not seemed like a 'stab in the back' when you were just in the thick of fighting to get your book done. They must no doubt have seemed very offensive to you, as apparently you are now shutting up altogether. I often think of you and our little quarrels and how I should blow them away if you were with me in this last beautiful undisturbed summer. I fear that for you it is everything else but undisturbed. In fact you will be a good deal disturbed because your friends are not as disturbed about the things that disturb you. In one of [y]our letters you talk of 'after the war' as if the impending war were a matter of fact already. And you describe to me the weekend when you all but had war. The first I think is a very bad way of going about things and the second confirms my belief that the powers (including Germany) will do everything possible to avoid a general European war as it will mean the end to them all. It had at one time to come out clearly that this war could no longer be a local matter and at that moment I grant you that your country has behaved like a European one and that perhaps quite a share of the credit for that goes to the Duff and her like.

But you must be generous too and admit some justice to the charge I have made against your *spirit* of defending Europe—a spirit I come up against more and more, i.e. one of blind denunciation of Germany's ills which although couched in phrases of liberal rights and progress is fundamentally drawing more and more on socially reactionary motives and those of nationalism which made the last war. Who am I, as a German, to make such a charge you may ask. Unless, again you are generous and admit that Germany was to a large extent (by no means wholly) driven into these ills, you accept by reacting to it on the same plane, the entire mess of pre-war sentiment and motivation and share in responsibility what will indeed inevitably ensue . . . I fear that the world of journalism in Europe is bound to drift into this rut again and I would truly hate to see you joining them in that direction, darling.

I have questioned myself often recently why I did not react much more violently against your following that trend when I still saw you sometimes. And I am afraid my answer was that the charm of your presence and all that seemed to remain *out*side politics made me take this other side of your life not so seriously. Even now I often think it's a lack of humour to become so serious about these general matters which do not as yet dominate either you or myself completely. But then I could not escape the simple animadversion that you had long ago given me to understand that this side *was* more important to you than any single human relationship. And perhaps it should be more important for you. But in that case, darling, you must admit that it becomes of paramount importance for the success of your continued friendships whether on these to you vital matters you can agree with your friends or not. And the feeling that more and more we do not really agree made me write in the [vein] I wrote.

I am not, as you might think, going over to some 'other side' or trying to escape or surrender my identity to whatever comes. It is true that this long journey has put me in a rather remote position and this last year in China has given me chance to think of things more objectively than I ever could before and I know now that as I am going back to my home country the basis for remaining true to the old fight will be very narrow and precarious indeed—especially if my nearest friends too begin to think that it is an impossible position which they must deny and fight.

I don't know whether you really do and it will come out clearly enough when we meet again. I should like to stay a fortnight or so in Oxford to finish off my summary report and size up the general situation before I return. If, however, I feel that the majority of my English friends think a war with Germany inevitable, I shall return there direct. The effect of morbid idiosyncracies may be greater than that of reason—but everything I have experienced in the outer world goes to convince me that we must work to the last moment for peaceful adjustment and only if violent destruction of the present national states proves inevitable fight for a united Europe.

There is no more room or paper, but I wanted to say that I am still sufficiently fond of you to think that this will remain so *whatever* happens.

Always love

A.

[1] The original of this letter is missing.

EDITOR'S NOTE

The following must be read against the background knowledge of the pre-Munich days in England in which, in anticipation of the worst, the public became conditioned to busy defence preparations like the filling of sandbags, the distribution of gas masks, etc.

The Clock House, High Elms Farm[1]
Farnborough, Kent.
Sept. 1 1938.

Darling Adam,

Thank you for your letter this morning.[2] It is lucky it came before I sent the passionate letters which had been accumulating in my mind and on paper. We cannot quarrel at a distance and I would probably be sorry if my letters landed you in jail even though I have more than once decided that is the suitable place for you. You are quite right that your letters are a 'stab in the back.' They are a real betrayal. . . . This side *is* more important than any single human relationship—and more and more my only deep and strong affections are for people who care for these things too, and if you do not—then we part.

It needs a long explanation before that, and I will try and give it. I do not know quite where to start. Your attacks are directed as much against the people as the things I care for, and I don't know whether you will understand better through the one or the other. . . .

In your last letter,[3] you protest against the *spirit* in which I defend Europe, and you attack my attachment to liberal rights as mere phrases.

It is very difficult to know what one's further political aims are. I think the only thing—or chief political good—is freedom, and every policy which one approves has some bearing on that. Policies of a socialist kind, i.e. the limitation of the power of the rich to dominate the poor, are good, but not beyond the point at which the dominion of the rich is given to the state, and the individual becomes the wage-slave, party-slave of the state. In a way, therefore, I suppose I am more of a Liberal than a Socialist. I think the good of the community can only be seen in the moral, intellectual, physical value of the individual, and the aim of the community must be to make good and free individuals.

By freedom for an individual I mean the widest possibility of choice in everything he does. For this, the first essential is that his own capacities must be developed to the utmost; secondly, that there must be a wide choice in the world around him—both for his work and for his pleasures. Finally, that there should be complete freedom of conscience, and the coercion of one man by another should be rigorously punished. The only limitation on freedom should be that which harms the community or other individuals—i.e. crime—and more things should be crimes than are today accounted criminal.

This is all very simple and would not pass even Fulton's eye,[4] but it is a sort of touchstone which I measure things by. My idea of Europe is of a continent based on these ideas, and one in which frontiers are no longer important. If frontiers are to disappear, they can only do so if the fundamental attitude to life on each side of them is the same. I think this is the fundamental attitude of the democracies.

There are many good things in Germany, and even in the Nazi regime, but you know as well as I that fundamentally there is no compromise between the attitude of Germany and Italy and the attitude of England and France. I do not even believe that the two can live side by side, and 'respect each other's internal regimes,' as my countrymen have constantly exhorted us to do with your country (your countrymen have never once done so). I believe, if Europe is ever to be united, one or other of these systems has got to disappear. It seems to me a Europe united under a despotism is not worth living in. Perhaps a new Dark Ages has got to come before a new Renaissance, but the civilised Romans can hardly have welcomed the Barbarian invasions.

Therefore I am passionate in my hatred of certain systems. I do not call on 'socially reactionary motives.' As luck has it, the Right here and in France is the last to turn against you. There is, dear Adam, still approval among the 'socially reactionary' for your countrymen.

Then you reproach me with nationalism and of war-1914-sentiments. You know, I have tried always to make a distinction between Governments and people. Germany is a beautiful country and I have many friends—but what has been done to show there is a distinction between government and people? Nothing. In moments of anger one thinks, 'They are the same, and I condemn them both' or 'They are different, and the people too cowardly and weak to say so.'

Then you say, how should I condemn when my countrymen commit these atrocities in the Empire? You know I condemn that, and would work against that too—and started to do so till I realised the greater danger was here at home, in Europe. The solution of one will be the solution of the other. I may feel I fight for my country. But I fight for a different country than the one I live in now. My brother says, how can he fight for his country, when he disagrees with the majority of his countrymen. One can—first one combines to oppose the greater evil—then one settles the other problems in peace. Perhaps we'll lose—perhaps the wrong people will come out on top again—then one fights against that. Perhaps one loses, but that is not a reason not to try.

. . . Does Hitler want war or not? You will remember there was a thing called the War Guilt Clause.[5] It has been disputed. If there is another war, there will be no dispute again. I deny we drove Germany to accept a regime which meant war. Suffering does harm only to the weak and the wicked. It taught you nothing—not even not to make a new war. Darling Adam, when one's friends and contemporaries are threatened with death in the trenches, one cannot but recall that the last generation was wiped out by war. Who threatens war today? Who started it in 1914? Perhaps one draws the wrong conclusions, but the most obvious is hard to overcome. I will admit to feeling wrongly, perhaps, but we were brought up to forgive—how have your countrymen been brought up? Can I forgive the person who brings them up now to think it glorious to murder my friends? No, dear Adam—it is something quite simple. It is not 'blind denunciation of Germany'—it is a hatred of what your country stands for—hatred of war, of cruelty, of coercion. You know as well as I do my country hates war. Even now, there are no flags and drums in our press. For 'European journalism' as you picture it, look to the violence of your press. Mine is still pacifist, quiet, pleading almost. I, myself, am far more bellicose than any of my countrymen. I hate war—but I have watched the fear of it bring it on.

Now we come to my friends. Of Mowrer in China I know nothing. Probably in three weeks he did not understand the 'real power which is moving China's resistance,' but he does care passionately for certain things I care for. I admire him morally and politically, and if you accept me you accept him—or neither.

Your criticism of Ripka too I despise as jealousy. Even if it is more, this is not the moment to utter it. He has worked more for Czech-German co-operation than any other Czech, and has failed because of the political crimes and follies of your countrymen. He is the most honest, brave, and disinterested man I have ever met. His love of his country and his idea of Europe is far more profound than any other I have met, and goes far beyond mere self-defence against your countrymen. But today, that alone requires heroism and unfaltering determination which I admire profoundly. I care for him very much, and he has come nearer than anyone else to replacing what I lost through your country 25 years ago.[6] That Germany again threatens that is not a reason for my feeling very calm about it, or my tolerating criticism of my friends from you. So there it is. Now you can judge whether we agree sufficiently to be friends. I retract absolutely nothing—either you accept me like that, or not. Now you are not in love with me, you can judge it better, perhaps. You could never have stopped me taking this trend except by proving your country did not mean these things, and your own countrymen would have disowned you.

I suppose you will go back and be part of it. I cannot condemn you, but I cannot approve either, and perhaps one day I shall think you did wrong. I should certainly like to see you first, since there will be no more of my going there after this autumn. I shall go to Berlin soon. I would like to see your family, but cannot, for their sake. I would like you to come to my house. It is so beautiful. The country is so rolling, green, and beautiful around here, and I discover it all again. I have my breakfast looking through a door to the farm yard, and that is where I am writing now, though it is late and dark outside. I wish you would come, but perhaps you never will. Many people think there will be war next week. It all depends on one man. I think your proper attitude would be shame and to ask forgiveness. Even I feel ashamed, and I am less guilty than you—but you only reproach me and declaim. Perhaps, after all, we cannot be friends. But we have been, and if there is war, and I survive, I shall try to remember. I shall try to remember Wickersdorf[7] and the country by your house, and your home; the little castles by Kassel, Hamburg, and even some parts of Berlin, the music and the country.[8]

Bless you,

[Shiela]

[1] One of the two cottages which comprised the old flint dower house of High Elms home farm had fallen empty, and Shiela's grandmother had offered it to her. It served her as a 'blessed shelter' during the difficult months following the Munich Agreement of Sept. 1938 in which Germany, Great Britain, France, and Italy forced Czechoslovakia to turn over the Sudeten areas to Germany; cf. Grant Duff, *The Parting of Ways*, pp. 189 ff.

[2] See letter Adam–Shiela, Peking, 10 Aug. 1938.

[3] See letter Adam–Shiela, Peking, 20 July 1938.

[4] John Scott Fulton (1902–86), from 1966 Lord Fulton of Falmer; Adam's and Shiela's philosophy tutor at Balliol.

[5] Art. 231 of the Treaty of Versailles (under Pt. VIII: Reparation): 'The Allied and Associated Powers affirm and Germany accepts the responsibility of Germany and her allies for causing all the loss and damage to which the Allied and Associated Governments and their nationals have been subjected as a consequence of the war imposed upon them by the aggression of Germany and her allies.' The war guilt clause was vehemently rejected by virtually all political parties in Germany of the Weimar Republic. The political right in particular used the so-called 'war guilt lie' as a rallying slogan.

[6] Reference to Shiela's father, Lieutenant Colonel Adrian Grant Duff, who died in Sept. 1914 in the Battle of the Aisne as Commanding Officer of the first battalion of the Black Watch.

[7] A well-known progressive boarding-school in Thuringia where Shiela stayed in the summer of 1932 with Goronwy Rees; see letter Adam–Shiela, Brussels, Dec. 1932?, n. 5.

[8] For Adam's reply see letter Adam–Shiela, Shanghai, 6 Oct. 1938.

[Peking,]
[8 August 1938]
as from c/o Am. Express Co., Hongkong.[1]

Darling Duff,

Have you written off the Trott, or decided one cannot write books
and letters at the same time? I longed to have a furious contradiction
from you of my theory on 'best European friendships'—and that
your silence may mean agreement seems particularly disappointing.
Or perhaps I have used clumsy stupid words which made you think it
all useless reiteration. Probably you are right in that, and it is high
time we should meet and quarrel or agree eye to eye.—Good God, I
don't seem to have seen a creature like yourself for years, and it is
very bad for my soul and—probably—style of writing to you. The
worse things got, actually, these last weeks, the more fondly I have
thought of you. I reproach myself for not, somehow, having succeeded in getting you away from Europe—but I don't see how it
could have been done. Had we been here together, for instance, we
would have both been in Europe all the time. But this is not the real
reason why I don't think you would have come to the East now. We
had something to achieve for ourselves, both of us. And when we
meet again, things will be new—and perhaps clearer and better. . . .

But I do not feel defeatist about our friendship. It may become different, but it will remain there even if one of your bullets should put
an end to Trott one day. The passion that binds us—or does this
sound silly in your green English fields—is the ambition of a new
common Europe, to which we must hold as tight as hell. The East
and the huge distance make this passion seem unreal and half forgotten. But though it has to lie low with me, it will not die or weaken. To
realise it, I believe Germany must contribute from its own stock, and
the others must accept that. You mistake that for a false backward
leaning on my part, and that makes you impatient and aggressive.
And you cannot help attacking me at times for what our stock at
present is like.

Distance has not made me grow a thick hide against that. I see,
even better, how viciously things are going wrong in Europe at present. This is the worst week. If peace remains, there seems a chance
that change will not destroy the whole past.

I hope you are not in Prague this moment.

Were you the special correspondent of 'Runciman's Mission' in
the Spectator, beginning of August?[2] If so, I congratulate you. Things
here, in the mean time, are equally on the fringe, or even in the midst
of cold catastrophe. Yesterday the village next to my servant's home

was shot up, three hundred killed. At night one has visions of the thousands now homeless and starving, dead peasants, poor children in rags groping and searching in the ruins of their homes.

This summer, at times extremely hot, was perhaps not very good for one. I spent it—with one exception—entirely alone, and lots of it in a temple outside the city. There was a strange deep peace there. Perhaps, one day, you will let me tell you about it all.

Now I am leaving Peking, and will try and reach Chungking,[3] the new capital, and then Yunnan,[4] possibly India for a few weeks, and then Europe soon after the new year.

Don't turn enemy or alien till then. Write and tell me about your life.

Love
A.

[1] Shiela's letter of 1 Sept. 1938 had not yet arrived.
[2] 'From a Special Correspondent', 'The Czechs and Lord Runciman', *Spectator*, 12 Aug. 1938. On 2 Aug. 1938 Neville Chamberlain sent a mission, led by Lord Runciman, to Czechoslovakia with the aim of obtaining an agreement between Czechs and Germans. Lord Runciman was favourably disposed towards the Sudeten Germans. The mission represented one of Britain's last exercises in appeasement. The article—not written by Shiela—gave expression to the Czechs' fear of being sold down the river; must they follow his advice that would spell the loss of their freedoms?
[3] City in the province of Szechwan in south-western China; it had become the new capital in Nov. 1937.
[4] Province in south-western China to the south of Szechwan.

[Peking,] as from American Express Hongkong.[1]
[8 September 1938]

Darling S,

I am breaking off here now just as it becomes most beautiful cool autumn. I long to come back to Europe. (How you must hate us!) But I feel I must try and get to the new capital before I leave China. Then I may stop over for a few weeks in India. But the East if I stay longer will be the end of your Trott. So I'll come back around the change of the years. Don't turn enemy or alien. Europe I am afraid is like that but our heart should remain bigger and firmer. I remain devoted to you. Write to me and I hope you are not having a heartbreaking time over it all. I hate the procedure but I see an inevitability in the process which we must later arrest and transform in peace. We still don't think there will be war in Europe. My love and thoughts are very much with you. Write.

A.

---

[1] This note was written on a postcard (crossed out from one corner to the other) inserted by Adam in letter Adam–Shiela, Tsingtao, 1 Oct. 1938.

Tsingtao
September 28, 1938[1]

My darling Zamecka,

This prolonged silence—at least from my side—and in these pitiful circumstances strikes me as altogether unnatural. My thoughts have of course been with you all along since things have begun to turn really bad. It proves you were right in many respects where I was foolhardy and optimistic. You can imagine that I feel badly out of place in the midst of this alien war and if worse comes to worse I shall be high and dry in the most unreal of worlds while all of you are undergoing hell. My sweet, I don't even know where you are at this moment—what is happening to you inside and out or whether I shall see or hear of you again. If you think I am blindly anxious to get home and take up arms against you and your country, you are very much mistaken. But the painful aloofness that this unreal continent has gradually steeped one in, is probably quite inconceivable to you in your eager anticipation. I am rather shocked with myself—although perhaps this aloofness is based on my incapacity yet to believe that such a thing can again happen to us. But I long to get home and be with you all. When I left Peking a fortnight ago, things looked very bad indeed but after a day or two in Tientsin it seemed better and I took a train south through areas which haven't really been opened to traffic again yet. I spent an interesting day in Tsinanfu[2] with Chinese and an old Catholic Bishop and since things looked still not desperate I went further inland to another mission and then cross country to Confucius' town Chu'fu[3] and to his tomb built in bandit territory. It is one of the most beautiful places I have ever been [to] in my life and I should like to one day take you there. But now, I fear, when you read all this, you will give me up as one gives up an opium eater. I feel a bit like one and it is not a nice feeling. But don't you give me up—I don't give you up when you are bad, even though I may write bad and stilted and unreal letters. Day after tomorrow I am sailing to Shanghai: There may be something from you but somehow I doubt it. I wish I didn't. In Shanghai I am going to finally decide which way I am coming back to your side of the globe. If there remains a threat of our countries going at each other, I shall try and return via America and Scandinavia, if not I may still get to Chungking, Kunming,[4] Rangoon, Calcutta, Bombay, Port Said, London. Gosh darling, I don't think you'll even recognise me. I really am bald and grey haired to a degree. But what does that matter in a war? You know, I have been enveloped in that feeling for some time here—perhaps that has taken the sap out of me or the hot summer or the dear Chinese. But the truth is that I cannot find myself getting, as I thought I might get, heavily enthusiastic or even concerned about sides in this pending struggle: I can't even get really excited—it seems utterly unreal and remote from my person as yet. You have been in my thoughts most and it is your views and hopes which to my horror I find myself increasingly sharing. But what a mess—what a dreary general mess! Here, you know, Nature goes on while a war is being fought. The peasants go on somehow and even trade does and you drive through where there has just been fighting and in the nights you hear shots and people screaming—but it's all still natural and enveloped in the greater rhythms of growth and decay which we have so hysterically forgotten in our parts. I don't want to praise what is going on here—it is ghastly enough, but hasn't this apocalyptic mechanical terror about it which is war in Europe. That, perhaps, is what isn't real to my imagination as yet while the necessity to die seems painless from here. Do we differ very profoundly in our views of this, I wonder? I just cannot imagine your heart to become all bound up with the wheel of events and I wished very much that what is constant and not bound up may have some quiet spot still for T.

Bless you always, sweet.

Love
A.

1   Harbour city in the province of Shantung.
2   City in the province of Shantung.
3   City in the province of Shantung; the proper spelling should be Ch'ü-fu.
4   City in the province of Yunnan.

Tsingtao
1.10.1938[1]

Shiela darling,

We have now heard of the Munich[2] accord, a solution which is no doubt very painful for you in many respects. I wish we could weigh together its probable ultimate outcome: I don't feel at all easy about it yet. Anyway the thing seems to be settled as a *European* and not as a German-Czech issue which, if people had sense, might lead to something really more satisfactory—but I participate in the fears you have previously expressed about exactly this contingency and I am with you in your present apprehensions. Considering that the European horizon is still considerably blacker than it ought to be for allowing one to stay away with equanimity—I think I shall return from Shanghai directly.

I am strongly tempted to go via America (this entirely between you and myself) to look for a place to work if our continent is really going to be what we both feel threatening now a conflict has been spared. It is a damned hard choice, but I'd rather be a beggar than a slave and I am not too old to start all over again and I have good friends in America. Going that way at present means, unfortunately, throwing up the sponge with my present work, is not going to see those parts of China which are absolutely essential for a fair analysis of the immediate and future possibilities. I long to be on the spot where real China is still fighting and it would seem more sensible also, once I am out here to return in the westward direction. I shall never get to India again, I suppose.

So if things really look safe enough at home, I shall probably proceed to Hongkong and Kunming from Shanghai and there cut across to Rangoon and India. But I shall weigh it very carefully and continue to think about America.

All is not well with the Trott, S. darling, as you may have noticed in his letters and perhaps in your own inhibition to write any longer. Perhaps I have opened myself too widely to the Orient and to certain weaknesses—like considering fate bigger than possible efforts and reclining into a passive contemplativeness which is no good for solving the problems right ahead of us nowadays. And you know how I got over from California into this vast impersonal world and its strong fateful ways—perhaps I have changed so much through it all that you find me too queer to deal with. . . .

I want very much and must come home, some time in not too distant a future. I want to see my old father, mother, my brothers and my fields (though I'm really quite unsentimental about all that now).

I want to see my friends because it does not do to isolate oneself from all those one cares for and who share one's real concerns. I want very much to see you, although I feel that too many things that used to pass freely between us, you probably will have hardened yourself—no, I don't know, I am very uncertain how much you can have continued to be interested. But I want very much to find out also whether your ambition is still greater than your affection for people and whether all these things in Europe have made you become more or less your own self. But darling I am not only curious but want terribly to have your company. We could once make between ourselves things seem clear and more whole than with other people and I don't think that can have been undone.—I want also very much to see my brothers and, if possible, start work in some university—but the prospects of Europe seem absolutely appalling and I feel I would have to stay away at least for another couple of years to be anywhere near capable of taking on what I should there. All this time away has done the very opposite to adapting one to 'fit in'.

The East as a permanent place to live is out of the question—the European problem is the only one that really concerns one. But one feels overwhelmingly at times that it can really no longer be solved in Europe—unless there has been in the last years a change to the better in my country that I cannot perceive from here. This is another reason why I must get back and make a last try.

America also is a prospect of considerable resignation—one has to sacrifice the things that Europe still gives freely for a mere potentiality but a potentiality which one may help to work out as a free and self-respecting individual.

Are you going to stay in Europe these next months?

I wish I knew who your present friends are—I would not like you to be friendless in this present situation.

The other night—I think in Tsinanfu—I dreamt that you were in Peking and that you were having a child and that we were standing with some other people under a leafy chestnut tree and I was leaving the next day and I longed to take you away to my temple in the country—when you said Let's all go to a film together! Silly dream—but you looked very charming. Sometimes I imagine you with your hair done up in a knot and rather superior and maturer than myself and in with all the fashionables. Or I remember some small gesture of yours that used to pain me—and the eager way in which you used to talk and how exciting it was to go to pubs with you. And the background to you is always green and never grey like Prague or Berlin.

Love always

A.

[1] The original of this letter is missing.
[2] Agreement between Germany, Great Britain, France, and Italy of 29 Sept. 1938 concerning the cession of the Sudeten areas by Czechoslovakia to Germany. It constituted the height of the appeasement policy of Western powers.

                                          Shanghai
                                          October 6 1938

Shiela my dear,
    Your letter[1] reached me here but the first days were too busy to sit down and write. The enclosed[2] was written before I got your letter: I send it along though it may have lost its point for you. There remains, I am afraid, a good deal in which we will continue to differ—but I wouldn't look on our differences in the light you do. You certainly have learnt to use strong language, that wasn't what seemed real and important in your letter. So that did not hurt and I don't feel at all as perhaps I ought that a strong letter should be written back. During the week you wrote it, it might have been the last letter I ever received from you and at the end of it, you did try to remedy that— The tone of anger and hate in the rest, I confess seems a little unreal and difficult to understand. Perhaps the distance of space and time in which it was written accounts for that. Or because in the meantime such stupendous happenings had taken place, as I felt, we had undergone in the solidaric spirit which I still believe continues to exist deeply between us, for if everything had broken up, I couldn't ever have remembered a single offence or attack we had ever levelled against each other. Also darling Shiela, there is a ground on which I feel completely to blame, i.e. that this whole extreme sharpening of the European conflict came as a complete surprise to me and I failed to understand that my attacks came at a time when you must have felt that they were conducted against you when you were entering the last stages of a desperate battle. Please understand this—it may explain the inconsistency of my last two letters with that aggressive one. I confess that I failed to realise the intrinsic turning point which came about with the Anschluss[3] and which opened up the path for a coercive settlement of the Central European problem—which I had never considered possible with the power, prestige and commitments of the Western democracies in that area. Though I did realise that there was in England a large body of opinion that favoured a negotiated settlement of the Sudeten question in Germany's favour, I believed that France and Russia would remain intransigeant on the

matter and your country would back up that ring. I argued against your propagating such a 'ring' (or the lid theory)[4] because I felt it must result in an explosion which would destroy the very suppositions on which Europe rests. But I did not realise the immediate threat as it must have existed all these last months of a unilateral settlement of the issue by Germany without the Western Powers carrying out their promises to your friends. I would not have written to you as I did had I been clear about the circumstances.

And let me add another confession which I hope you will not be too hostile about. It is not only this particular aspect of the mounting European crisis, but Europe itself, home and all I love there that I have really lost touch with to a degree which is beginning to worry me a good deal. You have, in none of your letters, made allowance for the fact that I have been living now for a considerable time in conditions which are not only completely and utterly different in many essentials, but in a country where there is war already and the horror of death and destruction no longer a threatening cloud but an actuality and part of life. This may be bad for one, especially as one is not suffering directly—but it brings about a difference of attitude to some things which makes the European reaction to them seem completely hysterical and useless. But it also encourages a type of indifference and passiveness which is utterly objectionable and however good it may be for getting out of the rut of morbid over-intensity from which we suffer and as a calm stratum to withdraw to from time to time, it is no way out of our bad troubles. In a sense, you are absolutely right—perhaps you remember my thinking years ago that the right place for me and my brothers would be the prison. But you do me an unjust wrong when you imply that being afraid of that makes us silent or subservient or escape into other continents. It is a horrible waste when the few human beings of different nationality who should continue trusting each other, contribute by unjust attacks to make life even more a hell than it is already. This applies to my inadequate attitude as well as to yours. I *am* ashamed to have introduced into our relationship the slightest note of nationalism. You must admit that it is not easy sometimes not to rise indignantly when one finds all one loves in one's country is slandered, along with the things one cannot defend. That it is wrong to try and return the blame, as if blaming each other's nation was not a meaner form of quarrelling than friends ever should descend to. And I still firmly adhere to the instinct that the whole *jargon* of mutual national blame in Europe belongs to the past, to the least agreeable characteristics of the last generation which survive in the present conduct of politics and publicity but by which we, honestly are really (should be) no more moved. And I think the bitter personal loss, darling Shiela, which you have suffered through my country[5] should not contradict but confirm this, as it does in the case of your good mother. The expressions of hatred against England which I have heard from elderly countrymen of mine who were treated badly, have always struck me as something so far from my own stirrings that I noted it as one would a fact in a history text book. Hate, surely, is blinding and cramping and nothing good can come of it—not even a victory, because one fails to understand one's opponent.

Our fundamental feelings about Europe are the same still. But it does not do merely to establish the axiom of individual liberty and fight or support things according to the prevalent notion whether they really mean liberty or the destruction of it. You do not really answer my reproach that perhaps capitalist and imperialist democracy uses liberty as a smoke screen for definite coercive policies whereas some aspects of 'authoritarian' systems may mean a more straightforward assertion of the rights of men in modern industrial society than its opponents realise. With other words, the conflict of ideologies may really be quite unrepresentative of and disguise the real nature of the conflict which may be based on rival but not different ambitions! I do not agree that the rival dynamic of the European Powers is ultimately incompatible and must result in the bloody victory of one ideology over the other. England and France, as every working State, have definitely authoritarian elements and I think it is vicious to put that down merely to capitalist flirtation with fascism— every socialist state must be to some extent authoritarian, if it is to survive. And, however narrow that may be, I still think that even the authoritarian state *must* allow for the development of free individual personality to survive. I believe, and I have seen that to some extent this is the case in Germany and it is my duty to try that out until I fail utterly. I often think I will, because I have not the strength—but I do not yet think it is impossible in principle.

Any system, however, which threatens to or actually dominates the whole rest of Europe and which cannot be changed from within must be considered as definitely coercive and to accept it as final would be the self-abandonment of Europe. I agree with you in this fundamental point and when I have seemed to introduce nationalistic arguments, it is not because I think that such a tendency in Europe can from any angle be supported, but because I believed and still think that it is not actually in existence and conjured up by the Western press to hide another unfair predominance and coerciveness. So I do not think we disagree in our motives but in our judgment of the European situation.

My attack against journalism which in principle I uphold is mainly that it moves in the medium of those viciously irreconcilable ideologies—instead of concentrating the mind, as I think we should, on the substance of what is to be reconciled in Europe. From here at least these rival ideologies seem like the fever and fantastic nightmares of one and the same whole organism, whereas the threat of violence behind seems like utter irrevocable disaster—extreme patience with the phenomenon of delirious dreams and time-saving healing methods seem the best—though the patient may still kill himself if his delirium . . . [*The rest of the sentence is scratched out.*]

I have to leave off in a minute. I only want to say it is probably jealousy mostly that turned me against Ripka—but that you should not be so terribly severe about that because after all it is *you* that I am jealous about. You say either I accept you and Mr. Mowrer or neither! How can I accept him when I don't even know him and when he refuses to confront 'Germans'—don't take that all so terribly seriously darling. How could I help feeling angry at them for chasing you all over the European continent just when I was leaving it and wanted to go skiing with you and when they appear to inspire you with so much more loyalty to them than to me. But that was, I know, the 'destiny of heaven' and no fault of yours, theirs or even mine. If I said in that offensive letter of mine that I was in love and therefore blinder to your overbearing ideomanias, you took it to mean something more and different: or we never understood each other. I still think that in our heart of hearts we agree as very few people in Europe agree and that we love each other for this and no other more important reason that we know each other really very well and for a long and important time in our life—but instead of being sensible and using this knowledge and sympathy of each other's faults and merits for an unbeatable human alliance, we spend most of our time (at least in letters) doubting and disapproving of each other's thoughts, words and actions. I don't mean to lose your friendship for one minute and allow you to turn into an indignant spinster or a jingoist British hostess or famed authoress in the ruts of Bloomsbury.[6] Perhaps the rather insufferable sides of my character which the Orient seems to have brought again more strongly may help you to practise the good European that really is in you, but which was not so very apparent in this last letter of yours.

But may I say at least without annoying you again, that after all I was happier to get this indignant letter from you than not getting any letters at all. I think I deserved part of your rage—but I realise very strongly that it is not good or right for you to have entertained it in exactly that way but you must not give up helping me not to deserve it. And now you must write me a nice letter and be a good friend again. I'll probably leave China soon.

Love always

T.

[1] See letter Shiela–Adam, The Clock House, 1 Sept. 1938.

[2] The previous letter.

[3] The annexation of Austria by Germany 11 Mar. 1938; see letters Shiela–Adam, 20 Mar. 1938 as from London; Adam–Shiela, Yumoto Nikko, Japan, 1 Apr. 38 and Adam–Shiela, Peking, 4 June 1938.

[4] See letter Adam–Shiela, Kassel, 24 Aug. 36, n. 2.

[5] See letter Shiela–Adam, The Clock House, 1 Sept. 1938, n. 6.

[6] Reference to the 'Bloomsbury Group' of early twentieth-century British intellectuals and artists that included Virginia Woolf, Lytton Strachey, John Maynard Keynes, and Roger Fry.

write to c/o American Express Hongkong

10.10.38.

Darling S,

All this I send off with hesitation.

I am so dissatisfied with all the writing between us—it is fundamentally wrong and unnecessary that this whole dispute arose. Friendships like ours are not based on the expounding of ideas but on much deeper faith and loyalty. If that is lacking, there is no point in disputing anyway. I have it for you still, my dear, and I think I deserve it from you still.

I wish you would leave Europe for a while and that we could meet outside Europe and get used to certain necessarily different habits of thought between us, gradually without haste and excitement. I must not ask you to come East because there would be no point for you if you did, unless you were staying for a good while.

Would Turkey be any good? I shall work on my final report (did you see the one of June?) in Ankara, I think, and then return (February). But my money shortage may force me to change plans.

I hate you thinking our friendship must break over these things—but it was me who put that idea into your nice head I'm afraid.

Love, my Sweet

A.

These days must have been very unhappy for you and I long to comfort you. I feel a bit more optimistic since Tsingtao, but the papers here are bound (for obvious reasons) to stress the constructive view. One should try to make it a reality, don't you agree?

[Adam]

Oct. 24th 1938

Darling Adam,

Thank you for your letter from Tsingtao[1] on such beautiful paper. I have not written to you for a long time purposely. The last letter, I wrote at the end of August I think[2]—was an answer to two of yours in which you attacked me and said we could not continue to be friends unless, fundamentally, we believed in the same things. I tried to write you what it was I believed in, and left it to you to judge if you wished to be friends. I'm afraid the faltering antipathies I had for certain things which concern you, when you left, are pale echoes of my passionate and profound hatred of them now. I don't know if you can tolerate that. I think we must meet and talk. If only we could, somehow, each in our own countries, continue to stand for certain things, uphold them, and oppose this terrible penetration of falsehood, lies, self-interest, and cowardice, it would be so important to go on being friends.

In all the horror of the last few months and weeks, it has only been the friendship and goodness and courage of my friends that has made it bearable. Affection and common endeavour and support of those temporarily defeated, is all that one can save from the wreckage of our life's esteems.

I cannot tell you what Europe, and especially England, has become since you left. Our rulers are people not only with second-class minds, but with second-class hearts. They are just morally bad.

I can't write to you now about all this. Perhaps one day you will find my book[3] somewhere, and read it and understand how I feel. I cannot expect you to understand the horror, despair, and defeat I feel. If you will come back via the Near East I would try and meet you there in the early months of 1939. I want to visit Roumania, Hungary, Yugoslavia—perhaps Turkey even.

Bless you. I think we can and must be friends.[4]

[Shiela]

[1] See letter Adam–Shiela, Tsingtao, 28 Sept. 38.
[2] See letter Shiela–Adam, The Clock House, 1 Sept. 1938.
[3] Shiela Grant Duff, *Europe and the Czechs* (Harmondsworth, 1938); the book appeared as a Penguin Special on 30 Sept. 1938.
[4] This letter missed Adam in Hongkong and reached him only after he had arrived home.

Peninsula Hotel, Kowloon, Hongkong,
Oct. 28, 1938.

Darling Shiela,

I wanted to write you a long letter to make quite sure that my last one from Tsingtao reached you properly. If it did I trust you will agree that national difference and all the painful confusion daily arising from it cannot conceivably scatter or destroy our friendship. I think I have been conscious of every pang of pain and disappointment that you must have gone through in these last weeks. I longed to be with you and convince you that though we may disagree on causes—our motives, hopes and apprehensions are exactly the same. They are, darling.

I am terribly sorry I slandered poor Ripka, but I really had no idea how serious things had become for him and his and your friends. Please tell me soon that you no longer consider my attitude to you a further cause of grief and disappointment in this awful collapse of things we both consider realities, though our angle to them differed.

Don't please let your mind get trapped in the hopeless view that only war can make things right again. Peace, even a painful peace is ultimately better and may still give us a chance to disentangle the destinies of our two countries.

Although Europe is in the end almost all important for the future of the world, I have concentrated firmly on this Far Eastern situation and this has kept me breathlessly busy in Shanghai and Hongkong from where I am writing you this note a few hours before sailing to Haiphong to get up through Indo-china to Kunming (my next address!) and Chungking. Then I hope to go through Burma to Rangoon, Calcutta, Bombay and home to England and Germany.

If you do know of anyone I ought to meet en route from Calcutta to Bombay do let them know. The safest address for that will be c/o American Express Co. Calcutta. But please darling write to Kunming too.

Will you post the enclosed note to my mother please? I have to pay too much otherwise!ˣ

I am sorry to be in such a hurry darling but I love you still and we must not write harsh distrustful letters to one another.

Bless you and be good

A.

ˣ I'm as poor as a tramp but beginning to borrow money now. I should otherwise ask you to please come and see at least India with me. But I'm afraid a Duff couldn't possibly travel with a poor white there.

Love always

A.

29/10/38

P.S. Since I wrote this letter I had telegrams from home saying that my father had had a stroke and that he died.

I am taking the next ship to Europe. It is the SS Ranchi (P & O) sailing in 2 hours. So I cannot write very much more—except that it arrives in Marseilles on Nov. 25 and that if you should happen to be in France, nothing would make me gladder than to be seeing you there first. We could travel back to Paris together and end this voyage there.

I do hope you got my last letter from Tsingtao, because what I wrote in it was the honest truth.

Bless you

A.

Colombo, Nov. 10th 1938.

[Ceylon]

Darling Duff,

Are you sitting in your nice room—the cat before the fireplace, twiddling your thumbs as to whether you should see the Trott in France or not?

You are probably saying to yourself: He has not really deserved it or at least his country hasn't deserved it (that's a very important confusion of thought already which you will no doubt correct).

In so far as he could I think he has deserved your coming—although it should be pointed out to you honestly that he is no longer the attractive boy but a gaunt bald worried individual that it will be no particular pleasure perhaps to encounter.

Then you will say, stroking your cat, I have more important duties to attend to in London or wherever they are. If it's a boy,[1] he must be taught to accept and wait for an old friend to be got out of the way. I had to do that so often (and they weren't ever got out of the way!) that he should learn that too. If it's a man to whom you must do a secretary's work, he must wait too: he could not alter the course of history if you had stayed, if he can't when you are gone—not that this implies that you couldn't have. But you might by going.

Finally, you will say, it is winter. France will be rainy and not at all attractive. Marseilles to the *ordinary* European seems very far away (for the extraordinary ones to whom we belong, of course, no place in Europe is far and its greatness rests on nothing else but on the fact that all its parts are so closely connected in every way). So even if Marseilles should be grey and wet, it isn't really far. And if we cannot, between us, overcome its greyness then good night to us anyway—besides it's the vastest criminal harbour Europe has and with all my experience of these harbours out here I shall be able to show you the brightest sides of it.

And quite finally you will say, no. it is too expensive. As far as Paris that is—well I don't know. You see not going up country from Haiphong[2] as I had hoped to has left me with the money I would have spent on that way: I would only too gladly spend it on yours now through France if you would meet me or, at least, entertain you once you get there. So that ultrafinal point doesn't hold either.

You may think then that having got so far in my reasoning I must be very happy and certain to find you when I get to Marseilles on the 25th. But I am not happy for many reasons which you can guess, besides this ship itself is like a big black coffin carrying me back to Europe to be buried there—and also there has been a persistent gale for the last twelve hours in this Indian Ocean of yours and has made me very sick of myself, life and the world and everything—and top of all I know with all the a priori reasoning within my power, there can be no certainty whatsoever that I shall see you in Marseilles. So I shall look in at the hotel de l'université when I pass through Paris (as a mere symbolic act because I cannot stay and wait there a while this time as I must fly home to help)—

But darling, understand and be there.

Love
A.[3]

[1] Boy-friend.

[2] The harbour of Hanoi, French Indo-China.

[3] In the correspondence with Shiela there is no reference to the anti-Jewish program of 9 Nov. (*Kristallnacht*), which does not in any way detract from their feelings about the matter. Adam expressed his in a letter to Diana at the end of Nov. on his voyage home: 'My thoughts have been with him [*Wilfrid Israel*] very much these last weeks—do you know where he is, how I can reach him? Give him my love if you can. You know that it is we who are humiliated by what has passed and it is for us to wonder whether our former friends wish to have anything more to do with one who, after all (in my case through my very absence) has to accept his full share of responsibility. I know that our friendship is too deeply rooted to be affected by all these developments, but I know of hardly another one I have abroad that in some way or other is not. This I think will be my hardest discovery on returning to Europe after these eventful months. I shall have to face it and set to work in other directions.' Hopkinson, 'Memoir', p. 127.

6

PARTING

THE 'PRIVATE' AND THE 'PUBLIC' WAR
ENGLAND AND GERMANY

17 November 1938–25 August 1939

EDITOR'S NOTE

Adam's return from the Far East did not bring him any closer to
Shiela. Their brief meeting in Paris made them aware that the political upheavals that had taken place during their separation had not
been shared in common. Nor did Adam's visits to England in February and June 1939 overcome their estrangement. Meanwhile Shiela,
after campaigning against the Chamberlain Government in two by-
elections, had more or less withdrawn from active political life, settling in at the Clock House on the family estate in Kent to write her
contribution to another 'Penguin Special' *Germany: What Next?*[1]
and await events. Adam's second visit involved a sudden venture on
his part into high diplomacy which, he had hoped, would, short of
war, prepare the ground for an erosion of Nazism in Germany.[2]
Adam did try to enlist Ripka's[3] support for his plan, and while he did
not inform Shiela of it, she nevertheless was apprised of it through
Ripka. They could not follow Adam's intricate dealings with British
Government circles and understood them to be yet another attempt
at appeasement. Further coldness and acrimony was perhaps the
inevitable outcome.

The correspondence broke up six days before the outbreak of the
Second World War.

[1] *Germany: What Next? Being an Examination of the German Menace So Far As
it Affects Great Britain* (Harmondsworth, 1939).
[2] See the account of William Douglas-Home, *Half-term Report: An Autobiography* (London, 1954), p. 113 and the report by David Astor to Lord Halifax of 9 July
1939 on a meeting in Berlin with Adam von Trott and some of his friends; FO 800/
316.
[3] Ripka left Czechoslovakia after Munich and was based in England in Shiela's
mother's house in Chelsea and her own in Clock House in Kent. Adam met him in
both places and broached his plan to him as the main Czechoslovak representative in
exile. Beneš and Jan Masaryk (1886–1948, son of Tomáš Garrigue Masaryk;
1925–39 Czech Minister to London and, thereafter in exile, a close collaborator of
Beneš) were in the United States at this time.

London.

17.11.38.[1]

Darling Trott,

By all means I'll see the Trott in France, but not in Marseilles unless some philanthropist hands me out a ticket and the Trott intimates he's staying a while in Marseilles—otherwise it means 24 hours travelling in 26 for the sake of a tired cross Duff keeping a tired cross Trott company on a journey—and perhaps not even that since you have a special P and O train to yourself. I'll send you my book[2] to Marseilles, and I assure you that it will be more lucid, expressive and revealing company to you than I would be myself. It is very important for you to read it if you want to know where the Duff's got to in the last one and a half years.

Please do not be cross or angry. I'm ill in bed with poisoning, so perhaps Marseilles seems to me a more unperformable request than it is. It is only a difference of twelve hours to our meeting. I will fetch you Friday evening from the Gare de Lyons—or whichever it is—and perhaps the next day we might go to Fontainebleau or somewhere for two days or as long as you can spare.

Darling Trott, I am glad you are coming home, tho' so very very sad for the reason which has brought you home sooner. Your return to your home ought at least to have been wholehearted happiness. You must not be discouraged, or hate returning. Europe has need of you, and there is so much to be done—but if you feel like that about it, how will you be able to accomplish a thing? Old gloomy.

Don't be depressed, don't be cross with your Duff, and be as pleased and happy to see her as she is to see you.

Love always,

S.

[1] This letter was sent to Malta to await Adam's arrival there.

[2] Shiela Grant Duff, *Europe and the Czechs*. In her memoirs Shiela herself comments that Adam must have regarded the book as a 'painful attack' since it constituted altogether a piece of 'political agitation with the objective of rallying the British to the side of the Czechs against the Germans'; Grant Duff, *Fünf Jahre*, p. 272.

Hotel Beaujolais
Paris[1]
Sunday night (end of November 1938)

Darling Duff,

So, you see, I did go back here—but not because I was homeless but because, wandering about I suddenly found myself confronted with it and decided it might be nice to write you a little letter.

I want you to know how much I appreciated your coming over to see me and how good it was to see you again.

Have you ever observed the attitudes of professional dancing partners in cabarets to each other? It is very nice and admirable sometimes—though they make sweet gestures in public their strenuous job makes them very matter of fact and unsentimental in their solidarity, and their attachment to each other is bound up with all the hard facts of life, and all the more real because it is unromantic.

Will we perhaps be a little like that one day?

Going back I feel a bit like a swimmer who is going to dive into a pool from a rather distant and high rock and does not quite know how cold, deep or rocky the pool itself is—but he dives quite cheerfully.

I am very glad to be in my home again—Europe and Imshausen (crossing the frontier will mean much less) though I know that not finding my old father again will seem real only when I get there. And everything will be very much changed.

My love to you, dear Duff, and try for a common policy for us from your end—Give my love to Goronwy.

A.

[1] Shiela met Adam on his return from the Far East in Paris between 24 and 27 Nov. 1938, at the Hotel Beaujolais.

[*about* 31 November 1938]

Darling Adam,

Thank you for your letter. I was rather depressed by the simile of professional dancers—perhaps it was just the effect of the Paris railway station which, already in the afternoon, you had thought beautiful and I had thought idealised. I find your simile more like my idea of the railway station than like yours. The 'hard facts of life' are both much harder and less grim than those.

It was strange to see you again and I have not quite grasped that you are back in Europe. Europe casts such a shadow on its inhabitants that it has somehow cast them into unimportance except as they are related to it. Sometimes people are not related at all and a sort of garden happiness is the result—mostly they are related and either that is purposeful or it is painful. With you it is painful. I suspect we are enemies. I do not know what you really care for and admire but suspect it is not what I care for. I suspect that even your feelings for me are now less affectionate acceptance than a sort of desire to conquer or at all costs stand up and differ. And I'm afraid it has to be like that. I have never met a German with a different patriotism and patriot one must be.

This is not the sort of letter I wanted to write to you. I am in my house and it really takes me away from all that and want only peace and private life. I feel I am no longer an actor on this stage and I need not be an onlooker. I wish you could visit my house and we could go back to Oxford in our hopes and fears. The post is going so I must finish. This is only a flag, as it were, from this dugout. Please give my love to your mother, your sister Vera and respects, as is only proper, for the male members of the family.

Much love.

Sh.   Z.

Imshausen
Dec. 6, 1938.

Darling,

Can you not postpone your suspicions till we meet again?

Partly, at any rate, I am certain they are wrong. My feelings for you are not only affectionate acceptance, but a real and tender care for your person—deepened I think by a growing recognition of your objective worth as well as a selfish wish to keep you as a friend. You are so suspicious of violent conquest or disagreement and you forget how little freedom our affections have been and are allowed now.

I got your good letter from Hongkong[1] the other day and was very glad of it. Had I received it before setting out for Europe I would probably have been in a better frame of mind and heart to meet you. As it was, you see, I had only your very hostile document from August and a benevolent note to Malta assuring me that you would postpone hostilities[2]—since apparently poor Trott needed your help and guidance. So, darling, I came armed with a lot of determined emotional independence and defiance of hostility. You were charming and, in Paris, almost not at all hostile. I was very glad: I am sorry for the 'professional dancer' simile. I was so relieved you still seemed to feel some kind of solidarity or readiness to feel it. But it was indeed strange to see you again so near. A lot of my defensive armour which I think consists of a cheap kind of hardness would not thaw up in this brief space of time.

Please be a little patient and not so suspicious. I wish I could be with you in your garden and let you look very critically at the Trott's shabby German armour. I think you would find me gladly surrendering piece by piece to you if only you will have the mercy of letting me be my own awful self in your presence. I am full of faults—like a plague bitten coolie—and perhaps we must be enemies. But don't let us become cold suspicious enemies but full-blooded loving ones. . . . I love you more where I feel I differ and where you feel, I suspect, that you ought really to differ from yourself. Certain kinds of admiration do cramp one's affections, as if one did not know perfectly well that the most enthusiastic virtue includes make believe and other tricks one plays on one's own nature. In short I must see and feel you again a bit more closely before I can feel free to quarrel with you, darling Duff. I think it would be bad before we meet again. So here is a white flag from the other dugout to accept.

Things here look more grim than hard although you kindly advise me that the actual facts of life are the other way. And I do not on the whole idealise railways stations, unless I see them on a picture of Monet[3] where it is more his bright heart than the station that delights one.

The fog around here—and I am afraid over the channel—is pretty grim. One does not see much from here at first—the papers are empty and the fields and woods received one in a deep and peaceful kind of joy. But soon enough one feels a sterile despair in most veins of life that one follows up and behind any sense of peace there is a deeper one of guilt and shame. But I do care intensely for my home and its people.

I spoke with a cousin in Frankfurt, a friend from Hamburg and an uncle from Berlin.[4] They all think nothing can be done without bowing to the formula.[5] The field after that is wide and full of opportunities but the starting point is evil and closes down the real wells of one's strength or possibilities.

My brother,[6] I am afraid, has reduced the struggle to a highly involved battle of ideas and beliefs within him, rendering him extremely vulnerable. I think he is on his way too to considering me an enemy—so far he blames an inherited difference of nature in me for antagonising him. He is very unhappy and very difficult.

There is some pleasure in the plain naive affection that meets one's return in the village and in Solz. But that is nothing and one would indeed welcome a true friend without suspicions. My mother is one and she says she would make you one too. She has just read your book which she found 'clear, intelligent and honest'. I think she is with you in most of your arguments.[7]

It would be good to see you again soon. But I must stick to this and clear up muddles and then I must go and explore things. It would be good to come and merely look after you for a little while in your house in the country or let you look after me and get it quite straight whether we are enemies or not.[8] Be good darling and let us fight through these clouds together.

Love always,
A.

My mother too sends her love.

[1] See letter Shiela–Adam, 24 Oct. 1938. Adam got this letter only after his return to Germany.

[2] Adam meant the letter Shiela–Adam, The Clock House, 1 Sept. 1938; for the note to Malta, see letter Shiela–Adam, London 17 Nov. 1938?

[3] Reference to Monet's 'Gare Saint-Lazare'.

[4] The cousin in Frankfurt: Adalbert von Unruh, Prof. of Aeronautical Law at the university. The friend from Hamburg: Dr Peter Bielenberg, who had planned to emigrate with his English-born wife Christabel (see, Christabel Bielenberg, *The Past is Myself* (London, 1969)) and his sons to Ireland but was dissuaded from doing so by Adam; Adam argued that it was important for him to stay and work against the Nazis from within. Peter Bielenberg subsequently obtained a post in the Reich Ministry of Economics. The uncle from Berlin: Eberhard von Schweinitz, youngest brother of his mother, who preceded Adam as Rhodes Scholar at Balliol (1903–5).

[5] Joining the Nazi Party.

[6] Werner von Trott; he fought fiercely to draw Adam into his orbit. He particularly disapproved of Adam's course of fighting Nazism by deceit accusing him of making a pact with the devil; cf. Sykes, *Loyalty*, pp. 31–4, 38, 417–19; cf. also, letter Shiela–Adam *middle of* June 1935, Paris, n. 2.

[7] Adam does not seem to have put his own views about the book on paper.

[8] A line is scratched out.

13.12.38.

My darling Z,

I did write at length and tried to explain why it was bad to 'suspect being enemies' these pestilential days. I am sorry that letter got lost[1] but it was not a very good document and I was thinking of following it up by another one when your charming little note with the book list came[2] and made me feel a little warm again in your presence.

Thank you for being rather worried as you say and for caring how I
found things here. They are difficult and I too find it difficult to get
down to my own work. But though the people are a rather thick and
sower [*sic*] nut to crack, homecoming to the woods and lands and
familiar horizons was lovely and reassuring. I still care intensely for
the country and its people and still believe in the fundamental integrity of Europe and its ultimate reassertion. All that is intermediate is
indeed bitter and disheartening and you are only too right in wondering whether the changes which are bound to come upon us all will
find us unprepared or not—I do not at present see a way out along
Ch's[3] line, but cannot see all I should before making up my mind—
from this angle in the country here. I hope we may meet sometime
soon next year and that till then suspicions against me will not have
bitten too deeply into your mind and heart. This picture[4] which
makes writing a little difficult was done as a coloured wood print by
nice old Ch'i Pai shih whom I knew in Peking. He had many children,
a wife and a concubine. He lived in a house guarded all round by
thick steel bars against robbers and grown all over with kreepers [*sic*]
and melons and vine. He showed me his coffin which had been made
and brought to him all the way from Honan, his home province,
where people use a different kind of coffin from the Peking
people. . .

  There are many ways, my sweet, in which it seems to me that we
would need and be of real help to each other and yet our world is so
constructed that what lies immediately ahead of us we must do alone
and that what may be best in each of us may imply a subtle kind of
pressure, diffidence and even enmity towards each other which is distinctly harmful unless we consciously size it up and bridge it by a bigger common aim beyond the things that are immediate. For this our
brief reunion the other day was too short but it filled me, as I said in
my last letter, not merely with 'affectionate acceptance' (which you
said I had lost) but with clear hope and joy in our friendship and with
renewed, and I think, deepened[5] . . . for your own self. You always
wanted me to and I think have hardened to a clearer view of the
limited realisation and potentiality of our mutual affection and to the
fact we are probably not meant to be supreme happiness to each
other. For me this does mean more of an adjustment than for you,
darling and I admit that I came to Paris with a bit of fear in my bones.
Be good and understand; also I had only had your hostile letter of
China[6] and your little one to Malta in which you did seem more prepared to be 'helpful' than affectionate too. So there darling are the
elements which went into making the Beaujolais[7] Trott whom you
got a little bit disgusted with in retrospect—now he's very much tied

up with Hessian pattern of his existence and it is not easy and he
wants you very much to be true and permanent as well.

Love always darling
T.

¹ The letter referred to, unless it was the one he wrote to Shiela from Imshausen,
6 Dec. 1938, must be lost.

² This note is lost; Adam had asked Shiela to send him a book list of recent books
on the Far East which she obtained from the library of the Royal Institute of International Affairs (Chatham House), to which she belonged.

³ Churchill's firm stand against appeasement.

⁴ Adam wrote on Chinese paper showing two frogs; Ch'i Pai-shih (1863–1957);
painter born during the late Ch'ing dynasty.

⁵ The paper is torn here; 'care'?

⁶ Letter Shiela–Adam, The Clock House, 1 Sept. 1938?

⁷ See letter Adam–Shiela, Hotel Beaujolais, Sunday night, end of Nov. 1938,
Adam was referring to himself in Paris.

Perthshire.
20.12.38.

Darling Adam,

Thank you very much for your letters, and for the two books
which look very useful tho' I have not yet embarked on them. Thank
you for sending them. I shall order yours for you as soon as I get
home.

At the present time I am here. It is the house of our former Liberal
War Minister, Lord Haldane, to whom Germany was his spiritual
home.¹ It didn't help very much. Now you will think that a hostile
remark. It isn't. Don't lets be enemies before we meet. We must sort
it out lots more. You must try and see for yourself what basis for political friendship there can be. I am making political speeches in the
election² not with much success. I am speaking badly, and I feel too
empty to go on. I'm afraid I have a terrible desire for peace and quiet,
a Shetland collie dog and a quiet home in my farm. I think the rest of
our lives will not be so quiet that we need give up what we have. I
wonder if you feel that about your home. I hope you do and can. I
feel what effort we must make must come later and now we need to
grow strong inside ourselves.

That your mother thought my book honest and intelligent is much
to be proud of. I so wanted to write a book of which good Germans
could approve. I have not got your letter here so you must forgive me
if I do not answer it. It was such a nice one and I agreed with so much
of what you said.

I'm sorry you felt angry and defensive in Paris, but glad it is not permanent. I'm afraid it made me feel just a little hopeless, as if we could not work together ever for the same things because we just did not want them. sometimes I am very frightened by the intellectual isolation of your country. Now that you are home, could you not teach me to read and study what you think is best in your country, what people you admire as good Germans. After Christmas I am going to start reading European history from the time of the French Revolution. I am really going to study and try not to write or speak much because I feel so empty.

Do you think I should join the Liberal Party? Like yourself, I prefer things that somehow connect one with the past, and mean a development all the way through history, and I'm afraid I prefer the personnel—but perhaps it is no longer a party but an attitude. There is a definite project in the constituency of my country home . . . .

I wonder how you are feeling. I'm afraid you find it rather hard. Your home must be covered in snow now. They say it is very very cold in Germany. I hope you are warm, that you will have a happy Christmas and no troubles. Please give very much love to your mother, your sister Vera, your brother and yourself. To Monika too if she is with you.

Bless you always,
Shiela.

[1] Richard Burdon Haldane, 1st Viscount (1856–1928); British statesman; Secretary of War 1906–12; responsible for the creation of the British General Staff; entered into unsuccessful negotiations with Germany in 1912 with the aim of naval disarmament (Haldane Mission). Haldane had studied at Göttingen where he read German philosophy.
[2] The by-election in Kinross and West Perth, Scotland, 22 Dec. 1938. The Duchess of Atholl who supported the Spanish Republican Government was opposed to the British Government's policy in the Spanish Civil War and to appeasement of the Dictators. Not willing to continue to sit as a Conservative in the House, she sought re-election as an Independent, but lost.

30.12.38.

Dear Duff,

Thank you for your letter from Cloan.[1] The place seemed quite familiar to me even before I read your letter—because I used to have quite an admiration for Haldane and read his books and saw a picture in one of them of his home. He was an intelligent admirer of Germany although his friends in that country had mostly been dead a hundred years. He knew Goethe—whom one must only read to know (especially his earlier poems and Egmont and Werther and Götz von Berlichingen)—and he knew the philosophers. But even them I think he would have been intelligent enough not to ask to his home. They would have been bored.

I was surprised when I got to Berlin. Instead of the triumphant capital of the future Empire of Europe, I found a sulky, disgruntled demoralised mess. Few if any see the Czech business as you do and I tend to: as the entry into unlimited economic and political possibilities.[2]

The attempt to couple the venture with a general overhaul[3] and readjustment of the inner gears of the machine was frustrated by your clever Neville and the only alternative is another 'venture' or an overhauling in the garage in which many chaps only disguised as mechanics would have to be squeezed out of the door as the engine is neither big nor tough enough to stand all their clumsy hands. At present the door is shut, the engine stinks and puffs the evillest poisons, suffocating all the more sensitive lungs while everybody gets more and more uneasy. Although some will still not believe that the gas is poisonous, all seem to agree that something must happen soon— push some men out or let the whole engine crash its way out so that all of them may remain under cover a little while longer. Schacht[4] whom I saw said there is no chance at all for a European war, now no longer, as clever Neville had been forging ahead with the other hand while holding out the one, and that the other with all that it could pull with it was ever ready and probably stronger already than both of ours.[5] His view of the garage door seemed cheerful but cynical and, I have been told, his predictions are often wrong. Anyway, all that is merely two days Berlin before Christmas and certainly one side of the matter. The country is magnificently industrious, full of new amazing achievement, but painfully resigned and spiritually asleep, if no worse. At home, at any rate part of it, I am having a hell of a time and wish you were nicer and wrote and understood[6] and be a little kinder and more alert to the requests of your Hun friend. I think you don't even come up to the standard of 'professional dancing partners'. What do you want then? Go into Parliament if you cannot help it and join the Liberal Party. For all I know an attitude may be better than a party. My sweet Duff, I haven't really seen[7] . . . you back again since China. I'll come in February.

Love and all blessings till then.

A.

[1] Lord Haldane's house.
[2] Adam meant to impart here the notion that with the fall of the Czechoslovak

bastion Germany would emerge most powerful. Both Shiela and Adam were apprehensive of this possibility.

[3] This paragraph constitutes an important contemporary documentation of the so-called 'Generals' Plot' under General Franz Halder who had succeeded General Ludwig Beck as Chief of Staff of the German Army on 27 Aug. 1938. The preparations for the coup went back to just about that time and the objective was to take the occasion of Hitler's aggression against Czechoslovakia to arrest or shoot him and to take over the government in Berlin. The leading figures in the conspiracy were, apart from Halder, the then Lieutenant Colonel Hans Oster who served as Chief of Staff to Admiral Wilhelm Canaris in the Armed Forces Intelligence (OKW Ausland/Abwehr), Dr Hans-Bernd Gisevius who had held various positions in the Ministry of Interior, with the Gestapo, and who was affiliated with the *Abwehr*, Generals Karl-Heinrich von Stülpnagel, Erwin von Witzleben, and Count Walter von Brockdorff-Ahlefeldt. Hjalmar Schacht, President of the *Reichsbank*, was also involved in the discussions. The failure of the coup to come off has variously been attributed to the over-cautiousness of in particular, General Halder and to insufficient preparations. One decisive factor in the collapse of the venture, emphasized in particular in the West German literature on the German Resistance, has been the last-minute decision of the British Prime Minister Neville Chamberlain to visit Berchtesgaden (15 Sept.) and Bad Godesberg (22–24 Sept.), and the conclusion of the Munich Agreement between the Western Powers, Germany, and Italy which maintained the peace at the expense of the truncation of Czechoslovakia. Adam in his letter clearly lends support to the view that Chamberlain's policy contributed to Hitler's triumph in Munich and thus foiled the plans of the Resistance. Adam's information about the 'Generals' Plot' came evidently from his friend Count Bernstorff; see Malone, *Adam von Trott* (diss.), p. 556.

[4] See letter Shiela–Adam, Prague, Sept. 1936 n. 2.

[5] Reference to Chamberlain's rearmament policy. Since Munich he had become convinced of the need to modify appeasement. He agreed to support the 'moderate' elements in Germany while at the same time hastening rearmament; see Sidney Aster, *1939, The Making of the Second World War* (London, 1973), pp. 41, 393.

[6] Shiela, alas, did not understand Adam's veiled message. She had not been privy to any active opposition in Germany and did not read these passages as intended to convey a particular message; see Grant Duff, *The Parting of Ways*, p. 206.

[7] A connecting sentence crossed out.

Imshausen.
Jan. 2nd, 1939.

Darling Duff,
    ... I miss you or somebody like you very much. I am not pessimistic about the local difficulties, they will be solved—but what comes after would be a hell of a lot better with at least one trustworthy comrade. Or are we at the mercy of 'this Europe' whatever it makes of others and oneself? ...

    You are right one must not think of 'relations' but of things in common or opposition and of decisions. But these it has exactly been the problem to reach and there the 'relation' of old failed—but still you are right. And strangely, as you again rightly remark, I don't think one should think too much: it spoils everything. But as you know it is easier to trust one's instincts in the country than in the town. There one must translate them and it's a hell of a language to understand and translate into. You have learnt it so rapidly—I think I am a good bit slower. But in the end I shall trust my own instincts even there. The great thing is to feel at home within oneself whether in town or country and then the instincts well up like French fountains. But what nonsense am I writing to you to-night, darling it is very late and I only wanted to undo a bit of fierceness, though I know it impressed me more than it did you. Do you think when I visit you or you visit me we will feel at home? I think I'm on the point of growing very bald a determined bachelor. Love my sweet and don't become too fierce. . . . Don't become too widely educated for your primitive old

Trott.

Berlin-Dahlem,
Helferichstr. 24
6.3.39.[1]

Darling Duff,
The sea and sky in Holland early Friday were extraordinarily beautiful and gave me a short vision and reminder of the vast wonderful world between our petty camps—which pervert even nature's innocence. Their very air contains the poison of wrong feeling and only the free and strong rooted in wider worlds survive it.

I was glad to find the 3 words from you in an envelope with two letters[2]—bless you too, darling. How typical of my whole stay this last day of misunderstanding and waiting between us. I truly imagined you had parted for good this time at the foreign office.[3]

I often dream that some supreme test is waiting between us after which life may be either rich and mutual, or hollow and full of irritation. But what that test is I do not somehow know. You think it is the 'dark hours'[4]—perhaps—I do not know. You sometimes think it is the test of action and change, and you sometimes used to think it was the risk of surrender.

Without the test won or lost, there is doubt, frustration—something untrue and static, apart from the rest of one's life and sometimes the 'dagger'—at least in my case. I'll try and find a German woman soon and tell you how things look afterwards.

Everything looks more serious from here than it does in England.

The thing that called me back is an almost hopeless piece of human worry. I am working hard for a remedy but probably there is none. . . . [5]

Be good and not rash.

Love

A.

[1] This letter was written following Adam's visit to England in Feb. 1939. In London he stayed with the Astors in their town house at St James's Square. But his first meeting after arrival early in the morning of 12 Feb. was with Diana. The reunion over breakfast at the Paddington Station Dining-room and a long walk in Kensington Gardens was a happy one. The visit to Oxford was less so. While he found the older men among his friends a cause for joy, he detected a distinct reserve among his contemporaries. The effects of the Nazi pogrom of Nov. of the previous year made themselves felt in the attitudes in England towards everything German. Adam also attended a weekend party at Clock House, High Elms, where he met Ripka, Diana, and her fiancé David whom he encountered for the first time. As for Adam's relations with the Astors, this visit was of great importance. It convinced Lady Astor that Adam's scheme for Anglo-German co-operation was in keeping with her and her husband's notion of appeasement, which in fact it was not exactly. But anyway this decided her to open the doors for Adam to the men around the Prime Minister Neville Chamberlain who frequented her London house as well as her country estate, Cliveden; cf. especially, Sykes, *Loyalty*, pp. 227 ff, Grant Duff, *The Parting of Ways*, p. 207, Hopkinson, 'Memoir', pp. 131 f.

[2] Presumably words such as 'bless you' accompanying letters which had been addressed to him at 16 Mulberry Walk, Shiela's London home.

[3] Adam evidently had an appointment at the Foreign Office which took place after the Clock House party. Shiela and Adam had arranged for her to pick him up after the appointment and to deliver any mail that had come for him. Whom Adam saw at the Foreign Office and the purpose of the visit could not be ascertained.

[4] War?

[5] Adam expressed here a variety of feelings which converged. His most recent visit to England in February had left him with the perception that the climate in the country, and especially among his Oxford contemporaries, had changed. His travels made him decide to return to live and work in Germany which, in turn, he described to Diana as 'my zoo'. Adam then saw the two countries which he loved, his native and his 'spiritual' home, drifting hopelessly apart. At the same time Adam got actively involved in conspiracy in his own country. A sense of isolation and fear lest his oppositional work be rendered futile by war threw Adam into a mood of deep depression. (Cf. Sykes, *Loyalty*, pp. 227 ff; also Hopkinson, 'Memoir', pp. 133 f.) Certainly Adam's mood had changed drastically since Jan. (see letter Adam–Shiela, Imshausen, 2 Jan. 1939, first para.).

[*2nd week of* March 1939]

Poor old Trott,
 . . . We seem to find it very hard to feel solidaric with each other's hardships. I wonder whether the fault is of the heart or of the mind. It is a general arrogance of feeling perhaps on both sides. I cannot help but feel that a word from you against the things which you know I passionately hate¹ might establish warmer relations. As it is, I'm afraid you resemble a larger number of my countrymen. You do not really care until your own skin is involved.

I don't seem to be as good as you are in changing the subject once I start an attack, though now I come to look at your letter, you have very conveniently ended it on the single sentence of reconciliation. It is a good discipline to continue.

I had lunch with your friend Mrs. Swinton² and met a number of imposing ladies. She is very nice and curiously like you in mentality. She thinks that the East has made you very serene—'too damn serene'—I wanted to answer but realised it would be rude to her as well as to you. I don't think that serenity is becoming in a lunatic asylum, do you? There it starts again. I shall try a little longer and if I can't help it, I shall finish. I liked Mrs. Swinton very much and I enormously enjoy the company of middle aged women—on condition they are fat and therefore kindly, qualities which should be confined to middle age or a very kindly world.

I am in my farm and the primroses are coming up in the woods and the birds begin to sing again. All the things natural to the world are so very pretty and only man is vile. I have finished turfing and sowing grass in the farmyard and have planted sweetpeas so that in summer my house will be full of flowers. I have moved to the top of the house and the sun shines in through a stained glass window. There is nothing in my nearest surroundings not to inspire the greatest tenderness and serenity—on which appeasing note, perhaps it would be wise to leave you. If things get worse, I shall go to Prague.³

[Shiela]

¹ Shiela meant the events leading up to the German annihilation of the Czechoslovak state in mid-Mar. 1939.
² A friend of Adam's mother.
³ This is the only extant letter by Shiela from the time just before the German occupation of Prague (15 Mar. 1939). It was this event which for the moment decided Shiela to break off relations with Adam.

[March ? 1939]

Darling Duff,

This can only be a brief note because someone is leaving for your country and will take it along. I wrote you a long letter two or three days after returning from England in which I asked you several important questions.[1] They cannot now be repeated but it would be a pity if you never got them.

If we relate all elements of friendship to the whirlpool of public events we will certainly be lost to each other in no time: it would be the devil's triumph to see us both dance to his pipe. When you address me in the collective 'You' I have no case to defend against you and I agree that serenity, kindliness etc. in an asylum are not only unbecoming but disgusting. Actually 'serenity' is utterly impossible and something else is more and more rapidly taking its place which you would find hard to attack, though possibly equally difficult to share.[2] You see, darling, I am back in that pool and from the first moment (that's why I said that your attack came at an ill-chosen moment) I was soaked right through, skin and all and the question is whether we have some common dry bank anywhere or not.

You are the truer child of our age now in merging personal and public relations completely—and by excluding your friends when you think of birds and beasts. How I long to convince you that all this is wrong—though I confess I would need convincing myself. It is so easy to be intimate when one is exuberant and so hellishly hard when one is sick and sore as we both are after these awful last weeks. This is the type of moment when the devil digs his dagger in to the few human relations which might remain. We had no chance ever really to get to know each other's human side again—away from other people and the bustle of the town and I am afraid I thought you rather avoided it, though like a fool and prejudiced by this forced return to the pool. One is bound, darling, by such general changes to falsify the heart of any situation and I am sorry I followed your lead into this thicket of mutual blame. The violence of your reaction contained a curious comfort, though your words in themselves were a bit bitter.

There's a big grey cat like Smoke on my window ledge and the sun is shining on the snow outside. Do you think, darling, we could meet somewhere in Spring? perhaps in the Rhineland or Imshausen, to 'have it out' and see some birds and beasts together (write me a little note to say you agree) and decide eye to eye and not scribble to scribble what we are going to do about the devil's pipe and dagger.

Love always, sweet Duff, your sad

T.

---

1 A number of letters of this period are missing.
2 An allusion of Adam's to his resistance activities?

Imshausen.
April 2, 1939.

Darling Shiela,

I do not accept your reasons for parting¹ but I see that part we must.

I do not see a 'barricade' separating us but a torrent of mixed passions, fears and hate. If you no longer feel it, I cannot convince you now that there is solid common ground even on the other side of that torrent and a similar though necessarily different struggle. Clearly we must first be as good and as brave as we possibly can at our end of it and if being friends hinders that we must part. But don't let us make culprits and enemies of each other when we cannot see through all the turmoil and clamour of our essential though separate solidarity. These may be mere words now—but I wish to God they will ring true when, in fight or peace, we should be near again.

And if we should be blasted off this inhospitable planet let us at least hope to meet in paradise and not that one will go to hell and the other alone to heaven. Won't we probably both be put in the same department of the latter? And may I then take you to the old garden and play there as happily as ever we did on Oxford's meadows of 1932? And² . . . remember the snake's foul impasse of worldly wisdom and the sour after taste of the apple and keep clear of both.

I hope, darling, your other friends all remain intact, for you need good friends to prevent you from hurting your own self through violence which is no help in defeating the sordid violence of our present world.

Bless you and always love

A.

---

1 Letter Shiela–Adam written after the Prague occupation lost?
2 Words crossed out.

Clock House,
May 21st, 1939.

Darling Adam,

Diana has asked me[1] to write you a note saying that Jane will not
be coming to Germany and reassuring you about all the contradic-
tory telegrams. She is not very well and finally decided to come home
and rest awhile. She must stay quiet for a bit so send her a nice letter—not about being ill but saying you will be able to see her.[2]

I saw Wilfrid who speaks very nicely of you. I hope your family are
well. My love to your mother. Diana and David seem very happy. I
hope you are.

Love
S.

[1] Notice that it was most likely upon Diana's prompting that Shiela resumed the
correspondence.
[2] This was the beginning of Jane Rendel's tragic mental illness.

EDITOR'S NOTE

In June Adam engaged in frantic efforts to reactivate his connections in England and commit them to an Anglo-German settlement
that would preserve the peace which, in turn, he thought, was a vital
precondition for a successful pursuit of conspiratorial work in Germany. Early in the month he set out for England where first he saw
his friend David Astor who arranged for him to spend the weekend
of 3–4 June at his parents' country estate Cliveden. At Cliveden he
met an assemblage of distinguished guests, among them Lord Halifax
and Lord Lothian, and, furthermore, Lord and Lady Astor arranged
for him to meet the Prime Minister. Indeed he was received at 10
Downing Street on 7 June. The Trott mission has been an object of
considerable controversy especially on the question of who author-
ized it and what its purpose was. While it is quite certain that the trip
was not initiated by Ernst von Weizsäcker, the Permanent State Secretary in the German Foreign Office, it was most likely co-ordinated
with him. It was also cleared with Walter Hewel, Ribbentrop's liai-
son officer with Hitler. The very fact that Adam came in a semi-
official capacity and that his hosts in England were the so-called
'Cliveden Set', which was identified with the appeasement policy,
caused a great deal of suspicion in England. Adam's specific proposal
to Lord Lothian and most likely also Lord Halifax, involving a swap
that would free the occupied territories in Bohemia and Moravia in
turn for a solution of the Danzig and Corridor questions, did not lead

to any result. Upon his return he wrote, with his friend Peter Bielenberg, a report about the Cliveden talks which was intended to impress upon the German leadership the need to proceed along the path of negotiation rather than resorting to war. Only the preservation of peace, so he and his friends in the opposition reasoned, could assure conditions necessary for staging a coup in Germany backed up by the military. While Adam's proposition did not meet outright rejection on the part of his British interlocutors, it encountered fierce rejection from Hubert Ripka to whom Adam insisted upon outlining it. Ripka in turn informed by letter Winston Churchill who assured him that nothing would come of it anyway.[1] As for Shiela, she was not drawn into Adam's confidence in this matter.

Soon after, on 11 June, Adam set out on another trip to England, first stopping at the Astors' and then proceeding to Oxford. This trip turned out to be a complete failure. At Oxford he saw his old friends again, but the after-dinner conversations at Balliol and All Souls left Adam's friends wondering whether he had gone over to the Nazis after all. The intimacy of the earlier Oxford days which had tied Adam to men like Stuart Hampshire and Isaiah Berlin now yielded to suspicion. Maurice Bowra (since 1938 Warden of Wadham College) indeed, though Adam confided in him that he was working for the opposition in Germany, decided that Adam was playing a double game and showed him the door ('I decided that von Trott was playing a double game and trying to weaken our resistance just when at last it was beginning to grow stronger. I was wrong. What I overestimated was the competence of the Gestapo, who could be extraordinarily blind and seem actually not to have known about von Trott's efforts against Hitler. So my reason for suspicion was actually quite unfounded. Von Trott was not only against Hitler, but after the failure of the plot of 20 July 1944, he was arrested and hung with a horrifying brutality on a wire cord. When I heard this, I saw how mistaken I had been, and my rejection of him remains one of my bitterest regrets'; C. M. Bowra, *Memories 1898–1939* (Cambridge, Mass., 1967), pp. 305 f.[2]

On 17–18 June Shiela gave a weekend party at Clock House, High Elms, to which she had invited also Churchill's daughter Diana and her husband Duncan Sandys, hoping thus somehow to pave the way for Adam to Churchill. But Adam resisted any suggestion of a meeting with him.

Shiela and Adam saw each other for the last time during this weekend at Clock House. In fact this visit was the last time that Adam saw most of his English friends; Diana he saw only once as she was in hospital recovering from an operation.

¹ Grant Duff, *The Parting of Ways*, pp. 209 f.

² For the main literature on the subject see Grant Duff, op. cit., pp. 209 f; Sykes, *Loyalty*, pp. 239 ff, 258 ff; Christabel Bielenberg, *The Past is Myself*, pp. 45 f; Marion Thielenhaus, *Zwischen Anpassung und Widerstand: Deutsche Diplomaten 1938–1941* (Paderborn, 1984), pp. 125 ff. For Adam's and Bielenberg's report see *Documents on German Foreign Policy 1918–1945* ser. D, vol. vi (London, 1950), Doc. 497, pp. 674–84. For a report by David Astor to Lord Halifax on Adam's position, dated 9 July 1939, see Public Record Office, FO 800/316.

Cliveden,
19.6.39. Sunday night¹

Darling S—

The week-end in your house did me a great deal of good—thank you a lot for it. Your apparent reluctance at the end we had not confided in each other more is a help for the future. I am sure it was to a large extent my clumsiness which has in the past and this time allowed us to develop this vicious circle of mutual diffidence. I am very very sorry about it.—

But since you *are*, darling, so fundamentally sure (much more than I am) that we are after different things and since neither verbal or other intimacy can dispel the clouds between us, we must I think let deeds speak for themselves later on. I feel that our mutual fondness could stand a long period of trial. . . .

I am sorry I had to go away so quickly, but I really had to.

Love and Auf Wiedersehen (in not too gloomy circumstances)

Adam

¹ June 19 was a Monday. On that day Adam left Clock House for Cliveden. The letter was therefore written most likely on Monday night.

Imshausen
August 2, 1939.

darling Shiela,

Thank you for your note, I think neglect has been at least mutual and perhaps to some extent timely. I have not been idling by lakesides, but read good books along with doing other things. I am sorry you are so vague with whom you are going to go to France and Switzerland alternatively. I think yours will be the fate of Caesar who was chilly to all men and finally got murdered by a Brutus with whom he believed to be on really familiar terms. I have always rather feared that your fondness of animals was an indication of your hatred of men. . . .

my love
[Adam]

[undated but must be mid-August 1939]

My darling Duff,
I have a feeling that my last letter was rather inadequate and somehow don't want to leave it at that just now especially since it is becoming highly doubtful whether my August trip to England and America can still come off. I hate this constant pathetic leave-taking, but when we are finally cut off, I do not want the smallest drop of bitterness to poison our mutual memory—let's bury the best European friendship deep in the soil, so it cannot be harmed by any winter or surface destruction and may blossom out again like these Chinese ones.[1]

Bless you sweet
A.

[1] This letter was written on brown Chinese paper with a blossoming fruit tree as watermark.

Paris
17th August, 1939.

Dear Trott,
I'm sorry about this paper. It's what this café thinks a girl should write on and perhaps, unable to emulate, it is as well to fall as low as possible from the standard of yours.

Thank you for your last letter. I appreciate the gesture but you always did believe the winter hadn't yet begun when it raged through Europe and froze all hearts. Or rather it made the world hard and glittering and the snow was white and the ice and the sky were black and there were no half shades and compromises but just a fight for the existence of what one cared for. But luckily the world doesn't seem to know how cold it is outside. Notre Dame shines in the evening sun and people fall in love and walk the streets hand in hand. Paris is full of memories but never one of great happiness but always of something unrealised and an urgent insistence that nothing exists but Paris itself and one is a stranger from another world.

Qu'as tu fait toi que voilà, pleurant sans cesse
Qu'as tu fait toi que voilà de ta jeunesse?[1]

It is a curious arrangement to make young people worry because of the troubles inside them—and when they learn to deal with those, to give them real trouble from without. Still there they are and perhaps it is the point of one's life to deal with them.

If we'd always been honest with each other we could bury a friendship deep but it is doubt that poisons not pain. Perhaps we will nevertheless survive and know fuller what things it was the other held dear. For now, I suppose, Goodbye. Be safe in body and mind.

S.

¹ From Paul Verlaine, 'Sagesse': Qu'as-tu fait, ô toi que voilà / Pleurant sans cesse, / Dis, qu'as-tu fait, toi que voilà / De ta jeunesse (Thou who so bitterly cries, what hast thou done, Pray tell me, what has of thy youth become?) St John Lucas (ed.), *The Oxford Book of French Verse XIIIth Century–XXth Century* (Oxford, 1926), p. 466.

Berlin.
August 25. 1939.

Dear Shiela,

The parting remark of your letter has made me angry, so that even at this time of day, I must add a few words.

You are right that distrust not pain poisons friendship. But if you imply that my reticence to you lately has in any way been dishonest you are viciously mistaken. I have never been consciously dishonest to you. To a great extent I have always believed that we did care for similar things and I loved and admired you for your single heartedness. But I also painfully and frequently experienced your complete incapacity to understand and sympathise with a natural ally when his battle had to be fought in an environment different from yours. You would from that incapacity even proceed to wreck a thing that you should have furthered, and fail to recognise values whose destruction were bound to hasten the defeat of your own cause. For that reason alone have I been reticent. I agree that a winter landscape is no subject for subtle colouring and ultimately levels a grim challenge to death or life of one's spark of right sense, but I cannot let that sneaking suspicion in the honesty of our friendship while it lasted pass without protest. It may not be fair or wise to write like this when there is hardly a chance for you to answer, but neither is it tolerable to let things stand as you did, or rather to let them rot away under poisonous suspicion as you intended. And finally, Darling S, I think these disputes are an awful silly waste and I'm sure should not have to arise. If it's part of the freezing of hearts you refer to, it is not me who has a right to blame you, but if it's part of your own ambitious coldness about your friend's battles, you should eradicate it.

A.[1]

[1] The whole letter, including the signature 'A', is typed, as was the unstamped envelope addressed to Shiela's country home, Clock House. Shiela has no recollection of how or when the letter reached her. War broke out on 1 Sept. and all communication between Adam and Shiela was broken.

POSTSCRIPT

'War broke out between us even before it broke out between our two countries. For this we were both guilty and both innocent. Innocent because neither of us really had this intention or harboured any ill-will in our hearts; guilty because we both allowed it to happen.' Thus far Shiela's memoirs.[1]

During the first war years Adam did manage to get a number of letters to Diana. The undertone of all these was a plea for continued trust among friends and sorrow over the break with England. In a letter written from Zurich on 5 December 1940 Adam told Diana that he had married.[2] On 8 June 1940 he had married Clarita Tiefenbacher, daughter of a prominent Hamburg lawyer, whom he had first met at a party in December 1935. It was Clarita who finally helped him come to terms with his situation and with the many strains in his character. Her devotion, her understanding, and her intelligent companionship enabled him to bring his 'private' and 'public' lives into tune with each other and to steel himself for his perilous tasks.[3]

Meanwhile Shiela took on official wartime assignments—she was in charge of Czechoslovak affairs in the Foreign Research and Press Service of the Foreign Office and subsequently started up the Czechoslovak Section of the BBC European Service.[4] For his part, Adam moved with striking persistence into the 'double life' of conspiracy. He divided his attention between his 'official' assignments for the Foreign Office and his stepped-up resistance activities. As emissary of the Resistance he undertook many journeys to neutral countries, inevitably risky ventures which more often than not

[1] Grant Duff, *The Parting of Ways*, p. 211.
[2] Letter Adam–Diana, 5 Dec. 1940, in Hopkinson, 'Memoir', pp. 150 f; the letter, signed 'E', did not reach Diana until Mar. the following year.
[3] Clarita and Adam had two daughters. After the war she studied medicine and settled in West Berlin as a practising psychoanalyst. She has five grandchildren.
[4] In 1942 Shiela published *A German Protectorate: The Czechs Under Nazi Rule* (London, 1942), which was one of the really important works on the Nazi Empire; in 1944 she resigned from public office. By that time she was married to Noel Newsome, the creator and wartime Director of the European Service, and had two children. After the war she married Michael Sokolov Grant, with whom she has farmed for the last thirty years, first in England and thereafter in the Republic of Ireland. She has two daughters, three sons, and three grandsons.

brought him to the brink of despair. But in the autumn of 1943 he met Count Claus Schenk von Stauffenberg, the officer who led the coup against Hitler in its last phases and was to set the bomb on the fatal 20 July, 1944. Adam and Stauffenberg before long developed a close friendship which for Adam meant a final confirmation of his commitment to resistance.

Shiela's and Adam's causes may not have been identical; they may have had to struggle separately. We can safely assume that the two correspondents on their separate journeys reached their destinations: Shiela in successfully alerting her country to the dangers of appeasement and committing herself to the liberation of the Czechoslovak nation from the Nazi yoke; Adam in upholding the honour of his country even at the price of the ultimate sacrifice.

Appendix

Letters between Shiela and Adam Not Included in the Edition

Chapter 1
A–Sh   Balliol, 1 Mar. [1932]
A–Sh   Balliol, Wed. [? May. 1932]
A–Sh   Balliol, Thur. [June 1932]
A–Sh   Sussex, [June 1932]
A–Sh   Balliol, [autumn term 1932]
Sh–A   note left in A.'s Balliol room on envelope of Diana to A. dated 10
Nov. 1932
A–Sh   (postcard) Brussels, 3 Jan. 1933
A–Sh   Boetzen b. Aachen, 5 Apr. 1933
Sh–A   20 Nov. 1933
Sh–A   London, 24 June 1934
Sh–A   Cumberland, 30 July 1934
A–Sh   Kassel, 2 Aug. 1934
Sh–A   Kent, 8 Aug. 1934
Sh–A   Basel, late Aug. 1934
A–Sh   Kassel, 23 Sept. 1934
Sh–A   Switzerland, 7 Sept. 1934
Sh–A   (postcard) Paris, 29 Oct. 1934
Sh–A   Chelsea, 31 Dec. 1934
Sh–A   London, Mar. 1935
Sh–A   Chelsea, 12 Mar. 1935
Sh–A   Chelsea, 16 Mar. 1935
Sh–A   [end of Mar. 1935]
Sh–A   Paris, 27 Apr. 1935
A–Sh   (postcard) Berlin, 28 Apr. 1935
Sh–A   Paris, 9 May 1935
Sh–A   Chelsea, 6 Aug. 1935
A–Sh   Berlin W 15, [mid-Aug. 1935]
A–Sh   (postcard) 16 Aug. 1935
A–Sh   (postcard) Kassel, 24 Aug. 1935
Sh–A   Berlin [end of Aug. 1935]
Sh–A   (postcard) Berlin, 8 Sept. [1935]
Sh–A   Berlin, 12 Sept. [1935]
Sh–A   Berlin, Sat., [?14 Sept. 1935]

Chapter 2
A–Sh   Hamburg, Wed. 16 Oct. 1935
A–Sh   Thurs., [31 Oct. 1935]
A–Sh   Mon. afternoon, [18 Nov. 1935]

Sh–A Chelsea, 22 Nov. 1935
Sh–A 13 Dec. [1935]
Sh–A Kent, 21 Dec. 1935
Sh–A Chelsea, 27 Dec. 1935
Sh–A Cardiff, 29 Dec. 1935
Sh–A 31 Dec. 1935
A–Sh Göttingen, 19 Mar. 1936
Sh–A Kent, 9 Apr. 1936
Sh–A London, 17 May 1936
Sh–A London, 29 May 1936
Sh–A Chelsea, 6 June 1936

Chapter 3
A–Sh Sun., almost midnight [most likely 12 July 1936]
      PS Mon. [most likely 13 July 1931]
A–Sh Imshausen, 14 July 1932
Sh–A Prague, Thurs., [16 July 1936] (first letter of the same date)
Sh–A Bratislava, 20 July [1936]
Sh–A in train from Bratislava, 22 July 1936
Sh–A Prague, 23 July 1936
A–Sh Kassel, 24 July 1936 (second letter of the same date)
A–Sh 26 July 1936
Sh–A Prague, 27 July 1936
A–Sh Kassel [end of July 1936]
A–Sh Bergstrasse 4 [c. 1 Aug. 1936]
A–Sh Leipzig, 5 Aug. 1936
Sh–A Prague, Wed. night [?5 Aug. 1936]
A–Sh Berlin, 10 Aug. 1936
A–Sh Imshausen, 12, 13, 14 Aug. 1936
Sh–A 13 Aug. 1936
A–Sh Imshausen, 6 Sept 1936
A–Sh Bellers, 13 Sept. 1936
Sh–A (postcard) Vienna, 20 Sept. 1936
A–Sh Berlin, 23 Sept. 1936
Sh–A Prague, 23 Sept. 1936
Sh–A Prague, 29 Sept. 1936
Sh–A 7 Oct. 1936
Sh–A 8 Oct. 1936
Sh–A Prague, 12 Oct. 1936
Sh–A Prague, 15 Oct. 1936
Sh–A 21 Oct. 1936
A–Sh 8 Nov. 1936
Sh–A Prague, 13 Nov. 1936
A–Sh Balliol, 15 Nov. 1936
Sh–A Prague, [15] Nov. 1936
A–Sh Surrey, 19 Nov. 1936; Sat; [21 Nov.]; Sun. [22 Nov.], New College
Sh–A Prague, 22 Nov. 1936

Sh–A Vienna, 18 Dec. 1936
A–Sh Berlin, Sat. [most likely 19 Dec.] 1936
A–Sh Berlin, 22 Dec. 1936
Sh–A Hofgastein, 5 Jan. 1937
Sh–A Hofgastein. 8 Jan. 1937
Sh–A Hofgastein, 13 Jan. 1937
Sh–A [22 Jan.] 1937
A–Sh Berlin, 29 Jan. 1937
Sh–A Prague, 2 Feb. 1937
Sh–A Prague, [Jan. or Feb.] 1937
Sh–A (postcard) [early Feb. 1937]
Sh–A Prague, 8 Feb. 1937
Sh–A 15 Feb. 1937
A–Sh Paris, 21 Feb. 1937

Chapter 4
A–Sh (postcard) New York, 13 Mar. 1937
A–Sh New York, 2 Apr. 1937
Sh–A Prague, 12 Apr. 1937
A–Sh Harvard, 23 Apr. 1937
Sh–A Prague, 26 Apr. 1937
Sh–A Slovakia, 16 May 1937 and Whit Monday
Sh–A Prague, 20 May 1937
A–Sh California, 20 May 1937
Sh–A 7 July 1937

Chapter 5
Sh–A Finisterre-France, 26 Aug. 1937
Sh–A London, 15 Sept. 1937
Sh–A London, 2 Oct. 1937
Sh–A 17 Oct. [1937]
Sh–A Prague, 11 Nov. 1937
A–Sh Peking, 15 Dec. 1937
Sh–A England, Christmas 1937
Sh–A [Prague] 7 Mar. 1938
Sh–A Prague, 2 June 1938

Chapter 6
A–Sh Christmas Day 1938
Sh–A [Clock House,] 28 Dec. [1938]
A–Sh Imshausen, 14 Jan. 1939
A–Sh Berlin W 15, [Jan. 1939]
A–Sh (postcard of an eagle) 21 Jan. 1939
Sh–A High Elms [6] Mar. 1939
A–Sh 9 Mar. 1939
A–Sh Imshausen, 2 Aug. 1939

INDEX